Shakespeare and the Comedy of Enchantment

Shakespeare and the Comedy of Enchantment

KENT CARTWRIGHT

OXFORD
UNIVERSITY PRESS

OXFORD
UNIVERSITY PRESS

Great Clarendon Street, Oxford, OX2 6DP,
United Kingdom

Oxford University Press is a department of the University of Oxford.
It furthers the University's objective of excellence in research, scholarship,
and education by publishing worldwide. Oxford is a registered trade mark of
Oxford University Press in the UK and in certain other countries

First Edition published in 2021

Impression: 1

Published in the United States of America by Oxford University Press
198 Madison Avenue, New York, NY 10016, United States of America

British Library Cataloguing in Publication Data
Data available

Library of Congress Control Number: 2021940050

ISBN 978–0–19–886889–7

DOI: 10.1093/oso/9780198868897.001.0001

Printed and bound by
CPI Group (UK) Ltd, Croydon, CR0 4YY

To

William C. Carroll
and
Ágnes M. Matuska

friends of comedy

Preface and Acknowledgments

This book makes a claim for the power of Shakespeare's comedies, and comedy more generally, to create deep responses, to provoke thought, to bring forth the world in new ways, and to create community. It does that by employing the inclusive notion of enchantment, which reveals in the comedies mysterious and enigmatic values that present-day commentary overlooks or recognizes only fleetingly or insufficiently. The book focuses on the emotional resonance, intellectual depth, uncanny force, and memorability of Shakespearean comedy, together with its questioning of mundane notions of causality and its broadening of the sense of etiological dynamics. It thus opens feelings and understandings to incipient new possibilities.

Literary scholarship may seem solitary, but it is as often social, for it thrives on the work, conversation, and advice of others. In that regard, I have been especially charmed in my colleagues and my discipline. One of the wonderful aspects of literary studies is working with fellow scholars and others who are astute, accomplished, and generous. The two long-time friends, William Carroll and Ágnes Matuska, from different countries and different generations, to whom this book is dedicated represent the best of the profession, and I have profited from their writing, their comments on this project, and their conversation about comedy, Shakespeare, and all things literary. My heartfelt thanks here are inadequate recompense. I also owe an enormous debt of gratitude to another long-time friend and a colleague from the University of Maryland English Department, Theodore Leinwand. Ted discussed this project with me, commented closely on several chapters, and, at a difficult stage, gave me invaluable help and advice. Among his other accomplishments, Ted has been legendary for the generous attention that he gives to graduate dissertations and to other people's work. I also wish to thank friends who have read chapters or discussed comedy and this project with me; they include Theresa Coletti, Katherine Eggert, Heather Hirschfeld, Robert Hornback, Carol Chillington Rutter, and Stuart Sillars. Fernando Cioni has also commented on parts of this material and has otherwise been an invaluable source of support.

I am grateful to Amanda Bailey, chair of English at the University of Maryland, who has provided financial assistance that has enabled crucial travel to libraries. As always, I also thank my extraordinary Medieval and Renaissance colleagues in the Maryland English Department, whose encouragement and example are a continuing source of inspiration; they include (during the writing of this book): Amanda Bailey, Kimberly Anne Coles, Theresa Coletti, Jane Donawerth, Donna

Hamilton, Theodore Leinwand, Thomas Moser, Michael Olmert, Gerard Passannante, Kellie Robertson, David Carroll Simon, and Scott Trudell. For some timely encouragement, thanks are due also to another departmental colleague, Neil Fraistat. At the University, I have been fortunate among my dissertation students to have some who shared the particular interests of this book; for their conversation and writing I extend special thanks to Kathleen Bossert, Jasmine Lellock, and Brandi Adams. I am appreciative, too, of the undergraduates who, over the years, have taken my courses on Shakespeare and on Tudor Drama; their lively observations have stimulated my own thinking immeasurably.

I have done the research for this book largely at the Folger Shakespeare Library, the British Library, and especially the Languages and Cultures Library of Ca' Foscari University of Venice. During the book's writing, I have been privileged to hold appointments as a Visiting Scholar in the Department of Linguistics and Comparative Cultures (*Dipartimento di Studi Linguistici e Culturali Comparati*) at Ca' Foscari University. The *dipartimento* has been my intellectual home-away-from-home, and I am deeply grateful for the hospitality and collegiality that I have been shown. At Ca' Foscari, I have had generous opportunities to discuss literature, Shakespeare, and my work, for which I thank my Venetian colleagues, who include Shaul Bassi, to whom I owe special gratitude, as well as Flavio Gregori, Loretta Innocenti, Geraldine Ludbrook, David Newbold, Valerio de Scarpis di Vianino, and Laura Tosi.

Parts of this book have been presented in seminar papers at the Shakespeare Association of America, and in talks at the University of North Carolina, Charlotte, the University of California, Irvine, Ca' Foscari University of Venice, the University of Padua, the Italian Association of Shakespeare and Early Modern Studies, the Italian Association of English Studies (*Associazione Italiana di Anglistica*), and the University of Szeged, Hungary. In one venue, more than any other, various strands of this book have been tried out, and that is the annual seminar-style gathering of the Bergen-Volda Shakespeare Network. I am deeply indebted to Stuart Sillars and Svenn-Arve Myklebost for serving successively as the Network's conveners, and I extend my enormous thanks to the numerous fellow scholars who have participated in these proceedings and provided me with insightful and helpful comments.

Chapter 3, "Place, Being, and Agency" is a revised version of a chapter, "Place and Being in Shakespearean Comedy," published in *The Oxford Handbook of Shakespearean Comedy*, ed. Heather Hirschfeld (Oxford: Oxford University Press, 2018). I thank the Press for permission to reprint, and, especially, I thank Professor Hirschfeld for inviting me to write the chapter and for her astute comments on drafts. Other chapters have not been previously published; limited debts to my previous publications are noted as appropriate.

At Oxford University Press, I was fortunate to have two external readers, James Bulman and an anonymous scholar, who saw value in the prospective book and who offered insightful questions, suggestions, and comments that have much improved it. Also, at the Press, I wish to thank Eleanor Collins, Senior Publishing Editor, who took an early interest in this project and then graciously and efficiently marshalled it through its various stages from proposal to final manuscript. My thanks also include Karen Raith, Commissioning Editor, Aimee Wright, Assistant Commissioning Editor, and Bheeman Dharuman, Project Manager, all of whom oversaw the book during the stages of its production.

Finally, I thank my wife, Pam, who is the center of my life and who has always believed in me and the work that I have tried to do. Lulu the cat has also graced me with her sleeping presence at odd hours as I have pondered this project.

In a book about enchantment it is perhaps fair to reiterate the sense of wonder and appreciation that I feel for the interest and encouragement given by the extraordinary group of people who have helped in a myriad of ways to bring this book to completion. As Sebastian puts it, "I can no other answer make but thanks, / And thanks, and ever thanks."

Contents

Shakespeare's Works Cited

Unless otherwise noted, references to Shakespeare's plays and poems are to the Arden Shakespeare, Third Series editions. The Arden standard abbreviations for titles will be used in parenthetical citations once the full title has been given in a chapter. In the entries below, abbreviations follow the citation.

All's Well That Ends Well. Edited by Suzanne Gossett and Helen Wilcox. London: Bloomsbury, 2018 (*AW*).

As You Like It. Edited by Juliet Dusinberre. London: Thomson Learning, 2006 (*AYL*).

The Comedy of Errors. Edited by Kent Cartwright. London: Bloomsbury, 2017 (*CE*).

Hamlet. Rev. edn. Edited by Ann Thompson and Neil Taylor. London: Bloomsbury (2006) 2016 (*Ham*).

King Henry IV, Part 1. Edited by David Scott Kastan. London: Thomson Learning, 2002.

King John. Edited by Jesse M. Lander and J. J. M. Tobin. London: Bloomsbury, 2018 (*KJ*).

Love's Labour's Lost. Edited by H. R. Woudhuysen. London: Cengage Learning, 1998 (*LLL*).

Measure for Measure. Edited by A. R. Braunmuller and Robert N. Watson. London: Bloomsbury, 2020 (*MM*).

The Merchant of Venice. Edited by John Drakakis. London: Bloomsbury, 2010 (*MV*).

The Merry Wives of Windsor. Edited by Giorgio Melchiori. London: Thomson Learning, 2000 (*MW*).

A Midsummer Night's Dream. Edited by Sukanta Chaudhuri. London: Bloomsbury, 2017 (*MND*).

Much Ado About Nothing. Rev. edn. Edited by Claire McEachern. London: Bloomsbury (2006) 2016 (*MA*).

Shakespeare's Poems. Edited by Katherine Duncan Jones and H. R. Woudhuysen. London: Thomson Learning, 2007.

The Taming of the Shrew. Edited by Barbara Hodgdon. London: Methuen, 2010 (*TS*).

Troilus and Cressida. Edited by David Bevington. London: Thomas Nelson and Sons, 1998.

Twelfth Night. Edited by Keir Elam. London: Cengage Learning, 2008 (*TN*).

Two Gentlemen of Verona. Edited by William C. Carroll. London: Thomson Learning, 2004 (*TGV*).

Introduction

Enchantment and Comedy

Believe in the simple magic of life...

Martin Buber
I and Thou

"Shakespeare did not believe in anything," asserted the famous writer and scholar. We were chatting at the reception following her poetry reading in my department a little earlier that evening. "Shakespeare did not believe in anything," she repeated, "except fairies." *Fairies*? "Yes," I responded agreeably—although not certain what she meant, her claim having perhaps turned more metaphorical than literal. Our conversation was then interrupted, leaving me in doubt. Fairies, of course, were a legacy to Shakespeare's world from medieval folk magic, preternatural beings abiding in the forest but partaking of the marvelous; to some degree like us, but vivid and intense with life.[1] They have at their disposal fairy dust, which, when sprinkled, enchants, or at least conveys the impression of enchantment. In Shakespeare's plays, fairy machinations are dangerous, yet not tragically but impishly so. They play on the border between the quotidian and the fantastical. So, our speaker may have been referring not so much to the numinous half-light of Shakespeare's beliefs as to a certain register in his artistry, to fairy dust—to Shakespeare's sense of the comic.

Enchantment, I would argue, constitutes the cause of Shakespearean comedy. Achieving a fact-based and rational conclusion—that the characters are not mad, say, but confused by twins—may be the ostensible goal of the comic action, but the plays distinguish themselves by their residual resistance to that very value. Such complexity is possible in part because Shakespeare's works build upon comedy's long development in England and pre-eminence as a Renaissance genre.[2] In the sixteenth century, comedy emerged before tragedy, rivaled it in achievement, surpassed it in volume, and persisted beyond its waning. Both in Italy and

---

[1] See C. S. Lewis, *The Discarded Image: An Introduction to Medieval and Renaissance Literature* (Cambridge: Cambridge University Press, 1964), 122–38.

[2] The present study employs both "Renaissance" and "early modern" for the era in question, recognizing that "Renaissance" leans towards certain cultural experiences (education, literature, art), while "early modern" emphasizes economic, social, and political conditions.

Shakespeare and the Comedy of Enchantment. Kent Cartwright, Oxford University Press. © Kent Cartwright 2021.
DOI: 10.1093/oso/9780198868897.003.0001

England, comedy, especially in the form of performances, adaptations, or imitations of Plautus and Terence, emerged earlier than did tragedy.[3] In the century's
opening decades, Italian playwrights such as Bibbiena, Ariosto, and Machiavelli,
writing mash-ups of classical plays, set the course for what would become
romantic comedy. Likewise, Italian comic theory, largely Aristotelian in spirit,
appeared long before, and considerably influenced, literary theory in England.
There in the sixteenth century, domestic comedy first flowered in the farcical
debate plays of John Heywood, followed Classical Roman patterns in the comedies
of Mr. S. (*Gammer Gurton's Needle*) and Nicholas Udall (*Ralph Roister Doister*),
found expressive form in the romantic comedies of John Lyly and Robert Greene,
and flourished in the comic works of Shakespeare, Ben Jonson, Thomas
Middleton, John Marston, Francis Beaumont and John Fletcher, and others.
Altogether, "comedies outnumber tragedies on the Elizabethan stage by nearly
three to one," observes Muriel Bradbrook.[4] Across the periods of Tudor and of
Stuart drama, the combination of comedies and tragicomedies much exceeded the
tally of any other genre, with their vitality extending deep into the seventeenth
century, even as tragedy lost steam. City comedy burst forth in the Jacobean
decades, and, during the reign of Charles I, the production of comedies and
tragicomedies vastly outpaced that of tragedies.[5] Today, with a few notable
exceptions, new tragedy is not being written, while comedy constitutes the most
continuous and pervasive of all dramatic kinds. And its most formative English
practitioner is Shakespeare.

Shakespeare inclined towards comedy. Although criticism has preferred his
tragedies and, in recent decades, his histories, Shakespeare's "natural disposition"
and "instinct," according to Samuel Johnson, were for comedy.[6] As John D. Cox
puts it, "the genre that arguably best represents [Shakespeare's] characteristic way
of thinking" is comedy.[7] Shakespeare wrote more comedies than plays in any
other genre. Of the First Folio's thirty-six works, fourteen are listed as comedies,
compared to ten histories and eleven tragedies. That list of comedies could be
culled by removing *The Tempest* and *The Winter's Tale*, but one would need to
acknowledge that those and other late romances continue to explore forms and

---

[3] On English comedy's emergence, see Bruce R. Smith, *Ancient Scripts and Modern Experience on
the English Stage, 1500–1700* (Princeton, NJ: Princeton University Press, 1988), 134–98. On the rise of
Italian sixteenth-century comedy, see Douglas Radcliff-Umstead, *The Birth of Modern Comedy in
Renaissance Italy* (Chicago, IL: University of Chicago Press, 1969). On the critical underestimation of
early comedy, see Robert Hornback, *The English Clown Tradition from the Middle Ages to Shakespeare*
(Cambridge: D. S. Brewer, 2009), 3–5.

[4] Muriel C. Bradbrook, *The Growth and Structure of Elizabethan Comedy* (London: Chatto &
Windus, 1955), 3.

[5] See Alfred Harbage, *Annals of English Drama, 970–1700*, rev. S. Schoenbaum; 3rd edn. rev. Sylvia
Stoler Wagonheim (London: Routledge, 1989).

[6] Samuel Johnson, *Mr. Johnson's Preface to his Edition of Shakespear's Plays* (London, 1765), xvii.

[7] John D. Cox, *Seeming Knowledge: Shakespeare and Skeptical Faith* (Waco, TX: Baylor University
Press, 2007), 34.

issues broached in the earlier comedies. Both the tragedies and especially the histories are rich in comic episodes, presided over by figures such as the grave-digger in *Hamlet* or Falstaff in *1–2 Henry IV*.[8] Shakespeare's comedies themselves constitute vibrantly restless experiments in the genre and its possibilities, from New Comedy romance, to comedy of manners, to pastoral comedy, to "problem" comedy.[9] As Bart van Es states, comedy was "the dominant form in [Shakespeare's] art."[10] Something about comedy called forth that monumental outpouring.

My Argument in a Nutshell

Let me summarize my approach here; later sections of this Introduction locate the argument amidst a range of critical issues. Although comedy has always been difficult to analyze, theoretical attention to the genre has recently ticked up. The present study addresses Shakespearean comedy as an encounter between its rationalizing dimensions and those extra-rational aspects that elude demystifica-tion and exert affective power, an encounter between what is explicable and what is inexplicable.[11] It situates itself in relation to the claim that scientific modernity is the age of disenchantment. Thus, my title foregrounds "enchantment" because my argument arises in the shadow of present-day disenchantment; because the comedies showcase the play of wonder and doubt; and because they often leave behind a sense of residual re-enchantment. The study also pays attention to comic theory. Generally, a Shakespearean comedy progresses from trickery or error, through confusion—with occurrences that seem magical or mad—to, finally, a rational sorting out of cause and effect, presided over by an authority figure, "the duke." Romantic love is usually at stake, heightening apprehensions of magic or madness. The resolution feels ingenious but apt, as in the way *As You Like It* deftly lines up its four couples for marriage, that neatness itself producing rational delight. For such reasons, the development of early modern comedy has been

---

[8] According to Susan Snyder, many of Shakespeare's tragedies are built upon comic form; *The Comic Matrix of Shakespeare's Tragedies* (Princeton, NJ: Princeton University Press, 1979).

[9] The present study encompasses the Shakespearean plays that modern criticism treats as comedies, through *All's Well That Ends Well*. *Troilus and Cressida* is omitted, being perhaps, as David Bevington puts it, "in a genre, or a *mélange* of genres, all to itself"; *Troilus and Cressida*, 4. This study makes occasional reference to the late romances, such as *The Winter's Tale*, but its subject is the earlier plays.

[10] Bart van Es, *Shakespeare's Comedies: A Very Short Introduction* (Oxford: Oxford University Press, 2016), 109; on Susan Snyder's argument, see van Es, 100–2.

[11] Heather Hirschfeld has recently stressed the term "encounter"—"a moment of contact marked by confrontation, opposition, or conflict as well as by the possibility or potential for future negotiation, amity, and even affection"—as a way of viewing comedy; "Introduction," *The Oxford Handbook of Shakespearean Comedy* (Oxford: Oxford University Press, 2018), 4, see 1–18. Hirschfeld takes special interest in the encounter with the cultural "other," typically understood in racial, ethnic, geographic, or gendered terms, but the notion of encounter can be helpfully extended to other confrontations, as between the rational and the extra-rational.

aligned with developments in the protocols for fact-finding and the juridical understanding of events.

Yet as the comic action advances, elements of mystery accrue—uncanny coincidences, magical sympathies, inexplicable repetitions, psychic influences, wonders, fears, and doubts about the meaning of events—all of whose effects linger after reason has apparently answered the play's questions. Another, mystifying order of affect and causation seems at work, albeit half-hidden, felt against the current. A Shakespearean comedy accumulates a sense of mystery that leaves a residue, an affective surplus, often extra-rational, that spills beyond the usual explanations. We might collect those effects into a soft-sided container marked "enchantment." The comic elements in question include the topics of the ensuing chapters: (1) magical clowns and fools who introduce disruptive, non-realistic 'time-out-of-time' moments that influence the protagonists, alter the flow of the main action, and shape meaning; (2) repetitions, such as within and among scenes, that evoke a seemingly uncanny dreamscape suggesting mysteriously converging destinies and opaque but providential outcomes; (3) places with differing affective and metaphorical characteristics and possibilities that frame encounters between the regulatory and the protean drives in human existence; (4) desires and utterances that magically generate, or 'manifest,' comically monstrous realities, including objects and individuals; (5) characters who return from the dead, reflecting a sense of the haunting of the present by the past, facilitated by the desires of the living; and (6) play-endings that traffic variously in wonder and wondering, including moments when wonder creates the irrational possibility of forgiveness. The term "enchantment" captures the agency of those encounters and their transformative immanence, as if haloed with meaning. They are like a grid of soft theatrical lights composed of different tones and luminosities, brightening at different times and to greater or lesser degrees, yet always radiating with interrelated significance. While some of our immediate attention to comedy focuses on its glittering surface, the chiaroscuro values of enchantment suggest alternative etiologies and add depth and staying power to the comic encounter; recognizing them can reformulate our sense of comedy's aims and effects. Enchantment, then, functions as reason's shadow. For playgoers and readers, like characters, the comic experience can feel both miraculously revealing and obscurely unsettling.[12]

"Enchantment" weaves together matters structural, characterological, and metaphorical. It also, as we shall see, gathers up certain Elizabethan habits of mind. The term helps to identify a Wittgensteinian family, or network, of values

---

[12] Richard C. McCoy argues that Shakespeare's plays use religious language as a source of purely dramatic and theatrical power so as to deny the possibility of supernatural truth; *Faith in Shakespeare* (Oxford: Oxford University Press, 2013). It is preferable, I think, to leave the question of metaphysics open.

and causes sifting through Shakespeare's comedies.[13] Present-day critics have begun to employ the language of actor-network theory, which can helpfully point towards newly conceived ways of organizing evidence. Bruno Latour developed the concept in order to reach across vast webs of causation whose interrelationships tend to disappear from view when information is divided into the spheres of formalized knowledge (science, politics, discourse). Actor-network theory allows one to jump the artificial boundaries of disciplines. In *We Have Never Been Modern*, Latour introduces "network" when discussing the example of AIDS, and one can see the usefulness of the concept for large-scale, multi-dimensional problems that involve data, social systems, and cultural interpretation.[14] It may be sleight of hand to try to refashion that term into a mode of literary analysis, yet Latour does draw from drama. In actor-network theory, action is "not a coherent, controlled, well-rounded, and clean-edged affair. By definition, action is *dislocated*. Action is borrowed, distributed, suggested, influenced, dominated, betrayed, translated," so that its source is always "uncertain."[15] In making that argument, Latour invokes the example of the theater, where "it's never clear who and what is acting."[16]

Comedy, like drama generally, functions as a Latourian network, we might say, by unleashing an overabundance of causes. Such overabundance in an artwork can undermine "official" explanations that would dominate conclusions and express the preferences of the prevailing power structure, argues Caroline Levine.[17] In Shakespearean comedy, the different vectors of enchantment make up such a network. They reveal a second experiential, sometimes causal layer that the surface narrative of rational, proto-scientific etiology cannot quite capture but that seems quietly, resiliently *there*. This encounter between rationality and enchantment recalls the more familiar aesthetic conflict between harmony and dissonance. For Paul B. Armstrong, that latter opposition is critical: "[L]iterature plays with the brain through experiences of harmony and dissonance that set in motion and help to negotiate oppositions that are fundamental to the neurobiology of mental functioning—basic tensions in the operation of the brain between the drive for pattern, synthesis, and constancy versus the need for flexibility,

---

[13] In such a grouping, set A overlaps with set B, B with set C, C with set D, such that although sets A and D do not overlap with each other, they are nonetheless linked within the same network; see Ludwig Wittgenstein, *Philosophical Investigations*, trans. G. E. M. Anscombe, 2nd edn (Oxford: Basil Blackwell, [1953] 1958), part I, section 65ff.

[14] Bruno Latour, *We Have Never Been Modern*, trans. Catherine Porter (Cambridge, MA: Harvard University Press, 1993; orig. pub. in French, 1991), 111.

[15] Bruno Latour, *Reassembling the Social: An Introduction to Actor-Network Theory* (Oxford: Oxford University Press, 2005), 46.

[16] Latour, *Reassembling*, 46.

[17] Caroline Levine, *Forms: Whole, Rhythm, Hierarchy, Network* (Princeton, NJ: Princeton University Press, 2015); see esp. 112–31.

adaptability, and openness to change."[18] Enchantment, with its ruffling undertow of doubts and questions, creates its own encounter between harmony and dissonance; therein lies its power.

In its various aspects, then, enchantment stands for the elusiveness of comic experience (indeed, even those characters representing rational authority can be deluded). A protagonist's invocations of the occult necessarily confuse our sense of causation, for the occult's workings are always occluded and often manifold, so that enchantment becomes a master trope for overdetermination, the surplus of explanations, described by Latour. Enchantment entails doubt and suspicion; it problematizes the business of explanation itself. With Shakespeare, enchantment evokes a double response, a sense of both its absurdity and yet its possibility (in contrast to Italian comedies, which often parody magic). Shakespeare's comedies create wonder and wondering—sometimes disturbingly so, as in *The Merchant of Venice*—which traverse the boundary between what yields to quotidian explanation and what resists.

Comedy's interest in causation and explanation makes it a genre of the moment; we need more of it, especially the Shakespearean sort. In a social and political world of hardening ideological conflicts, works that empower Armstrong's "flexibility, adaptability, and openness to change" call for fresh cultivation. No wonder that the genre of comedy, with its capacity for both objectivity and openness, could take on the sixteenth-century world of upheaval and alteration. Shakespeare's comedies have not only the power to satirize fantasies and false preconceptions and to prompt moral insight but also the perhaps more important power to celebrate human irrepressibility, to animate utopian dreams, and to forge community. Those works show the potential of comic form to be morally inquisitive as well as visionary. As John Cox puts it, Shakespeare's comedies "affirm the possibility of repairing and renewing individuals and communities."[19] Behind comic laughter hums a love song to the extravagant possibilities of the human condition. Since Shakespeare's is the richest, most diverse, and most influential body of comedy ever written, the claims made about its powers of enchantment bear directly on how we understand comedy as a form—a set of structural, conceptual, experiential, and cultural latencies—that speaks to us today. Although comedy may resist rules and systems, a study of Shakespeare's oeuvre casts a reflected light on the potentialities of the genre, whether it takes the form of Greek and Roman New Comedy, Renaissance English and Italian comedy, Restoration comedy of manners, the works of Oscar Wilde and G. B. Shaw, Hollywood screwball comedy, or film and television romantic comedy.

---

[18] Paul B. Armstrong, *How Literature Plays with the Brain: The Neuroscience of Reading and Art* (Baltimore, MD: Johns Hopkins University Press, 2013), ix.
[19] Cox, *Seeming Knowledge*, 35.

Theories of Comedy and the Rational Dimension

As commentators remark, comedy constitutes the least understood and least studied of genres. We lack "any satisfactory definition of comedy," declares Wylie Sypher bluntly.[20] Yet a number of theoretical works on comedy have appeared of late, including Agnes Heller's *Immortal Comedy*, Jan Walsh Hokenson's *The Idea of Comedy*, William Demastes's *Comedy Matters*, Alenka Zupančič's *The Odd One In*, Dmitri Nikulin's *Comedy, Seriously*, Todd McGowan's *Only a Joke Can Save Us*, and Terry Eagleton's *Humour*.[21] That upsurge of interest argues for the importance of comedy as the genre of the moment. Notwithstanding, comedy offers difficult terrain, criss-crossed with pathways leading in opposite directions, the same comedy, as Scott Shershow notes, capable of producing incompatible interpretations.[22] Modern critics, observes Richard Keller Simon,

> have argued that comedy is a force for civilization (Meredith) and a force of nature against the repressions of civilization (Freud, Santayana); that the comic corrects aberrant behavior (Bergson) and that the comic does not correct aberrant behavior (Smith); that comedy celebrates what is (Scott) and that it celebrates what should be (Feibleman); that it represents detachment from life (Bergson) and that it represents engagement with life (Burke); that it is an irrational attitude (Sypher), a rational attitude (Swabey), and a force both rational and irrational (Gurewitsch [*sic.*]); that it is politically left (Feibleman) and politically right (Cook); that it affirms freedom (Kaul, McFadden) and that it denies freedom (Girard); that it shows the victory of the individual (Torrance) and that it shows the victory of society over the individual (Bergson, Duncan); that its subject is carnival (Santayana) and that its subject is everyday life (Kaul); that it requires self-consciousness (Burke) and that it requires a lack of self-consciousness (Mack).[23]

---

[20] Wylie Sypher, "The Meaning of Comedy," in *Comedy:* An Essay on Comedy *by George Meredith;* Laughter *by Henri Bergson; Introduction and Appendix,* "The Meanings of Comedy," *by Wylie Sypher,* ed. Wylie Sypher (Garden City, NY: Doubleday Anchor, 1956), 191–255, on 206.

[21] Agnes Heller, *Immortal Comedy: The Comic Phenomenon in Art, Literature, and Life* (Lanham, MD: Lexington Books, 2005); Jan Walsh Hokenson, *The Idea of Comedy: History, Theory, Critique* (Madison, NJ: Fairleigh Dickinson University Press, 2006); William W. Demastes, *Comedy Matters: From Shakespeare to Stoppard* (New York: Palgrave Macmillan, 2008); Alenka Zupančič, *The Odd One In: On Comedy* (Cambridge, MA: MIT Press, 2008); Dmitri Nikulin, *Comedy, Seriously: A Philosophical Study* (New York: Palgrave Macmillan, 2014); Todd McGowen, *Only a Joke Can Save Us: A Theory of Comedy* (Evanston, IL: Northwestern University Press, 2017); Terry Eagleton, *Humour* (New Haven, CT: Yale University Press, 2019). For an historical survey of comedy, see Andrew McConnell Stott and Eric Weitz, eds., *A Cultural History of Comedy,* 6 vols. (London: Bloomsbury, 2020).

[22] Scott Cutler Shershow, *Laughing Matters: The Paradox of Comedy* (Amherst, MA: University of Massachusetts Press, 1986), 26.

[23] Richard Keller Simon, *The Labyrinth of the Comic: Theory and Practice from Fielding to Freud* (Tallahassee, FL: Florida State University, 1985), 239–40; Simon's summary has been often noted. To

Of course, a specific work might invoke only some of the binaries on Simon's amusing list, or it might contain both sides of an opposition, as when the everyday coexists with the carnivalesque. An era's critical interest will shift, winnowing the reigning number of antitheses—or even moving beyond the idea itself of antithesis. Of Simon's descriptors, pertinent for Shakespeare and the present study is the difficult relationship between comedy and rationality. Heller points out that "laughter is rational, not emotional" and that any "therapeutic effect" of comic experience "is mediated by reflection, by understanding, by the work of the intellect" (*Immortal*, 8, 11). Relatedly, Nikulin has argued that comedy is a philosophical genre in which "the realization of human well-being and freedom" in society is achieved through an action that reflects "careful and consequential— 'logical'—reasoning"; "comedy reproduces the structure of philosophical reasoning in its very plot."[24] Here comedy's project is to advance human fulfillment, found in community, through the sophisticated exercise of rationality. Meredith, too, felt that "comic intelligence" promoted civilized society.[25] Positions such as Nikulin's sound like defenses of Enlightenment values, with comedy as the field of contest, intended implicitly to rebut the modern and postmodern "devaluation of reason" that, for Hokenson, is the "one governing principle of recent comic theory."[26]

Nikulin's argument squares with the literary and historical analysis of Lorna Hutson, who sees Renaissance comedy as crucial to the emergence of protocols for modern rational thinking and communal problem-solving. In that view, early modern English comedy reflects rhetorical training in grammar schools along with rising evidentiary standards and coherent explanatory narratives in jurisprudence.[27] Hutson's perspective aligns with the work of historians such as Barbara Shapiro, who identifies in the early modern period the crystalizing of the notion of "fact" in the arena of law.[28] Shapiro sees her study as intersecting with "the innovative work of Steven Shapin and Simon Schaffer on the construction of early modern English empirical natural philosophy, Lorraine Daston's on the history of objectivity and marvels, and Peter Dear's on 'experience' and

---

this list might be added Nelson's opposition between causing laughter or moving towards reconciliation; T. G. A. Nelson, *Comedy: An Introduction of Comedy in Literature, Drama, and Culture* (Oxford: Oxford University Press, 1990). Hokenson sees the splintering of views as a modern phenomenon (174); her *The Idea of Comedy* provides a helpful history of theories of comedy. For a collection of extracts from historical works on comic theory, see Magda Romanska and Alan Ackerman, *Reader in Comedy: An Anthology in Theory & Criticism* (London: Bloomsbury, 2017).

[24] Nikulin, *Seriously*, viii, ix; he draws his examples largely from Greek and Roman New Comedy.

[25] George Meredith, "An Essay on Comedy," in Sypher, *Comedy*, 3–57, on 33. From an ecological perspective, Demastes argues that comedy helps us to recognize ourselves not as "discrete, individuated life forms" but "as environmented parts of some larger whole"; *Comedy Matters*, 2.

[26] Hokenson, *Idea*, 185.

[27] Lorna Hutson, *The Invention of Suspicion: Law and Mimesis in Shakespeare and Renaissance Drama* (Oxford: Oxford University Press, 2007).

[28] Barbara J. Shapiro, *A Culture of Fact: England, 1550–1720* (Ithaca, NY: Cornell University Press, 2000).

'experiment'" (2). An argument for comedy's rationalism, that is, can be located in a large and complex historical, philosophical, and literary project to understand developments in epistemology and proto-scientific ways of knowing in the early modern period.

From the perspective of Nikulin and Hutson, comedy becomes partner to the intellectual and cultural trends that produce the scientific revolution and eventually the modern sense of disenchantment. Comedies turn on errors and deceptions, of course, and, in Shakespeare, as noted, the comic knots are unraveled in the denouement typically by a rational authority figure who compares conflicting narratives, sorts out inconsistencies, brings forth the truth, and, on those grounds, passes moral judgment.[29] Thus, *Much Ado About Nothing*'s Friar Francis achieves insight about Hero's honesty by applying trained knowledge and disinterested observation of physical details. The "pragmatic and practical skill" of "careful noting" that *Much Ado* depicts is, according to Jean Howard, "more congruent with the dawning scientific age than with the age of faith."[30] Yet truth-seeking can encounter roadblocks, and those obstacles interested Renaissance Italian theorists of comedy. Ludovico Castelvetro's *Commentary of Aristotle's Poetics* (1570) discusses the multiple ways that comic characters can be deceived,[31] and Francesco Robortello's *On Comedy* (1548) feels compelled to enumerate the types of discovery—through memory, reasoning, and signs—that can be employed to uncover the truth.[32] Those matters troubled the Renaissance, which—given its religious controversies and the rise of the Machiavellian state—has been called "'the age of dissimulation.'"[33] Comedy, notes Eric Bentley, "makes much of appearances."[34] How does one discover the truth?

Comedy's rational dimension connects to a host of cognate values, including inductive thinking, based on empirical evidence, and careful, unbiased attention to details, especially physical facts and reliable testimony, parallel to the processes of judicial forensics, as in Hutson's model. Such rationality undertakes a comprehensive and systematic interpretation of its data, all puzzle-pieces fitted

[29] In Tudor comedy, this figure already appears: for example Bailey, the bailiff, in *Gammer Gurton's Needle* (c. 1553). Paul A. Olson sees Shakespeare's introduction of the duke figure as his "first significant invention or expansion" from New Comedy, noting that such characters are almost entirely absent in Plautus and Terence; *Beyond a Common Joy: An Introduction to Shakespearean Comedy* (Lincoln, NE: University of Nebraska Press, 2008), 31–2.
[30] Jean E. Howard, *The Stage and Social Struggle in Early Modern England* (New York: Routledge, 1994), 60.
[31] Lodovico Castelvetro, from "Commentary on Aristotle's 'Poetics'" (1570), trans. Andrew Bongiorno, in *Theories of Comedy*, ed. Paul Lauter (Garden City, NY: Anchor Books, 1964), 87–97.
[32] Franciscus Robortellus, "On Comedy" (1548), trans. Marvin T. Herrick, in Marvin T. Herrick, *Comic Theory in the Sixteenth Century* (Urbana, IL: University of Illinois Press, 1964), 227–39, on 233.
[33] Jon R. Snyder, *Dissimulation and the Culture of Secrecy in Early Modern Europe* (Berkeley, CA: University of California Press, 2009), 5. Likewise the Renaissance seems to have been fascinated with the idea of error; François Rigolot, "The Renaissance Fascination with Error: Mannerism and Early Modern Poetry," *Renaissance Quarterly* 57, no. 4 (Winter 2004): 1219–34.
[34] Eric Bentley, *The Life of Drama* (New York: Atheneum, 1983), 242.

into place in a way that produces overall coherence. It thus moves towards a rational demystification of seemingly magical events, as happens variously in plays from *The Comedy of Errors* and *A Midsummer Night's Dream* to *All's Well That Ends Well*. In comedy's rational dimension, human affairs reveal themselves as governed by contingencies and forces that can be discovered by intellect. Crucially, truth emerges only in the community of characters, for truth must comprehend the different experiences of those participants, and it receives implicit validation by communal acceptance. The rational dimension of comedy brings great satisfactions not only to characters but also to spectators and readers, who take pleasure in an unraveling of mysteries that organizes past events into a surprising and coherent narrative, or in seeing a character finally achieve those recognitions possessed before only by them.[35]

But a comedy's official narrative seldom eradicates every doubt. Even an authority figure might not seem entirely objective. The Duke in *Two Gentlemen* acts capriciously at the close and seems deceived about certain characters. Duke Solinus in *Errors* does not recognize his own desire to free Egeon out of sympathy, surely a partial motivator of his actions. In *Much Ado*'s ending, neither Leonato nor Don Pedro, despite their self-satisfaction, grasps fully the emotional facts. The King in *All's Well* becomes so exasperated in the denouement that he almost prevents the truth from coming out. His behavior illuminates the dangers of the authority figure's peremptoriness and sense of privilege. Evidence gets left out, too. The trick in *Much Ado* is never fully revealed to Beatrice and Benedick. In *Errors*, after the Duke has sorted out the confusions of the double doubles and the separated couples, with the whole party heading into the abbey to celebrate, the Abbess remarks on "this sympathized one-day's error." The phrase might slip by, except that it lands the phosphorescent word "sympathized," recalling magical theories of sympathy and antipathy, attraction and repulsion relevant to the preceding events. What the Duke cannot explain, and what the Abbess breaks open for consideration, is the working of psychic or cosmic forces that have brought characters together, even allowed them dimly to share thoughts.

Shakespeare's comic endings provoke other uneasy wonderings. Can the Egeon-family's joy at reunion compensate for their prior sufferings? Might Beatrice and Benedick actually talk each other to marital death? Will Viola remain partially Cesario? Can Vienna achieve justice? Will Bertram actually cherish Helen? We wonder, and part of that wondering, the enchantment of the moment, is our fascinated scrutinizing of those characters' attitudes and responses left enigmatical in Shakespeare's endings. In the wake of harmony, the plays leave a backwash of dissonance. On a broader level of potential dissonance, Shakespeare's comedies frequently introduce large-scale social problems but solve them only

---

[35] See Claire McEachern, *Believing in Shakespeare: Studies in Longing* (Cambridge: Cambridge University Press, 2018).

pragmatically, contingently. The 'problem' that critics see in a play such as *Measure for Measure*—that it raises issues of moral corruption in the social body and of abuse of power in the body politic but can only sort them out through a bed trick—is the extreme version of the dilemma that haunts all the comedies: systematic wrongs addressed by situational remedies. Other comedies of the period, as in Italian cinquecento comedy and Tudor comedy, reflect that conundrum. Its pervasiveness suggests that Renaissance comedy operates, not as bad faith, but as the groundwork for, and provocation to, further thought.[36] Wondering turns not conclusive but generative.

Enchantment and Shakespearean Comedy

Comedy's rational dimension carries us from the demystifying of magic to Max Weber's famous, albeit cryptic, notion of "disenchantment." The term derives from a 1917 lecture by Weber, "Science as Vocation," in which he characterizes the modern drive towards "rationalization" and "intellectualization" as "the disenchantment of the world."[37] Weber insists uneasily that by "[t]echnical means and calculation" humans can control "all things" without the need for magic or prayer, so that "disenchantment" becomes a byword for the centuries-long "progress" presided over by science (35). For Weber, disenchantment initiates an historically "inexorable and self-compounding" movement towards rationality and human domination.[38] Disenchantment, then, has come to stand for a set of social values and trends—rationalism, scientism, bureaucracy, capitalism—and with them a disregard of cultural and ethnic differences and a reification of sameness. The term has organized a sustained discussion about the nature of modernism.[39]

---

[36] Jeremy Lopez argues for the thought-provoking complexity of Elizabethan drama; *Theatrical Convention and Audience Response* (Cambridge: Cambridge University Press, 2004), esp. 37, 131–3, 170–200. Robert Hornback sees intellectual, aesthetic, and emotional complexity in Elizabethan stage clowning; *Clown Tradition*, 9.

[37] Max Weber, "Science as Vocation," in *Max Weber's Complete Writings on Academic and Political Vocations*, ed. John Dreijmanis, trans. Gordon C. Wells (New York: Algora Publishing, 2008), 25–52, on 51. Weber is here alluding to a thesis that he had previously developed; see his *The Protestant Ethic and the Spirit of Capitalism*, trans. Talcott Parsons (London: George Allen and Unwin Ltd., 1930; orig. pub. in German, 1904–5). For an influential related work, see Keith Thomas, *Religion and the Decline of Magic: Studies in Popular Beliefs in Sixteenth and Seventeenth Century England* (Harmondsworth: Penguin, [1971] 1973).

[38] Nandini Das and Nick Davis, "Introduction," in *Enchantment and Dis-enchantment in Shakespeare and Early Modern Drama: Wonder, the Sacred, and the Supernatural*, ed. Das and Davis (New York: Routledge, 2017), 1–17, on 3.

[39] In the foundational document of Critical Theory, Max Horkheimer and Theodor W. Adorno invoke Weber's term "disenchantment" and critique the modern failure of Enlightenment reason; *Dialectic of Enlightenment: Philosophical Fragments*, ed. G. S. Noerr, trans. E. Jephcott (Stanford, CA: Stanford University Press, 2002; orig. pub. in German, 1947).

Resisting the presumably de-humanizing effects of disenchantment, a literature has grown up around the idea of "re-enchantment."[40] Sociologist Nicholas Gane, for example, has written about Weber's own discomfort with modern disenchantment and about arguments that imagine re-enchantment, as offered by Jacques Lyotard, Michel Foucault, and Jean Baudrillard.[41] Thus, the idea of "disenchantment" has entailed a counter-movement, with notions of secularity and religion typically becoming inextricable. According to Joshua Landy and Michael Saler, the void left by disenchantment has been filled by philosophers, artists, writers, and others with new secular strategies for re-enchantment: "[T]he progressive disenchantment of the world was thus accompanied, from the start and continually, by its progressive re-enchantment."[42] Landy and Saler favor what they call an "antinomial" position that acknowledges in modern life the contraries of "rationality and wonder, secularism and faith" (3): "[M]odernity is characterized by fruitful tensions between seemingly irreconcilable forces and ideas … [by] contradictions, oppositions, and antinomies: modernity is messy" (6–7).[43] They propose that "[i]f the world is to be re-enchanted," it must be re-imbued with mystery and wonder, order and purpose, even the possibility of redemption: "[T]here must be everyday *miracles*, exceptional events which go against (and perhaps even alter) the accepted order of things" (2).[44] The modern fiction of magical realism, among other types, might be understood in that spirit.

---

[40] Besides works subsequently named in this chapter, see Marlies Kronegger and Anna-Teresa Tymieniecka, eds., *Analecta Husserliana*, vol. 65: *The Aesthetics of Enchantment in the Fine Arts* (Dordrecht, The Netherlands: Springer Science+Business Media, 2000). The volume's typical model for enchantment is the Siren's song in *The Odyssey*; see the contributions by Anna-Teresa Tymieniecka, Gary Backhaus, Steven Leuthold, and David Brubaker. A significant interest in enchantment has arisen in the fine arts; see, for example, James Elkins and David Morgan, eds., *The Art Seminar*, vol. 7: *Re-Enchantment* (New York: Routledge, 2009), and in that collection David Morgan, "Enchantment, Disenchantment, Re-Enchantment," 3–23. On the early modern period's polemical use of narratives of enchantment and disenchantment, see Jason Crawford, *Allegory and Enchantment: An Early Modern Poetics* (Oxford: Oxford University Press, 2017).

[41] Nicholas Gane, *Max Weber: Rationalization versus Re-enchantment* (Houndmills, Basingstoke: Palgrave, 2002).

[42] Joshua Landy and Michael Saler, *The Re-Enchantment of the World* (Stanford, CA: Stanford University Press, 2009), 1–14, on 2. Interested readers might consult Landy and Saler's bibliography; also 281, n. 28. An early sociological work in this mode is Morris Berman, *The Reenchantment of the World* (Cornell, NY: Cornell University Press, 1981). See also Joshua Landy, *How To Do Things with Fictions* (Oxford: Oxford University Press, 2012), 43–92; and Michael Saler, *As If: Modern Enchantment and the Literary Prehistory of Virtual Reality* (Oxford: Oxford University Press, 2011).

[43] Sianne Ngai, among others, looks at certain modern forms of "enchantment" as affects of capitalism; *Theory of the Gimmick: Aesthetic Judgment and Capitalist Form* (Cambridge, MA: The Belknap Press of Harvard University Press, 2020). Seeing the power of enchantment in early modern drama, however, broadens its cultural relevance beyond the devices of a later capitalism.

[44] For a suggestive itemizing of the challenges to the teleology of disenchantment, see Das and Davis, *Enchantment*, 4–6. Science itself often defies everyday logic, as in quantum mechanics's wave / particle paradox, dark energy, string theory, Schrödinger's cat, or quantum entanglement (which Einstein famously called "spooky"). "[R]eality," says physicist Carlo Rovelli, "seems to be made up of the same stuff that our dreams are made of"; *Seven Brief Lessons on Physics* (New York: Riverhead Books, 2016), 11.

Jane Bennett argues that "contemporary life" is sprinkled with "moments of enchantment" and—importantly for this study—that the "affective force of those moments might be deployed to propel ethical generosity"; that is, the "mood of enchantment may be valuable for ethical life."[45] "*[E]nchantment* entails a state of wonder," Bennett argues, a "temporary suspension of chronological time and bodily movement" that attests to the sense of the uniqueness that surrounds the object (4; see 4–6). Enchantment involves "exhilaration" and "acute sensory activity"; indeed, wonder can prompt a close looking at the particularities of things, a heightened scrutiny of details, coupled to the experience of being "carried away" (5), our perceptions focused, "sharpen[ed]," and "intensif[ied]" (5). It can also be prompted by "complexity."[46] Thus, wonder occurs as different from, but not opposite to, rationality, with the suggestion that intense rational observation could even expand into the experience of awe. Wonder takes the form of engagement with life in its immediacy, "overflow[ing] familiar categories of perception."[47] For Bennett, enchantment brings surprise, sometimes fear, certainly pleasure, along with a sense of the uncanny and "a mood of fullness, plenitude, or liveliness."[48] She cites Gilles Deleuze and Felix Guattari to the effect that enchantment can feel transformative, partly by increasing the speed of one's reactions and also by networking together objects presumably devoid of "'natural affinity'" (6). Thus, wonder and enchantment enable the breaching of boundaries and nurture "ethical generosity" (3). Enchantment, then, is not anti-rational; we should be cautious of a false dichotomy. The qualities described by Bennett will come into play in our ensuing discussions.

Bennett's view fits with the perspectives of Shakespeare scholars who have discussed wonder in the comedies. For T. G. Bishop, Shakespearean wonder identifies an inbetweenness, especially a capacity to frame and inspect "the emotions it generates"; it thus becomes a "'switchpoint' for transactions between emotional and rational responses," registering "significance."[49] In comedy, Bishop observes, "wonder absorbs into itself the resistance of skepticism" (73) yet accepts skepticism's force; the "tempering of wonder and skepticism against one another" mark out "Shakespeare's comic practice" (74), for wonder identifies the plays' "simultaneous desires for continuity and discontinuity" (73). According to Peter G. Platt, wonder exercises a "continuing, if tenuous, power" for Renaissance

---

[45] Jane Bennett, *The Enchantment of Modern Life: Attachments, Crossings, and Ethics* (Princeton, NJ: Princeton University Press, 2001), 3, 2. In a related argument, Genevieve Guenther sees the intentions of Renaissance literature as analogous to magic, with its transport of delight undertaking to alter readers or spectators ethically; *Magical Imaginations: Instrumental Aesthetics in the English Renaissance* (Toronto: University of Toronto Press, 2012).

[46] Bennett, *Enchantment*, 10, see 91–110.   [47] Das and Davis, *Enchantment*, 2.

[48] Bennet, *Enchantment*, 5.

[49] T. G. Bishop, *Shakespeare and the Theatre of Wonder* (Cambridge: Cambridge University Press, 1996), 3, 4.

writers.[50] Platt underscores wonder as an experience that lasts rather than one (in Aristotle's view) diminished quickly by reason, and he notes wonder's capacity to challenge and alter "ways of knowing and perceiving the world" (xv). In that argument, Platt draws upon the anti-Aristotelian poetical theories, perhaps underappreciated, of the cinquecento Italian Platonist Francesco Patrizi (2–18 and passim.).[51] Like Bennett and Bishop, Platt explores wonder as simultaneously "an ongoing inquiry and an aesthetic astonishment" (125) (although the late plays privilege wonder over skepticism).[52]

In the world of late cinquecento Italian comedy—such as Girolamo Bargagli's *La pellegrina* ("The Female Pilgrim") *c.*1568—wonder can be prolonged and experienced as extended transport, ecstasy, as in Platt's view. Shakespeare's comedies likewise contain examples of wonder sustained through a series of speeches and discoveries, as in the endings of *The Comedy of Errors*, *As You Like It*, and *Twelfth Night*; but often, too, wonder is acknowledged but not given long duration, as in the unveiling of Hero in *Much Ado About Nothing*. There Claudio and Don Pedro's wonder is interrupted by the Friar, who wants to urge the wedding along, while he in turn is interrupted by Benedick, who wants to be married to Beatrice. Wonder is here not so much "qualif[ied]" (i.e., proven) (5.4.67) or intensified as it is diffused into other concerns. Elsewhere, as in *The Comedy of Errors*, wonder at the close will encourage characters and spectators to scrutinize those on stage (Who is who? Who thinks what?), exemplifying Bennett's claim that wonder can draw attention to particularities. Wonder can likewise lead to ethical responses, especially the possibility of forgiveness, as we shall see. Yet it can be moderated in intensity—not every occurrence of wonder in the comedies need be a sublime, top-of-the-mountain emotion—and ironized, too, as happens with Lorenzo's effort, undercut by Jessica, to sprinkle his own fairy dust in the last scene of *The Merchant of Venice*. In *The Taming of the Shrew*, onstage spectators often experience something like wonder at Kate's last speech, but observers off-stage can be left in a state of puzzlement about its meaning. These endings invoke wonder as a significant condition of the plays but surround it with the sardonic, the anxious, the prosaic, the wondering at wonder—with comedy.

[50]   Peter G. Platt, *Reason Diminished: Shakespeare and the Marvelous* (Lincoln, NE: University of Nebraska Press, 1997), xiv.

[51]   For Patrizi, the goal of a poetic work is to induce wonder in its audience. He argues that poetry calls a new faculty into being, the "*potenza ammirativa*," at the intersection of the cognitive and the affective; Bernard Weinberg, *A History of Literary Criticism in the Italian Renaissance*, vol. 2 of 2 (Chicago, IL: University of Chicago Press, 1961), 774, see 772–5. Patrizi's *Della poetica* was published in Venice in Italian in 1586.

[52]   In an influential essay with a different perspective, Stephen J. Greenblatt associates the Renaissance "experience of wonder" with "the spectacle of proprietorship" (179), although he cites Patrizi in discussing Renaissance wonder as initially a kind of textual ravishment; "Resonance and Wonder," in *Learning to Curse: Essays in Early Modern Culture* (New York: Routledge, 1990), 161–83.

The Comic Surplus

Enchantment's affective residue can be compared to the critical concept of the "surplus." The term "surplus" was coined by Karl Marx to indicate the monetary exchange-value of a commodity produced by labor, in excess of the cost of the labor itself: Labor goes into the commodity, and both the cost of labor and surplus-value come out. Some theorists of literature, and specifically of comedy, have adapted the idea of surplus or surplus-value.[53] Notably, Paul Ricoeur uses the phrase "surplus of meaning" to indicate the potential of a literary work to accumulate meanings beyond its author's intention and even the work's time period. Comedy as a form, argues Scott Shershow, depicts the tension among the biases, ideologies, and realities of an age, that tension bringing the surplus into view, as exemplified in the glimmerings of utopian community in a play's end-ing.[54] Shershow invokes the Marxist cultural philosopher Ernst Bloch's phrase, "cultural surplus," for the dimension of a work that "'persists through the ages, once the social basis and ideology of an epoch have decayed.'"[55] Bloch sees the utopian energies of an artwork as inchoate, even "preconscious," glimpses of future possibilities, a cultural surplus to be fully grasped by later generations.[56] To Shershow, comedy offers the perfect aesthetic genre for Bloch's utopian surplus. The dream of utopianism colors moments of Shakespearean comic enchantment, as when, in *The Comedy of Errors*, the Abbess marks the magical "sympathized one day's error" that has led to the "nativity" of the present moment (5.1.397; 403, 406).[57] To crown this enchanted experience, she invites Duke Solinus to a "gossips' feast," an inherently communal and non-hierarchical bap-tismal celebration—here of rebirth and new life—and he enthusiastically accepts (*CE* 5.1.405). Hymen in *As You Like It* also catches that glimpse of transformative communalism: "Then is there mirth in heaven / When earthly things made even / Atone together" (5.4.106–8).[58] Wondrous comic gatherings become infused with the surplus of spirit, blessed mirth, that includes a new possibility in human relationships.

[53] Ricoeur also uses "surplus" to discuss the tension in metaphor between tenor and vehicle; see, for example, his *Interpretation Theory: Discourse and the Surplus of Meaning* (Fort Worth, TX: Texas Christian University, 1976).

[54] Shershow, *Laughing Matters*, x, 103, 107; on utopianism in Shakespeare's comedies, see Kiernan Ryan, *Shakespeare*, 3rd edn. (Houndmills, Basingstoke: Palgrave, [1989] 2002), 102–21.

[55] Shershow, *Laughing Matters*, 103, quoting Ernst Bloch, *A Philosophy of the Future*, trans. John Cumming (New York: Herder and Herder, 1970), 94–5.

[56] Neville Plaice, Stephen Plaice, and Paul Knight, "Translators' Introduction," in *The Principle of Hope*, vol. 1 of 3, ed. Ernst Bloch, trans. Neville Plaice, Stephen Plaice, and Paul Knight (Cambridge, MA: MIT Press, 1986; orig. pub. in German, 1958), xix–xxxiii, on xxvii.

[57] The Abbess's "sympathized," a theoretical term for magical affinities, foregrounds the way that characters in *CE* share or transfer psychologies, as if humans were living in profoundly communicative and dependent relationships with each other but which they perceive only obscurely; see Cartwright, *CE*, 5.1.397n.

[58] On mirth, see Dusinberre, *AYLI*, 5.4.106n.

A related dimension of comic surplus occurs in the mask of the *commedia dell'* *arte* figure; as Mikhail Bakhtin argues, the mask identity exceeds any specific circumstances of fate that entangle the character.[59] The surplus of the clown, Shakespearean comedy's preeminent mask character, will feature prominently in our discussion of clowns and fools, for they bear meaning into the play from a realm outside its confines. Their very alienness and repeatability gives them a larger-than-life dimension, a surplus that glows like an aura around their momentary embodiment. As Bakhtin puts it, mask characters "are heroes... of a life process that is imperishable and forever renewing itself" (37). The surplus of the mask, then, entails a mysterious transcendence of the immediate circumstances—and hence the clown's association with enchantment and with the utopian values of comedy recognized by theorists of comedy.

Finally, the most developed application to comedy of the idea of surplus appears in the Lacanian study of Alenka Zupančič.[60] Zupančič contends that comedy exposes, or enacts, the split in subjectivity between the ego (the conventional self that assumes its own oneness) and the id (the Other, unknown to consciousness, who speaks through one's discourse). In the incursions of the Other, comedy lets "the odd one in," as Zupančič's title suggests; hence comedy's special fascination with doubleness. Zupančič's fresh insights into comedy will figure variously in the chapters below. Here we can note how much, for her, comedy is characterized by the creation of surplus. Zupančič explores forms of dividedness in comedy, such as a comic character's inherent indestructibility despite his or her propensity to be upended by banana peels; or comedy's capacity to invoke two simultaneously present but incommensurate domains of experience, as in the ego and the id, the mundane and the unreal, or the mechanistic and the vital identified by Bergson.[61] As comedy stages such splits, it undermines unity of being by generating a surplus. Zupančič frames it thus: "[W]hen in comedy some (imaginary) Oneness or Unity splits in two, the sum of these two parts never again amounts to the inaugural One; there is a surplus that emerges in this split, and constantly disturbs the One" (185). That in-between dimension constitutes a space for comic surplus, as when love conflicts split the "incorporate" "double cherry" of Hermia and Helena, two halves of an apparent whole (*MND* 3.2.208, 209). Hermia, who had been ironic and reserved towards Lysander, now turns

---

[59] M. M. Bakhtin, *The Dialogic Imagination: Four Essays*, ed. Michael Holquist, trans. Caryl Emerson and Michael Holquist (Austin, TX: University of Texas Press, 1981; orig. pub. in Russian, 1975), 36.

[60] McGowan cites Zupančič's theory as one of the three most important in the last hundred years (*Joke*, 50) (Bergson's and Freud's are the others). He also calls hers "the most convincing theory of comedy that anyone has yet advanced" (60); see 60–4. McGowan's own view, which he sees as compatible with Zupančič's, is that comedy is marked by a revelatory convergence of lack and excess.

[61] In Bergson's famous phrase, the comic is produced by *"something mechanical encrusted on the living"*; Henri Bergson, "Laughter," in *Comedy*, ed. Sypher, 60–190, on 84.

emotionally volatile and violent, while Helena, who had been aggressive towards Demetrius, becomes timid and fearful. In Zupančič's terms, the surplus arrives as the transformation of the two women and their relationship, double cherries no more. They will move towards a new, egalitarian separateness, especially as Helena discovers wisdom and integrity, a view not unlike Shershow's and Bloch's. Zupančič also sees another kind of surplus that shows itself in the new and extravagant slap-stick energy of the *Midsummer* characters' bruhaha in 3.2, a revelatory marker for the ferocity of love. For audiences, the scene's surplus comes as joyful hilarity (and wins perhaps some admiration for Helena). Laughter especially releases the energy of the magical surplus into the world, much as a joke generates an excess of energy.[62]

Zupančič's affective sense of surplus helps in describing comic enchantment. Comedy, she argues, characteristically generates for the audience more satisfaction than we demand and of a kind that varies from our expectations:

> Comedy or, more precisely, comic sequence is always inaugurated by some unexpected surplus-realization. This surplus-realization may well be produced by failure, by a mistake, an error, through misunderstanding (and it usually is), but the moment it occurs it changes the very structure of the field. The field of comedy is essentially a field in which the answer precedes the question, satisfaction precedes the demand. Not only do we (or the comic characters) not get what we asked for, on top of it (and not instead of it) we get something we haven't even asked for at all. And we have to cope with this surprising surplus, respond to it (this is the imperative of the genre).[63]   (132)

Within the action, comic errors and misrecognitions are problems to be solved, but at the level of spectatorial or readerly experience, they are to be savored as sources of laughter and insight—surplus pleasure—such that a comedy's ending will bring a let-down (130).[64] That surplus is something, to quote Sianne Ngai from a different context, "that cannot be reabsorbed" into the artifact and that

---

[62] As Freud describes it, the inhibitory energy discharged when one hears the punch line of a joke constitutes an "innervatory expenditure which has become an unusable surplus"; Sigmund Freud, *Jokes and Their Relation to the Unconscious*, trans. James Strachey (London: Routledge & Kegan Paul, 1960; orig. pub. in German, 1905), 194. For books that describe and critique the dominant theories of laughter, including Freud's, see, among others, John Morreall, *Taking Laughter Seriously* (Albany, NY: State University of New York Press, 1983); Michael Billig, *Laughter and Ridicule: Towards a Social Critique of Humour* (London: Sage Publications, 2005); and Eagleton, *Humour*, 67–93. Like Morreall, I accept the "incongruity theory" as the most useful general explanation of what causes laughter.

[63] By "the answer precedes the question," Zupančič means that, in an example such as *The Comedy of Errors*, we perceive the solution to the misrecognitions long in advance of the characters. Zupančič's sense of characters getting not what they asked for but something different fits the Shakespearean comic canon: for example, *Errors*, *A Midsummer Night's Dream*, and *Twelfth Night*.

[64] Zupančič is anticipated in this idea by Morton Gurewitch, *Comedy: The Irrational Vision* (Ithaca, NY: Cornell University Press, 1975), 90.

constitutes "a form of surplus resonance or feedback *that intensifies engagement with an aesthetic object.*"[65] Zupančič sees such comic experience as parallel to love experience, for love "always involves a dimension of an unexpected and surprising satisfaction"; indeed, the love-encounter "is always accompanied by a feeling of perplexity, confusion, a feeling that we've got something that we don't know exactly what to do with, and yet something rather pleasant"—the surplus (134).

Although Zupančič does not precisely say so, the affective similarities between comedy and love surely help to explain why the one so often involves the other. As illustration, Beatrice and Benedick declare that they love each other "no more than reason" (*MA* 5.4.74, 77)—but, of course, the play's ending rejects that dispirited position, for love and comedy are always "more than reason": That is their point. The 'moreness' is the special realm of experience—"a miracle," says Benedick (91), or an enchanted surplus—that love and comedy bring into being. Describing the sense of the real manifested in the comic surplus, Zupančič uses the kind of language—something out of nothing—associated with conjuration or enchantment: "the mysterious 'something more,'" "*transcendent* and *accessible*", "the miracle of its [i.e., nonsense's] real effects," "inexplicable," "something that appears where there should be nothing," "the mysterious Thing that lies somewhere beyond representation."[66] "The miracle of love" she describes as "a funny miracle" (174). From Zupančič, a formidable argument emerges that comedy introduces a surplus of utopian meaning into relationships and produces, for characters and audiences, surplus pleasures and recognitions to be understood in the language of magic and wonder.

Renaissance Comedy, Magic, and Medievalism

Magic was already being woven into the fabric of comic form when Shakespeare began making his contribution.[67] John Lyly's comedies, like earlier Elizabethan romance drama, regularly feature sorcery, enchantments, and pagan god-magic, as in *Endymion* (*c*.1588) and *Gallathea* (*c*.1584). Magicians, fairies, or enchantresses figure in each of Robert Greene's comedies. Italian comedy in the late decades of the sixteenth century, as Louise George Clubb notes, regularly taps magic as a theme, and that oeuvre may have influenced Shakespeare.[68] Indeed, one of the earliest of those comedies, Cardinal Bibbiena's *La calandria* (*c*.1513),

---

[65] Sianne Ngai, *Ugly Feelings* (Cambridge, MA: Harvard University Press, 2005), 79, 80.

[66] Alenka Zupančič, *The Shortest Shadow: Nietzsche's Philosophy of the Two* (Cambridge, MA: MIT Press, 2003), 169, 171, 172, 173; see 164–81.

[67] For a classic inventory of magic in Elizabethan drama, see H. W. Herrington, "Witchcraft and Magic in the Elizabethan Drama," *The Journal of American Folklore* 32, no. 126 (October–December 1919): 447–85; see http://www.jstor.org/stable/535187.

[68] Louise George Clubb, *Italian Drama in Shakespeare's Time* (New Haven, CT: Yale University Press, 1989), see 59–60, 93–123.

employs the necromancer Ruffo, presumably possessing the power to turn a man into a woman, a key plot element. Cinquecento Italian comedies were full of sorcerers, who express "the dark features of Italian Renaissance society" but whom the plays treat with "rational skepticism."[69] Two of the three Italian comedies translated or adapted into English introduce occultist themes: *The Bugbears* (John Jefferey?, *c.*1566) trades humorously on fears of haunting and magic, while *Fedele and Fortunio* (Anthony Munday, 1585) employs an "enchantress," Medusa, who carries a "box of enchantments" that can compel characters to fall in love.[70] The late Elizabethan and early Jacobean decades saw a keen interest in magic, expressed in various witchcraft crazes, and during the early 1590s and 1600s, the London stage enjoyed a raft of productions and revivals of plays featuring magic.[71]

Contributing to that Elizabethan upsurge of interest were the writings on magic by various late medieval and humanistic thinkers, including Marsilio Ficino, Pico della Mirandola, Heinrich Cornelius Agrippa, Paracelsus, and Giordano Bruno, who will figure in the following chapters. Magic was a "core problem" of the Renaissance,[72] not only because the era inherited traditional beliefs in demons, fairies, ghosts, charms, magical locales, and alchemical transformations but also because humanist figures such as Ficino, Pico, and Bruno, recovering and investigating the writings of the ancients, developed a vision of natural magic in which all the elements of heaven and earth were connected by sympathies and antipathies, those elements linked and enlivened by a universal "spiritus" whose power could be harnessed and manipulated by man.[73] As Brian Copenhaver puts it in describing Ficino's influential theories, the "natural and the supernatural form a continuum," and all things are connected by a "World Soul" that "animates them all and unites them, opening channels for magical action."[74] Thus, mind, plants,

---

[69] Douglas Radcliff-Umstead, "The Sorcerer in Italian Renaissance Comedy," in *Comparative Critical Approaches to Renaissance Comedy*, ed. Donald Beecher and Massimo Ciavolella (Ottawa: Dovehouse Editions Canada, 1986), 73–98, on 73.

[70] Anthony Munday, *A Critical Edition of Anthony Munday's* Fedele and Fortunio, ed. Richard Hosley (New York: Garland, 1981), s.d. at 4.3.02–03.

[71] Roslyn Lander Knutson, *The Repertory of Shakespeare's Company, 1594–1613* (Fayetteville, AR: University of Arkansas Press, 1991), 143.

[72] Brian P. Copenhaver credits Aby Warburg with identifying "magic as a core problem in the development of Western Culture"; "Introduction," to D. P. Walker, *Spiritual and Demonic Magic: From Ficino to Campanella* (University Park, PA: Pennsylvania State University Press, [1958] 2000), viii–xi, on viii.

[73] On the Renaissance recovery of classical theories of magic, see, among others, Brian P. Copenhaver, *Magic in Western Culture: From Antiquity to the Enlightenment* (Cambridge: Cambridge University Press, 2015). On dark and natural magic, see Paola Zambelli, *White Magic, Black Magic in the European Renaissance* (Leiden: Brill, 2007). For a summary of Ficino's paradigmatic theories, see Brian P. Copenhaver, "How to Do Magic, and Why: Philosophical Prescriptions," in *The Cambridge Companion to Renaissance Philosophy*, ed. James Hankins (Cambridge: Cambridge University Press, 2007), 137–69.

[74] Copenhaver, "How to Do Magic," 148, 155.

objects, images, music, and words have the power to call forth heavenly assistance, as for medical healing,[75] a theory suggestive for incidents such as Lorenzo's invoking of music in *The Merchant of Venice*. According to Mikhail Bakhtin, Renaissance ideas of natural magic, sympathy, and "'universal animatization'" "played a considerable role in destroying the medieval notion of hierarchical space in which natural phenomena had their own distinct levels. The new ideas brought together that which was divided, effacing false boundaries, contributing to the transfer of all to one horizontal plane of the becoming of the cosmos in time."[76] In essence, he implies, theories of sympathetic magic replaced notions of hierarchy with more democratizing ones of relatedness and correspondence.

For Shakespeare, scholarship on magic and enchantment has focused on *The Tempest, Macbeth, A Midsummer Night's Dream*, and *The Winter's Tale*, while just one monograph, Elissa Beatrice Hare's *Enchanted Shows*, studies magic specifically in early modern comedy, including *A Midsummer Night's Dream* and *The Tempest*.[77] In Hare's view, Elizabethan playwrights introduce magicians typically to account for a play's structural discontinuities, such as breaks in cause and effect. But criticism lacks any comprehensive treatment of enchantment in relation to Shakespearean comedy.[78] Nonetheless, Shakespeare's plays, argues Linda Woodbridge, generally reflect "magical thinking," a residue of belief in magic inherited from the Middle Ages that, though disavowed by some of Shakespeare's contemporaries, remained embedded subconsciously in individual and collective psyches, providing explanations and structuring experiences.[79] Mary Floyd-Wilson explores the magical dialectic of sympathy and antipathy, arguing perceptively that "a pervasive belief in sympathies and antipathies shaped

[75] Copenhaver, "How to Do Magic," 156–61. See also Marsilio Ficino, "Book Three: The Book on 'Obtaining Life from the Heavens,'" in Marsilio Ficino, *Three Books on Life: A Critical Edition and Translation*, ed. and trans. Carol V. Kaske and John R. Clark (Tempe, AZ: Medieval and Renaissance Texts and Studies, [1989] 1998), 236–393.

[76] Mikhail Bakhtin, *Rabelais and His World*, trans. Helene Iswolsky (Bloomington, IN: Indiana University Press, 1984; orig. pub. in Russian, 1965), 364–5.

[77] Elissa Beatrice Hare, *Enchanted Shows: Vision and Structure in Elizabethan and Shakespearean Comedy about Magic* (New York: Garland, 1988). Recent works on magic and early modern drama include Das and Davis, *Enchantment and Dis-enchantment*; Mary Floyd-Wilson, *Occult Knowledge, Science, and Gender on the Shakespearean Stage* (Cambridge: Cambridge University Press, 2013); Gabriela Dragnea Horvath, *Theatre, Magic, and Philosophy: William Shakespeare, John Dee and the Italian Legacy* (New York: Routledge, 2017); Helen Ostovich and Lisa Hopkins, eds., *Magical Transformations on the Early Modern English Stage* (New York: Routledge, 2014); and Linda Woodbridge, *The Scythe of Saturn: Shakespeare and Magical Thinking* (Urbana, IL: University of Illinois Press, 1994).

[78] One might wonder why. Some speculative answers would be that the history of criticism has preferred tragedy over comedy, finding in the latter more the stuff of entertainment than of complex thought; that enchantment as a motif looks quaint and archaic; and that, as indicated, modernity has privileged a teleology of scientism, rationalism, and secularism. For these notions, I am indebted to a private email exchange with Robert Hornback, May 2019.

[79] Woodbridge, *Scythe of Saturn*, 5.

early modern interpretation of affective experiences";[80] that these forces were regarded as hidden and occult but yet consistent with naturalistic interpretations; and that, consequently, the early modern search for a systematic understanding of them, using "new experimental methods that emphasized the observation of effects over theoretical causation" (4), contributed crucially to the emergence of the new science.[81] A world that entertains such occult knowledge, we might say, is neither entirely enchanted nor entirely disenchanted. Relatedly, Kristen Poole demonstrates how, during Shakespeare's era, two conflicting models of space encountered each other simultaneously, the one a geocentric, religiously inflected conception of space as "fluid and metamorphic," in which supernatural beings operated freely; the other a heliocentric, proto-scientific conception of space as geometric and regular, governed by natural law yet capable of being "violated by the demonic."[82] Such paradoxes are the stuff of drama, and they are consistent with the sense of a postmodern enchantment that juxtaposes the wondrous with the familiar, allowing them to "pull against each other."[83]

For Shakespearean comedy, those studies help to establish magic and enchantment as Elizabethan habits of mind, culturally powerful metaphors, that acknowledge an extra-rational dimension of human experience, while yet embracing it qualifiedly, even sometimes ironically. They put the wondrous sense of human possibility in tension with its potential ridiculousness, as Zupančič might argue. Shakespearean comedy, perhaps all comedy, calls forth that interplay of the affective and the cognitive postulated by Patrizi; it identifies moments of what Hans Ulrich Gumbrecht calls "presence," when the affective impact of something is felt before meaning is attributed to it and its force dissipated.[84] Such

[80] Floyd-Wilson, *Occult Knowledge*, 6. According to the principle of sympathy and antipathy, all beings and objects in the natural world have properties that relate them to each other on a continuum from twinness to opposition, so that objects can attract, repel, and affect each other even at a distance; see Floyd-Wilson, *Occult Knowledge*, 6–14. On the transformation of sympathy from a magical to a moral concept in the seventeenth century, see Seth Lobis, *The Virtue of Sympathy: Magic, Philosophy, and Literature in Seventeenth-Century England* (New Haven, CT: Yale University Press, 2015).

[81] Floyd-Wilson argues that the study of magical causes overlapped the study of natural causes, making complex any case for early modern "disenchantment." On magic and the development of scientific thinking, see Floyd-Wilson, *Occult Knowledge*, 2–6, 141–2, 18n, 24n. On the scholarly debate about early modern disenchantment, see the seminal analysis by Alexandra Walsham, "The Reformation and 'The Disenchantment of the World' Reassessed," *The Historical Journal* 51, no. 2 (June 2008): 497–528. Walsham argues that recent scholarship has "seriously complicated, challenged, and undercut" the Weberian thesis that the Protestant Reformation launched the historical shift towards "modernity and secularization" (497). She traces in detail, furthermore, a persistent "Protestant culture of the supernatural" (515). See also Euan Cameron, *Enchanted Europe: Superstition, Reason, and Religion: 1250–1750* (Oxford: Oxford University Press, 2010), e.g., 14–18.

[82] Kristen Poole, *Supernatural Environments in Shakespeare's England: Spaces of Demonism, Divinity, and Drama* (Cambridge: Cambridge University Press, 2011), 10, 9; "One of the great social paradoxes of the period was the simultaneity of a heightened geometrical awareness and a widespread fascination with supernatural, especially demonic behavior that refuted a fixed sense of space" (10).

[83] Poole, *Supernatural Environments*, 7, see 7–12; see also Landy and Saler, *Re-Enchantment*, 3.

[84] Hans Ulrich Gumbrecht, *Production of Presence: What Meaning Cannot Convey* (Stanford, CA: Stanford University Press, 2003), xiv.

considerations have relevance for the modern world. Shakespeare's comedies are detailed with forms of enchantment, including spells and transformations (*A Midsummer Night's Dream*); fairies and gods (*A Midsummer Night's Dream*, *As You Like It*); sympathetic effects (*The Comedy of Errors*, *Twelfth Night*); magical repetitions in scenic structure (*Twelfth Night*); figurative revenants (*The Two Gentlemen of Verona*, *Much Ado About Nothing*, *Twelfth Night*, *All's Well That Ends Well*); wonderments (virtually all the comedies); and plastic time, magical locales, and "green worlds" (all the comedies). Those devices—structural and formal elements used to create meaning and emphasis—reflect the fantastical and anti-realistic underside of Shakespearean comedy and of comedy in general. They create a force field of enchantment, for exactly by their means can Shakespeare the craftsman bring the comedy of enchantment into being.

Shakespeare's comic fantasticality vies with awareness of the temporal present; comedies, as Agnes Heller puts it, are "experiences of, and about, absolute present time" (13). While history plays and tragedies are historically rooted, there is no such thing, argues Heller, as an historical comedy. Not only does comedy speak to audiences about present concerns, but the experience of comedy itself carries a fundamental sense of presentness, lacking any "past-oriented emotion" (13). In a famous line from *Twelfth Night*, Fabian says of the gulling of Malvolio, "If this were played upon a stage now, I could condemn it as an improbable fiction" (3.4.123–4). As editor Keir Elam notes, "Fabian's *now* conflates dramatic or fictional time with the 'real' time of the performance" (*TN*, 3.4.123–4n). Fabian's remark exemplifies metadrama (or metatheater), a speech, action, or device in a play that calls attention overtly to the play's status as a fiction. Fabian's comment, coming from inside the world of play but looking at it from outside, from Heller's "absolute present," recalls Zupančič's sense of comedy's "impossible sustained encounter between two excluding realities."[85] That encounter helps us understand the often fancifully mixed sense of time in Shakespeare. Even when a work such as *The Comedy of Errors* adopts a vaguely Classical Mediterranean setting, its Ephesus resembles modern London, yet immanent with an older Catholicism of prayer beads and abbeys, a place of temporal density.

Shakespeare's comedies are often colored with medieval elements, sometimes related to Catholicism, that can feel anachronistic, partly because they were being challenged by England's emergent Protestantism.[86] A considerable amount of current scholarship rightly resists treating medieval and Catholic habits of thought

---

[85] Zupančič, *Odd One*, 57. Such presentness helps to explain how clowns can enter comedy as if from another dimension, trailing clouds of utopianism (as we shall see) and how they can violate the 'fourth wall.'

[86] Of course, early moderns did not necessarily have the same sense as we do today about what is medieval, nor necessarily any sense of the medieval at all; see Deanne Williams, "Shakespearean Medievalism and the Limits of Periodization in *Cymbeline*," *Literature Compass* 8, no. 6 (June 2011): 390–403. See also Helen Cooper, *Shakespeare and the Medieval World* (London: Bloomsbury, 2010).

as consciously abandoned in sixteenth-century England, a perspective that the present study adopts and one relevant for the comedies.[87] Various of the comedies stage friars as characters or refer to them (for example, *The Two Gentlemen of Verona*, *Much Ado About Nothing*, *Measure for Measure*). An abbess and her abbey function importantly in *The Comedy of Errors*. An allusion to Popish "incensing relics" sounds a key note in *All's Well That Ends Well* (5.3.25), referring to Helen, apparently deceased, who has earlier gone on a pilgrimage to St. James Campostela in Spain (the image of pilgrimage also occurs in other comedies, such as *Two Gentlemen*), and in this play Helen is both a modern woman and a messenger from a past world of Catholic wonders.[88] While only one of the tragedies mentions miracles, seven of the comedies invoke them. Likewise, many of Shakespeare's comic narratives draw on medieval sources, while medieval folk festivity has been seen by C. L. Barber as crucial to the tone of Shakespearean comedy.[89] Relationships among characters in the comedies appeal to a mystical medieval sense of community[90]—the sense of its members being mysteriously linked to each other socially and sacramentally—just as medieval and Catholic values also shine through the comic device (developed in the late romances) of the return from the dead. These values, still vibrant, clash with Protestantism and evoke an older yet influential world order. Thus, although comedies operate in an "absolute present time," Shakespeare's are layered deep with other times and places, part of that "sustained encounter between two excluding realities."

Shakespearean Comedy and Present-Day Criticism

Enchantment should be viewed in relation to the prevailing interests in criticism of the comedies, those interests including festivity, psychology, and politics (others will be treated in the subsequent chapters). Regarding festivity,

---

[87] For a recent contribution among many, see Curtis Perry and John Watkins, eds., *Shakespeare and the Middle Ages* (Oxford: Oxford University Press, 2009). Comedies have generally not been the focus for discussions of the medieval; Lucy Munro observes that "scholars interested in the interactions between the medieval and early modern periods have focused much of their attention on Shakespeare's history plays"; "Shakespeare and the Uses of the Past: Critical Approaches and Current Debates," *Shakespeare* 7, no. 1 (April 2011): 102–25, on 108.

[88] Kent Cartwright, "Secularity Meets Wonder Woman in *All's Well That Ends Well*," in *Sacred and Secular Transactions in the Age of Shakespeare*, ed. Katherine Steele Brokaw and Jay Zysk (Evanston, IL: Northwestern University Press, 2019), 49–67.

[89] C. L. Barber, *Shakespeare's Festive Comedy: A Study of Dramatic Form and Its Relation to Social Custom* (Princeton, NJ: Princeton University Press, 1959). Phebe Jensen sees festivity in some of Shakespeare's comedies as not nostalgic but contemporaneous in its employment of Catholic values; *Religion and Revelry in Shakespeare's Festive World* (Cambridge: Cambridge University Press, 2008).

[90] For one of several discussions of the communalism of medieval life, see Ronald Hutton, *The Rise and Fall of Merry England: The Ritual Year 1400-1700* (Oxford: Oxford University Press, 1994); Hutton details the typical ritual year in late medieval England, with ongoing religious and seasonal customs, sacred and secular, that were public and communal, saturating the year.

Northrop Frye saw magic, along with dreams and "spiritual energy," as features of the "green world" retreat from which characters emerge at the ends of the comedies, while C. L. Barber argued influentially that what appears as holiday magic in the comedies is revealed, instead, as the action of the artistic imagination.[91] The present study questions those views by proposing that the values constellated around enchantment are so multifarious, enigmatical, and subtly influential, and so much features of their play-worlds, that they cannot be written off as only dramatic contrivances.[92] According to Michael Bristol, "Barber's reading of festivity and of social life in general necessarily favors a benevolent repression as the source of collective harmony."[93] While not explicitly about a Bakhtinian carnivalesque inversion, the present study of enchantment argues for an encounter between an overt harmony and an undertow of dissonance as a key feature of the comedies.

The poetics of enchantment can also be juxtaposed with Barbara Freedman's political and psychological approach in *Staging the Gaze*.[94] To Freedman, the comedies steadily undercut any secure purchase on knowledge: "[T]hey no sooner tantalize us with a stable position of mastery than they mock this stance by staging audience, character, plot, and theme as sites of misrecognition" (2). Doing so, they

---

[91] Northrop Frye, *A Natural Perspective: The Development of Shakespearean Comedy and Romance* (New York: Columbia University Press, 1965), 143; Barber, *Festive Comedy*, 139, see 139–48. The study of Shakespearean festivity, launched by Frye and Barber, has generated a considerable body of important work; see also, for example: Northrop Frye, "The Argument of Comedy," *English Institute Essays 1948*, ed. D. A. Robertson (New York: Columbia University Press, 1949), 58–73; William C. Carroll, *The Metamorphoses of Shakespearean Comedy* (Princeton, NJ: Princeton University Press, 1985); François Laroque, *Shakespeare's Festive World: Elizabethan Seasonal Entertainment and the Professional Stage*, trans. Janet Lloyd (Cambridge: Cambridge University Press, 1991); and Jensen, *Religion and Revelry*. Robert Weimann opened up the sociological aspects of festivity by connecting Shakespearean comedy with the "popular tradition"; *Shakespeare and the Popular Tradition of the Theater: Studies in the Social Dimension of Dramatic Form and Function*, ed. Robert Schwartz (Baltimore, MD: The Johns Hopkins University Press, 1978; orig. pub. in German, 1967). Likewise influential is Mikhail Bakhtin's vision of carnivalesque popular culture in *Rabelais and His World*; see also Michael D. Bristol, *Carnival and Theater: Plebeian Culture and the Structure of Authority in Renaissance England* (New York: Methuen, 1985).

[92] Northrop Frye's *Natural Perspective* shows important sensitivity to fantasy, magic, and dream in the comedies. Frye contends that comedy expresses the mythic rhythms of nature, from winter to spring. Consequently, his discussion of features such as the green world repeatedly invokes ideas of "natural cycle," "natural society," and "renewal," the green world becoming a symbolic place where a dream-like loss of identity gives way to the discovery of a new or renewed self in harmony with the processes of nature, the "harmony of a world below the heavenly spheres" (154). Rather than seeing the comic ending as resolving conflicts in a tidy harmoniousness, I find a residual mystery that provokes doubt and thought. That errant dimension brings a special, unsettling energy and power to the comedies. Frye tends generally to "naturalize" mystery; the present project does the opposite.

[93] Bristol, *Carnival and Theater*, 32.

[94] Barbara Freedman, *Staging the Gaze: Postmodernism, Psychoanalysis and Shakespearean Comedy* (Ithaca, NY: Cornell University Press, 1991). *Staging the Gaze* shares Lacanian interests with Zupančič's *Odd One*. Other works and collections that encompass political and psychological approaches include: Richard Dutton and Jean E. Howard, eds., *A Companion to Shakespeare*, vol. 3 of 3: *The Comedies* (Oxford: Blackwell, 2003); Alexander Leggatt, ed., *The Cambridge Companion to Shakespearean Comedy* (Cambridge: Cambridge University Press, 2004); Emma Smith, ed., *Shakespeare's Comedies* (Oxford: Blackwell, 2004); and Hirschfeld, *Oxford Handbook*.

mirror the "Renaissance preoccupation with undermining right sight through trick perspective pictures and paradoxes, unreason or folly, and theatrical games that confuse spectator and spectacle" (9). The comedies reveal ideological, class, or gendered positions, and thus constitute an argument against any claims to exclusive truth. Freedman embraces a paradoxical "knowing unknowingness," derived from Nicholas of Cusa and Erasmus (10, 4), by which she seeks herself to avoid declaring specific truths (a difficult task). The present study will share the concern for misrecognitions and instabilities in comedy, especially in relation to enchantment, for the plays often keep their points of view in motion, the lens twisting to bring objects into and out of focus. Freedman, however, treats the comedies as radically skeptical, a position that seems extreme and contrary to their moments of communal joy, their sense of comic surplus, and their utopian pulsations (although the later comedies become increasingly skeptical). The question of Shakespeare's skepticism will be in the background of our discussion.[95]

In the comedies, individual truth-claims may be revealed as partial, obscured, or interested without, I would argue, negating the existence of truth or the possibility that some views of it are more inclusive and accurate than others. Elizabethan comedy in the 1590s and early 1600s does move towards a newly satirical and ironic perspective, exemplified by Jonson's comedies and by others as disparate as Dekker's *Satiromastix* (1602) and the anonymous *The Second Part of the Return to Parnassus* (c.1602). Such works introduce a critical, Juvenalian vein into late sixteenth-century comedy and poetry.[96] Yet, while Shakespeare's later comedies, such as *As You Like It*, showcase moments of satire, they still keep celebrative possibilities alive; even the 'problem' comedies can be interpreted in ways less or more cynical. In the late comedies, to be sure, marriage can appear as equally coerced as chosen, but Shakespeare's comic plays never arrive at an ending as cynical as that of, say, Jonson's *The Alchemist* (1610). Comic enchantment allows the possibility that truths do exist, if sometimes beyond our reach. Freedman's "unknowing knowingness" suggests a distanced, even detached stance towards the artifact: "[I]n Shakespearean comedy, it is the mind . . . that sees itself seen as that which can never be seen" (20). Such a complicated, ironic intellectualism bypasses an audience's emotional engagements with the characters and

---

[95] For Derek Gottlieb, the comedies explore ways to live affirmatively in the face of skepticism; *Skepticism and Belonging in Shakespeare's Comedies* (New York: Routledge, 2016). In a related vein, J. F. Bernard argues that melancholy becomes an increasingly shaping, even liminal, force in Shakespeare's comedies; *Shakespearean Melancholy: Philosophy, Form and the Transformation of Comedy* (Edinburgh: Edinburgh University Press, 2018).

[96] On the tension between the Horatian and Juvenalian strains in Jonson's early comedies, see Victoria Moul, *Jonson, Horace and the Classical Tradition* (Cambridge: Cambridge University Press, 2010), 98–106.

their worlds, engagements kept in play by experiences such as wonder and enchantment.[97]

More political, R. W. Maslen's *Shakespeare and Comedy* emphasizes the subversive social potential of comedy; he sees Shakespeare as exploring especially the precariousness of comic timing, as in the hilarious moment that can turn violent.[98] Central to comedy is gender conflict, argues Maslen, and that problem brings with it the issue of Otherness, the treatment of those who are racially, ethnically, or culturally different.[99] For the present study, gender relations figure intermittently, as in the male–female conflicts of *Much Ado* or in the doubt about marital success or even marital prospects that weaves through the endings. Issues of ethnicity also arise, illustrated by the figure of the Jew that haunts the ending of *The Merchant of Venice*. An indirect means of addressing these matters comes in the places that Shakespeare chooses as comic settings. He locates many of the plays, says Geraldo de Sousa, in "the Mediterranean region, known as a crossroads of ethnicity and one of the most racially and culturally diverse regions of the world,"[100] the arena where a Spaniard and a Moor can vie for Portia's hand. Such places in the comedies function as enchanted locales that question gender roles and signal generally the instability of identity categories.

Another line of political criticism focuses on a play's ideological faultlines, which expose the dissemblings of the ruling power structure and its deceptive telos of harmonious, transcendent values.[101] From that perspective, Jean Howard disputes Frye and Barber's sense of festive reconciliation by noting the high "degree of unresolved turbulence and contradiction present in [the comedies] and present in the audience's aesthetic experience of them."[102] For John Drakakis, Elizabethan theater often works to "recuperate for its practices those images of the

---

[97] On postmodern aesthetic distance, see Rita Felski, *The Limits of Critique* (Chicago, IL: University of Chicago Press, 2015), esp. 52–84.

[98] R. W. Maslen, *Shakespeare and Comedy* (London: Thomson Learning, 2005), see esp. 1–37. Critics have stressed the political dimensions of the tragedies and histories more than of the comedies; those aspects include: centralization of state power; proto-capitalism; Protestantism; and, pre-eminently, inwardness and subjectivity. The comedies have attracted interest regarding companionate marriage, mercantilism, middling class values, and education. Camille Wells Slights observes that New Historicism's "primary concern with manifestations of political power has directed attention for the most part to Shakespeare's histories and tragedies, rather than to the early comedies," a claim that could include many of the later ones; Camille Wells Slights, *Shakespeare's Comic Commonwealths* (Toronto: University of Toronto Press, 1993), 5.

[99] See also Geraldo U. de Sousa, "Shakespearean Comedy and the Question of Race," in Hirschfeld, *Oxford Handbook, op. cit.*, 172–89.

[100] De Sousa, "Question of Race," 184.

[101] For the now-classic work in this regard, see Jonathan Dollimore, *Radical Tragedy: Religion, Ideology, Power in the Drama of Shakespeare and his Contemporaries*, 3rd edn. (Houndmills, Basingstoke: Palgrave Macmillan, [1984] 2004). For a critique of such work, see Felski, *Limits of Critique*, esp. 62–84.

[102] Jean E. Howard, "The Difficulties of Closure: An Approach to the Problematic in Shakespearean Comedy," in *Comedy from Shakespeare to Sheridan: Change and Continuity in the English and European Dramatic Traditions*, ed. A. R. Braunmuller and J. C. Bulman (Cranbury, NJ: Associated University Presses, 1986), 113–28, on 113.

dominant order, at times simply representing them, at others inverting them, but always rendering them 'open': at times reinforcing their ideological power, while at others exposing the inadequacies of ideology to contain contradiction."[103] In the case of *The Merchant of Venice*, Drakakis sees the ending as exercising bad faith, because its "ritualized" comic closure in marriage deflects attention from the play's contradictions, thus falling back on the resolution "legitimized and authorized by the dominant ideology of patriarchy" (52, 51). Here *Merchant*'s ending becomes an exercise in elitist tidying up, given the lie by the play's prior contradictions and "openness." But concerns might be raised about that model. First, it can represent the conclusions of suspect comedies as more neat and orderly, "ritualized," than they really are; likewise, it assumes that the "turbulences and contradictions" that have raged through a play can vanish from the audience's consciousness under the weight of the ending. While finales may partake of dominant values, they do not necessarily eradicate from memory, or always attempt to eradicate, a play's contradictions.[104] Second, the model implies that a comedy can be properly analyzed in terms of a sociological paradigm; that is, it assumes that a comedy is fundamentally realistic, and it can ignore for argumentative purposes any concern about how comic fantasticality and comic distance intervene in meaning. Third, as a disenchanting approach, it tends to de-mystify romantic love by treating it as an illusion or a sublimation of power relations. Such tendencies look reductive. Fourth, it misses the generic tension in Shakespeare's comedies and in Renaissance comedy overall between the abstract and the particular. The problems raised in those comedies, I would argue, tend to be global and pervasive, while resolutions are local and provisional; thus, although comic endings may ease the mind regarding immediate circumstances, they also provoke thought about deeper, residual conflicts. Political models might be adjusted to allow for the play of both enchantment and disenchantment in the comedies.

Experiences of wonder and enchantment occur as responses to events that characters find incomprehensible, paradoxical, or self-contradictory, amounting precisely to moments of "openness," when meanings and causal interpretations hang in the balance. In the spirit of Patrizi and Gumbrecht, we might view such instances of suspended understanding as occasions for a pause, short or sustained, tinged with both awe and uncertainty, before full conceptualization takes form. Thus wonder, when read as intense doubt, can put doctrinaire systems in question, especially when it arises out of distrust for proffered explanations of a play's events, leading potentially to ideas and possibilities not before imagined. As

---

[103] John Drakakis, "Historical Difference and Venetian Patriarchy," in *The Merchant of Venice*, ed. Nigel Wood (Buckingham: Open University Press, 1996), 23–56, on 29.

[104] For an argument from that viewpoint, see Ejner Jensen, *Shakespeare and the Ends of Comedy* (Bloomington, IN: Indiana University Press, 1991).

Cornelis Verhoeven puts it, "Wonder sets thought in motion."[105] The invocation of magic, as we have noted, inherently both raises and clouds the task of determining causation; enchantment brings its own dissonance. We might think of it as a way of allowing both pleasure and suspicion into the culminating experience of a play, remembering Bennett's associating of wonder with scrutiny and complexity. That view of enchantment squares with claims, such as Freedman's, that comic denouements are layered and multifaceted. Although Shakespearean comedy can achieve moments of profound joy, its endings show far more emotional restraint than, say, the typical endings in late cinquecento Italian comedy.[106] More generally, one might wisely allow for both consonance and dissonance in the form of comic closings, the interplay of those opposite dimensions being arguably foundational to literary response. Enchantment in Shakespearean comedy forms a nexus for both.

*   *   *   *   *

The present study focuses on formal comic devices and techniques that arise in a particular historical and literary environment, yet which help to explain the particular staying power of Shakespeare's comic oeuvre and the possibilities of the genre. Developments such as humanism, religious change, magical theorizing, incipient science, and medieval influences will sift through the following discussions. Chapters will also attend, as appropriate, to comic theory and to literary comparisons, especially of Shakespearean comedy to Tudor and cinquecento Italian comedy, so as to suggest the larger shape of the genre in the period and to signal its possibilities. Chapter 1, on clowns, fools, and folly treats the clown-figure in terms of his magical ontology and analyzes moments of folly that intervene—transformatively, enchantingly—in a comic narrative, as in the way Feste's fantastical chop-logical interview with the lachrymose Olivia in *Twelfth Night* seems to make possible her becoming suddenly possessed by infatuation. Clowns and fools, slightly otherworldly figures, introduce magical stop-time interludes into the narrative. Rather than being 'marginal,' they can influence the protagonists, the action, and the play's meaning, as do the consummate figures of Dogberry and Bottom. Chapter 2, treating comic doubleness as a structural matter, explores the way scenes, actions, and plot lines reflect each other, as if to create an uncanny closed circuit or dream-world. Those reflections call up a long-standing critical recognition of "magical parallelisms" that express the Renaissance fascination with analogy and with occult theories of sympathetic

---

[105] Cornelis Verhoeven, *The Philosophy of Wonder*, trans. Mary Foran (New York: Macmillan, 1972; orig. pub in Dutch, 1967), 63.

[106] On the pleasure of "intense emotion" for early modern theatergoers (tears in tragedy; uncontrollable laughter and sexual desire in comedy), see Tanya Pollard, "Audience Reception," in *The Oxford Handbook of Shakespeare*, ed. Arthur Kinney (Oxford: Oxford University Press, 2012), 458–73, on 461.

influence. Focusing on *Twelfth Night*, this chapter considers how the play creates the sense of a numinous but opaque providentialism. Chapter 3 identifies the special world of Shakespearean comedy in terms of the multiple dimensions of place, of which comedy seems especially aware. The association of place with Italy in the comedies calls upon popular notions of that land as dichotomous, yet open. The comedies often organize locale in terms of a contrast between "regulative" and "protean" places (the latter recalling Frye's "green world"). Protean environs are enchanted and can enchant, as in *As You Like It*; they make metamorphosis possible; and yet they exhibit different degrees of agency in different plays. Notwithstanding its power, the protean world is a nice place to visit, but one would not want to live there. Chapter 4 conceptualizes the device of 'manifest-ation,' the term identifying the causal power of desires, thoughts, and words to call forth objects and even characters in Shakespeare's comic world. In the spirit of Zupančič, the device shows, among other things, the way that comedy can surface the amusing monstrousness and presumptuousness of human wishes. The chapter formalizes and theorizes a quality found variously in early literature and in present-day commentary. *The Comedy of Errors*, *A Midsummer Night's Dream*, and *The Merry Wives of Windsor* receive extended discussion. Chapter 5 argues for the lingering power of medieval values and imaginative forms in its attention to characters who seemingly return from the dead. While this motif is usually discussed in relation to Shakespeare's late romances, such as *Pericles*, *The Winter's Tale*, and *The Tempest*, it is more pervasive, influential, and mysterious in the earlier comic works than criticism has recognized, as suggested by characters ranging from *Two Gentlemen*'s Julia to *All's Well*'s Helen. The motif lends uncanny power, emotional and intellectual depth, and memorability to Shakespearean comedy. Chapter 6 on endings discusses harmony and dissonance, and explores relevant Renaissance theories of comedy. It concludes with three sections, the first ("Exclusion") taking up the problem of how the Other (here Shylock), seemingly excluded from the "harmonious" ending, can retain a ghostly presence; the second ("Delusion") addressing the question of what protagonists and authority figures (and audiences) are left not knowing by the end, as seen in *Much Ado About Nothing*; and the third ("Forgiveness") focusing on the special way that the comedies employ wonder to make forgiveness possible (as with Proteus, Claudio, Angelo, and Bertram), a process different from that of the late romances, where forgiveness precedes wonder. These chapters typically take up a range of plays, though lingering on certain ones for special attention. The present approach generally avoids assessing the development of comedy across Shakespeare's career and likewise avoids making distinctions such as "apprentice" or "mature." Rather, it identifies recurrent comic devices, techniques, and values that have not been fully recognized or credited but that carry unusual cultural energy and that help to explain, in new ways, the continuing power of Shakespearean comedy.

Coda: Playgoing, Reading, and Response

I have been treating together playgoing and reading, as if they produced comparable responses, yet those dramatic encounters differ in certain ways. Readers typically read silently and in isolation; they can re-read passages, appeal to glosses, flip back to early scenes, or just raise their heads from the text and think at their leisure. Spectators, on the other hand, respond in a usually darkened space, in synch with the pace and dynamics of the performance, and in communal relation with others. Bits that do not get much of a smile from a reader can become hilarious on stage, and the shape of a production, a scene, or an individual performance can deeply affect a spectator's interpretation. Feelings can be contagious in the theater in a way that they are not in solitary reading.

But recent scholarship has been bringing spectatorship and reading into alignment. In Barbara Mowat's view, "the boundary between theater and literary culture" was becoming "increasingly porous" in Shakespeare's time, such that one might speak of the "semi-identity" of the two cultures.[107] Mowat points at the fact that performed plays were printed, and the printed text used (adapted, edited, altered) for further performances, and she notes, too, the strongly literary allusions in many plays. Lukas Erne argues—influentially, if controversially—that Shakespeare wrote his plays to be both seen and read.[108] He employs Mowat's term, "porous," for the relationship between page and stage (4). Charles Whitney defends analyzing theatrical and reading responses together, partly because performance provokes the audience's thinking beyond the immediate play-watching experience.[109] Likewise, Tiffany Stern rejects the "divided binaries" of "theatrical and literary" texts.[110] Akihiro Yamada strongly affirms "the interrelation between the reader and the audience of Shakespeare's time," given drama's growing reading public, and given playwrights' composing with an eye towards both performance and reading (adopting Erne's view; Stern takes a similar position).[111] Studying a large Shakespearean print archive of marginalia in the seventeenth and eighteenth centuries, Jean-Christophe Mayer also rejects "the all-too-often assumed divide"

[107] Barbara Mowat, "The Theater and Literary Culture," in *A New History of Early English Drama*, ed. John D. Cox and David Scott Kastan (New York: Columbia University Press, 1997), 213–30, on 217, 228.

[108] Lukas Erne, *Shakespeare as Literary Dramatist*, 2nd edn. (Cambridge: Cambridge University Press, [2003] 2013).

[109] Charles Whitney, *Early Responses to Renaissance Drama* (Cambridge: Cambridge University Press, 2006).

[110] Tiffany Stern, *Documents of Performance in Early Modern England* (Cambridge: Cambridge University Press, 2009), 254.

[111] Akihiro Yamada, *Experiencing Drama in the English Renaissance: Readers and Audiences* (New York: Routledge, 2017), 200. Amy J. Rodgers posits a "discursive playgoer," an image produced by literary culture that informed the Renaissance sense of how one watched a play: *A Monster with a Thousand Hands: The Discursive Spectator in Early Modern England* (Philadelphia, PA: University of Pennsylvania Press, 2018).

between the worlds of print and theater.[112] "[M]any playwrights were themselves scholarly readers," observes Mayer, "while a number of so-called serious readers showed an interest in performance" (107).

Likewise, Renaissance playwrights surely expected at least some playgoers to bring their reading experiences with them into the theater, as evident from Elizabethan dramatists'—including Shakespeare's—extensive references to Greek and Roman mythology, as Mowat observes. Many plays stage scenes of reading and writing—markedly so in Shakespeare. Various of Shakespeare's plays assume the observer's knowledge of sonnets and other literary works. In the case of *Love's Labour's Lost*, *Romeo and Juliet*, and *Twelfth Night*, David Schalkwyk sees the sonnet form as "literally incorporated into the material space of the theatre."[113] Title pages of Renaissance printed drama sometimes call attention to a play's success in performance, an implicit encouragement to read theatrically. Students at grammar schools both read and performed Plautus and Terence. Literary works, surely including plays, were read aloud in households, giving performative voice to the reading experience; indeed, reading aloud, alone or communally, says Heidi Brayman Hackel, may have been as common as reading silently.[114] According to Tiffany Stern, books might be read aloud by spectators at a play-house before performance time and, further, playbooks themselves were some-times sold at theaters.[115] It seems unwise, then, to insist on a strict separation between early modern playgoing and reading. Thus, the term "audience" in the present study can apply to both spectators and readers.

Something similar can be argued for the present day. Teachers sometimes suggest to student readers that they listen to an audio recording and follow along in the text, and they regularly use video clips of performances in the classroom or in public workshops while looking at the printed text, the performa-tive approach enhancing the readerly one and vice versa. Shakespearean theatrical performances often involve pre- and post-performance discussions that include Shakespearean scholars who bring their literary expertise into the conversation. Not uncommonly, a production of Shakespeare will have a program with an essay by the dramaturg, the director, or a scholar, drawing together elements of the play and citing literary criticism. And, of course, YouTube and podcast sites are rich with discussions of Shakespeare. Perhaps because of Shakespeare's unique pos-ition in world literature, it is fair to say that many playgoers try to educate

---

[112] Jean-Christophe Mayer, *Shakespeare's Early Readers* (Cambridge: Cambridge University Press, 2018), 11, 106.

[113] David Schalkwyk, *Speech and Performance in Shakespeare's Sonnets and Plays* (Cambridge: Cambridge University Press, 2002), 60.

[114] Heidi Brayman Hackel, *Reading Material in Early Modern England: Print, Gender, and Literacy* (Cambridge: Cambridge University Press, 2005), 43–52.

[115] Tiffany Stern, "Watching as Reading: The Audience and Written Text in Shakespeare's Playhouse," in *How to Do Things with Shakespeare: New Approaches, New Essays*, ed. Laurie Maguire (Malden, MA: Blackwell, 2008), 136–59.

themselves about the plays in ways that draw upon academic knowledge. On the theatrical side, many actors and directors consult carefully edited and annotated modern texts of Shakespeare and take a sampling of scholarship when they begin to work on a play. It is reasonable to argue that, today, reading and seeing Shakespeare are mutually informing approaches.

Thus, one of the goals of this study is, through reading, to reveal possibilities in performance, and, by attending to theatricality, to enrich the reading experience. Regarding enchantment, one advantage of the term is that it can be applied both inside the play, to characters, and outside the play, to spectators and readers. Words such as "magical," "charming," and "enchanting" attach traditionally to theatrical experience. "Enchantment" is also a term that arises among reading theorists, such as Rita Felski, to describe the way that readers can become absorbed in a narrative.[116] Given its adaptability for reading and play-watching, the term identifies a useful nexus for thinking about either kind of experience.

Early modern playgoing itself may have developed as a literary as well as a theatrical experience. According to Whitney, Christopher Marlowe's *Tamburlaine* helped to establish a pattern of response that might involve a strong, immediate affective or emotional reaction at the theater, followed by a more discursive, post-performance rumination on the "moral and practical benefit and use" of the work.[117] Whitney argues that theater is both visceral and discursive, and that even in watching a play, metatheatrical moments that break the illusion can induce reflection and provide fodder for subsequent thinking. As Whitney observes, "Playgoers carry their theatrical experiences with them from the theatre and continue to absorb, assimilate, and apply them," so that dramatic response becomes "an extended process" (3). The interplay of affect and intellect applies especially well to Shakespearean comedy, which mixes fantasticality with realism, regularly violates the 'fourth wall,' and employs motifs such as enchantment to create a backwash of unresolved but provocative meaning. As Northrop Frye points out, comedy excels in the use of dramatic conventions that playgoers and readers will recognize and that provide occasions for momentarily disengaged experiences of recognition.[118] That dimension of comedy draws our attention to genre and structure (8). One of the interests of Shakespeare's comedies, we might conclude, is their special jostling between feeling and thought.

---

[116] Rita Felski, *The Uses of Literature* (Malden, MA: Blackwell, 2008), 51–76.
[117] Whitney, *Early Responses*, 2.   [118] See Frye, *Natural Perspective*, 4–8.

1

Clowns, Fools, and Folly

FOLLY HERSELF SPEAKS: Whatever mortals commonly say about me...I and I alone, through my divine radiance, pour forth joy into the hearts of gods and men alike.

Erasmus
The Praise of Folly

In Knoxville, Tennessee in 2007, a white supremacist march brought out, in reaction, an unusual group of counter-protestors: not anti-fascist street fighters but the Coup Clutz Clowns.[1] Scores of individuals dressed in clown suits marched comically alongside the demonstrators, staging their own funny burlesques and chants (e.g., "White Flour" for White Power, with flour thrown into the air). The counter-event won popular approval, with newspaper commentators hailing the capacity of humor and parody to defang right-wing intimidators. Yes, humor can be surprisingly compelling as a political weapon.[2] But, if the jokesters had dressed in ordinary street clothes, their effect would have been far less devastating. The crucial difference was that the counter-demonstrators were *clowns*. Besides causing laughter, clowns reinvent the environment; they establish a different world, a different beingness from that of the political agitator. Psychologically, they incapacitate their objects. A neo-Nazi militia costume cannot match the power of a clown suit.

How does one understand a clown? In Shakespeare's comedies, fools and clowns show up repeatedly and to our delight, but what should we make of them? As the figure of the clown or fool—Launce, the Dromios, Grumio, Costard, Launcelet, Bottom, Dogberry, Touchstone, Feste, Lavatch, Pompey[3]—asserts his engaging presence, the attitude of the audience shifts from its narrative

---

[1] The clowning in Knoxville adopted a tactic used against neo-Nazi demonstrators in Olympia, Washington in 2005, and it was followed by a similar anti-right-wing clown event in Charlotte, NC in 2012; Tina Rosenberg, "Neo-Nazis in Your Street? Send in the Coup Clutz Clowns," *The New York Times*, September 6, 2017. Similar events have been staged in Finland, Germany, and elsewhere. The tactic was devised in the United Kingdom in 2003 by a group calling itself the Clandestine Insurgent Rebel Clown Army (CIRCA).

[2] As playwright Joe Orton put it, "[L]aughter is a serious business, and comedy a weapon more dangerous than tragedy. Which is why tyrants treat it with caution"; *Radio Times*, August 29, 1964.

[3] For "Launcelet," I follow Q1's spelling rather than Arden Three's "Lancelet" (or "Clown" in the speech prefixes) because the former retains the suggestions both of mock-heroism and thrusting lancet. "Launcelet" is the spelling in the Clown's opening speech in the First Folio. I omit Falstaff in *The Merry Wives of Windsor* because he functions there as a protagonist.

Shakespeare and the Comedy of Enchantment. Kent Cartwright, Oxford University Press. © Kent Cartwright 2021.
DOI: 10.1093/oso/9780198868897.003.0002

mode, relaxes into the moment's enchantment, and surrenders to the figure's playfulness. Although the clown can create a charmed interlude—a temporary, humor-filled time-out-of-time—the notion of comic relief seems too reductive to explain his role. Robert Hornback rightly calls "comic relief" a "critical chimera"[4]—and what sense does comic relief make in a comedy, anyway? Present-day scholars, as we shall see, highlight various dimensions of the clown's presence: festive, parodic, contrarious. Pervasively, the clown has been seen as an essentially marginal figure, a commentator, a reflector, but not a protagonist. This chapter takes a different position, that the clown and his enigmatical charm influence a Shakespearean comedy's action, meaning, and experience.

While the terms "clown" and "fool" have individualizing and overlapping meanings, the ensuing discussion will not, for the most part, differentiate between them in function and effect.[5] For Shakespeare, as David Wiles shows, "clown" typically designates a specialized actor who performs a specific kind of dramatic role.[6] Thus, we can distinguish the company clown from the play clown. Within a play, the clown is typically a rustic figure, like Costard, the opposite of the gentry, free of speech, oriented towards bodily matters, yet able to move among the upper social classes. Such roles would be undertaken by the company clown, who might also play the 'fool' or jester characters, like Touchstone, witty and chop-logical, able to roam noble or courtly households. The clown's range also extends to mechanicals, tinkers, constables, bawds, servants, messengers, and the like,[7] such as Dogberry, played by the clown, called a fool, but neither jester nor rustic. Altogether, clowns and fools stand apart in similar ways from other characters.

Clowns and fools possess an ontological and performative Otherness and an inherent magic, expressed through costume, paradoxes, puns, imitations, and, fundamentally, play. Fools and clowns introduce a surplus-effect and hint at utopian values. Not necessarily marginal, they can influence a play's action by promoting confusion, amplifying a protagonist's misprision, or reorienting his or her behavior: They are beings of disruption. They also can affect the meaning of a play by representing alternatives—even if risibly presented, as with Dogberry—to the way that misguided protagonists view things. The unpredictable, transformative presence of clowns and fools aligns them conceptually with romantic characters, for lovers are repeatedly called fools by others, while love, something also transformative, is often regarded as folly. Love and folly, as Erasmus might say, pour an irrational joy into the human heart. Yet Shakespeare's clowns also retain,

---

[4] Robert Hornback, *The English Clown Tradition from the Middle Ages to Shakespeare* (Cambridge: D. S. Brewer, 2009), 12, see 12–13.

[5] The position here follows that of Hornback, *Clown Tradition*, 1–3.

[6] David Wiles, *Shakespeare's Clown: Actor and Text in the Elizabethan Playhouse* (Cambridge: Cambridge University Press, 1987); see 61–72.

[7] Bente A. Videbaek, *The Stage Clown in Shakespeare's Theatre* (Westport, CT: Greenwood Press, 1996), 3.

like the folly of love, a potential for anarchy and amorality, a latency opposed to comedy's presumed goal of harmony. Here the behavior of clown characters emphasizes their connection with the otherworldly medieval Vice. Fools advance the enchantments of comedy; they factor in the comic action, meaning, and experience; but they also claim a certain unruliness or impishness, an element of comic form never quite sublimated within any system of harmonics. Fools are magical—even disturbingly so.

Criticism and the Marginal Clown

Much criticism since the mid-twentieth century has conceived of the clown as a sociological figure whose function is to voice popular or folk values. In Shakespeare's "festive" comedies, according to C. L. Barber, the clown stages "a burlesque version" of the main action, in the spirit of holiday saturnalia.[8] In Barber's model, "clowning could provide both release for impulses which run counter to decency and decorum, and the clarification about limits which comes from going beyond the limit" (13): release and enlightenment together. Barber's ground-breaking formula has been deeply influential, even though some critics fault it for underwriting the status quo. Similar to Barber, Northrop Frye describes the "dominating mood" of Shakespearean comedy as "festive," while seeing the clown, like the spectator, as a figure standing apart from the main narrative, sometimes linked oddly to an anti-comic character in a play of perspectives.[9] Mikhail Bakhtin conceives of the clown as representing the values of carnival, a sociologically and ideologically charged vision of festivity expressing a mystically perpetual folk humor that levels hierarchy, mocks and ridicules decorum, embraces the body, and affirms the utopian energies of the common people.[10] Likewise, François Laroque calls the clown "one of the foremost representatives and spokesmen of popular culture."[11]

Subsequent approaches accept the clown as an embodiment of non-elite popular values and thus embrace his marginality. According to David Wiles, Shakespeare's clown, linked to "the popular tradition,"[12] establishes direct rapport with the audience, sometimes improvises, but largely moves within his own "self-contained sub-plot" (44). The clown-actor Will Kemp (Wiles's focus) gained fame

[8] C. L. Barber, *Shakespeare's Festive Comedy: A Study of Dramatic Form and its Relation to Social Custom* (Princeton, NJ: Princeton University Press, 1959), 12, 13.

[9] Northrop Frye, *A Natural Perspective: The Development of Shakespeare's Comedies and Romances* (New York: Columbia University Press, 1965), 49; on the clown, see 92–7.

[10] Mikhail Bakhtin, *Rabelais and His World*, trans. Helene Iswolsky (Bloomington, IN: Indiana University Press, 1984; orig. pub. in Russian, 1965).

[11] François Laroque, *Shakespeare's Festive World: Elizabethan Seasonal Entertainment and the Professional Stage* (Cambridge: Cambridge University Press, 1991), 42.

[12] Wiles, *Shakespeare's Clown*, ix.

for his postlude performances of jigs, mini-narratives of dance and mime that burlesque romantic love but also express communal and "Utopian" elements (56, 44). For Wiles, the clown stands at the perimeter of the central narrative, casting an ironic eye on it, like Bakhtin's clown; he is a "liminal figure" operating on the "margins" of the dramatic "structure" and the "stage" (174).

The clown's marginality is theorized in the work of Robert Weimann. His *Shakespeare and the Popular Tradition* and subsequent studies establish the distinction between the stage *locus*, the physically and conceptually central space in which the main, realistic narrative takes place, and the *platea*, the physically and conceptually liminal space bordering the narrative site and positioned close to the audience.[13] The clown ranges in that latter area. For Weimann, the *platea* and the clown together express a popular, plebeian attitude of parody and critique antagonistic to the privileged, "elevated," upper-class characters.[14] The clown becomes a vitalistic figure displaying "extemporal wit, 'jestures,' bodily dexterity, song, dance, and related forms of juggling, posturing, and exhibiting" (181), a view not unlike Wiles's. While the play's *locus* crystalizes values of verisimilitude and representation, the "contrarious" *platea* turns unlocalized, resists closure, violates the fourth wall by reaching out to the audience, and "prob[es] the limits of dramatic representation" (193) by showing—as in the case of Launce and his dog in *The Two Gentlemen of Verona*—what is beyond imitation, "nonrepresentable" (195). According to Weimann, then, Shakespeare's clown critiques and evaluates the behavior of the privileged class from a perspective of popular values that comprehends, but remains outside, the zone of the elites: The "popular vision," embodied in the clown, gave Shakespeare, broadly, "the freedom, the detachment, and the imagination" to critique the conflicting mores of his time (177). Although Weimann recognizes the clown's power both to enchant and to disenchant, the clown serves largely as a force of disenchantment towards the central dramatic action and its social values: "[T]he age-old conventions of disenchanting and irreverent parody," represented by Richard Tarleton, had become "integrated within the public theater of the Renaissance" (187). Weimann importantly recognizes the clown's enigmaticalness, his role in forging contrapuntal meaning, and his capacity for magic, but the clown constitutes, nonetheless, an essentially

---

[13] Robert Weimann, *Shakespeare and the Popular Tradition of the Theater: Studies in the Social Dimension of Dramatic Form and Function*, ed. Robert Schwartz (Baltimore, MD: The Johns Hopkins University Press, 1978; orig. pub. in German, 1967). See also Robert Weimann, *Author's Pen and Actor's Voice: Playing and Writing in Shakespeare's Theatre* (Cambridge: Cambridge University Press, 2000); and Robert Weimann and Douglas Bruster, *Shakespeare and the Power of Performance: Stage and Page in the Elizabethan Theatre* (Cambridge: Cambridge University Press, 2008). For a critique of Weimann's *locus* and *platea*, see Erika T. Lin, "Performance Practice and Theatrical Privilege: Rethinking Weimann's Concept of *Locus* and *Platea*," *New Theatre Quarterly* 22, no. 3 (August 2006): 283–98; see also Lin, *Shakespeare and the Materiality of Performance* (New York: Palgrave Macmillan, 2012), 23–69.

[14] Weimann, *Actor's Pen*, 195.

disenchanting and marginal figure. Weimann and Bruster sum up the clown's marginality thus:

> Shakespeare's clowns and fools...may wittily deflate the dominant representations in either genre, but their role in the dramatic formation of "worthy matter" remains marginal...[T]heir comic orbit of performance holds them aloof... from any decisive dramatic action.[15]

Weimann's views have been deservedly influential, yet one might entertain them with certain reservations. First, Weimann often emphasizes the clown as essentially oppositional. In *Author's Pen*, for example, Weimann discusses the *platea* and the clown in terms of nonrepresentation, "nonidentity," "a gap," "disinterest," "a certain defiance," "resistance," and "contrariety" (196). Suggestive as these negations are, one might wish to see them squared with the familiar popular sense of dramatic clowns and fools as focused on matters such as comfort, sensuality, and food. Second, Weimann applies his model substantially to the tragedies (e.g., *Lear*'s Fool) and the histories (e.g., Jack Cade) but less to the comedies. Weimann in *Author's Pen* spends a little over a page discussing Launce and Crab and, in the same chapter, eleven and a half pages treating the Porter in *Macbeth*. The discrepancy may arise because, although the clown always possesses an ontology that distinguishes him as Other, he still hews closer in the comedies to the narrative world—is far less marginal to it—than he does in the tragedies. The difference is critical. In the comedies the clown's influence can leak into the main action, as we shall see, partly because, in that world, the gods of folly distribute their gifts democratically, to main characters as well as to 'peripheral' ones. In such a genre, the clown can hardly be so sharply adversarial or oppositional or remote as in other forms. That difference makes room not only for his charmed and charming aspects but also for his involvement in the action. Third, Weimann argues for the importance of the clown to meaning while restricting him to the narrative margins. Meaningful critique occurs, but outside the action, on the perimeter; sociologically, the clown must be kept aloof from the privileged characters who drive Shakespeare's comic action. That position seems problematic, even a little self-contradictory, for it makes the clown simultaneously important but nonfunctional, integral yet not integral to our understanding of the play. I want to embrace Weimann's sense of the significance of the clown but to give the figure more direct pertinence by pulling him back from the margins and bringing his aura of enchantment more directly into the action.

---

[15] Weimann and Bruster, *Performance*, 78.

Certain studies coming after Weimann's have subtly moved beyond his analysis. The most important is Robert Hornback's *The English Clown Tradition from
the Middle Ages to Shakespeare*. Hornback's goal is to "reclaim . . . an ideological
dimension" of early comedy, particularly the "clown's role in a tradition of
religious and political theatrical satire," which he finds underestimated by criticism.[16] For Hornback, clowns require "layers and ranges of audience response,"
not just laughter but also, crucially, a complex intellectual engagement. *The
English Clown Tradition* analyzes a history of blackface clowns that associates
blackness with evil and folly, recovers clowning practices of evangelical comedy,
and identifies the satirizing of "a stereotyped rustic, ignorant puritan clown type"
(22). Hornback's predominant focus is not Shakespeare, but he demonstrates the
complex, multi-directional power that the clown-figure could assert. Here the
clown steps in from the margins.

Relatedly, Robert H. Bell, connecting Shakespeare's clown with Erasmus's
enigmatic holy fool, argues that "[f]ools illustrate Shakespeare's hybridity and
liminality, . . . excess or extravagance, resistance to resolution, antic discombobula-
tion, and infinite supplementarity"; in that respect they provide a *"mise en abyme"* of
the comedy.[17] The clown's paradoxicality makes him central. Thinking about the
theatrical event, Richard Preiss posits the clown as marginal to the playtext but
central to the performance because of his combative relationship with the audience.[18]
My own argument identifies ways in which the clown invades the main action and its
tones and meanings. That is not to make him into a force for thematic unity, for he
can function as the opposite. Helpful here is the term "ludic," which Douglas
Peterson contrasts to "mimetic" (the two terms reformulating *platea* and *locus*):
The clown is a "ludic" figure, while the more narrative characters are "mimetic."[19]
"Ludic" evokes play, ritual, and communal experience; it takes in the clown's magical
aura and interpretive complexity. The clown in his ludic dimension—influencing
characters and events, shaping our experiences and interpretations—stands for the
comedy of enchantment.

In the following sections, we will explore: (1) the facets and complexities of the
clown that establish his magical aura and empower his crucial interventions in
action; (2) his influences on other characters; (3) his effects on the action; and (4)
his potential for moral salience, as in the case of Bottom. Shakespeare's clown

---

[16] Hornback, *Clown Tradition*, 1; on Weimann, *Shakespeare and the Popular Tradition*, see 18–20.

[17] Robert H. Bell, *Shakespeare's Great Stage of Fools* (New York: Palgrave Macmillan, 2011), 5.

[18] Richard Preiss, *Clowning and Authorship in Early Modern England* (Cambridge: Cambridge
University Press, 2014). Preiss envisions an adversarial relationship between play and audience wherein
the clown serves as a lightning rod for the latter's aggressive energies. Preiss's description of play-
audience relationships would leave little room for the magical dimension that the present chapter sees
in the clown.

[19] Douglas L. Peterson, "Beginnings and Endings: Structure and Mimesis in Shakespeare's
Comedies," in *Entering the Maze: Shakespeare's Art of Beginning*, ed. Robert F. Willson, Jr. (New
York: Peter Lang, 1995), 37–53.

brings a sense of magical possibility that can reach from the periphery to the center of a comedy.

The Clown as Magical

Our understanding of the clown changes when we focus on not just his sociology but also his charmed and otherworldly ontology. Fools in Shakespeare's comedies possess a magical aura, and they take fellow characters into a magical temporal zone. As Weimann himself notes, the Elizabethan fool descends from a tradition in which he possesses the powers to enchant, for he can "generate a ritual dimension through the fantasy and madness of his topsy-turvydom or through his inversion of values and transformation of reality into something strange, sad or comical."[20] In those aspects, the fool evokes a utopian and "visionary" world (11). But Weimann's emphasis falls on a play's capacity to produce demotic social criticism. More ontologically, for the philosopher Peter Berger, fools and clowns are "magicians," and "the comic should be understood as a form of magic."[21] For that, we need to inventory the clown's specialness.

Costume

The clown manifests his magical otherness in costume. The clown-as-jester, fully turned out, wears identifying apparel that might include: a motley jerkin (or a long coat), a pair of baggy gaskins, and a clown's cap with a cockscomb (or asses' ears, bells, or a large feather). He sometimes carries a bauble or a marotte (a wand with a clown's head on it);[22] Lavatch, for example, makes a phallic reference to his fool's "bauble" (AW 4.5.29). Wiles names yellow and blue, or yellow and green, as colors for a traditional fool's coat,[23] which was motley, or "patched." Feste invokes his "motley" (TN 1.5.53), and Jaques describes Touchstone as "a motley fool" (AYL 2.7.13). "The patch is kind enough," says Shylock of Launcelet (MV 2.5.44). In his rustic incarnation the clown or fool might wear a jerkin or a country-looking russet coat.[24] Such paraphernalia, or just a piece of it, would mark out the folly-character: Thus, Lavatch suggestively describes Bertram, home from the wars, as wearing "a patch of velvet on's face" (4.5.91–2).

---

[20] Weimann, *Popular Tradition*, 11.

[21] Peter L. Berger, *Redeeming Laughter: The Comic Dimension of Human Experience* (Berlin: Walter de Gruyter, 1997), 77, 117.

[22] On the clown's costume, see the index entries under "clown" and "fool" in Wiles, *Shakespeare's Clown*.

[23] Wiles, *Shakespeare's Clown*, 5, 183.   [24] Noted in Weimann and Bruster, *Performance*, 79.

Surplus

As scholarship has established, the Elizabethan clown descends, in large part, from the medieval dramatic Vice.[25] The quasi-occult Vice-figure of medieval and Tudor morality drama directs characters towards sin, comments cynically upon events, changes his mind willfully, works to produce mayhem, and generates a sometimes amoral humor and laughter.[26] He moves easily between *locus* and *platea* and takes the audience into his confidence as he mocks and betrays characters, as Ambidexter does in Thomas Preston's *Cambyses* (c.1561).[27] The Vice-figure arrives from a world beyond the narrative, and, as Wiles says of Mischief in *Mankind*, he "has the power to juggle layers of reality," so that he can seem simultaneously both a metaphysical excrescence of evil and a "carnivalesque celebrant,"[28] a bit numinous in both respects. As Weimann acknowledges, Mischief is a "magician, doctor, and fool all in one."[29] The Vice always survives the play's action, ready, in effect, for the next narrative. Such a figure carries an inherent surplus of being and meaning. The clowns and fools who succeed the Vice of the early morality plays—down to pre-Shakespearean embodiments such as Miles in *Friar Bacon and Friar Bungay* (c.1589)—inherit some of that mystery and surplus.

The Elizabethan clown Richard Tarleton could famously inspire laughter simply by poking his head out from behind the stage curtain. Tarleton possessed superb comic skills, yet his laughter-inducing power also derived from the audience's knowing in advance not only who he was but what he was. Like the Vice or the popular mask figures of *commedia dell' arte*, the Renaissance clown exists generically prior to, and independent of, any particular manifestation. As Mikhail Bakhtin says of mask-figures:

> [P]opular masks...are able to assume any destiny and can figure into any situation...but they cannot exhaust their possibilities by those situations alone; they always retain, in any situation and in any destiny, a happy surplus of their own, their own rudimentary but inexhaustible human face.[30]

---

[25] For the most influential of many studies on this subject, see Bernard Spivack, *Shakespeare and the Allegory of Evil* (New York: Columbia University Press, 1958); see also, Weimann, *Popular Tradition*.
[26] Ágnes Matuska argues that the Tudor Vice epitomizes the spirit of "play and mirth," a potentially liberating force that exposes the differences between signs and meanings in representational systems undergoing challenge; *The Vice-Device: Iago and Lear's Fool as Agents of Representational Crisis* (Szeged, Hungary: Institute of English and American Studies, University of Szeged, 2011), 13.
[27] See Kent Cartwright, *Theatre and Humanism: English Drama in the Sixteenth Century* (Cambridge: Cambridge University Press, 1999), 102–8.
[28] Wiles, *Shakespeare's Clown*, 3, 2.   [29] Weimann, *Popular Tradition*, 114.
[30] M. M. Bakhtin, "Epic and the Novel," in *The Dialogic Imagination: Four Essays*, ed. Michael Holquist, trans. Caryl Emerson and Michael Holquist (Austin, TX: University of Texas Press, 1981; orig. pub. in Russian, 1975), 3–40, 36.

The popular clown's excess over his narrative circumstances—the quality that makes audiences laugh when Tarlton merely peeks—constitutes a comic "surplus," Bakhtin argues, an "inexhaustibility of [the] self," "an unrealized potential."[31] The clown exists, doubly, because a part of him always transcends his localized identity. Bakhtin, in discussing surplus in the novel, speaks of "the field of vision" that the surplus brings into play[32] (he is interested in the author, but the concept can migrate to "mask characters" in comedy). For Bakhtin, the Renaissance clown induces a carnival laughter that is festive and vivifying, inclusive and universalizing, and paradoxically both gay and mocking.[33] Those dimensions give the clown's perspective and inferentially the comic surplus a "special philosophical and utopian character" (12). In Renaissance Italy, comedies were publicly acted during the Carnival season.[34] Thus, in the spirit of carnivalesque utopianism, the sixteenth-century plebeian Paduan playwright Ruzante can promote to general audiences a "philosophy of 'natural' values" that draws him close to Bakhtin, observes Richard Andrews.[35] Within the clown's special "field of vision," the human world occurs as dynamic, material, and communal, with its utopianism oriented towards the future, "another world" beyond the stage, a "friendly world," a "golden age."[36] (The sometime sadness or bitterness of a clown might be interpreted as the failure of the world against the possibility of his dream.) When the clown enters the audience's field of vision, he bears his surplus of utopian qualities like a halo around him.

Qualities of Being

Along with his symbolic costume and magical surplus, the clown has other special ontological qualities. Most famously, clowns cannot be injured or die; their beingness is governed by an enchanted cartoon logic in which they survive every slip on a banana peel or fall from a cliff's edge unscathed. This is the logic of fantasies, daydreams, and childlike imaginings. Often clowns do not share the protagonists' nationality or any connection with the play's locale. *The Two Gentlemen of Verona* may be set in Italy, but Launce and Speed sound English and have English names. For the most part, clowns also lack personal history or

---

[31] Bakhtin, "Epic and the Novel," 35, 37.

[32] Mikhail Bakhtin, *Problems of Dostoevsky's Poetics*, ed. and trans. Caryl Emerson (Minneapolis, MN: University of Minnesota Press, 1984; from expanded Russian edition in 1963; first Russian edition, 1929), 70.

[33] Bakhtin, *Rabelais*, 11–12.

[34] See, e.g., Leo Salingar, *Shakespeare and the Traditions of Comedy* (Cambridge: Cambridge University Press, 1974), 121, 176, 177, 180, 182, 183, 191; *commedia erudita*, performed during carnival, often celebrates its city, manifesting its ruler's ideal fantasy (176, 184) even while it expresses carnivalesque values.

[35] Richard Andrews, *Scripts and Scenarios: The Performance of Comedy in Renaissance Italy* (Cambridge: Cambridge University Press, 1993), 133.

[36] Bakhtin, *Rabelais*, 48.

even family (with some exceptions, such as Launce and Launcelot). "[T]he clown is a pretend person," says Robert Bell;[37] individual psychologies are limited or absent, as are objectives in the narrative; the clown's goals are generic, such as escaping punishment, sleeping, and gourmandizing. Clowns, too, are always a little bit in trouble, in danger of being dismissed, beaten, or starved: Launce loses his position, the Dromios keep getting cuffed, Costard is arrested, Launcelot is virtually dismissed by Shylock, Feste is in hot water with Olivia and Lavatch with the Countess, Pompey lands in prison. Additionally, Shakespeare's clowns speak in prose or tumbling verse instead of the blank verse of the romantic or higher status characters, although they can use regular verse and rhyme when warranted. They comment without much 'filter'; that is, without the internalized conventions of social restraint that prevent embarrassment to others. Lack of inhibition unleashes their angular perspectives, and it privileges their close contact with the audience, so that the clown carries a special verbal, psychic, and social coloring. Company clowns, too, often have an unusual appearance: Will Kemp was unhandsome and big of build; Robert Armin was unhandsome and dwarfish. But each compensated for his appearance by means of uncommon gifts and skills: Kemp was a famed dancer and leaper, being swift and light of foot, and a skilled physical mime; Armin could sing, improvise rhymes, and impersonate different voices (presumably even using ventriloquism).[38] Clowns thus inject their own oblique field of vision and their performative surplus into a narrative milieu that can never quite explain or contain them.

Stop-Time

Shakespeare's comic interludes within the narrative begin to show how clowning can reshape the action. Renaissance comedies typically contain 'set-pieces,' self-contained moments that develop a comic exchange exceeding the plot's requirements. Narrative time temporarily stops for play time. Italian comedy is full of such moments. An early example occurs in Bernardo Dovizi da Bibbiena's influential *La calandra* (1513). Here the servant Fessenio, employed by the foolish old husband Calandro but working on behalf of the young lover Lidio, enjoys duping the *vecchio*. Fessenio engages in comic 'bits' with Calandro meant simply to be amusing, as when he describes to the latter how to drink a woman, or when he discusses dismembering and reassembling Calandro so that he can be conveyed clandestinely into Santilla's bedroom. This last gag affords Fessenio the opportunity to yank Calandro's arm painfully to see if it will come off. These incidents

---

[37] Bell, *Stage of Fools*, 10.
[38] On Kemp, see Wiles, *Shakespeare's Clown*, 22, 24–42 and passim.; on Armin, see Wiles, *Shakespeare's Clown*, 136–63.

suspend the plot temporarily to illustrate the dupe's stupidity and create farcical humor. Italian comedies are rife with such *beffe*, tricks or deceptions, aimed at ridiculing their dupes or at bringing illicit lovers together. Servant-tricksters typically enact the *beffa*, taking fool-figures as their victims. The shenanigans in Italian comedy help to generate a set of commonly recognized, interchangeable plot devices, "theatergrams," as Louise George Clubb terms them.[39] The victims tend to be stock comic butts: old husbands, misers, pedants, and braggart soldiers from *commedia dell' arte* transmuted into the humanistic *commedia erudita*. Tudor comedy has its counterpart parodies, as in MerryGreek's various self-amused mockeries of Ralph in *Ralph Roister Doister* (c.1551). According to Richard Andrews, Italian and Shakespearean comedy are related in their sharing of common theatrical plots, devices, and details, but their clowns do not translate directly from one tradition to the other: "[T]here are very few of Shakespeare's clowns...who evoke the comic masks of the Italian tradition."[40] Likewise, Shakespeare's comic interludes differ significantly from Fessenio's brand of trickery.

Shakespeare's digressive bits are performed by clowns rather than tricksters, a significant difference from Italian comedy that allows the in-sets to express the clown's aura of enchantment. Philosopher Peter Berger, analyzing comedy, draws upon the concept of different kinds of realities in daily human experience occurring inside a dominant reality, a theory developed by phenomenological sociologist Alfred Schutz.[41] Those discrete sub-realities entail their own "'provinces of meaning'" (7). Like jokes, clown interludes constitute one of those sub-realities. In clown interludes, characters and audiences join in a suspension of the narrative, a stop-time, as participants and observers relax into a new condition where normal social rules and expectations are suspended and participants experience themselves, and are taken by others, as being at "play" (with permission to say things unacceptable in the dominant reality). Such moments break into quotidian affairs or into comedy as "momentary, even fugitive" alternative zones of meaning,[42] but they constitute integral parts of the rhythm of life and are hardly marginal. In Shakespeare, stop-times, because fueled by clowns as opposed to tricksters, can become magical.

Shakespeare's clowns enter, spilling forth puns, inversions, paradoxes, improvisations, and even utopian hypotheses, all destabilizing conventional meaning

---

[39] Louise George Clubb, *Italian Drama in Shakespeare's Time* (New Haven, CT: Yale University Press, 1989), 1–26.

[40] Richard Andrews, "Resources in Common: Shakespeare and Faminio Scala," in *Transnational Mobilities in Early Modern Theater*, ed. Robert Henke and Eric Nicholson (Farnham, Surrey: Ashgate, 2014), 37–52, on 38.

[41] Berger, *Redeeming Laughter*, 7–8, 29, 65–6; for Schutz, see his essay "On Multiple Realities" (1945), in Alfred Schutz, *The Problem of Social Reality: Collected Papers I*, ed. Maurice Natanson (The Hague: Martinus Nijhoff, 1962), 207–59.

[42] Berger, *Redeeming Laughter*, 6.

and hinting at new possibilities and ways of thinking, thus creating a new sub-reality. What Berger says of circus clowns applies to Shakespeare's dramatic ones: They are "magician[s]" who, by ushering other characters into "the world of folly," create "an oasis of enchantment within the reality of modern rationality" (77).[43] Because the clown comes from an ontological domain different from that of other characters, because he can freely criss-cross storylines, and because he takes others into an experiential zone sheared away from the everyday, Shakespeare's comic interludes become their own moments of suspended and enchanted temporality.[44] They interrupt immediate events but re-enforce a larger narrative rhythm. These moments of stop-time folly resemble "festive time," being "qualitatively differentiated" from the "measured time of towns and businesses," and they evoke dreams, topsy-turvydom, utopianism, and other carnival values.[45] The clown's stop-time interludes break into the everyday with an alternative, even numinous, "province of meaning."

And put everything back together differently. Consider an exchange between Syracusan Antipholus and Dromio early in *The Comedy of Errors*. The play's action builds upon the pressure of time; characters fuss about it; and discussions of temporality sift into the play's comic interludes. In 1.2, Ephesian Dromio bursts in upon Syracusan Antipholus, as if from another reality, jabbering crazily about time: "'Returned so soon'? Rather approached too late! / The capon burns, the pig falls from the spit; / The clock hath strucken twelve upon the bell" (1.2.43–5). Much later, Syracusan Dromio will veer into a hyper-caffeinated rhapsody about the Officer as a figure of Biblical Adam (or possibly a sixteenth-century London tapster [4.3.13–20]). Midway between those bits comes a moment, in 2.2, when the Syracusans shift their conversation into a comic zone released from the narrative flow, a change that will, however, alter the possibilities of the narrative. Antipholus strikes his servant Dromio for denying (truthfully) that he (Dromio) had barged in upon Antipholus in 1.2 to insist that his master urgently return home to his wife. Antipholus grows angry at Dromio's denials, smacking him and justifying the blow because of Dromio's "jest[ing]" during Antipholus's "serious hours" (28, 29).

Like other Shakespearean clowns, Dromio defends himself with puns, improvising upon "sconce" as not head but head-covering (35–9). Using a familiar clown stratagem, Dromio asserts a paradox, that by beating him "out of season" (47), Antipholus has given him something for nothing. When Antipholus prefers to ask about "dinner-time" (54), Dromio puts off an answer with quibbles, and the

---

[43] Citing Schutz, Berger observes that comic interludes, like other province of meaning, have a "'cognitive style,'" an internal consistency, and an "exclusive sense of reality" (*Redeeming Laughter*, 8). One enters the comic moment, like others, in a "'leap'" (8).

[44] On suspended time, see Matthew D. Wagner, *Shakespeare, Theatre, and Time* (New York: Routledge, 2012).

[45] Laroque, *Festive World*, 174.

two fall into what becomes the throughline argument of the exchange, whether or not, as Antipholus claims, "there's a time for all things" (67). Dromio denies that "rule" (70) and even invokes Father Time in the ensuing *disputatio*, in which he holds his own against, or even betters, Antipholus. Throughout this exchange both characters employ 'connective repetition,' the *commedia dell' arte* and comedy-duo tactic of picking up a word or phrase from the other speaker and turning it improvisationally in a new direction with a surprise meaning.

The pair's exchange, so much about time, lasts over a hundred lines and constitutes a self-contained, magical stop-time, rife with destabilizing puns, para-doxes, and mock assertions. As play, it leavens the comic violence with humor and removes Antipholus's attention from his confusion about Dromio. But it is hardly 'comic relief,' for, in a play that entails conflicting senses of farcical time and romance time, it demonstrates Schutz's layeredness of reality as an experiential fact. Is there a time for all things? Although Dromio's demurral argues the impossibility of recovering lost hair, *Errors* will ultimately have much to say about the possibility of recovering other, more dear things lost to time.

But the episode shadows the action more directly still. While *post hoc, ego propter hoc* (after that, because of that) constitutes a fallacy in logic, it frequently makes for a truth in drama. With their time-for-all-things stop-time, the Syracusans have moved into the domain of exploratory ideas, unstable meanings, and shifting levels of reality. The characters' talk of contradictory possibilities in time supplies the theme to their own time-out-of-time interlude. Under those conditions, the action might go anywhere. Thus, when Adriana and Luciana disrupt Antipholus and Dromio's exchange, a transformative moment ensues, wherein the two outsiders will surrender to the experiences of "fairy land" and "dream"-world (195, 188). Given the Syracusans' prior, strongly registered fear of Ephesian magic, what makes them now willing to immerse themselves in this alien enchantment? The preceding, magical intrusion of play-time, I would argue, creates the necessary condition, the openness, for the mock bewitchment: "What, was I married to her in my dream?"; "This is fairy land"; "I am trans-formed, master, am I not? / I think thou art in mind, and so am I" (188, 195, 201–2). So, in an enchanted "mist" (222), the Syracusan men go off with the Ephesian women, and the whole course of the action takes a turn. If the clowning stop-time authorizes and makes credible the characters' "metamorphosis"—if, Puck-like, it ushers new possibilities and actions into the narrative—then we can think of Shakespeare's comedic clowns as sometimes functioning in ways more crucial than marginal. We will see other such effects.

The stop-time interlude in *Errors* 2.2 shows off several of clowning's ingredi-ents: improvisations, puns, paradoxes, and magical impossibilities. Dromio and Antipholus's various quibbles—"sconce," "basting," "dry," "fine and recovery," and the like—dismantle fixed meanings; social roles fall away; realities bend. Dromio's very first pun establishes a paradox: Antipholus has claimed that he must beat Dromio in order to instill understanding into his hard head, his "sconce"; Dromio replies that what he needs at that moment is a "sconce," i.e., a helmet, to protect him from beating. Thus, "sconce" becomes paradoxically both what is to be penetrated and what resists penetration. In such ways, Dromio drives the *disputatio*, deploying pseudo-paradoxes ("something for nothing") and riddling mock-aphorisms: "Was there any man thus beaten out of season" (47); "the meat wants what I have" (55–6); "what he [i.e., Time] hath scanted men in hair he hath given them in wit" (83–4). Dromio wields the forms of rational argument to make ridiculous assertions and deploys apothegmatic thinking to cast doubt on conventional proverbs ("there is a time for all things"). Many of Shakespeare's clowns speak similarly, as in the much later example of Pompey Bum: "[H]e that drinks all night and is hanged betimes in the morning may sleep the sounder all the next day" (*MM* 4.3.44–6). As Laroque puts it, the clown revels in ambivalences and contraries, his "function" being "to draw attention to the limits of the world of the intellect."[46] And to expand that world.

Paradox

As with Dromio, Shakespeare's clowns gleefully spout paradoxes. According to Peter G. Platt, the Renaissance was an age of paradox, founded, first, on a Ciceronian and Erasmian rhetorical tradition and, second, on the belief that rhetorical paradoxes complimented Christianity's logical paradoxes.[47] For the Renaissance, Platt argues, paradoxes "challenge common opinion," received wisdom, *doxa* (4); they can be more than merely nonsensical pronouncements or self-contradictions. Citing Cicero, Henry Peacham, and the Renaissance Italian theorist Francesco Patrizi, Platt links paradox to wonder, admiration, and the marvelous.[48] For Shakespeare, likewise, paradox operates as "a way of questioning conventional teaching and fostering debate" (52). It enlarges conceptual possibilities.

If comedies employ paradox at the level of theme, clowns invoke it at the level of language and experience, often generating key ideas. Paradoxes might emerge from the clown's intentional or unintentional puns, mix-ups, and reversals of meaning. In *Love's Labour's Lost*, Costard quips aptly and presciently about suffering for love: "[W]elcome the sour cup of prosperity! Affliction may one day smile again" (1.1.297–8). Launcelet finds himself in an ethical quandary close to the texture of *The Merchant of Venice* when his conscience advises him to stay

---

[46] Laroque, *Festive World*, 42.

[47] Peter G. Platt, *Shakespeare and the Culture of Paradox* (New York: Routledge, 2009), see esp. 17–55. Regarding Christian paradoxes, see R. Chris Hassel, Jr., *Faith and Folly in Shakespeare's Romantic Comedies* (Athens, GA: University of Georgia Press, 1980).

[48] Platt, *Culture*, 17–18, 19–20; Patrizi will be noted in Chapter 6 in relation to the wonder of comic endings.

with his master, who is a kind of devil, while the "devil himself" advises him to leave (*MV* 2.2.21, 23): Can devilry be avoided? Dogberry's instructions to the Watch weave a network of paradoxes that, in the face of misdemeanor and crime, counsel inaction under the guise of action (*MA* 3.3.24–59): They give exquisite form to the penchant of other characters for rationalization. And when Touchstone opines, "the truest poetry is the most feigning, and lovers are given to poetry, and what they swear in poetry may be said, as lovers, they do feign" (3.3.17–19),[49] he reaches into the heart of *As You Like It*. The paradoxes of the presumably marginal clown often become mysteriously central to capturing a comedy's narrative implications.

Utopianism

The clown is touched by a utopian vision, made possible by his ontological difference from other characters. He carries echoes of a world better, more congenial, more bountiful, and more egalitarian than the present one. "'Twas never merry world," says Pompey, wittily sizing up inequalities, "since of two usuries the merriest was put down and the worser allowed by order of law a furred gown to keep him warm" (*MM* 3.1.276–7). Such background utopian visions deserve emphasis in criticism, for, argues Hugh Grady, approaches that are anti-aesthetic can overlook a work's "utopian potential."[50] The reigning model acknowledges the clown's utopianism, as Weimann does,[51] but sees it implicitly as remote and marginal, a kind of outer rim of critique, just as the clown is marginal. Recognizing the clown's utopianism as apposite to the action, then, helps to bring it back from the play's edges. For Mikhail Bakhtin, as we noted, carnival calls forth a plebeian utopian ideal in which official "prohibitions" and "hierarchical barriers" are supplanted by a "sphere of freedom," a "radical[]" space of brotherhood.[52] In the clowning interlude between Antipholus and Dromio, Dromio achieves a moment of socially inverting parity: He may have just been beaten by Antipholus, but in the *disputatio* he converts himself, through spontaneous wit and linguistic facility, into his master's equal, even partner. This stop-time brotherhood has benefits. By leveling intellectual differences, the clowning interlude energizes not only Dromio but also Antipholus—making each alert, quick—and, as we have seen, shifts their moods and opens them up to transformational possibility. Thus, the utopian leveling of clowning assumes instrumental value.

---

[49] In place of the First Folio and Arden's "faining," I have adopted Rowe's emendation, "feigning," followed by virtually all editors.

[50] Hugh Grady, "Shakespeare and Impure Aesthetics: The Case of *A Midsummer Night's Dream*," *Shakespeare Quarterly* 59, no. 3 (Fall 2008): 274–302, on 276.

[51] Weimann, *Popular Tradition*, 11, 31.   [52] Bakhtin, *Rabelais*, 89, 90.

Other comedies likewise show utopian influences. At the far end of the canon from Dromio, Lavatch in *All's Well* calls himself a "prophet" (1.3.58) and adopts a comically visionary, sometimes apocalyptic tone: "[']T]is not so well that I am poor, though many of the rich are damned" (17–18); "I am for the house with the narrow gate, which I take to be too little for pomp to enter. Some that humble themselves may" (4.5.51–4). That last remark arouses in Lafew, its object, a sudden discomfort: "Go thy ways. I begin to be aweary of thee" (4.5.57). Lavatch's sense of utopian justice works similar effects on others, fluttering the play's already problematic moral surface.

A comedy's ideals can even be foregrounded in the clown's utopianism, as with Dogberry in *Much Ado*. That might seem surprising, since critics typically treat Dogberry as long-winded and pompous but inarticulate. Arden editor Claire McEachern quotes A. P. Rossiter's statement that "'[a]s a real official, Dogberry would be a terror.'"[53] Citing Thomas Dekker's *Gull's Hornbook* (1609), McEachern aligns with critics who interpret the Watch as parodying the "realities of Elizabethan policing," including the general slothfulness of the constabulary and its preferential treatment of the gentry (23–4).[54] But when we consider Dogberry (played by both Will Kemp and Robert Armin) as a clown-figure, utopian and carnival values appear. Instructing the Watch, Dogberry speaks paradoxically, as we have noted, his every injunction to enforce the law being undone by an exception to leave malefactors at peace: "[F]or indeed the watch ought to offend no man, and it is an offense to stay a man against his will" (3.3.78–80). "[C]all at all the alehouses," he tells his men, "and bid those that are drunk to get them to bed," but should they refuse, "let them alone till they are sober" (42–5). Viewed one way, these orders will fail to enforce good behavior, yet viewed another, they exhibit a serene generosity, even indulgence, towards humankind: "You have always been called a merciful man," says Verges, and Dogberry responds, "Truly, I would not hang a dog by my will, much more a man that hath any honesty in him" (59, 61–2). If there is rationalized ineptitude here, there is also a protest against the cruelties of Elizabethan legal punishment—a protest that resounds in other plays, from *Errors* to *Measure for Measure*. Dogberry perceives his citizen constables as "good men and true" (1), towards whom he feels friendly benevolence—"neighbor" is his preferred address—and expresses a kind of utopian fellowship, no matter if naïve. That good will, lodged in the comic spirit of his instructions, explains Dogberry's likeability. Officious,

---

[53] McEachern, *MA*, 25. Robert Hornback sees Dogberry as, in part, a parody of Puritan pomposity; *Clown Tradition*, 135–40.

[54] See Duncan Salkeld, "New Directions: Letting Wonder Seem Familiar—Italy and London in *Much Ado About Nothing*," in *Much Ado About Nothing: A Critical Reader*, ed. Deborah Cartmell and Peter J. Smith (London: Bloomsbury, 2018), 89–109, on 100–5. On Dogberry as illustrating how the dominant class must "negotiate" with and partially accommodate the lower ones, see Theodore B. Leinwand, "Negotiation and New Historicism," *PMLA* 105, no. 3 (May 1990): 477–90, esp. 483–5.

egotistical, Dogberry yet speaks for a Golden-Age behavior towards others that offers a corrective to *Much Ado*'s world of social cruelty. As R. W. Maslen argues, Dogberry crystallizes popular values—those of "good men and true"—that make their way into the play as counterweights to the gentry's deceptions and failures.[55] The clown's charmed utopianism breaks into the narrative and introduces the possibility of revising one's way of relating to others.

Dark Magic

But utopianism's light is dimmed by shadows, the dark side of the clown, who, as Wiles suggests, moves among differing realities. The comedies often include a threatening background presence, sometimes imaged in the forest or the violent, uncontrollable sea: the dangerous woods in *Two Gentlemen of Verona* and *A Midsummer Night's Dream*; the hazardous seas in *The Comedy of Errors*, *The Merchant of Venice*, and *Twelfth Night* (we shall return to places in Chapter 3). In parallel fashion, clowns possess a vein of anarchic energy—a reason, perhaps, why a melancholic and anti-comic character such as Jaques might be drawn to them. Clowns and fools can appear a bit louche. In *Merchant*, Launcelet earns a nervous warning from Lorenzo over his intimacy with Jessica: "I shall grow jealous of you shortly, Lancelet, if you thus get my wife into dark corners" (3.5.26–7). Jessica dispels any suggestion of impropriety, but Lorenzo persists, admonishing Launcelet for "getting up of the negro's belly: the Moor is with child by you" (3.5.35–6). The clown responds merely with confusing quibbles: "... but if she be less than an honest woman, she is indeed more than I took her for" (38–9). Launcelet's remark amplifies the Venetians' racism, while its pun-based rationalization individualizes the misdeed. We might call his behavior immoral, and it joins unpleasantly with Launcelet's view that Jessica will be damned for her father's Jewishness (3.5.1–5); but it also could be called amoral, the behavior of a being for whom responsibility for a pregnancy vanishes by means of word-magic. Here the clown's special ontology negates his social accountability.

Other clowns and fools, too, dally with sex. Launce and Lavatch each intend to marry (although the latter changes his mind); Touchstone will wed Audrey with carnal intent and in hopes that he might easily abandon her; and Pompey earns his living as a bawd. *Love's Labour's Lost* begins with Costard's arrest for consorting in "the manner" with Jaquenetta (1.1.206). Whether he or Don Armado is the real father of Jaquenetta's child will remain a mystery: Armado takes responsibility; no such idea occurs to Costard, as with Launcelet. A strain of lasciviousness and indifference runs through the clown. It constitutes a given, one low-key but

---

[55] R. W. Maslen, *Shakespeare and Comedy* (London: Bloomsbury, 2005), 89, 169–70.

inconsistent with the comedies' implicit ethics, a wave of waywardness invading a play from a different domain.

The magic can get even darker. Shakespeare's clowns and fools, as we have noted, descend from the medieval Vice, and the comedies sometimes remind us directly about that mischievous figure. "Well, your old vice still: mistake the word," rejoins Speed to Launce, noting the Vice-business of purposely confusing "Mastership" with "master's ship" (*TGV* 3.1.278, 276, 277). In the same scene, Launce delays informing Speed that his master Valentine awaits him at the North Gate, and he proclaims that he will "rejoice" in the "unmannerly slave" being beaten by Valentine, "swinged," for the nonsensical offence of reading Launce's letter (in which Launce had seemed to take pleasure) (383, 382, 381). There is a bit of the Vice, too, in Launce's bizarre claim that the lapdog meant for Sylvia was stolen by "the hangman's boy" and Launce's ill-conceived replacement of it with the "currish" Crab (4.4.58, 48) (the misbehaving mutt effectively symbolizes Proteus's infatuation). Launcelet, too, aligns with the Vice as he parodies the medieval psychomachia in describing his conscience (or Good Angel) whispering into one ear and the "fiend" into the other (2.2.2).[56]

Grumio typically functions as the amplifier of his master's statements, but he also goes further by displaying his own nasty streak. When he arrives at Petruccio's estate, he strikes Curtis a blow on the ear for no apparent reason beyond the pleasure of it (*TS* s.d. at 4.1.55). A few scenes later, with Petruccio absent, Grumio undertakes to torment Kate on his own by offering her meat, beef, and mustard and then withholding them (4.3.1–35). Kate finally beats him (s.d. at 31), getting some revenge if not meat. Later in the same scene, Grumio provokes a verbal altercation with the Tailor, a conflict without point other than its own perverse pleasure. In tormenting Kate, Grumio presumes to be Petruccio's factor, but he lacks Petruccio's charm and amusingly extravagant rhetoric, so that Grumio's standing-in feels reductive, crude. His attempt to ape his master by abusing Kate receives the violent retaliation that she never offers to Petruccio—who enters moments later, thankfully, to redirect the flow of the scene. Feste possesses a bit of a mean streak, too, made full-blown in his tormenting of Malvolio. The clown-figure, then, sometimes behaves cruelly, acting by nature, and exceeding the play's thematic requirements.

That latent callousness flares up in minor ways. Costard calls the Princess thick-waisted (at which she takes offense) (*LLL* 4.1.5). Launcelet causes his father grief over his son's alleged death merely to amuse himself. Feste claims to Viola that he does not care for her (*TN* 3.1.28). In the spirit of the Vice, Lavatch informs the Countess that the "devil" drives his desire for marriage (*AW* 1.3.29); later he tells

---

[56] Launcelot's self-alignment with the devil may stain Bassanio: When Bassanio dresses Launcelet in gaudy livery, argues Wiles, he "identifies the Vice as one of his party, and himself as one of the Vice's party"; *Shakespeare's Clown*, 10.

Lafew that he can serve a prince as great as he, that being "the prince of darkness, alias the devil" (4.5.41–2), a comment that disparages Lafew and comes out of nowhere. Lavatch offers Helen a cruel paradox, that the Countess "has her health" but "is not well" because "she's not in heaven, whither God send her quickly" (a suggestion that he repeats) (2.4.2, 10–11). Much earlier the Countess takes offense at the Fool's foul mouth and "calumnious" speech, and he admits to her that he has been "a wicked creature" and is "out o'friends" (1.3.57, 35, 39). Lavatch's discontent exceeds any local causes, being a ready-made irritability that keeps barely on the safe side of rage. Like the threatening edge-world of the forest or the sea, the clown harbors a dark, anarchic, sometimes cruel streak that can flare up unprovoked, a mysterious whiff of sulfur passed down to him from his forefather the Vice.

In predecessor Elizabethan comedies, clowns likewise exhibit Vice-characteristics and behave impertinently towards their betters; they even enjoy or suffer extremes of fortune. Taking an example from an enormously popular late sixteenth-century play, *Mucedorus* (c.1590), we might compare Mouse the Clown to Costard. Like Costard, the rustic Mouse mishears words, misunderstands metaphoric statements, and falls into apt blunders (such as referring to Captain Tremelio as Captain Treble Knave). Mouse possesses Costard's irreverence and dogged independence of mind. He is opportunistic, amoral, and distracted by food and drink, yet, surprisingly, he ends up with gold, silver, and new apparel, simply because he bears celebratory news to the King: The clown, often favored by providence, can be blessed by changeable Fortune.[57] Mouse participates in the play's action but, unlike Costard (as we shall see), does not influence it, although, as the villain Segasto's man, he serves as an index to Segasto's essential folly. A contrasting figure is Miles in Robert Greene's *Friar Bacon and Friar Bungay* (c.1589), another popular play of the period. The educated Miles, Friar Bacon's scholar, stands in relief to the more self-consciously comic Ralph Simnel, the royal fool. Miles makes jokes in Latin, needles Friar Bacon's adversaries, offers cheeky rejoinders, breaks out in witty Skeltonics, and proclaims his skill in eating—behaving always a bit outlandishly for the circumstance. But Miles, whom Bacon disparages as a blockhead, plays an instrumental part in the action. Ordered by Bacon to stand guard over the magical Brazen Head while Bacon rests, Miles arrives comically overburdened with weapons. But when the head utters enigmatic pronouncements, Miles becomes carried away with his own commentary and fails disastrously to rouse Bacon, resulting in the Brazen Head's destruction. Bacon's work and his dream shattered, the magus sends a devil to carry Miles away to hell (where he will become a tapster), perhaps not a punishment so much as a recognition of Miles's true affinities. The figure of folly seems only marginally amusing in this play until

---

[57] Autolycus in *The Winter's Tale* likewise enjoys an opportunistic and unmerited good fortune.

it's almost demonic ineptitude becomes the turning point of the action. While Ben Jonson's *à la mode* humours comedy did away with clowns, Shakespeare held onto those out-of-step and teasingly otherworldly figures. They evoke the pseudo-Catholicism of an anachronistic, slightly anarchic dramatic world, and from that mysterious place they, like Miles, intermittently affect the course of the play.

The Clown's Transformative Influence on Other Characters

Not so marginal, clowns and fools can substantially influence other characters. They might do so straightforwardly, as in Speed's explanation to Valentine of Sylvia's letter-trick verifying her love for him (*TGV* 2.1.135–55). Or more indirectly, as in *Love's Labour's Lost*, where Costard, under arrest for being taken with a woman, interrupts the nobles' oath-signing scene. Costard represents, for Berowne, an object lesson to the lords that they will forsake their vows, Berowne now pushing them towards their eventual capitulation to love: "I'll lay my head to any goodman's hat, / These oaths and laws will prove an idle scorn" (1.1.292–3). In other plays, clown-servants reverberate and amplify their master's thoughts and emotions (as we noted of Grumio) in a way that confirms them. When that function mixes with the clown's superstitiousness, the results can be combustive, as with Syracusan Dromio and Antipholus. Addressed by Adriana, who mistakes him for her husband, Antipholus wonders whether she is some dream-remnant; or he is now sleeping; or some "error" or "fallacy" is at work (*CE* 2.2.190, 192). Dromio, stupefied, reacts with amped-up credulity and an instant conviction that occult forces have intervened: "O for my beads! . . . / This is the fairy land; . . . / We talk with goblins, owls and sprites!" (194–6). As Dromio exclaims, "I am transformed, master, am I not?" Antipholus adopts his servant's frame of mind: "I think thou art in mind, and so am I" (201, 202). After Dromio's further imaginings of himself morphed into an ass, Antipholus exits amazed: "Am I in earth, in heaven or in hell?" he asks, feeling himself enveloped in a "mist" of enchantment (218, 222). The events may be inexplicable, but Antipholus and Dromio also operate inside their own feedback loop, amplifying each other reciprocally, until both are vibrating with superstition and wonder. The clown's heightened echo-chamber mentality helps to convince Antipholus to follow Adriana, with consequences.

A similar process occurs after Antipholus professes love to Luciana, calling her "divine" and comparing her to "our earth's wonder" (3.2.32). "Are you a god?" he asks, offering himself for transformation (39). He takes Luciana as a "sweet mermaid," a "siren" upon whom he will "dote" (45, 47), displacing any ominous thoughts in a vision of "dying" joyfully in her lap (51). Luciana is here the sublime object of desire. But after Luciana's departure, Dromio enters and effects an enormous shift in the scene's tone and in Antipholus's mind. Dromio, agitated, questioning who he is, declares that he has been "haunt[ed]" by a woman who claims to be his husband, leaving him distracted, "besides" himself (79, 76). On Antipholus's inquiry, Dromio embarks on an extended, comic stop-time catalog of Nell the kitchen wench's gargantuan features—typically hilarious in performance. Nell is "beastly," "fat," "all grease"; one could "make a lamp of her" and "run from her by her own light" (85, 91, 95, 96–7). From there the counter-Petrarchan inventory becomes only more inventive and grotesque. Concluding, Dromio describes her as a sorceress ("diviner"), says that, "amazed," he "ran from her as a witch," and invokes the biblical armor of faith for protection (145, 148). Dromio's superstition and horror cause an instant transformation in Antipholus. Completely reversing his benign view of Luciana from moments ago, he now decides that he and Dromio must depart Ephesus immediately and that he will forthwith stop his ears to her dangerous "mermaid's song," for "none but witches do inhabit here" (169, 161). At work again is the revved-up feedback loop, whereby Dromio amplifies ideas or emotions latent in Antipholus, arousing his apprehensions and changing his actions (other examples occur elsewhere). To Antipholus's growing fear of enchanters and magic spells, the clownish Dromio turns out to be not marginal but integral.

Another example of the clown's agency occurs later in the comic oeuvre. In *Twelfth Night*, 1.5, Feste's exchange with Olivia before her interview with Viola upends Olivia's melancholy and creates the condition for the lady's subsequent transformation by love. Critics sometimes conclude that Feste's conversation with Olivia has no impact on her: "When Feste proves her a fool . . . she also does not heed the real import of his words. Before Viola is admitted, Olivia calls for her veil and her old posture is resumed."[58] But Feste does influence the lady by engaging her in the pleasure of improvisatory play, breaking down her defenses, facilitating a shift in perspective, and constructing the pattern by which Viola will charm her.

Feste has been long absent from Olivia's household. The exigency of his return becomes clear in the form of the episode itself. It immediately spotlights Feste's mental agility and assumed insouciance: When Maria warns him of banishment or worse, he turns the threat into puns and jokes: "Let her hang me. He that is well hanged in this world need fear no colours" (4–5)—puns and jokes with an ominous tone. We enter into an environment, says Geoffrey Hartman, of "improvisations beyond the ordinary scope of wit,"[59] with the clown's well-being potentially at stake, a crisis that Feste himself emphasizes (30). Feste refuses to explain his absence to Maria, who, although brushing aside his jokes, establishes for the

---

[58] Jean E. Howard, *Shakespeare's Art of Orchestration: Stage Technique and Audience Response* (Urbana, IL: University of Illinois Press, 1984), 184.

[59] Geoffrey H. Hartman, "Shakespeare's Poetical Character in *Twelfth Night*," in *Shakespeare and the Question of Theory*, ed. Patricia Parker and Geoffrey Hartman (New York: Methuen, 1985), 37–53, on 50.

audience an attitude of goodwill towards the clown.[60] Originally played by Robert Armin, Feste, the text hints, comes outfitted in an identifying motely jerkin, a similar fool's cap, and big gaskins;[61] one might speculate that he carries a fool's bauble or marotte.[62] Feste alludes to "motley," he puns on "patch," and Maria mentions his "gaskins" (53, 44–5, 23), so that the dialogue reinforces Feste's status as clown. The text does not specifically identify a bauble, but the phallic joke on "hanging" (5) would make a good opportunity to use such a prop, as would Feste's quoting of "Quinapalus" (33), which would allow him to throw his voice so that the bauble speaks.[63] Armin was celebrated for his skill with voices, apparently including ventriloquism; later he will employ different vocalizations when he play-acts Sir Topas and recites Malvolio's letter.[64] Thus, Feste steps forth as a classic stage clown, mysteriously arrived, visibly of another ontology, full of chop-logic and multiple voices, awash with the clown's special mystique and magic: He is an intervention personified.

Feste affects Olivia in ways that anticipate, make possible, and empower her subsequent "enchantment" by Viola (3.1.110). Feste and Viola are surrogates of each other as fools; later, Viola will say to Olivia, "for now I am your fool" (3.1.142). Feste's playing breaks down Olivia's defenses and reconstructs her perspective, with the effect that she progressively opens herself to folly's life-giving improvisations. Confirming that significance, remnants of Feste's interview will return in the conversation between Olivia and Viola. When she enters to Feste, Olivia says brusquely, "Take the fool away" (35).[65] To forestall the conversation's sudden end and his punishment, Feste intervenes with a comically assertive air: "Do you not hear, fellows? Take the lady away" (36), a quick-witted ploy if Olivia's attendants are offering to take hold of him. Feste's standing his ground here looks forward to Viola's similar resistance to dismissal, "fortified against all denial" (141) and to the airs of self-assertion that she will muster. To Olivia's accusations, Feste's response about the dishonest man becoming, through amendment, "patched with virtue" employs the clown's costume as a metaphor

---

[60] In the First Folio (1623) Feste's entrance direction and speech headings identify him as "Clo [wne]."

[61] On Feste's costume, see Wiles, *Shakespeare's Clown*, 187–8, 182.

[62] Latvatch, also played by Armin, in *All's Well That Ends Well* apparently carries a bauble (4.5.29). Feste seems associated with props: He plays on a pipe and tabor (3.1.0.2, 1–2); he dons a beard and gown to play Sir Topas (4.2.63–4); he will enter with a letter (5.1); and, in performances, he sometimes accompanies his singing with a guitar in 2.4.

[63] On the fool's marotte, see Wiles, *Shakespeare's Clown*, 190–1.

[64] On Armin's ventriloquism, see Wiles, *Shakespeare's Clown*, 138; Richard Preiss, "Robert Armin Do the Police in Different Voices," in *From Performance to Print in Shakespeare's England*, ed. Peter Holland and Stephen Orgel (Houndmills, Basingstoke: Palgrave Macmillan, 2006), 208–27, on 220. On Armin's style of clowning, including his skill at mimicry and improvisation, see Wiles, *Shakespeare's Clown*, 136–53.

[65] What does "Take the fool away" mean? Unfortunately, editors do not comment on what Olivia intends; Maria's suggestion of hanging sounds exaggerated, but the danger of physical punishment would not be. Elsewhere in Shakespeare (and in reality) fools were subject to beating and whipping.

for humankind's imperfect mixture of vice and morality. He adds ambiguously, "As there is no true cuckold but calamity, so beauty's a flower" (47–8). According to Elizabeth Story Donno, the first claim means that "a calamitous state of affairs necessarily alters for the better,"[66] while the second implies, perhaps contrarily, that beauty fades. Feste's faded-flower image might return to Olivia's mind when Viola expresses admiration, "'Tis beauty truly blent" (231). Patchedness and impermanence color one's virtue, features, affairs, Feste's whole comment implies, and the insight hangs like a cloud over *Twelfth Night*, even to his final song.

Now Feste changes again to an assertive tone: "The lady bade take away the fool" (49). With Olivia not yet moved, Feste cites a Latin phrase (perhaps throwing his voice into his bauble) and asks permission to prove Olivia a fool. "Can you do it?...Make your proof" she responds (55–7). Her language recalls Maria's "Make that good" (6) and anticipates her own later words to Viola: "Speak your office" (202; cf. 187). Like Maria before and her own self later, Olivia has become hooked into the conversation, her detachment crumbling. Feste will "catechize" Olivia, using the kind of question-and-answer repartee that Armin specialized in and that illustrates his 'dexterity' in clowning (58, 56). Moments later, Olivia will turn tables and catechize Viola with a series of challenges—"Now sir, what is your text?"—along with ripostes to Viola's answers (214). As John R. Ford observes, "Olivia quickly adapts her perspective, offering a parody of Feste's catechism."[67] In Feste's clownish catechizing, Armin might well have employed once more his skill in changing voices, and the tactic will find its twin in Viola's on-again-off-again, sometimes grandiloquent, sometimes awkward speaking stances, as she assumes an attitude and then comments on it or positions herself both inside and outside her putative role. Thus, when Olivia questions her, "Are you a comedian?" (177), she seems to be remembering the scene's prior thespian model, Feste.

Feste, finishing his "proof" of Olivia's folly, switches voices again to repeat triumphantly, "Take away the fool, gentlemen" (67–8). Now almost won over, Olivia turns to her steward for agreement: "What think you of this fool, Malvolio, doth he not mend?" (69–70). Olivia's "mend" takes possession of Feste's word and with it his faux-logic and patched vision, the power of the fool not only to mend himself but, like the tailor, to mend others, including Olivia.[68] For the steward, however, those who laugh at fools are no more than "the fool's zanies" (85), one of the meanings of "zany" being, according to Elam, a "poor imitator."[69] In the form of an insult, he recognizes the fool's ability to inspire imitation, as Olivia is proving. Yet Malvolio's mean-spiritedness and inflexibility, so opposite in style from Feste's good humor and 'dexterity,' move Olivia decisively into a defense of

---

[66] Elizabeth Story Donno, ed., *Twelfth Night* (Cambridge: Cambridge University Press, 2003), 1.5.41–2n.
[67] John R. Ford, Twelfth Night: *A Guide to the Play* (Westport, CT: Greenwood Press, 2006), 76.
[68] Matuska, *Vice-Device*, 74.   [69] Elam, *TN*, 1.4.85n.

folly: "There is no slander in an allowed fool"; further, she asserts, listening with equanimity shows the auditor as "generous, guiltless and of free disposition" (89–90, 87–8). A key lesson of folly, Olivia grasps, is that one must transform oneself in responding to it.

Feste succeeds through performance as much as through message. His claim that death is not mournful if it brings heavenly salvation was an Elizabethan cliché—one that could hardly have been satisfying. But Feste's greater persuasiveness resides in his capacity to multiply himself, to speak verbally from alternating positions and with different rhetorical and perhaps physical voices, illustrating the argument for shifting one's perspective. His performance looks forward to the subsequent "comedian" immersed in, yet ironically separate from, the roles she plays. Olivia picks up that very stance when, with Viola, she "draws the curtain" of her veil and shows the "picture": "[S]uch a one I was this present" (226, 227), she says, as if a former self were displaced into her present image—as if she were double. Perhaps the idea of the fool's marotte has morphed into that of a mirror, Olivia's "picture" of herself. The line is also a joke—from the person, moments before, the least likely in Ilyria to pass a witticism. If, when Feste makes his proof, Olivia laughs, even a little (as in all productions she does), her laughter becomes the embodiment of a changed mental position, just as her internalizing of "mend" becomes its linguistic counterpart. Where there is laughter, so the saying goes, there is hope. Even more, Olivia shows that she, unlike Malvolio, can take a joke. Where there is self-laughter, there is self-knowledge—and those make the foundation for transformation; Olivia's defense of the clown Feste constitutes, then, her declaration of receptiveness to the comedian Cesario. Laughter opens a future for Olivia. That change is possible because Feste's conversation with her conjures forth an interval of time-out-of-time, an enchanted space where the listener's defenses drop away, as she relaxes into the 'catechism' of the joke and comes back rejuvenated. The parallels between Olivia's interviews with Feste and with Viola suggest that the first creates the possibility of the second. Folly has transformative agency.

But we should be cautious, too, about interpreting Feste as precisely a moral reformer. His idea of mending, after all, involves listening to "good counsel" while becoming inebriated. Likewise, Olivia's rediscovered receptiveness to life will lead her into self-embarrassment before it leads her to reciprocal love. Folly transforms, and that is a good thing: It is better to be Olivia than Malvolio. But folly, always a bit unwitting, is not overly scrupulous or moral about its effects and the results they might produce.

The Clown's Critical Influence on the Action

Clowns reshape not only characters but also events. Their misadventures in delivering messages, for example, inject disorder and unpredictability into the plots, manifesting the clown's pull towards chaos. Launce, as we have noted, delivers the wrong dog to Sylvia, the currish gift reinforcing her contempt for Valentine instead of winning her sympathy. The Dromios repeatedly, if unintentionally, transport messages or objects to the wrong person. Costard confuses the two love letters that he is to deliver, handing to Rosaline the one intended for Jaquenetta from Armado, and to Jaquenetta the one meant for Rosaline from Berowne. The first mix-up means that Berowne's infatuation can be inferred by Rosaline through a means that devalues it (similar to the dog Crab given to Sylvia). The second mix-up causes more disruption, for Jaquenetta turns the letter over to the King at exactly the moment when Berowne is puffing himself up for resisting love while his fellows have succumbed: "I, that am honest, I that hold it sin / To break the vow I am engaged in" (*LLL* 4.3.174–5). Costard's misdelivered letter presciently exposes Berowne's oath-breaking and, more importantly, green-lights the lords' collapse into self-indulgent love-longings. Dismissed by the embarrassed King, Costard quips accurately, "Walk aside the true folk and let the traitors stay" (209). *Love's Labour's Lost*'s scenes are frequently interrupted; little works out in the manner its characters intend; and the preternaturally clever yet unreliable Costard stands Vice-like as agent and emblem of misadventure.

In *Much Ado About Nothing*, Dogberry likewise exercises unwitting agency. The mood of *Much Ado* shifts hopefully when Dogberry, Verges, and the Watch showily proceed onstage (3.3), effecting the kind of familiar, tone-changing group entrance that flips a comedy into the clown-world. The procession, according to Duncan Salkeld, is a "reworking" of those by "Petruccio's servants in *The Taming of the Shrew*, or...Peter Quince and the mechanicals in *A Midsummer Night's Dream*,"[70] a tactic for sharply re-orienting a play's direction. Coming after Don John's disastrous misleading of Claudio and Don Pedro, the entrance of the Watch (3.3) defines the middle and turning point of the plot, promising an eventual sorting-out of problems. In this intrusion, Dogberry "serves as a special kind of *deus ex machina*," argues John Allen; "the fates have mustered" Dogberry "to come between disaster and ourselves."[71] Indeed, the clown-figure stands in here for fate itself. With the "air and mannerisms of a veritable sage" but the speech and behavior of a bona fide fool (36), Dogberry offers a perfect Erasmian combination of prophet and *moros*, the avatar of a well-intentioned providence but one never quite coherent or reliable.

As *deus ex machina*, Dogberry intervenes in the action ironically, first by launching the catastrophe, then by saving the protagonists from self-destruction. The constable shares Costard's fascination for, and ineptitude with, language, and he adds loquaciousness. In 3.5, Verges begins to reveal Don John's treachery—"our watch...Ha' ta'en a couple of arrant knaves as any in Messina" (3.5.29–31)—when

---

[70] Salkeld, "New Directions," 100.
[71] John A. Allen, "Dogberry," *Shakespeare Quarterly* 24, no. 1 (Winter 1973): 35–53, on 36, 43.

Dogberry interrupts condescendingly to expatiate upon Verges's lack of wit, eventually returning confusingly to the subject: "Our watch hath indeed, sir, comprehended two aspicious persons" (43–4). Baffled and rushed, Leonato dismisses the matter by telling Dogberry to examine the prisoners himself. As Don Pedro will remark, Dogberry "is too cunning to be understood" (5.1.220). By failing to communicate, Dogberry facilitates Hero's humiliation; foolish while thinking himself witty (like other characters), he becomes, Costard-like, an emblem of his play's confusions. Yet, oppositely, Dogberry and the Watch famously work another effect: As Borachio says to Claudio, Don Pedro, and Leonato, "What your wisdoms could not discover, these shallow fools have brought to light" (5.1.223–5). That Dogberry, "this foolish everyman," "is instrumental in creating the happy ending," says Alison Findlay, evokes "a sense of optimistic wonder."[72] That wonder, both transformative and precarious, expresses the slightly inscrutable spirit of clownish enchantment.

The clown works not only a causal but also a thematic intrusion. As Lynne Magnusson has argued, Dogberry's "'peaceable way'" re-instills in the play the "politeness" and "courtesy" that the aristocratic world should mirror but seems to have forgotten.[73] Yet the constabulary infuses the play with a new class perspective, too, one of popular, plebeian rectitude, according to Robert Maslen. The men of the Watch, in confronting Conrade and Borachio, spot what is self-evident: "Some treason, masters" (3.3.103), and, as the "lower classes" are wont to do, they progressively become "a kind of unruly jury, always testing and unsettling the judgements of their superiors."[74] The Dogberrian sense of utopian rectitude, then, affects the play's meaning just as his intervention affects the action.

In that spirit, Dogberry imagines himself something of a moral philosopher, exemplified in his judiciously reasoned, if self-contradictory, instructions to the Watch or in his incidental observations, such as "Comparisons are odorous" (3.5.15). Dogberry's utterances offer the *reductiones ad absurdum* of deft Ciceronian maxims and dense Sibylline pronouncements. Yet the constable possesses a "spiritual generosity" comparable only to that of Friar Frances[75] and suggestive of his utopianism. Dogberry's frequent invoking of God, his awe for the Prince, and even his reverence for the truth of the written word associate him with religious and quasi-spiritual values. Thus, as scholars note, Dogberry often speaks with a mysterious aptness: "By this time our sexton hath reformed Signor Leonato of the matter" (5.1.243–5); "I leave an arrant knave with your worship, which I beseech your worship to correct yourself, for the example of others . . . God

---

[72] Alison Findlay, "The Critical Backstory," in *Much Ado About Nothing: A Critical Reader*, ed. Deborah Cartmell and Peter J. Smith (London: Bloomsbury, 2018), 21–39, on 23.

[73] Lynne Magnusson, *Shakespeare and Social Dialogue: Dramatic Language and Elizabethan Letters* (Cambridge: Cambridge University Press, 2004), 160–1.

[74] Maslen, *Shakespeare and Comedy*, 87. Dogberry and the Watch, observes Carol Cook, shift the play's focus from misogyny to law; "'The Sign and Semblance of Her Honor': Reading Gender Differences in Much Ado About Nothing," *PMLA* 101, no. 2 (March 1986): 186–202, on 199.

[75] Allen, "Dogberry," 48.

restore you to health!" (5.1.210–14). "O villain! Thou wilt be condemned into everlasting redemption for this" (4.2.58–9), Dogberry says to Borachio, who will subsequently begin to "correct himself" by confessing the truth and clearing Margaret. As Findlay puts it, "the play invests the everyman role with a mysterious wisdom,"[76] providence working through, but also a little beyond, its ken.

Just as Dogberry speaks with prescience, so his qualities illuminate truths about other characters. As Allen argues, Dogberry functions as Don John's antagonist and possesses traits likening him to the Friar, yet his egotism mirrors Leonato's, while his desire to be seen as witty reflects the like ambition in Benedick, Beatrice, and others of the gentry. With the "mentally intoxicated" Dogberry, the theme of self-deception, says Graham Storey, "reaches miraculous proportions."[77] He is, then, "a source of illumination as well as of laughter."[78] Dogberry also receives a humanizing touch, for, as E. W. Sievers observes, Conrade's slander of him as an ass "metamorph[oses]" the constable into a figure of wounded honor meriting "pathos."[79] Both *deus-ex-machina* and everyman, Dogberry becomes a complexly symbolic, even transcendent, personage. As the nineteenth-century critic Henrich Ulrici observes, Dogberry's contradictions reach into the essence of the play.[80] Thus, Dogberry can claim climactically a universal, albeit comic, perspective towards a world grown cold from corruption, as symbolized by Deformed: "[T]hey say he...borrows money in God's name, the which he hath used so long, and never paid, that now men grow hard-hearted and will lend nothing for God's sake" (5.1.297–302). In figurative response to his own sentiments, Dogberry stands as the cock-eyed deity who just barely salvages the hard-hearted play-world from self-destruction.

The more Dogberry is investigated, the more multitudinous he becomes. Exuding the clown's mystique, he transforms the tone of the play, functions as an everyman figure, mysteriously proclaims truths, corrects the play-world's ethics with a plebian sensibility, crucially alters the action, stands for the workings of providence or fate, and yet transcends all categories in both his sympathetic humanity and his obliviousness. The hard-won good-naturedness of *Much Ado About Nothing* would be impossible without the enchanted and enchanting Dogberry.

---

[76] Findlay, "Critical Backstory," 24. Despite Dogberry's malapropisms, he is actually not so difficult for audiences to understand, thanks, as Magnusson points out (*Social Dialogue*, 159–60), to the redundancy built into conversational speech: "You are thought here to be the most senseless and fit man" (3.3.22–3).

[77] Graham Storey, "The Success of *Much Ado About Nothing*," in *More Talking of Shakespeare*, ed. John Garrett (New York: Theatre Arts Books, 1959), 128–43, on 133.

[78] Allen, "Dogberry," 38.

[79] E. W. Sievers, excerpt from *William Shakespeare* (1866), in *Bloom's Shakespeare Through the Ages:* Much Ado About Nothing, ed. Harold Bloom (New York: Infobase Publishing, 2010), 86–8, on 88.

[80] Heinrich Ulrici, excerpt from *Shakespeare's Dramatic Art* (1839), in *Bloom's Shakespeare Through the Ages:* Much Ado About Nothing, ed. Harold Bloom (New York: Infobase Publishing, 2010), 78–9.

Bottom and the Moral Center

Let us complete this reassessment of the clown's marginality by considering the clown or fool most associated with enchantment, Bottom, who plays a "central role in bringing about the reunion of Oberon and Titania."[81] Syracusan Dromio may believe himself bewitched, but Bottom is the only clown or fool who actually is transformed, or "translated," by magic (*MND* 3.1.115). He also casts a spell: For centuries, critics have considered him *Dream*'s most fascinating and charming character, just as his fellow artisan actors treat him as their most charismatic colleague. In his first scene, he bubbles irrepressibility, interrupting Peter Quince in order to make suggestions, to raise performance questions, and to offer to act every role in *Pyramus and Thisbe* himself. (Bottom showcases the clown's ability to shift voices and perspectives.) Quince may direct, but Bottom leads, and all the mechanicals lavish praise and admiration on him. Quince insists flatteringly that only Bottom can play Pyramus because the character is "a sweet-faced man," "a proper man," "a most lovely gentlemanlike man," implicitly like Bottom himself (1.2.80–1). Later, the artisans laud him for having "a sweet voice," "the best person," and "the best wit of any handicraftsman in Athens" (4.2.12, 11, 9–10). Bottom has charm.

Beyond the claim of those gifts, Bottom's charisma derives equally from his naïve enthusiasm and, not least, his pleasure in self-presentation, a trait that clowns share with actors. In the spirit of the clown's fantastical nature, Bottom shows off a detailed, impossible knowledge of theater. He comprehends different genres of drama and the character conventions associated with them. He knows what passions must be represented in different types of plays and what emotions to induce in the audience. He can modulate his voice, raging loftily "to make all split" like a tyrant or adopting "a monstrous little voice" like Thisbe's (1.2.25–6, 48). He has conned and can recite great swathes of pseudo-Senecan tragic dialogue in doggerel verse—here lines that parody John Studley's alliterative translation of *Hercules Oetaeus* (1581).[82] He knows stage wigs and beards, their colors and textures. He recognizes production values (without quite understanding them), and he shows a heightened, if errant, sense of Classical theatrical decorum, as in his concern that an on-stage suicide will vex the audience's ladies. He grasps, too, the regulatory virtue of prologues. We accept Bottom's mastery of such extravagant knowledge because we apprehend him as not a simple weaver but a figure of, and for, the theater. Bottom embodies, then, clown and actor together, bathed in the aura of both mysteries.[83]

---

[81] Karen Newman, *Shakespeare's Rhetoric of Comic Character: Dramatic Convention in Classical and Renaissance Comedy* (New York: Methuen, 1985), 86.

[82] On *Dream* and Seneca, see Chaudhuri, *MND*, 56–7, 1.2.27–34n.

[83] Shakespeare plays with the relationship of clown to actor to very different effect with Christopher Sly in *The Taming of the Shrew*.

Puck despises Bottom instantaneously, perhaps in part because Puck sees himself as a superior thespian (if, that is, Puck possesses motives). Earlier, he had bragged to Titania's fairy of his ability, like an actor, to imitate voices and to adopt various guises in disrupting the daily lives of country folk (2.1.43–58). When he intervenes in the rehearsal of *Pyramus and Thisbe*, he imagines taking a part—"I'll be an auditor; / An actor too, perhaps" (3.1.74–5)—and proceeds, like a director or playwright, to interfere by reordering the action, and then, like an actor, to call out in different voices, much as Bottom had in the first rehearsal scene, as if Puck were illustrating the skill of a real thespian.[84]

Emphasizing theater as a context for understanding Bottom (and Puck) helps to redirect critical attention away from Bottom's asininity and to showcase his comic complexity and mystery. Bottom is more than a buffoon only and merits more than bemused condescension as a response. Puck—perhaps prompted by Thisbe's description of Pyramus as "*as true as truest horse*" (3.1.97)—famously affixes an ass's head to Bottom. Now the play's so-far lightly registered donkey references burgeon exponentially, as if Bottom were metamorphosing into the identity with which Puck has saddled him—wanting to be scratched, finding his face hairy, longing for provender. But Puck, no careful observer, exaggerates Bottom's asininity, especially if we compare Bottom with that other accused ass, Dogberry. Bottom utters occasional malapropisms—"there is not a more fearful wildfowl than your lion living" (3.1.29–30)—but hardly in Dogberrian torrents. More often, he spills over with exuberance for theater—acting points, production values, audience effects. Bottom never reaches Dogberry's level of donkey-like obtuseness. Critics sometimes argue that Bottom's transformation reveals his essence; the claim has a satisfying *contrapasso* quality, but would we say then that Titania's enchantment exposes her essential love of bestiality?[85] "Bottom radiates good will and good sense," says Harold Bloom; "he is sound at the core, and is the skein upon which the play's elaborate design is wound"; criticism "tends to underestimate his innate dignity."[86] For Bloom, Bottom has "sublimity" (2), a quality attributed by other critics. Perhaps Bottom's enchantment only heightens certain potentialities while suppressing others without finally revealing any single essence.

More than being asinine, Bottom is a dreamer, a fantasist (are not all thespians?), an inhabitant of different personae. He gives himself over to the experience of enchantment and the fairy world, courteously befriending Cobweb, Peaseblossom, and Mustardseed, detailing in his imagination the usefulness of

---

[84] In *Dream*, the errant, uncontrollable, and even dangerous energy of the clown is displaced into Puck.

[85] Likewise, the lovers in their confusion behave with an animalism that, if anything, surpasses Bottom's.

[86] Harold Bloom, "Introduction," in *William Shakespeare's Comedies: New Edition*, ed. Harold Bloom (New York: Infobase, 2009), 1.

the one, the lineage of the second, and the patience of the third. Later he will ask Cobweb to go kill "a red-hipped humble-bee on the top of a thistle; and, good Mounsieur, bring me the honey-bag... [H]ave a care the honey-bag break not; I would be loath to have you overflown with a honey-bag, signior," projecting himself expansively into the fairies' world (4.1.11–15). He conjures forth the joys of "a peck of provender," "good dry oats," "a bottle of hay," and "a handful or two of dried peas" (29–30, 34)—evocatively concrete images—while seeming indifferent to Titania's efforts to feed him nuts, adorn his head with musk-roses, and kiss his ears. Bottom may slip so comfortably into enchantment because, as C. L. Barber observes, he is "literal about fiction."[87] That is, he can be magically transformed because he already awards to imaginative events the effects that he would attribute to real ones.[88] With Bottom that attitude becomes ridiculous, but, properly qualified, it approaches Elizabethan justifications for (and attacks upon) theater. Barber calls Bottom "antipoetic" (155), but perhaps inaptly so, for the epithet misses Bottom's imagination and occasional lyricism, no matter that they express themselves as the donkeyfied version of the clown's utopia of camaraderie, physical comfort, and food. Bottom can gleek upon occasion, too, and in well-constructed figures, not only with his epigrammatic "reason and love keep little company together nowadays" but also with more complicated witticisms such as, "Who would give a bird the lie, though he cry cuckoo never so" (4.1.139–41, 3.1.131–2).[89] These quips differ from showing prescience by malapropism.

If translated to an ass, this weaver of fantasies has also metamorphosed magically from wanna-be romance actor to putative romance hero, transported into an otherworldly dream-narrative, Walter Mitty *avant la lettre*. Bottom is the one figure in *Midsummer* who interacts directly with fairyland (in conversation, touch, and presumably more) and who can subsequently recall his otherworldly experiences, because he himself is magical. Akin to Erasmus's Folly, Bottom has special access to the spiritual realm.[90] Like a waking knight, he recognizes that he has had "a most rare vision" (4.1.203), one that recalls the unfathomability of God's love in 1 Corinthians 2.9. "The eye of man hath not heard, the ear of man hath not seen, man's hand is not able to taste, his tongue to conceive, nor his heart to report what my dream is," says Bottom (409–11). In attempting to utter the ineffable, using synesthesia (if accidentally) seems excusable, even helpful—and there is something fitting in his image of the heart's report. According to Raphael

---

[87] Barber, *Festive Comedy*, 151.

[88] As William C. Carroll observes, "Bottom's imagination is, if anything, *too* inclusive and encompassing. It recognizes no distinctions"; *The Metamorphoses of Shakespearean Comedy* (Princeton, NJ: Princeton University Press, 1985), 151.

[89] I take Bottom's second comment to mean that it is foolish, perhaps self-incriminating, to dispute with a bird, especially a bird whose cry sounds salacious.

[90] On the relationship between *Dream* and Erasmus, see Thelma N. Greenfield, "*A Midsummer Night's Dream* and *The Praise of Folly*," *Comparative Literature* 20, no. 3 (Summer 1968): 236–44; Greenfield calls Bottom "Folly's man of action" (243).

Lyne, Bottom's form of "heuristic cognition" is "surprisingly close to" that of "Hamlet's soliloquies."[91] The 1 Corinthians passage figured centrally in Elizabethan conceptions of the afterlife, argues Stuart Sillars, for whom Bottom's allusion embraces also the First Epistle of St. John and Erasmus's *Praise of Folly*.[92] Sillars traces the influential Corinthians verse as it appears in the works of Nicholas of Cusa, Pico della Mirandola, and Queen Elizabeth. Bottom's Dream resonates powerfully, if comically, then, with the Elizabethan sense of the inexplicable power of transcendent vision. Like "the deepe things of God,"[93] it "hath no bottom" (214); unfathomability and self-negation constitute the paradox of "discours[ing] wonders" (4.2.28). As Leonard Barkan notes, Bottom's "vision" exceeds that of the young lovers, and his dream expands the play to its greatest range, becoming "an experience simultaneously beastly, human, divine."[94] Bottom recalls *Praise*'s "personification" of Folly, for he has become enigmatically wise, even holy, observes Helen Hackett: In his "transcendental revelation," he has "fleetingly touched the divine."[95]

In *Dream*, only a clown can peer into the mysteries of the spirit world, for he exists outside of normal ontology, embraces paradox, and violates instrumental rationalism, his wisdom infused from other sources. Bottom is, after all, the player-hero allowed to return from the dead—twice. Because Bottom's dream-vision is "nonrepresentable," in Weimann's terms, it must be "translated" "to the aesthetic realm" via ballad and performance, as Hugh Grady notes.[96] Indeed, for Sillars, Bottom represents values that align with Hyppolita's respect for intuition and narration and that show the limitations of Theseus's ultra-rationalism. Bottom recounts his dream with disarming authenticity. Whereas the awakening lovers seem increasingly distanced from the night's "dream," Bottom exhibits a sense of "immediacy" and "speculative inner life."[97] Bottom thus becomes a central figure in defining the play's contest of values.

Bottom constitutes the clown as actor, playwright, and fictional hero who translates into art what can be expressed by no other means, while verging simultaneously on the ridiculous. He evokes in the young lovers only laughter and scorn, yet various critics and productions have taken Hyppolita's "Beshrew my heart, but I pity the man" (5.1.283) as evidence of the power of dramatic

---

[91] Raphael Lyne, *Shakespeare, Rhetoric and Cognition* (Cambridge: Cambridge University Press, 2011), 102.

[92] Stuart John Sillars, "'Howsoever, strange and admirable:' *A Midsummer Night's Dream* as *Via Stultitiae*," *Archiv für das Studium der Neueren Sprachen und Literaturen* 244, no. 1 (2007): 27–39.

[93] Chaudhuri cites this language from 1 Corinthians used in versions of the Geneva Bible after the first edition; *MND* 4.1.209–11n.

[94] Leonard Barkan, "Diana and Acteon: The Myth of Synthesis," *English Literary Renaissance* 10, no. 3 (Autumn 1980): 317–59, on 358.

[95] Helen Hackett, "Introduction," in *A Midsummer Night's Dream*, ed. Stanley Wells (London: Penguin Books, 2005), xxi–lxxxvii, on lvii, lviii.

[96] Grady, "Shakespeare and Impure Aesthetics," 274–302, on 296.

[97] Karen Newman, *Comic Character*, 85.

narrative to move, even when performed ineptly. Bottom is beloved of all and shines his good-will on all, while his capacity for transport affirms the possibility of love, perhaps more deeply, if more indirectly, than do the affections of the lovers themselves. In those aspects, Bottom stands for the inalienable magic of theater. In *A Midsummer Night's Dream*, Shakespeare takes the presumably marginal figure of the clown and makes him, as Peter Holbrook says, the "moral center" of the play.[98] When Hyppolita refers to "the story of the night" as growing to something credible yet "strange and admirable" (5.1.23, 27), she might as easily be describing the clown's comedy of enchantment.

*   *   *   *   *

Bottom's experience with Titania parodies the follies of the young lovers in the woods, as implied in the clown's comment about reason and love keeping little company. Yet, in the conflict between reason and the madness of love, which runs like a scarlet thread through the warp and woof of Shakespearean comedy, we are always on the side of the lunatics. At the end of *Much Ado About Nothing*, when Beatrice and Benedick almost renounce the possibility of love, each saying that they love the other "no more than reason" (5.4.74, 76), the heart sinks. Shakespeare's comedies constitute an ongoing exploration of the meaning, danger, possibility, and difficulty of love in all its folly.[99] Clowns are not romantic lovers, but they are the avatars of that folly's strange, admirable, and irreducible magic.

---

[98] Peter Holbrook, "Class X: Shakespeare, Class, and Comedy," in *A Companion to Shakespeare's Works*, vol. 3 of 3, *The Comedies*, ed. Richard Dutton and Jean E. Howard (Malden, MA: Blackwell, 2003), 67–89, on 84. In this regard, argues Holbrook, Bottom "challenges" the "snobbery" of the elite, and their "claim to natural superiority" (84).

[99] Except for "in all its folly," this thought was crystalized for me in a lecture by Carol Chillington Rutter, July 2016.

2

Structural Doubleness and Repetition

> Wherever there is repetition or
> complete similarity, we always suspect
> some mechanism at work behind the living.
>
> Henri Bergson
> *On Laughter*

Think of doubleness in comedy and you think of twins. They are funny because a bit hysterical, a bit uncanny, maybe magical, an impossibility in nature come true: seemingly exact replication.[1] Comedy obsesses over uncanny likenesses, which possess the power to disrupt our sense of reality, and those patterns of recursion illuminate something fundamental to the genre. Such patterns characterize Shakespearean comedy, pre-eminently *Twelfth Night*.[2] The play contains scenes whose actions constitute uncanny repetitions of actions in other scenes; likewise, those scenes themselves sometimes reprise their own actions or employ self-reflecting symmetries in events. That structural dimension of *Twelfth Night* is empowered, furthermore, by notions of occult sympathy and providentialism, so that both generic and cultural values emphasize enchantment.

Those qualities appear variously in other Shakespearean comedies and predecessor plays. Early comedy is fascinated with twinness and likeness,[3] suggesting that beneath the form lies a vision, older than liberal humanism, of a strange

---

[1] John Morreall says we laugh at twins because we are "surprised" by two people who "look alike," and he cites Henri Bergson's notion that "identical twins look as if they were manufactured"; *Taking Laughter Seriously* (Albany, NY: State University of New York, 1982), 68–9. In the dominant theory of humor (see 15–19), identical twins are funny because incongruous. The theory foregrounds the violation of a category—here the fundamental non-identity of different people—thereby forcing an expansion of the observer's understanding of that category. But, one might argue, twins suggest more than the breaching of categorical boundaries, since they seem to deny the category itself, the uniqueness of the individual.

[2] Frank Kermode links *Twelfth Night* to *Hamlet* and "The Phoenix and the Turtle," all marking a period in Shakespeare's life, around 1600, when he was fascinated by doubles; "Voltimand and Cornelius: Doubles in *Hamlet*," in *Forms of Attention: Botticelli and* Hamlet (Chicago, IL: University of Chicago Press, 1985), 33–63, on 61.

[3] For Roman comedy, Plautus introduced real and metaphorical twinness in *Amphitruo, Miles Gloriosus, Persa, Menaechmi*, and *Bacchides*. Following the Roman lead, in cinquecento Italy Bernardo Dovizi da Bibbiena's landmark comedy *La calandria* (*c.* 1513) twists together the alternating actions of a twin brother and sister separated by war. The influential Sienese *Gl' ingannati* ("The Deceived") (Anon., 1531), likewise features dispersed twins; it may have been a source text for *Twelfth Night*. The main characters of Annibal Caro's *Gli straccioni* ("The Ragged Brothers") (1543) are twin-like siblings, and Giambattista della Porta's *La sorella* ("The Sister") (*c.* 1591) presents twin sisters with contrasting

Shakespeare and the Comedy of Enchantment. Kent Cartwright, Oxford University Press. © Kent Cartwright 2021.
DOI: 10.1093/oso/9780198868897.003.0003

relatedness among people that crosses social, ethnic, or racial differences and hints at reproducible identities and mutual destinies that manifest mysterious, recursive patterns of order.[4] Twinning bespeaks a compulsion for reiterating and mirroring, and a potential for uncanniness, central to comedy. The double, argues Alenka Zupančič, is a "structural theme" on which comedy thrives, a position echoed by Andrew Stott's claim that "divided and doubled experience" forms the "theme of comedy."[5]

Doubleness extends to other genres, of course: It occurs with the doppelgängers and psychic hauntings of Gothic fiction, elements perhaps less remote from comedy than we expect. Twinned characters, recurrent types of incidents, and mirrored storylines also inform romance fiction, as with Edmund Spenser's *The Faerie Queene*. There doubleness reveals the duplicity of reality, the feebleness of one's capacity to grasp it, and the distortions of it caused by repressed desires, while the action responds to those problems with the single, true light of Protestantism. Symmetry and doubleness figure in the tradition of romance from the Middle Ages to the Renaissance, often with a sense of eeriness or imminent meaning poised uncannily at the edge of apprehension.[6] Shakespeare draws from those dynamics.[7] Doubleness has its own literary life, but the widely felt Renaissance anxiety about dissimulation and misprision likely contributed to its vitality during the period (see Introduction); so, too, arguably even more, did the Renaissance tendency to reason by analogy and the Calvinist emphasis on double predestination, discussed later.

Doubleness and reiterated actions occur in Shakespearean plays besides the comedies. In *Henry IV, Part 1*, according to A. R. Humphreys, the "comic and

characters. Tudor stage comedy trafficked in metaphoric twinship, as in the allegorical doubling of Ignorance for Wit in Redford's *Wit and Science* (c. 1530) or of Confusion for Moros in Wager's *The Longer Thou Livest the More Fool Thou Art* (c. 1568), while Nicholas Udall adapted Plautus's *Amphitruo* into the satirical, identity-troubling *Jack Juggler* (pub. 1562). John Lyly's *Gallathea* concerns two young women in love with each other who, if not twins, appear virtually identical and have virtually identical storylines. Regarding Shakespeare, twins feature in *Twelfth Night* and *The Comedy of Errors*, and doubleness in the comedies includes similar, linked characters (Hermia and Helena), character foils (Malvolio and Orsino), initially differentiated but ultimately homologous protagonists (Antonio and Shylock), and paired couples (Theseus and Hyppolita / Oberon and Titania).

[4] A "fascination with identity" along with a paradoxical telos of "providential fortune" were the features of *Menaechmi* that, according to Richard F. Hardin, accounted for its popularity in the Renaissance; "*Menaechmi* and the Renaissance of Comedy," *Comparative Drama* 37, nos. 3, 4 (2003–4): 255–74, on 269, 263.

[5] Alenka Zupančič, *The Odd One In: On Comedy* (Cambridge, MA: MIT Press, 2008), 73; Andrew Stott, *Comedy* (New York: Routledge, 2005), 8. Similarly, Wylie Sypher observes, "comedy is built upon double occasions, double premises, double values"; "The Meaning of Comedy," in *Comedy: An Essay on Comedy by George Meredith; Laughter by Henri Bergson*; Introduction and Appendix, "The Meanings of Comedy," by Wylie Sypher, ed. Wylie Sypher (Garden City, NY: Doubleday Anchor, 1956), 191–255, on 213.

[6] See Helen Cooper, *The English Romance in Time: Transforming Motifs from Geoffrey of Monmouth to the Death of Shakespeare* (Oxford: Oxford University Press, 2004).

[7] See Helen Cooper, *Shakespeare and the Medieval World* (London: Bloomsbury, 2010), esp. 171–203.

serious plots" show relationships, "sometimes of parallelism and reinforcement, sometimes of antithesis and contrast, sometimes of reversal";[8] likewise, the notion of counterfeiting is one of the play's key images. In *1 Henry IV*, the main function of doubleness seems to be parody, and, as David Scott Kastan notes, the play is almost evenly split between its serious and comic actions.[9] Paired characters and mirrored scenes also occur in tragedy, as in *Hamlet* or *King Lear*, allowing such plays to refine their values. But in tragedy, an "emphasis on repetitive patterns," as René Girard says of *Oedipus Rex*, runs the risk of giving the play "a slightly parodic flavor" such that the sense of tragedy "immediately . . . evaporates."[10] In neither the histories nor the tragedies does doubleness express something transcendent about the form.

Not so Shakespeare's comedies, which are fascinated with doubleness in plot lines, locales, verbal *entendres*, allusions, objects, characters, marriages, deceptions and disguises, parodies and impersonations, and clowns and straight men: multiples everywhere.[11] That profuseness of paired elements suggests that the genre harbors a submerged dimension brought variously to the surface. In Renaissance comedy, according to Francesco Loriggio, underneath the overt narrative progression of boy-wins-girl, there often lurks a covert narrative of uncanny repetition.[12] What Northrop Frye says of repeated themes and words in comedy might be applied to all its self-echoings: "Such repetitions seem to have something oracular about them, as though arranging them in the right way would provide a key to some occult and profound process of thought."[13] The uncanniness of doubling figures centrally in Alenka Zupančič's discussion of comedy, evidenced as she considers Bergson's theory of laughter: "something mechanical encrusted upon the living, the mechanical and the living dovetailed into each other. For what else is the stuff that the genre of the uncanny is made of—machines, automata that come to life, mortifying doubles, living dead . . . ?"[14] Such doubleness becomes the sign of enchantment.

Critics often apply terms like "magical," "miraculous," and "wondrous" to the events and experiences of *Twelfth Night*; as John R. Ford says, the play evokes a sense of "spirituality," of "a mystery beyond the reach of rationality."[15] In *Twelfth*

---

[8] A. R. Humphries, ed., *The First Part of Henry IV* (London: Methuen, 1960), xlvi.

[9] David Scott Kastan, ed., *King Henry IV, Part 1* (London: Thomson Learning, 2002), 14.

[10] René Girard, "Perilous Balance: A Comic Hypothesis," *Modern Language Notes* 87, no. 7 (December 1972): 811–26, on 816.

[11] The present discussion does not consider actors' doubling in different roles; on that topic, see Brett Gamboa, *Shakespeare's Double Plays: Dramatic Economy on the Early Modern Stage* (Cambridge: Cambridge University Press, 2018).

[12] Francesco Loriggio, "Prefacing Renaissance Comedy: The Double, Laughter, and Comic Structure," in *Comparative Critical Approaches to Renaissance Comedy*, ed. Donald Beecher and Massimo Ciavolella (Ottawa: Dovehouse Editions, 1986), 99–118.

[13] Northrop Frye, *A Natural Perspective: The Development of Shakespearean Comedy and Romance* (New York: Columbia University Press, 1965), 25.

[14] Zupančič, *Odd One*, 114.

[15] John R. Ford, Twelfth Night: *A Guide to the Play* (Westport, CT: Greenwood Press, 2006), 28.

Night, doubleness manifests that mystery through patterns of uncanny repetition among and within scenes that draw attention to the temporal dimension of comedy. Structural repetitions generate an obscure dreamworld imbued with an equivocal sense of the providential. To see comic doubleness as mysterious is to discover alongside the plot a supplemental dramatic dimension, a weird mirroring, that casts an unsettling influence over the beholder's feelings, impressions, and imaginings. Comedy operates, we might say, with a mystifying double vision.

Analogy, Sympathetic Magic, and Causation

On its surface, *Twelfth Night* tells of characters successfully puzzling out romantic love in a world of confused identities, while, on a less obvious level, it whispers of threatening seas, miraculous double rescues, beneficent mistakes, and recursions signifying mysterious laws and forces. The play showcases scenes, episodes, and related details that are similar enough to each other as to constitute reflections.[16] We might call these occurrences structural repetitions or structural doubles, and they feature not only here but elsewhere in Shakespeare's comedies (as we shall note later). In *Twelfth Night* and other plays, structural recurrences generate responses and expectations that steadily turn the narrative form itself into content. In Shakespeare's first *Henriad*, notes Marjorie Garber, "repeated events" and "scenes that echo one another with a difference" can "carry a considerable weight of meaning."[17] Similarly, argues Leah Scragg, a play's paralleling of actions "contributes to the meaning through the relationship between those events and the experience which forms the principal focus of audience attention."[18] Parallel scenes make for analogies. In Shakespeare, Joan Hartwig observes, "scenes tend to progress because of their analogical relationships with what precedes and what follows as much as narrative causality."[19] Renaissance dramatists, Hartwig argues, were attuned to their audiences' awareness of analogical thinking, and they used "parallel scene structure" to "energize[]" their audiences' sensibilities (3). That

---

[16] Doubleness saturates *Twelfth Night*: the play's double title (implying both Epiphany and revelry); its two households; its double mournings (Olivia and Viola); its double set of fools (Feste and Viola); its double lords of misrule (Sir Toby and Maria); its double time scheme (two days or three months); its double anagrammatical names (Olivia and Viola, plus the fake anagram of M.O.A.I.); its double marriage couples; its double modes, romantic and satiric, distributed between its double upstairs-downstairs storylines; and even the redoubled refrain of Feste's last song. On the auditorial experience of doubleness, see J. P. C. Brown, "Seeing Double: Dramaturgy and the Experience of *Twelfth Night*," *Shakespeare* 10, no. 3 (April 2014): 293–308.

[17] Marjorie Garber, *Shakespeare After All* (New York: Anchor Books, 2005), 305.

[18] Leah Scragg, *Discovering Shakespeare's Meaning* (Houndmills, Basingstoke: Macmillan, 1988), 114. Mark Rose argues that Shakespeare's scenes are arranged and juxtaposed for not just narrative but also thematic purposes; *Shakespearean Design* (Boston, MA: Belknap Press of Harvard University Press, 1972).

[19] Joan Hartwig, *Shakespeare's Analogical Scene: Parody as Structural Syntax* (Lincoln, NE: University of Nebraska Press, 1983), 3.

energizing occurs because analogy possesses "a mysterious power to create a sense of wholeness in human perception of the world" (3). A Renaissance playwright sets up scenic parallels, concludes Hartwig, expecting that they will provoke specta- tors' post-performance thoughts about matters hinted but never fully expressed, matters lingering in the mind for "retrospective" "comprehension" (12).

Hartwig's claim for the "mysterious power" of analogy "to create a sense of wholeness" echoes William Empson's position that the double plot in Renaissance drama "mak[es] you feel the play deals with life as a whole."[20] Discussing Robert Greene's *Friar Bacon and Friar Bungay* (c.1589), Empson argues that its double plots—one involving Bacon's necromancy, the other Margaret's beauty—function analogously such that Margaret's beauty takes on some of Bacon's magic, con- verting Margaret into an "earth-goddess" (33). In *Troilus and Cressida*, such transference or contamination formulates into: "'Cressida will bring Troy bad luck because she is bad'" (34). The double plots here "encourage primitive ways of thought ... This power of suggestion is the strength of the double plot; once you take the two parts to correspond, any character may take on *mana* because he seems to cause what he corresponds to" (34). Angus Fletcher cites that argument approvingly as "the Empsonian concept of magical causation," and holds "that double plots are related to each other so as to produce magical interaction."[21] Richard Levin brings Empson's and Fletcher's arguments for magical parallelisms to bear broadly on Renaissance drama's multiple plots: "Some of these equations, as Empson remarked, may even evoke primitive notions of a hidden causal connection linking the plots ... this is the causation of homeopathic magic, pro- duced not by the action of cause and effect but by the analogy constructed between them."[22] (Homeopathic, or imitative, causation refers essentially to like affecting like: Make an effigy of your enemy, stick it with a pin, and he will feel the pain.[23]) For Levin, "analogical" etiology constitutes, in Aristotelian terms, "formal" rather than "efficient" causation (10, 11). Analogies in the Renaissance, then, activate a preternatural, meaning-making power: A thing effects a magical transference of quality or form or meaning or energy to another to which it is related or that it resembles. Thus, likenesses exude a "primitive" psychic aura.[24] To occult ana- logical effects working at a distance should be added those working close up,

[20] William Empson, *Some Versions of the Pastoral* (London: Chatto & Windus, 1950), 27, see 27–86.

[21] Angus Fletcher, *Allegory: The Theory of a Symbolic Mode* (Ithaca, NY: Cornell University Press, 1964), 187, 184. Such "magical parallelisms" apply to many kinds of literature (186).

[22] Richard Levin, *The Multiple Plot in English Renaissance Drama* (Chicago, IL: University of Chicago Press, 1973), 10.

[23] On homeopathic magic and contagious magic, see Fletcher, *Allegory*, 188–219.

[24] Renaissance rhetorical treatises are full of terms for forms of verbal repetition that make vivid emotional appeals; see Richard A. Lanham, *A Handlist of Rhetorical Terms*, 2nd edn. (Berkeley, CA: University of California Press, 1991). As Fletcher observes, "Aristotle points out that to achieve a marvelous, magical effect in a mimetic drama you must introduce ornamental language. The implica- tion would be that the language of cosmic correspondences is an inherently magical language"; *Allegory*, 193.

described by James G. Frazer in terms of "the Law of Contact or Contagion," really a subset of sympathetic magic, in which an object exerts magical influence on another object or a person via contact or close proximity, transmitted through "a kind of invisible ether."[25] The magic of contiguity produces effects like those of analogy.

"Up to the end of the sixteenth century," argues Michel Foucault, "resemblance played a constructive role in the knowledge of Western culture."[26] Foucault describes four essential "figures" for organizing knowledge according to resemblance (19): convenience, emulation, analogy, and sympathy (see 19–28; "convenience" is Foucault's term for contiguity). Analogy "makes possible the marvelous confrontation of resemblances across space ... Its power is immense," and it extends to the heavens, to the earth, to plants and minerals, to flora and fauna, and to the human body (24). Its "reversibility and polyvalency" allow it vast fields of application (24). The secret to the relationship between worldly entities is that they are governed and animated by sympathy and antipathy. Through the magical power of sympathy, like things are drawn toward and affect each other, while antipathy makes dissimilar things repel one another. Sympathy, says Foucault, "has the dangerous power of *assimilating*, of rendering things identical to one another, of mingling them, of causing their individuality to disappear ... Sympathy transforms" (26). Indeed, it functions so powerfully that it must be restrained by antipathy. For his other similitudes, "the linkages of analogy" "are supported, maintained, and doubled by ... sympathy and antipathy, which are ceaselessly drawing things together and holding them apart" (28). Writing on magical theories of sympathy in the Renaissance, Henry S. Turner similarly describes "all occult sciences as *mimetic*, since they presume an underlying principle of resemblance and grant to imitation a causal power."[27]

In that spirit, Renaissance treatises on magic can be understood as extended discussions of the power of objects, feelings, and desires, in all sorts of domains, to cause effects upon other objects through likeness, analogy, as well as proximity. Theorists such as Marsilio Ficino, Heinrich Cornelius Agrippa, and Giordano Bruno embraced the notion of a principle of "universal analogy" operating between the microcosm and macrocosm, the physical and spiritual, the human soul and the *anima mundi*, the individual and world. Analogies operate with causal power. In Ficino's *Three Books of Life* (1489), write editors Carol V. Kaske and John R. Clark, "[a]rgument from analogy crowds out argument from those material causes and effects which are the staple of modern science ... [T]he macrocosm-microcosm analogy is more than rhetorical, more than heuristic;

[25] James George Frazer, *The Golden Bough: A Study of Magic and Religion*, abridged edn. (London: Palgrave Macmillan, [1890] 1990), 11, 12.
[26] Michel Foucault, *The Order of Things: An Archeology of the Human Sciences* (London: Routledge, 1989; orig. pub. in French 1966), 19.
[27] Henry S. Turner, *Shakespeare's Double Helix* (New York: Continuum, 2007), 42.

analogy is the very energy that holds the Neoplatonic cosmos together and hence the basis of those sympathies by which sympathetic magic operates."[28] Ficino states, for example, that when a person studies science,

> the soul must draw in upon itself from external things to internal as from the circumference to the center, and while it speculates, it must stay immovably at the very center (as I might say) of man. Now to collect oneself from the circumference to the center, and to be fixed in the center, is above all the property of the Earth itself, to which black bile is analogous. Therefore black bile continually incites the soul both to collect itself together into one and to dwell on itself and to contemplate itself. And being analogous to the world's center, it forces the investigation to the center of individual subjects, and it carries one to the contemplation of whatever is highest...Contemplation itself, in its turn, by a continual recollection and compression, as it were, brings on a nature similar to black bile.   (*Three Books*, Bk 1, ch. 4, 113)

Through the analogic powers of black bile, the earth influences the human spirit as it contemplates, so that it functions in a manner parallel to that of "the world's center." By means of resemblance, one object can infuse its properties into another, energize it. Speaking of a certain "nourishing oil," which has virtues such as airiness, purity, and strength, Ficino observes that "[w]hat we get from taking a little of it is that not only are we made equal to it, but made like it."[29]

As Joseph A. Mazzeo says, the universal principle of analogy in the Renaissance formed the basis of "a new theory of knowledge."[30] In this analogical theory, things are not simply themselves but also "signs" that "reveal the marks of the Creator"; "[t]he analogical and symbolic potentiality of a thing is therefore not exterior or accidental to the thing but is derived from the very nature of creatures themselves" (302). Mazzeo concludes, as does Foucault later, that "[t]he Renaissance emphasis on universal analogy and cosmic affinities helped make the *forma mentis* of Renaissance men richly metaphorical and symbolic" (303).

The early period's recognition of the power of analogy complements current cognitive theories. Encompassing not only objects but also complex temporal processes, analogies allow us to map a new domain of knowledge into an old one, "do the reasoning in the old, and map the result back into the new,"

---

[28] Marsilio Ficino, *Three Books on Life*, trans. and ed. Carol V. Kaske and John R. Clark (Tempe, AZ: Medieval and Renaissance Texts and Studies, Arizona State University, [1989] 1998; orig. pub. in Latin, 1489), Introduction, 40.

[29] Marsilio Ficino, *The Book of Life*, trans. Charles Boer (Dallas, TX: Spring Publications, 1980; orig. pub. in Latin, 1489), Bk 2, ch. 3, p. 41.

[30] Joseph A. Mazzeo, "Universal Analogy and the Culture of the Renaissance," *Journal of the History of Ideas* 12, no. 2 (April 1954): 299–304, on 302.

permitting those domains to intermingle, argues Jerry Hobbs.[31] According to Giles Fauconnier and Mark Turner, analogy has emerged in recent years as an important subject for cognitive psychologists.[32] Analogy works imaginatively and typically unconsciously to create complex likenesses that take up existence in our minds as if they were facts of the world.[33] Analogies also bring information from the right side of the brain, associated with emotion, to bear on the left side, associated with reason.[34] That capacity of analogies to bridge domains of experience, link different kinds of brain activity, fire up the mind's imaginative processes, and generate insight helps to explain why Hartwig and Empson argue that analogy creates an experience of "wholeness." Present-day research enhances appreciation of some of the intuitions behind the Renaissance conception of sympathetic powers and magical parallelisms.

In the spirit of magical parallelisms, objects and situations can call forth other objects and situations related to them through inherent likeness. Foucault illuminates analogy as a Renaissance epistemological system; cognitive scientists affirm analogy's force and spontaneous realism; Empson frames analogy as a character's ability "to cause what he corresponds to"; and, in literature, Fletcher and others argue, magical parallelisms work etiologically. A psychically deep and energizing principle seems to operate in the perceiving and experiencing of structural parallels, for which comedy emerges as the generic home. In concrete literary terms, we might say that, in a play such as *Twelfth Night*, when an action in one storyline mirrors that in another, then a principle of mysterious sympathy, apparent through analogy, is revealing likeness in the two narratives and raising questions of causation.[35] Accumulated likenesses or sympathies in the play hint additionally at a metaphysical causal principle, one related to providence. Yet magical resemblances can still remain opaque in meaning, as we shall see. Taking the example of *The Comedy of Errors*, Barbara Freedman argues that repetitions of action create an uncanniness that works as resistance to closure and keeps meanings open.[36] Curiously, analogies and structural repetitions draw our attention towards wholeness but, in their complexity, resist final or exclusive meanings. Shakespearean comedy, then, echoes the occult nature of analogy and likeness, stimulating the mind to discern significance while creating the tension—a potentially lingering and productive one—of interpretive opacity.

---

[31] Jerry R. Hobbs, *Literature and Cognition* (Stanford, CA: Center for Study of Language and Information, Stanford University, 1990), 71.

[32] Gilles Fauconnier and Mark Turner, *The Way We Think: Conceptual Blending and the Mind's Hidden Complexities* (New York: Basic Books, 2002).

[33] Fauconnier and Turner, *Way We Think*, 19.

[34] Reuven Tsur, *Poetic Conventions as Cognitive Fossils* (Oxford: Oxford University Press, 2017), 38.

[35] According to Mary Floyd-Wilson, *Twelfth Night* identifies its "organizing structure" by its many references to "occult properties, sympathies, and antipathies"; *Occult Knowledge, Science, and Gender on the Shakespearean Stage* (Cambridge: Cambridge University Press, 2013), 73.

[36] Barbara Freedman, *Staging the Gaze: Postmodernism, Psychoanalysis, and Shakespearean Comedy* (Ithaca, NY: Cornell University Press, 1991), 90.

Patterns of Structural Doubleness in *Twelfth Night*

In *Twelfth Night*, magically paralleled actions suffuse the narrative yet sometimes remains difficult to grasp or even recognize, their presence becoming most obvious when they are most madcap. Isomorphism can entail a range of effects that we will explore in subsequent sections. First, strongly registered patterns of recurrence (even involving objects) within a plot line can foster a pervasive feeling of *paralysis* and *frustration*, as we will see with Viola's wooings. In *Twelfth Night*, the danger of enervation is partially mitigated by the engagingly uncanny sense that recurrences are weirdly self-duplicating. Thus, second, when details start to repeat each other analogically between separate plot lines—Toby's downstairs and Olivia's upstairs, for example—they foretell *convergence* and even hint at *fatedness* in those streams of action. Within a scene, likewise, mirrored actions imply that some special mechanism or sympathetic agency has supervened. Third, uncanny repetitions, when under pressure, can *accelerate* and *intensify manically*, plunging towards chaos (negative for characters, amusing for the audience), an effect of Toby's trickster line of action. But, fourth, reiterations can produce *differences*, multiple models, even within a process that appears to work by replication. A duplicated action might magnify qualities of the original, becoming an inspired transformation or a comic hyperbole. The same scheme of action might reveal variations in how different characters respond to similar circumstances, as illustrated by Sebastian, introducing the possibility of alternative destinies and spotlighting new agents who augur release from entrapment and its frustrations. The effect recalls Freedman's notion that repetitions can produce a sense of openness.[37] Just as enchantment can have its positive or negative valences, counterforces of restriction and expansiveness work paradoxical effects in *Twelfth Night*. Repetition, at its visible extreme, creates a wondrous, hallucinatory, yet periodically threatening experience.[38] It has a nightmare side as well as a happier dimension, and *Twelfth Night* passes through one to get to the other.

Certain of repetition's structural effects—paralysis, uncanniness, and manic fatedness—move *Twelfth Night* towards farce, sometimes plunging the play over the fence entirely. According to Eric Bentley, farce acknowledges our repressed

---

[37] In *Much Ado About Nothing*, argues Claire McEachern, patterns of repetition reassure the audience; *Believing in Shakespeare: Studies in Longing* (Cambridge: Cambridge University Press, 2018), 158. Something different is occurring in *Twelfth Night*.

[38] That effect is abetted by the unusual intimacy that critics see between the play's characters and audiences: see e.g., Freedman, *Staging*, 201. Freedman stresses the experience of loss and disillusionment in *Twelfth Night*, bypassing—unfortunately, I think—the play's joy and its affirming values, including love's ability to respond to loss; see 192–235. Allison P. Hobgood sees generally a "dangerously vibrant interplay between theatergoers and the English Renaissance stage"; in the case of *Twelfth Night*, playgoers especially provide "emotional collaboration" in creating Malvolio's experience of shame; *Passionate Playgoing in Early Modern England* (Cambridge: Cambridge University Press, 2014), 2, 129.

pleasure in aggression and violence; it indulges "wild fantasies" and imagines a phantasmagorical, incipiently paranoid world.[39] It ramps up repetitive actions to the point that a Bergsonian mechanicalness, or some other determinant, appears to have imposed itself on the spontaneous or vital—the effect that Zupančič sees as uncanny. Farce depends on a structure of "coincidences" that, to the audience, are not coincidences at all but, rather, intimations of destiny.[40] Thus, "[t]he heaping up of crazy intersections in farce creates a world in which the happily fortuitous seems inevitable" (245), an apt description of *Twelfth Night*. For all its "maniacal [ness]" (247), farce constitutes a complex causal system that illuminates *Twelfth Night*'s network of repetitions. Structural recurrence thus implies a kind of magical providentialism—helping to explain the staying power of romantic comedy.

Twelfth Night works up to its farcical episodes, but long before those it establishes an aesthetic of doubleness. Consider the way the motifs of repetition, analogy, and providence are silted into the play's second scene. "And what should I do in Illyria," says Viola at the outset, "My brother he is in Elysium" (1.2.2–3), with the assonance of the two place names pairing as much as contrasting them. Both characters will experience, we might say, qualities of both places. Hearing the captain's description of how Sebastian had ridden the waves, and thinking of her own rescue, Viola concludes, "Mine own escape unfoldeth to mine hope— / Whereto thy speech serves for authority— / The like of him" (18–20): Here likeness in events already implies a quasi-causal power that justifies hope. When the captain tells Viola of the recent death of Olivia's brother and her consequent withdrawal from the world, Viola, recognizing instantly their analogous situations, exclaims, "O that I served that lady," and imagines herself pursuing a course like Olivia's: "And might not be delivered to the world / Till I had made mine own occasion mellow— / What my estate is" (38–41). Viola's thoughts display the sympathetic influence of resemblance. Notions of fate and providence dot the exchange between Viola and the captain, as in the hopefulness of their reiterated "perchance" tossed between the two (4, 5, 6) or in the captain's hint of the providential: "I saw your brother / Most provident in peril" (10–11). The language of time and process subtly peppers the dialogue: "three hours," "a month ago," "twelvemonth," "shortly," "what else may hap to time I will commit" (21, 28, 34, 36, 57). The energies of the scene apparently carry over into and shape the next: "What a plague means my niece to take the death of her brother thus?" asks Sir Toby peevishly (1.3.1–2). On display here are qualities of repetition, analogical thinking, and incipient providentialism that will continue and multiply.

[39] Eric Bentley, *The Life of Drama* (New York: Atheneum, 1983), 241; on farce, see 219–56.
[40] Bentley, *Life of Drama*, 245.

Static Repetitions

A mode of static repetition possesses *Twelfth Night*'s opening scene. Orsino enters, of course, luxuriating in a self-obsessed fantasy of love and departs to immerse himself further in "[l]ove-thoughts" while lounging on "beds of flowers" (1.1.40, 39). His opening speech dallies with repetition: "That strain again, it had a dying fall. / . . . Enough, no more" (4–7), as he commands the musicians to stop and replay a passage and then to stop again, "excess" producing enervation: "'Tis not so sweet now as it was before" (2, 8). Lassitude eventually directs Orsino to return to his flowerbeds. In the interval, his business is once more to send his messenger profitlessly to Olivia, who will once more demur. Olivia practices her own cycle of ineffectual repetition, as she wanders "round" her chamber each day "like a cloistress," watering it with tears (28, 27) and clinging almost pathologically to the "sad remembrance" of her "brother's dead love" (31, 30).[41] Such repetitions, critics agree, bespeak narcissism and promise only dead ends.

Enter Viola, a potentially disruptive agent. As the first scene closes with Orsino hastening away, comforted only by his "love-thoughts" (1.1.40), the next answers it by ushering on stage the empathic Viola / violet (although her name is as yet undisclosed), who will become the object of those thoughts and who alludes indirectly to him: "What country, friends, is this?" (1.2.1), as if she were harking to some peculiar, responsive agency, much in the spirit of Northrop Frye's observation that thematic and verbal repetitions in comedy "echo and call and respond" to each other in ways that generate "fascination."[42] These first two scenes are paired also, according to John R. Ford, by means of a crafted set of contrasts involving inward-turned versus outward-turned perspectives.[43] We might add the contrast of passive and active. Yet soon enough Viola finds herself coopted by Orsino's fruitless fixation on Olivia and by her own fruitless suppression of her feelings for Orsino (restated frequently), as she engages as his proxy wooer. These related character stories come to reflect the torpor first projected by Orsino.

The narrative now takes its rhythm from Viola's to-and-fro embassies to Olivia and that lady's repeated refusals of Orsino's tenders of affection, doubled by Olivia's own reiterated wooing of Viola and Viola's repeated rebuffs, the business thus spawning mirror images of itself. At work is a kind of viral self-replication,

---

[41] The image is disturbing, as if Olivia hopes that by "season[ing]" (29) what is dead, she will somehow rejuvenate it. It anticipates Viola's more efficacious keeping alive of her brother's memory.

[42] Frye, *Natural Perspective*, 25. Relatedly, for G. R. Elliott, details of *The Comedy of Errors*' first scene are repeated in its second scene such that the one seems to have fathered the other; "Weirdness in *The Comedy of Errors*," *University of Toronto Quarterly* 9, no. 1 (October 1939): 95–106.

[43] Ford, *Guide*, 59–61. Viola's outward-looking, sympathetic, and interested nature, argues Ford, gradually captures Orsino's attention. For a reading that emphasizes the differences between the first two scenes and among the scenes of the different storylines, see Jean E. Howard, *Shakespeare's Art of Orchestration: Stage Technique and Audience Response* (Urbana, IL: University of Illinois Press, 1984), 172–206.

like cells that reproduce themselves, sometimes generating variant strains but staying within the same static system. The process has a snowballing dynamism, yet conditions remain largely unchanged, a craziness bottled-up. Orsino can only keep sending Viola to Olivia, and Olivia can only keep asking her to return.[44] The play gives us four courting scenes, three of them unproductive (1.5, 3.1, 3.4), followed by a successful fourth (4.1) when Olivia (who had just sent Feste to fetch Cesario [4.1.8]) wins Sebastian.

Within that circuit of duplicated actions are salted even more repetitions (or sub-repetitions), ones that make potential meanings multiple and doubtful. Take entrance announcements. In 1.5, Viola's imminent arrival at Olivia's gate is proclaimed three times, first by Maria, next by Toby, finally by Malvolio (95–6, 114, 116, 121–2, 135–6).[45] Likewise, Viola's second and third appearances before Olivia are both announced, the one promised by Feste (3.1.54–5), the other made by a servant (3.4.54–6). Echoing that pattern of deferral, Viola, in 3.1, has two exits, one called back and the other finally completed (132–4, 162). Such repetition, here and elsewhere, produces complicated, even paradoxical, effects. Delay can heighten expectation (as it does for Sebastian's entrance in 5.1), but it can recall other repetitions to make the action feel stuck (a secondary effect in 5.1). Recursion also produces enigmatical meaning: For Maria, in 1.5, Cesario is a "fair young man" (98); for Toby, "the devil" for all he cares (124); and for Malvolio, an "ill-manner[ed]" "fellow," neither boy nor man (149, 135), those repetitions hinting at alternative realities and trajectories.[46]

Other small details repeat uncannily.[47] Duplicitous or distracted letters recur, as one example. As another, Olivia initially presses a purse of money upon Viola, which she refuses (1.5.275–6).[48] Following Viola's departure, Olivia renews the offer by sending Malvolio after Viola presumably to return a ring, which Viola

[44] As Laurie E. Osborne notes, 2.4, in which Orsino talks about his love and prepares to send Viola again to Olivia, itself breaks into two parts, divided by Feste's entrance, that repeat each other thematically; " 'The marriage of true minds': Amity, Twinning, and Comic Closure in *Twelfth Night*," in Twelfth Night: *Critical Essays*, ed. James Schiffer (London: Routledge, 2011), 99–113, on 107.

[45] Lois Potter observes, "*Twelfth Night* is unusual in the amount of attention that is paid to the business of getting in and out of…doors"; Twelfth Night: *Text and Performance* (London: Macmillan, 1985), 25. Potter notes that the play's scenes often have symmetry, characters entering in one order and exiting in reverse order (24–5).

[46] The play, Ford argues, gives us multiple and differing views of Olivia before she actually appears, making her character mysterious; *Guide*, 61–5. He also finds 1.5, when we finally meet Olivia, to resemble "parodic[ly]" the later scene of misunderstanding, 5.1 (65).

[47] *Twelfth Night* also plays with verbal repetitions. Sir Andrew turns serial repeater, for example, as he attempts to woo Maria (e.g., 1.3.59–62) or as he copies Sir Toby's phrases and attitudes (e.g., 2.5.177, 180, 183, 185, 201). Later, Sir Andrew, hearing Viola use evocative words, says he will himself "get 'em all three all ready" (3.1.83, 87–9). Doubling extends to forms of play-acting: Orsino imitates a lover; Viola duplicates her brother and play-acts a wooer for Olivia; in the prison scene (4.2), Feste doubles as Sir Topas (and quizzes Malvolio on Pythagorean reincarnation), then play-acts himself (and the "old Vice" of Tudor interludes [4.2.123]), and later reads Malvolio's letter as if he were the madman.

[48] Picking up that play of objects, Antonio will later induce Sebastian to take a purse of money (3.2) whose subsequent apparent absence will figure in the action.

also declines, after which Malvolio repeats Olivia's request that she come again (294–9, 2.2.12). In 2.4, Orsino—who enters calling once more for music and specifically for the repetition of the previous night's song (3)—sends a "jewel" with Viola as a gift to Olivia (123), the idea appearing as if by osmosis from Olivia's prior attempted ring-gift. Orsino's jewel goes unmentioned thereafter, but it finds its counterpart in Olivia's pressing of a "jewel" upon Viola (3.4.203), the image flickering in and out of the action. (Feste calls Orsino's mind a changeable "opal" (2.4.75); he himself will later play a changeable "topas.") Olivia's jewel contains her "picture" (3.4.203), repeating the lady's earlier action of unveiling the "picture" of her face to Cesario (1.5.226) (both anticipated by Toby's reference to "Mistress Mall's picture" [1.3.123]). Later, Sebastian will return from Olivia with another jewel, a pearl, that she has given him (4.3.2).[49] Objects keep returning irrepressibly across this play-world, as if they were really the same object presented again and again, pulling the events that surround them into a subtle, shared sense of hallucinatory stasis.

Besides drifting and replicating objects, speech formulas also repeat themselves. In his first wooing instructions, Orsino tells Viola:

> Be not denied access, stand at her doors
> And tell them there thy fixed foot shall grow
> Till thou have audience.
> . . . .
> Be clamorous and leap all civil bounds
> . . . .
> It shall become thee well to act my woes.
>
> (1.4.15–26)

Such images arise in Viola's "willow cabin" speech (1.5.260–8), when she, in a lover's persona, imagines planting herself at Olivia's "gate" and singing, hallowing, and crying out until Olivia takes pity on her. (Feste's subsequent song to Orsino envisages such a lover having failed and now lying shrouded in "cypress," an alternative, if extreme, destiny [2.4.52].)[50] Just as Viola will hear Feste's song of unrequited passion as an "echo" from the seat of love (2.4.21–2), she—being herself a form of echo[51]—replicates in her "willow cabin" speech, perhaps unconsciously, Orsino's instructions (see Chapter 5). For Ficino, the echo is an image of

---

[49] On tokens, see Alan W. Powers, "'What he wills': Early Modern Rings and Vows in *Twelfth Night*," in Schiffer, *Critical Essays, op. cit.*, 217–28.

[50] The image of the cruelly rejected lover and of "cypress" will find a second life in Olivia's lament to Viola, as she accuses 'Cesario' of possessing a "tyrannous heart," in contrast to her suffering one: "a cypress . . . / Hides my heart" (3.1.118, 119–20).

[51] And, like the nymph, she is in danger of fading away from the narcissism of her beloved; Viola's association with Echo highlights her peculiar passivity.

sympathetic harmony.[52] More broadly, the Orsino–Olivia circuit is itself a static echo chamber, a magical hall of mirrors, able only endlessly to multiply elements and implications.

Yet in her willow-cabin speech, Viola also becomes an 'echo-plus,' for she extends the idea of multiplication and points towards newness arising out of repetition. As Lois Potter argues, Viola has a sympathetic capacity to "enter into [Orsino's] language," to internalize his cadences and diction.[53] Conjuring the willow cabin, Viola echoes, embodies, and transcends Orsino's instructions. By "imaginatively entering into [Orsino's] feelings" and by heightening his sense of "desperate determination," argues Potter, Viola moves beyond parody (24); sympathetic echoing here paradoxically hints at an authenticity of expression not otherwise available.

Fatedness, Opacity, Possibility

An implacable teleology seems always to be hovering on the horizon in *Twelfth Night*, the play driving a considerable business in background references to death, decay, and life processes. According to Thad Jenkins Logan, the play refers thirty-seven times to "death and destruction."[54] Orsino asks Feste for his "old plain song," saying, "The spinsters, and knitters in the sun / And the free maids that weave their thread with bones / Do use to chaunt it" (2.4.44–6), lines that invoke "images of the Fates," Leah Scragg points out, "spinning the thread of human life" as they chant ritualistically (215). Through their analogous lines of action and networks of correspondence, structural doublings in *Twelfth Night* likewise introduce the question of fatedness: Fixed or unfixed? Closed or open? Patterns and details from different storylines repeat to suggest paralleled and mutual destinies, but elusively so, evoking uncanniness while keeping open the possibility of alternative outcomes. Most obviously here, Sebastian's storyline reiterates Viola's. While Viola loops and re-loops through her rounds, Sebastian enters the play with Antonio, the sea captain who has saved him from shipwreck. Sebastian imagines tearfully that his sister has drowned, intends now to make his way to Orsino's court, and departs from Antonio at scene's end (2.1). The episode blatantly recapitulates the details of Viola's entrance scene at the play's beginning (1.2), as if the two characters had parallel or conjoined destinies or even as if Viola's action had, in the spirit of Ficino, magically authored Sebastian's.

[52] Ficino, *Three Books*, 40, 261.

[53] Potter, Twelfth Night: *Text and Performance*, 22; on repetitions, see 20–6.

[54] Thad Jenkins Logan, "*Twelfth Night*: The Limits of Festivity," *Studies in English Literature* 22, no. 2 (1982): 223–38, on 236. On the instructiveness of ideas of death in *Twelfth Night*, see Lisa Marciano, "The Serious Comedy of *Twelfth Night*: Dark Didacticism in Illyria," *Renascence: Essays on Values in Literature* 56, no. 1 (Fall 2003): 3–19.

Contiguous details, in parallel, from different lines of action conjure the sense of inchoate but possibly causal relationships. Sebastian departs from Antonio at the end of their first scene, but then Antonio reverses his agreement and decides to chase after the departed Sebastian: "I do adore thee so / That danger shall seem sport, and I will go" (2.1.43–4). As if occultly influenced by proximity, Antonio's about-face echoes the scene immediately preceding, replaying a version of Olivia's self-reversal towards Viola, when Olivia, feeling herself taken over by an irresistible force ("Even so quickly may one catch the plague?" [1.5.287]), instructs Malvolio to "run after the peevish messenger" and to give him the ring (293).[55] Adoration, emotional compulsion, rescinded resolve: The episodes' parallel events couple Antonio and Olivia through their mirrored feelings. One character will suffer love unrequited; the other will nearly do so—or perhaps, in some sense, does. The two destinies are linked, not only by the characters' common infatuation with 'Sebastian' but also by the strange mirroring of their actions.

But fate can be two-faced. "*Thy fates open their hands: let thy blood and spirit embrace them*," reads the forged letter to Malvolio (2.5.143–4). Fate apparently calls to Malvolio as something not fixed but only possible, an invitation that he must "embrace." At the end of the first wooing scene, Olivia may think that she has been clutched by fate, but she also wants fate to conform to her own ends: "Fate, show thy force, ourselves we do not owe. / What is decreed must be—and be this so" (1.5.303–4). Those closing lines are answered eerily at the outset of the very next scene by Sebastian's entrance with Antonio, for Sebastian arrives in the play as Olivia's fate, both beyond her control yet paradoxically fulfilling her desire.[56] In this play, you can have whatever you wish for, as long as you accept that it might not take the form you expected. Sebastian himself emphasizes his sense of being governed by "fate" (imagined as "malignan[t]"), as if hearing the echo of Olivia's language (2.1.4; see also 18–19). He refuses Antonio's further company so as not to shed (magically, by proximity) his bad fortune on his friend. The reflected actions of rejection—Olivia by Viola, Sebastian of Antonio—establish the necessary condition for the eventual convergence of the two fatalists, so that Olivia and Sebastian's scenes link together and show destiny coming into being through a doubled pattern. Yet, in another regard, Sebastian's emergence as the repeat of Viola's action puts in relief the twins' effective differences, for Viola has become passively engulfed by the Orsino–Olivia circuit, while Sebastian

---

[55] One might think of this device as a scenic version of rhetorical anadiplosis, wherein the last word of a sentence becomes the first word in the next; see Rose, *Shakespearean Design*, 76. We might also call it the "pick-up effect," the ending of one scene picking up and replaying enigmatically the qualities of a previous one. The motif is captured metaphorically in the scene of Malvolio's deception: When Maria plants a letter, presumably from Olivia, in his path, he picks it up, misinterprets its contents, and transforms his behavior into that recommended by the letter.

[56] Lois Potter observes that 1.5 ends with Olivia sending Malvolio after Viola, leaving audiences to expect the next scene to open with Viola, so that their encountering of Sebastian instead might evoke confusion (26)—and perhaps a sense of the uncanny.

sweeps forward with the new energy necessary to break that maddening loop. Repetition now brings the promise of release from stasis.

Relationships created by repetition can remain enigmatical, foregrounding communal likenesses among characters and events but keeping meanings and destinies opaque. Orsino's first line in 2.4, "Give me some music" (1), recalls not only his opening music speech in 1.1 but also the previous evening of "caterwauling" by the downstairs characters (2.3.71).[57] Does the linking of the two scenes by action and proximity suggest that music serves a comparably enchanting function in each, or even that Orsino's sentimentality has something in common with Toby's nostalgia? Perhaps. Orsino's concentration on music in 1.1 has sent a sympathetic shock wave through other scenes of the play, but their implications for Toby's episodes remain mysterious.

The ending of a scene might speak curiously to the beginning of another. Act Four, scene two closes with Malvolio's being left in the dark and accused of madness; the next scene opens with Sebastian's saluting of the "glorious sun" and his confirming to himself that his "wonder" is not "madness" (4.3.1, 3–4).[58] These events are juxtaposed and linked contrastively but left with their implications hanging in the air. The two characters are connected, of course, through Olivia—one aspires to her, the other seems almost aspired by her—but their circumstances are so matched in opposition that they seem to be undergoing positive and negative versions of the identical experience, like batteries with the same current flowing in different directions. To similar effect, at the culmination of 3.1, Viola states, with perhaps a touch of pique, that she will give up her surrogate wooing and withdraw from Olivia—"And so adieu, good madam, never more / Will I my master's tears to you deplore" (3.1.159–60)—upon which, in the scene's penultimate line, Olivia urges her desperately, "Yet come again" (161). The very next scene, as if oddly replaying that exchange, begins with an irritated Andrew Aguecheek insisting, "I'll not stay a jot longer" (3.2.1), prompting Sir Toby to convince him to abide and renew his suit to Olivia, the prior scene seeming to generate by mimetic magic its satiric reflection in the

---

[57] David Schalkwyk, "Music, Food, and Love in the Affective Landscape of *Twelfth Night*," in Twelfth Night: *New Critical Essays, op cit.*, ed. James Schiffer (New York: Routledge, 2011), 81–98, on 85. Schalkwyk sees Feste's late entrance into 2.4 as a device linking the scene to 2.3; in addition, he describes 2.4 as a "recapitulation" of 1.1 (85). Schalkwyk discusses music in *Twelfth Night* as "a structured kind of repetition and variation in time," apt phrasing that helps us understand the strong presence of music in this play of magic parallelisms.

[58] Noted by Potter, Twelfth Night: *Text and Performance*, 26. Ford observes that in a John Barton 1969 Royal Shakespeare Company production of *Twelfth Night*, a sobbing Malvolio could be heard in the background of Sebastian's entrance, "suggesting a surprising psychological link between two sharply distinct characters and the equally distinct plots they inhabit" (*Guide*, 59). As Brown notes, Sebastian meets and marries Olivia in a dream, while Malvolio in an adjacent scene is imprisoned for "the same dream"; "Seeing Double," 305. Howard argues for a further parallel, in that Malvolio's "claustrophobic dark hole" crystallizes Orsino's "languid passivity" and Olivia's "living entombment"; *Orchestration*, 177.

subsequent one. We might not be ready to liken Viola and Olivia to Andrew and Toby, but, as with Malvolio and Sebastian, and Olivia and Antonio, the suggestion that their different domains have something absurdly in common enters the play. Sometimes such linkages suggest fatedness or uncanny causation; at other times they reveal a commonality of behavior in storylines that never quite converge: Those ambiguities establishes the play's atmosphere. For auditors, patterns of repetition generally remain submerged but poised on the brink of awareness, slipping intermittently into conscious view. They hint broadly but often defy exact interpretation, keeping implications numinous and speculative. Repetitions and doubles hold open alternative possibilities even as they suggest a mysterious order bringing its form into being.[59] Doubleness, Zupančič argues, lets "the odd one in," but Shakespeare keeps the odd one's meaning in doubt.

Structural doublings—Malvolio's chasing after Viola in 2.2 as the odd sequel to Antonio's departure to find Sebastian in 2.1—might look coincidental, a kind of accident, as do other repetitions and doublings in scenic form. Or they might be explained away in terms of Shakespeare's skill at juxtaposition, nothing more than artistry. But, as Michael Witmore makes clear, accidents fascinated Renaissance writers and Protestant theologians because they carried potentially metaphysical import (see also Chapter 4).[60] In the Renaissance, "accidents have the power to startle and amaze," to convey "wonder," to the extent that they have "the appearance of design," as if they were "a spontaneous form of revelation" (1, 2, 3). In that sense, accidents are made for comedy, and they relate to occult theories of resemblance and analogy. Accidents as "early modern wonders" "straddle important ontological divisions between the natural and the supernatural, the fictional and the real" (5). Narrative coincidences constitute such accidents (see 62–81), which challenge the boundaries of categories in a way pertinent to comedy. To the hermeneutics of accidents might be added that of biblical typology, in which early modern Christian thinkers read characters and actions in the Old Testament as 'types' prefiguring individuals and events in the New Testament; indeed, such thinking allowed Catholic and Protestant polemicists to construe their own contemporary history in terms of biblical models, as in the way reform theologians fashioned the Pope as the Antichrist. Accidents and types, convergences and recurrences with metaphysical import are all partners to the mysterious forces of likenesses and parallels theorized by Ficino and described by Foucault and others. To the Renaissance observer, then, the structural repetitions of *Twelfth*

---

[59] The sense of alternative possibilities is built into the play's ending with Malvolio, argues Brown; he disrupts the finale but does not know of, or participate in, its discoveries and reconciliations: "Malvolio represents an alternative vision which the miracle of the twins' reunion and the consequent resolution of the play's romantic plots cannot eliminate"; "Seeing Double," 306.

[60] Michael Witmore, *The Culture of Accidents: Unexpected Knowledges in Early Modern England* (Stanford, CA: Stanford University Press, 2001); see esp. 1–16, although Witmore's study emphasizes genuine accidents rather than coincidences that hint of metaphysics.

Night could have been auspicious—"oracular" to use Frye's term—the poetic and the providential overlapping, pregnant with imminent meanings. Such doublings layer mystery into the comedy.

Manic Repetitions

The downstairs world of *Twelfth Night* mirrors the upstairs one—anticipating the intersection of the two domains and the pull towards mutual mania. The downstairs scenes of 1.3 and 2.3 "parallel" and echo each other, observes Keir Elam.[61] The latter scene even contains its own internal echoes: Toby calls for Maria to bring "a stoup of wine" (2.3.13), but Feste enters instead; later Toby asks Maria again for "[a] stoup of wine" (117), but Malvolio now enters (Elam, 2.3.13n). The scenic action advances by a pile-up of repeated entrances keyed to sounds: Feste at Sir Toby's call; Maria at the "caterwauling" of the "catch" (71, 57); Malvolio at the subsequent singing and "gabbl[ing]" (86) (a catch is, appropriately, a song in which singers repeat the same melody but begin at different measures). The scene finally turns cacophonous, with angry characters threatening and sniping at each other. (The action is shaped symmetrically, with Toby and Andrew ending, as they had begun, alone on stage, talking of staying up late.) Later, the would-be duel between Viola and Sir Andrew, with Sir Toby ready to step in (3.4), is doubled, of course, by the nascent fight between Sebastian and Sir Toby (4.1) and tripled by Sebastian's more bloody clash with Andrew and Toby (reported in 5.1). In 5.1, Andrew sees his broken head as completing grievously his near-confrontation with Viola in 3.4 (see 5.1.175–7). Through such scenes of replayed action, momentum accelerates, tempers inflame, and violence erupts, as repetition takes on an obsessive, inexorable drive. That steady build-up of repetitions argues that an unarticulated but feverish force of sympathy is at work in events.

The most important repetitions within the 'downstairs' plot line derive from the gulling of Malvolio, which leads to the play-acted treatment of him as demonically possessed (3.4), which leads to further treatment (by Feste) of him, when jailed, as inhabited by demons (4.2). In the prison scene, Feste takes a triple part: He play-acts himself and Sir Topas (a fictitious character who doubles for Sir Toby), while functioning figuratively "as a glass reflecting the 'madness' of the imprisoned steward."[62] Later, Feste will read aloud Malvolio's letter in the manner of the madman (5.1.285–91).[63] Thus, Malvolio's agitation in the prison scene (4.2)

---

[61] Elam, *TN*, 2.3n.; Elam also calls 1.3 "a third 'opening' to the play," another form of repetition; 1.3n.

[62] Elam, *TN*, 26.

[63] Malvolio's self-justifying letter re-employs the letter-device by which he was deluded (Sir Andrew also pens a letter, this of challenge, which Sir Toby recites aloud and dubs the work of, if not a madman, a "clod-pole," anticipating Feste's reading out loud of a letter [3.4.185]).

brings to the audience the sense of being themselves trapped, emblematically imprisoned, in a reiterated game that never stops, "the joke that goes too far."[64] It is a "knavery" that Sir Toby would be well "rid of," if he knew how (4.2.67), but this loop of manic repetition has become mysteriously self-driven. Feste imagines Malvolio as taken over by a "hyperbolical fiend" (25), and audiences themselves may experience, too, something of the "hideous darkness" (30) to which the gulling has brought events. Malvolio's 'possession' becomes a metaphor for the action. Feste addresses Malvolio as if he were "Satan," and the steward describes his room as dark "as hell" (4.2.31, 35). For Alexander Leggatt, the scene "brings to a head references to hell and devils scattered throughout the play."[65] Feste even likens himself to the "old Vice," the evil tempter of morality drama (123). The gulling of Malvolio has doubled and redoubled to the point of intractable, demonic nightmare.

With Malvolio's pathos and Feste's purposeless taunting, the downstairs action reaches its manic version of Viola's entrapment, the frenetic double of the endless loop that captures Viola, with the steward now trapped like the messenger—as if vast structures of the play were doubling themselves. The imprisonment scene's grotesquery and shadowiness ("hideous darkness" [30]) realize tonally the bad-dream world of farce. The scene feels urgent, hurried: "Do it quickly," says Maria (2–3); "To him, Sir Topas," prompts Sir Toby (17); "Sir Topas, Sir Topas, good Sir Topas, go to my lady," implores Malvolio (23–4). Yet it also feels excruciatingly drawn out, as "Sir Topas" debates with Malvolio about the darkness of the house, or as Feste sings while Malvolio desperately seeks his attention, or as Feste baffles Malvolio first in one guise, then all over again in another, deferral piled upon deferral. The scene is thus both agitating and enervating. One's sympathies may slide towards Malvolio,[66] while Feste works to distract or compensate by riffing like a stand-up comic or play-acting an internal dialogue with himself.[67] Meanwhile, the plot line grinds to a halt, almost as if the form of the scene were divided against itself. This is the dark side of uncanny repetition, the spiraling nightmare. The downstairs storyline, which began in the spirit of spontaneity and festivity, has itself morphed into self-replicating cycles of abusive revenge and nascent violence. Such are the manic dimensions of *Twelfth Night*, its building frenzy, its resemblance to a runaway train operating by its own demonic rules. The action augurs a Bergsonian mechanicalness or something worse, a mysterious madcap agency, a strange black hole drawing the circling events ineluctably into

---

[64] Ralph Berry, "*Twelfth Night*: The Experience of the Audience," *Shakespeare Survey* 34 (1981): 111–19, on 111.

[65] Alexander Leggatt, *Shakespeare's Comedy of Love* (London: Methuen, 1973), 244.

[66] Allison Hobgood discusses the sense, shared by many critics, that the audience becomes emotionally and complexly involved in the shaming of Malvolio; *Passionate Playgoing*, 128–58.

[67] In Shakespeare's time, the uncanniness of the scene might have been augmented by the reputed ventriloquism skills of Robert Armin, who played Feste.

its vortex. The downstairs domain has come to display, in farcical excess, the unsettling potential of the upstairs world.

Negative and Positive Enchantment

Both the upstairs and downstairs plot lines become trapped in self-reduplicating patterns of repetition—enchantment's negative valence—weirdly accepted as beyond anyone's control. We want Viola to break out of the Orsino–Olivia loop, even as she states repeatedly that she cannot (e.g., 2.2.33–41); her passivity feels inexplicable and exasperating. We want to get out of Malvolio's prison. The action proceeds as if under the sway of occult forces. As R. W. Maslen puts it, Illyria "grows progressively darker and more sinister from one scene to the next, with proliferating references to devils, witchcraft, hell, madness, and heresy, as the errors that beset its inhabitants multiply and the fears of its visitors grow more intense."[68] In that aura of dark enchantment, characters such as Olivia, Viola, and Sebastian yield themselves to a mechanistic yet strangely purposive fate and to an action enclosed yet volatile, as in the enchanted dream-world of farce.

But relief hovers in the air, too. The constriction of the plot lines is balanced by their intimations of multiplying possibilities, differences in detail or effect signifying openness and even indeterminacy. Here uncanny repetitions create a paradoxical resistance to closure, just as they do in *Errors*, according to Freedman. Since a repetition is never exact, it always makes for emphasis, exaggeration, or distinction. Similarly, repetition's multiplier effect suggests fecundity and surplus: "Would not a pair of these have bred, sir?" asks Feste, angling for yet another coin (3.1.48).[69] These features can induce auditorial restlessness, frustrated hope, and even anxiety, all to be given relief by Sebastian's returning from the sea and his injection into the action of combustive self-assertiveness. Throughout, an aura of enchantment flickers around both twins: Viola fears that she has "charmed" Olivia (2.2.18); Olivia refers to Viola as having performed an "enchantment" (3.1.110); Sebastian "wonder[s]" at Olivia; Antonio denounces the spell cast over him by Sebastian as "witchcraft" (5.1.72). The ending, of course, brings the plot lines into convergence and concludes their mimetic parallelisms. Yet, I would propose, the denouement allows notions of magical multiplicity to saturate the ending in other ways, including not only the occultism of twins but also the scene's diction and especially its allusion, including the image of "natural perspective" and the

---

[68] R. W. Maslen, *Shakespeare and Comedy* (London: Bloomsbury, 2005), 193.

[69] According to Gertrude Stein, what we take erroneously as repetition really constitutes, by its very emphasis or insistence, a new action; "Portraits and Repetition," in *Stein: Writings 1932–1946*, ed. Catharine R. Stimpson and Harriet Chessman (New York: Library of America, 1998), 287–312.

references to Platonic androgynes and to ghost figures and demonic doubles—features that cannot be explored in detail here.[70]

With repetition, sets of events or domains of experience that seem unrelated, even incommensurate, become linked: Such is the business of comedy. Repetitions and parallelisms in *Twelfth Night* will often remain a little buried, the reader or spectator registering them as much subconsciously as consciously, with occasional, small jolts of surprise and of wonder and wondering as things subliminal become apparent. Doubleness can function uncannily because comparisons are obscure or because they occur across separate strands of action or domains of experience. Repetitions thus create an atmosphere of hauntedness, of a compulsive force field organizing the action in a way difficult to define[71] and reminiscent of the elusiveness of such patterns in the romance narratives that Shakespeare knew so well. That feeling of an opaquely enchanted world charges *Twelfth Night* with mysterious power. Something significant but inexpressible appears to be taking form, just under the radar, an uncanny, looming power capable of malevolence or beneficence. Later, we will call it providence.

Structural Repetition in Other Comedies

Comedies prior to *Twelfth Night* may lack its rich uncanniness, but they do incubate qualities that Shakespeare cultivates and transforms. Earlier comedies show structural repetitions and imitations that attest to an incipient order coming into being, linked to providence. Shakespeare grasps those manifestations of an underlying causal power and builds upon them. As often noted, *Twelfth Night* apparently arises from the matrix of what Louise George Clubb cites as the "'*Ingannati* family'" of Italian comedies, the phrase deriving from the famous Sienese drama of 1532.[72] The great ancestor is *Parthenio* (1516), a romance drama

---

[70] These ideas have been presented in my paper, "The Occultism of Twins and Doubles in *Twelfth Night*," for the seminar on "The Occult in Shakespeare," at the Shakespeare Association of America conference, 2019.

[71] Leggatt speaks of the "implacable, mysterious sea" that looms in the play's background, suggesting "both destruction and new life," yet also "restless, pointless wandering"; the sea represents "a power beyond human will—frightening, destructive, yet finally benevolent"; *Love*, 221, 223, 224, 249. See also Brown, "Seeing Double," 300. Steve Mentz emphasizes the figurative importance in *Twelfth Night* of the beach, a "liminal" place, posed between the raging of the sea and its life-giving power; *At the Bottom of Shakespeare's Ocean* (New York: Continuum, 2009), 55. A vague but ominous power appears in other of the comedies. Studying the language of disruption in nature caused by the rift between Oberon and Titania in *A Midsummer Night's Dream*, Turner sees "something much more sinister" than "generic images of cosmic imbalance"; rather, "a grotesque but nevertheless still entirely 'natural' order that lives immanently and in potential," realized only dimly by humans; *Double Helix*, 36.

[72] Louise George Clubb, *Pollastra and the Origins of* Twelfth Night: Parthenio, commedia *(1516) with an English Translation* (Farnham, Surrey: Ashgate, 2011), 55. On John Manningham's famous comment comparing *Twelfth Night* to "Inganni," see Elam, *TN*, 3–4. John R. Ford sees *Gl' ingannati* as "filled with details that strongly link it to *Twelfth Night*," details that Shakespeare treats as "foils" for his own version; *Guide*, 21, see 21–5.

in which happenstance keeps revealing itself as destiny, assisted by the actions of the plucky, cross-dressed, magnetically attractive heroine Gallicella (who effects not one but two bed tricks); such is the formula passed on to Shakespeare. The later, famous *Gl' ingannati* concerns the look-alike twins Lelia and Fabrizio, separated by the sack of Rome, with the father, Virginio, and the daughter (Lelia) having escaped to Modena. Lelia has disguised herself as a boy in a white suit in order to be close to, and serve, her beloved, Flamminio, now besotted with Isabella. Fabrizio, wearing an identical white suit, turns up in Modena seeking his lost family. Everyone—man or woman, young or old—who comes in contact with Lelia-as-boy falls in love with "him"; she, like Viola, is the play's avatar of personal magic. *Gl' ingannati* sets up various mirrored actions: Lelia wants to avoid getting trapped into marriage with an older suitor, while, in a parallel action, she attempts, in disguise, to prevent Flamminio from successfully wooing Isabella; likewise Lelia-as-Fabio discourages Flamminio from pursuing a non-reciprocating woman and then applies the same reasoning to herself. Repetition and double-plot mirroring give the action inevitability, the values abstracted by the separated but converging twins. Fortune presides over this comedy, with the Prologue itself stressing the importance of good fortune and patience. At critical moments, characters bemoan their evil fortune or credit Fortune with a happy twist of events. The play does not aim for uncanniness, but its materials carry that potential.

A different step towards *Twelfth Night* appears in chivalric fiction set on stage; for example, *Clyomon and Clamydes* (pub. 1599). This double-plotter concerns the eponymous young knights who at first dangerously oppose each other but who are drawn closer and closer by their paired destiny. The self-sacrificing heroine, Neronis, serves her beloved, Clyomon, while impersonating a page, in the mode of Gallicella, Lelia, and Viola. The romance proceeds by means of alternating, sometimes intersecting, strands of action in loosely parallel scenes that shift between the two protagonists. In the opening, Clamydes is given safe harbor from a tempest by Juliana, Clyomon's sister; later Neronis saves the life of the ailing Clyomon, who has been set ashore from another tempest, and then, in disguise, saves him again after he has been wounded. Early in the action, Clyomon thrusts Clamydes aside, interposes himself, and steals the honor of being dubbed a knight. That device puts the two at potentially mortal odds, but it also hints at their essential interchangeability, a near identicalness that the action progressively makes manifest. Although the contending knights agree to meet at Alexander's court for combat, each is prevented; when they finally converge, they are prevented again from fighting. To win his love, Juliana, Clamydes must kill a flying serpent that despoils virgins; to recover his beloved, Neronis, Clyomon must kill the bestial king who has abducted her. Through various means, we come to see the two knights not as opponents but as mirror figures, kindred souls, the pair eventually becoming brothers-in-law. Crucial to the play is the sense that metaphysical forces guide its action; speakers invoke Fortune twenty-three times, fate another eight, the will of the gods some twenty-seven. At one point the god Providence even materializes comically to prevent Neronis from mistakenly committing suicide. Disguised as a page, Neronis becomes herself a kind of agent of destiny. The play, then, combines doublings of action and of identity with a powerfully registered sense of providence forcing characters away from violence and towards convergence and comity.

No playwright understood that doubleness entails an almost magical multiplier effect better than John Lyly, as illustrated by his middling-sort comedy *Mother Bombie* (pub. 1594).[73] Lyly is justly famous for his sense of symmetry and parallelism, in both syntax and dramatic structure. Pairs beget more pairs, quartets emerge, figures appear on stage in inevitable, shifting combinations, and the advancing action keeps spawning additional character sets, mostly occurring in scenes of mirrored events whose characters even echo each other's speeches. A wealthy father wishes to marry off his dim-witted son (who has been kept from public view) to his wealthy neighbor's daughter (likewise kept private). As it turns out, the daughter is also slow of mind, and her father seeks the same goal as does the other. Each ignorant of the foolishness of the other's child and each wanting to hide that of his own, the fathers similarly turn to their servants for stratagems. The servants, in response, plot against the masters. Another set of young lovers emerges, blocked in their romance by their fathers. More servants follow, with more stratagems. Finally, the plot brings forth a wet nurse, with two more children: She had switched sets of babies at birth, and the revelation effects a reorganizing of the families, a sorting out of difficulties, and a further imbricating of relationships. The play's humor is driven by the expanding cast of servant figures improvising new tricks and devices. A central pleasure arises in the action's doubling, reformulating, and redoubling of character sets until the stage, which begins with two figures, becomes crowded with a miscellany of pairs and types. Over all the action presides the cunning woman Mother Bombie, consulted repeatedly and dispensing her sibylline knowledge in rhymed riddles, her paradoxes multiplying until they finally dissolve.

Mirroring effects occur in Shakespeare's early comedies.[74] The cunning man Dr. Pinch, one might say, broods over Shakespeare's *The Comedy of Errors*, for he manifests the play's aura of magic as both ridiculous and slightly disturbing: its doubled pairs of twins and its mirrored events, with misunderstandings multiplying and potential resolutions continually deferred. Intertwined and recurrent

---

[73] Shakespeare may have seen *Mother Bombie* performed by the Children of St. Paul's before its publication, and he may have read it in print. *The Comedy of Errors* adopts the name of *Mother Bombie*'s leading servant, Dromio, for its own twin servants.

[74] David P. Young emphasizes their sophistication in *A Midsummer Night's Dream; Something of Great Constancy: The Art of 'A Midsummer Night's Dream'* (New Haven, CT: Yale University Press, 1966).

events—symbolized by the play's circulating chain—establish a sense of mad and magical, looped action. As with *Twelfth Night, Errors* builds frenetically towards a near-violent conclusion, farce and romance crowding one another out by turns. Scenes repeat in action and pattern: The play begins with dual arrival scenes; as it advances, the same Dromio is beaten by characters first from one line of action then from another; both Dromios dash back and forth, repeatedly interrupting their real or presumed masters; two exorcism scenes occur as do two wooings and two lock-outs; the real denouement is anticipated by a false one; and more.[75] Some of these actions, such as the wooings, are treated to over-the-top parody, and other parodic elements salt the advancing action. The characters' sense of madness or magic finds its counterpart, then, in a structure whereby events repeat and multiply uncannily, and with increasing mayhem. The narrative seems resistant to closure, absent some surprise intervention from outside, which arrives in the person of Emilia, who brings events full circle but who also generates an unanticipated additional married couple. Barbara Freedman rightly links uncanny repetitions in *Errors* to unpredictably open possibilities.

Other of Shakespeare's early comedies take up the genre's penchant for doubled and paired action. Scenes in *Love's Labour's Lost*, for example, display a much-noted, artificial symmetry: Different couples take the limelight successively for brief conversations, then step away; characters speak in stichomythia; prospective suitors pop sequentially in and out of a scene to ask the name of a mistress; the lords enter a scene one after another, each presumably in private, with a self-composed poem announcing his love, overheard by the preceding lord; the gentlemen come to the ladies disguised as Muscovites and then as themselves, the entertainment of the 'Russians' paralleled and parodied later by the Pageant of Nine Worthies. The structure of action is regularly likened to a courtly dance (a metaphor often applied as well to *Much Ado About Nothing*, a play characterized by "repetition, with variation"[76]). Yet a pattern of disruption also runs through

---

[75] See Cartwright, *CE*, 80–1.

[76] In *Much Ado*, "everything seems to happen twice (or even three times). The conversation between Claudio and Don Pedro is overheard by two others (Antonio's man and Borachio) who report it in two further scenes. Benedict is fooled, then Beatrice by the same device (and then the Watch, as a kind of counterpoint, overhears Borachio and Conrade). There is a masked dance, and a final scene when Hero and the other ladies all enter 'masked.' The Prince engages in two plots: one to woo Hero for Claudio, the other 'to bring Signior Benedict and the Lady Beatrice into a mountain of affection th' one with th' other.' Claudio is twice deceived by Don John and Borachio: once into thinking that Don Pedro has wooed Hero for himself, and again when he is convinced that Hero is dishonest. And to match Don John and Borachio's villainy (and evil plot), there is Friar Francis's goodness (and helpful plan). There are two dances, two sets of lovers, two old men, two 'gentlewomen attending on Hero,' two 'followers of Don John,' two named clowns, Dogberry and Verges, and the play ends, just as it began, with the appearance of a messenger. (There are even two songs, Balthasar's 'Sigh no more' and 'Pardon, goddess of the night,' which is sung in the churchyard.)"; Marvin Felheim, "Comic Realism in *Much Ado About Nothing*," in *Bloom's Shakespeare Through the Ages*: Much Ado About Nothing, ed. Harold Bloom (New York: Infobase Publishing, 2010), 194–210, on 199; orig. pub. in *Philologica Pragensia* 7 (1964): 213–25.

many of the scenes of *Love's Labour's Lost*. Berowne disrupts the first-scene signing ceremony; Dull and Costard disrupt it further; Costard and Boyet will continue to puncture scenes and re-direct their course; the ladies even refuse to dance. That patterning is not exactly magical, but cumulatively it becomes a formal cause in the play, predicating its possibilities. The failed courtship fulfills that implicit schema, but it also shocks with a disruption on a scale so great that the play catapults into a different mode. In *Love's Labour's Lost*, repetition provides structure but also leads, again, to unexpected possibilities. *The Merchant of Venice*, like other comedies, employs Hartwig's analogical scenes, as when Jessica's elopement in 2.6 is followed directly by Morocco's unsuccessful wooing of Portia in 2.7; or even small analogical details, as when Antonio's sadness in 1.1 seems to call forth Portia's weariness in 1.3. Kenneth Gross notes the way common elements weave through the two main storylines of *Merchant*, and comments, "As William Empson says of double plots more generally, the two worlds are positioned so as to suggest the maximum amount of magic in their connection combined with the maximum possibility for critical judgment."[77] Gross's observation rings true regarding this chapter's arguments about Shakespeare's comedies more generally.

Romantic Comedy and Providence

Those sample plays illustrate the patterns and effects that Shakespeare built upon and extended in *Twelfth Night*. Doubleness shapes the comic world by bringing with it a numinous sense of both endless self-replication and providentialism. Fortune entails alternative possibilities, and its happiest outcomes can turn on not only the will of the gods but also, paradoxically, the initiative of the characters. Comic doubleness bespeaks a universe of providential patterning but also of potentially infinite multiplicity and variability, a kind of comic fecundity; the metaphysical circuit asserts itself but remains open to unexpected or alternative destinies. In *Twelfth Night*, Shakespeare brings an aura of uncanniness and enchantment to this comic world; it is pregnant with the pressure of imminent destiny and yet with amorphousness, too, resisting final definition. Forms of dramatic mirroring "stimulate[] thought" in audiences, argues David Young;[78] Shakespeare in *Twelfth Night* infuses that reflection additionally with a sense of wonder.

Twelfth Night and its cognate plays give their own peculiar spin to the mash-up of English Renaissance beliefs about providence, fate, fortune, and the marvelous. According to Alexandra Walsham, "the doctrine of providence" constituted the

---

[77] Kenneth Gross, *Shylock Is Shakespeare* (Chicago, IL: University of Chicago Press, 2006), 30.
[78] Young, *Great Constancy*, 97, see 97–106.

"kernel and keystone" of Calvinistic Protestant life and thought.[79] Protestant providence, however, offered two potentially contradictory propositions: one, that all of human destiny was preordained, immutable, and foreknown by God, but, two, that God intervened actively and directly in human and worldly affairs in forwarding his purposes, even in contravention of the normal workings of nature. Because God could withdraw "his protection and grace" and because divine actions were secret and inscrutable, the individual was under pressure to conform her behavior to the divine order (14). Thus, "an all compelling providence was not incompatible with free will" (15). As an important corollary, Calvinism required individuals to scrutinize their lives for assurance of God's enigmatical favor, that search capable of encouraging, at its extremes, false egotism or "debilitating despair" (17).

Yet, in England, observes Walsham, Calvinist doctrine confronted a host of pre-existing popular attitudes and presumptions not easily dislodged; those included beliefs in chance and random fortune ("the fickle goddess Fortuna" [21]); fate as a "remote, inexorable force" (22); the workings of Dame Nature, entailing an "almost animistic trust in a self-evolving universe" (23); astrology; magical witchcraft (bringing with it witches and cunning men and women); and even atheism. Those popular beliefs—inconsistent among themselves—overlapped, intermingled with, and sometimes resisted the rigorous Protestantism echoed from the pulpit, with the result, we might infer, that popular literature and drama tend to be profoundly hybrid.

If an array of metaphysical values colors *Twelfth Night*, one of them is time. Just as we have noted the time markers in 1.2, numerous other critics have drawn attention to the prominence of time throughout the play. Keir Elam points out that it is "full of clocks and watches" and other references to time[80]—moon-time, musical time, wasted time, and the like. Although time might be "perceived with anxiety," it is also, he argues, "the medium of redemption" (77); those divergent values map onto the play's sense of time as both compressed and hurried yet also slow in development, when "occasion" is allowed to "mellow" (1.2.40). Thus, the whirligig of time, Lois Potter argues, spins energetically "within a more gradual and spacious process."[81] Through the thematic of time, *Twelfth Night* emphasizes processual experience, enhancing thereby the significance of its providential dimension. Time, argues Ford, reminds us "of the play's attentiveness to spiritual concerns" (94).

---

[79] Alexandra Walsham, *Providence in Early Modern England* (Oxford: Oxford University Press, 1999), 8. My discussion of providence relies substantially on Walsham's account; see esp. 8–64. Historically, it is tempting to see in *Twelfth Night* a middle point between official Calvinist prelapsarianism and an incipient Arminianism; on the latter, see Alison Shell, *Shakespeare and Religion* (London: Bloomsbury, 2010), 196–202.

[80] Elam, *TN*, 77.   [81] Potter, Twelfth Night: *Text and Performance*, 17.

While comic time evokes an image of lateral space, as Potter suggests, it also possesses both voltage and density. Frank Kermode, whose *The Sense of an Ending* considers the way that ancient teleological myths structure our present relationships to existence, introduces the term "*kairos*" as "our way of bundling together perception of the present, memory of the past, and expectation of the future, in a common organization. Within this organization that which was conceived of as simply successive becomes charged with past and future: what was chronos becomes *kairos*."[82] According to Matthew Wagner, Shakespeare creates moments of "thick" time, when the sense of the present, past, and the future converge intensely in a single moment.[83] *Twelfth Night*'s frequent references to time establish that sense of the present as dense, electrically charged with the past and the future: "What else may hap to time I will commit" (1.2.57); "O time, thou must untangle this, not I" (2.2.40); "And what's her history? / A blank my lord... She sat like Patience on a monument" (2.4.109–13); "till each circumstance / Of place, time, fortune do cohere" (5.1.247–8). Perhaps paradigmatically, the fleeting present, the mourned past, and the longed-for future all inform Viola's willow-cabin speech, its images of echo and reverberation applying temporally as well as spatially. The play's very structure of magical doubleness—scenes and episodes repeatedly recalling or anticipating others, insisting on the play's temporal and processual quality—constitutes itself a profound sense of *kairos*. The mystery of structural parallels conjoins not only with the mystery of providential power but also with the mystery of teleological time. Wagner describes time generally in *Twelfth Night* as "hovering in mid-air, as it were, above or beside the time of the world" (79), his language evoking other-worldliness, even spirituality. The layering of dense and pregnant time, and the slow yielding of tumult to an imminent albeit obscure providence infuse the play with hauntedness.

The romantic comedies that we have been exploring entail a strong, structural sense of providential, if inscrutable, forces at work, reinforced by the characters' frequent allusions to unseen agencies. *Twelfth Night*, like many of its predecessor plays, is dense with references to providence,[84] God's will, chance, time, and especially fortune, that last word occurring some eighteen times, most famously in Malvolio's declaration that "all is Fortune" (2.5.21) (hardly an orthodox Puritan slogan). Romantic comedy carries, we might say, an incipient metaphysical dimension, oriented towards providence; such a dimension appears far less

---

[82] Frank Kermode, *The Sense of an Ending: Studies in the Theory of Fiction* (Oxford: Oxford University Press, [1967] 2000), 46.

[83] Matthew D. Wagner, *Shakespeare, Theatre, and Time* (New York: Routledge, 2012), 6; on *Twelfth Night*, see 78–86; Wagner does not mention Kermode or *kairos*.

[84] Concerning providence in *Twelfth Night*, Maurice Hunt argues that "Shakespeare endorses" the notion of a deity "who works through secondary agents such as the sea to reward individuals who have had to earn their blessing by selflessly serving others," a description that fits Viola; "Malvolio, Viola, and the Question of Instrumentality: Defining Providence in *Twelfth Night*," *Studies in Philology* 99, no. 3 (Summer 1993): 277–97, on 278.

obvious in satiric comedy, and its suffusing presence in romantic comedy reveals much about the form's scope, magnetism, and staying power. *Twelfth Night*, in particular, comports easily with Protestant providentialism, along with related popular values. Fortune and chance reveal themselves as fundamentally providential aspects of design, as implied in the play's culminating image of "the whirligig of time" (5.1.370), whose turnings embody the logic of what appears accidental. Yet this metaphysical force ultimately encourages human attention and initiative. Characters invoke it, refer to it, seek to direct it, puzzle about it, all with an anxious Protestant intensity.[85] As with many of the plays associated with *Twelfth Night*, an active, interventionist, even responsive, providence broods over the action and radiates through its unfolding structure; yet that force, even when beneficent, always feels a little contingent, always keeps its properties blurry and its meanings enigmatical. That doubleness of what is imminent yet somehow absent looks like a blueprint of, and for, enchantment.

---

[85] Claire McEachern sees the Protestant emphasis on searching for signs that foretell one's destiny as a formative influence on Shakespearean drama; *Believing in Shakespeare*.

3

Place, Being, and Agency

I tell thee...magic haunts the ground.

Robert Greene
Friar Bacon and Friar Bungay

"[To] exist in any way," observes Edward Casey, "is to be somewhere"; "place is an
a priori of our existence on earth."[1] How strange, then, is Shakespearean comedy,
where place is not a given but a question. *Hamlet* may ask, "Who's there?" (1.1.1),
but *Twelfth Night* ponders, "What country, friends, is this?" (1.2.1). The *a priori* of
comic existence is not emplacement but displacement. Shakespeare's comic characters are in motion and typically a bit lost. As travelers, they arrive in strange
cities or depart familiar ones, wander in woods, escape from threatening locales,
wash up on alien seashores, and wonder where they are. Many of the locales they
encounter appear fantastical, even enchanted, as if passing through mysterious
landscapes had something to do with the protagonists' discovering their identities.

In comedy, *where* has much to do with *who*, for the nature of place can anchor
or change one's self-perception, as if place had agency. On the negative side, to
lose one's sense of place is to lose one's sense of self: "Am I in earth, in heaven or in
hell? / Sleeping or waking? Mad or well advised? / Known unto to these, and to
myself disguised?" asks Antipholus of Syracuse (*CE* 2.2.218–20). Yet Antipholus
may be more willing than he acknowledges to surrender his cognizance of place
and self. Although he fears dislocation, he also desires it for reuniting with his
brother—and perhaps subconsciously for conjoining with his romantic other self
(Luciana). Behind Antipholus's question lies what Kristen Poole describes as "the
almost ubiquitous understanding [in the Renaissance] that the universe is organized according to a homologous and interconnected relationship between body
and world."[2] In that spirit, one of Shakespeare's characteristic strategies, according
to Harry Berger, Jr., is to invest dramatic locales with metaphoric and psychological meaning, making them "the external correlatives of the speaker's character,

---

[1] Edward S. Casey, *The Fate of Place: A Philosophical History* (Berkeley, CA: University of California
Press, 1998), ix, x.
[2] Kristen Poole, *Supernatural Environments in Shakespeare's England: Spaces of Demonism,
Divinity, and Drama* (Cambridge: Cambridge University Press, 2011), 12. For an historical study, see
Alexandra Walsham, *The Reformation of the Landscape: Religion, Identity, and Memory in Early
Modern Britain and Ireland* (Oxford: Oxford University Press, 2011).

Shakespeare and the Comedy of Enchantment. Kent Cartwright, Oxford University Press. © Kent Cartwright 2021.
DOI: 10.1093/oso/9780198868897.003.0004

concern, or world view,"[3] a strategy that Shakespeare employs more systematically than do any of his predecessors. In the comedies, identity and locale act almost magically upon each other.

The locale recurrently associated with Shakespeare's comedies, as we shall see, is the fantasy land of Italy. 'Italy,' as an imagined construct, contains heightened civility yet also volatility and danger; at its best it facilitates new possibilities for the self and for human relations. That imagined Italy stands for the non-realistic and psychological dimensions of Shakespearean comedy and for the plasticity of its environment. Within the tragedies and histories, by contrast, places are comparatively stable and reflect the conditions of the worlds in which characters find themselves.[4] But in comedy, place is mixed and palimpsestic, a changeable taffeta. For Shakespeare, comedy offers the genre most self-conscious about geography, as its action typically proceeds by movement between symbolic locales of conflicting potentialities, such as the court or city and a zone of nature. Place and character interact, too, giving the impression that, under certain circumstances, the one influences the other. Because of its metaphoric richness and reach, place in Shakespearean comedy emerges as crucial, yet a bit mysterious.

The several sections of this chapter take up four interconnected topics: first, competing Renaissance perceptions of places either as undifferentiated or as magical and 'poetical' second, Italy as a poetical locale and the metaphoric home of Shakespeare's comedies; third, comic places within the comedies as regulative or protean; and fourth, causality as it operates in protean sites. Ultimately, the chapter asks how locale affects who characters are or what they become: What is the agency of place?

Measurable and Magical Geographies

Shakespeare wrote at a time when two notions of place were coming into conflict: an older mystical world view that accepted some locations as charmed, magical, or charged with unique properties; and an emergent proto-scientific conception that viewed place and space as both quantitatively measurable and qualitatively undifferentiated. Illustrative of that second view, in the early fourteenth century, European maps began to appear with markings that identified known, charted routes, navigable by magnetic compass, across bodies of water such as the

---

[3] Harry Berger, Jr., *Second World and Green World: Studies in Renaissance Fiction-Making* (Berkeley, CA: University of California Press, 1988), 128.

[4] The tragedy whose geographic coordinates most resemble those of comedy is *Antony and Cleopatra*, with its dialectic of Rome and Alexandria, an opposition that helps to underwrite the play's sense of romance and comedy. In the tragedies, place can sometimes mirror character.

Mediterranean.[5] Mapmaking advanced exponentially with the recovery, c.1400, of a copy of Ptolemy's *Geographia*, which demonstrated how the earth's curved surface could be represented two-dimensionally and divided linearly with "a crosshatch of coordinates"—latitudes and longitudes.[6] Thinkers such as Nicholas of Cusa, in the fifteenth century, moved correspondingly away from a vision of space as bounded and hierarchical and towards a vision of it as infinite and homogenous.[7] Signally, in 1543 Nicolaus Copernicus published his finding that the sun, rather than the earth, constituted the center of the universe. These developments had pragmatic consequences; in England in 1592, for example, Emery Molyneux began to manufacture his large terrestrial globes, graphed with latitudes, longitudes, and the routes of Sir Francis Drake and Thomas Cavendish.

Thus, at the end of the sixteenth century, according to Poole, a notion of natural space—"absolute" and "rigorously geometric"—was posed against one of super-natural space—"labile, fluid, and plastic."[8] Naturalistic and heliocentric concepts worked against the religious and cultural view of space as hierarchical and of place as potentially numinous.[9] The residual view recalls the enchanted woods, sacred springs, haunted grounds, and talking trees that abound in Malory's *Morte d'Arthur*, Ariosto's *Orlando Furioso*, and Spenser's *The Faerie Queene*. In a similar spirit, according to John Gillies, Renaissance maps were still deeply poetical, reflecting an axis of bounded, normative centers (cities, homes) rimmed by threatening margins or fluid borderlands populated with barbarians and gro-tesques, a "poetical geography" (Gillies borrows the term from Giambattista Vico).[10] Such binaries reenact a hierarchical medieval view of the four-cornered world, with Jerusalem as its spiritual, moral, and geographical center and with corruption and wildness increasing as one moves progressively away from it, as in John Mandeville's *Travels* (c.1357). For Gillies and other critics, Shakespeare's geographies are "conceptual structure[s]," intellectual models, whose import resides in their metaphoric, symbolic, and characterological meanings.[11] These

---

[5] This and the subsequent summary of scientific advances rely on Alfred W. Crosby, *The Measure of Reality: Quantification and Western Society, 1250–1600* (Cambridge: Cambridge University Press, 1996), see esp. 95–108, 227–40.

[6] Crosby, *Measure of Reality*, 98.   [7] See Casey's magisterial *Fate of Place*, esp. 1–129.

[8] Poole, *Supernatural Environments*, 9.

[9] A developing body of medieval thought had explored the question of Nature's orderly rule over the universe versus God's power to intervene miraculously; see Kellie Robertson, *Nature Speaks: Medieval Literature and Aristotelian Philosophy* (Philadelphia, PA: University of Pennsylvania Press, 2017).

[10] John Gillies, *Shakespeare and the Geography of Difference* (Cambridge: Cambridge University Press, 1994). On the contrast of old and new, see Garrett A. Sullivan, Jr., "Shakespeare's Comic Geographies," in *A Companion to Shakespeare's Works*, vol. 3 of 3, *The Comedies*, ed. Richard Dutton and Jean P. Howard (Oxford: Blackwell, 2003), 182–99.

[11] Sullivan, "Comic Geographies," 182. Gillies's work draws him close to recent French theorists of place, several of whom he cites approvingly (*Geography of Difference*, 4). See Gaston Bachelard, *The Poetics of Space*, trans. Maria Jolas (Boston, MA: Beacon Press, [1964] 1994; orig. pub. in French, 1958); Michel Foucault, "Of Other Spaces: Utopias and Heterotopias," trans. Jay Miskowiec, *Architecture/ Mouvement/Continuité* 5 (October 1984): 46–9; orig. delivered as a lecture in French, March 1967; quotations are taken from the Internet transcription, see http://web.mit.edu/allanmc/www/foucault1.

arguments are strengthened by Harry Berger, Jr.'s concept of the "second world." In Berger's analysis, Renaissance fiction differs from medieval by having increased greatly fiction's distance from the actual, thereby demonstrating Renaissance culture's valorization of the human mind and its imaginative power, a key index to what we think of as "Renaissance."[12] The play-world thus becomes fundamentally imaginative, self-contained, and even oppositional to the first world of actuality; indeed the cool "scientific" view of an indifferent primary world inspires in reaction a human and affect-rich second world. Berger thus establishes an historical foundation for poetical geography that puts it productively in tension with the undifferentiated space of scientific history: Here literature's figurative vision of place displays not simply a latent medievalism or reactionary cosmology but rather the vitalizing energies of the mind, including "the power of fiction to manipulate realities and to create a common ethos."[13]

Shakespearean Comedy and the Fascination with Italy

The prototypical second world of Shakespearean comedy is a fictionalized Italy, envisioned as a place of contradiction and transformation. Although certain of Shakespeare's other plays (*Romeo and Juliet, Othello, The Winter's Tale, Cymbeline*) employ Italian settings and although only a minority, five (*The Two Gentlemen of Verona, The Taming of the Shrew, The Merchant of Venice, Much Ado About Nothing*, and *All's Well That Ends Well*), of Shakespeare's some thirteen comedies are set entirely or partly there, Italy still functions as their emotional and conceptual motherland.[14] Yet Shakespeare possessed no first-hand knowledge of Italy; likewise, Elizabethans experienced the country as intensely real but also intensely evocative for the imagination. Not surprisingly, then, Shakespeare takes little interest in accuracy over details of Italian geography.[15]

---

pdf; Henri Lefebvre, *The Production of Space*, trans. Donald Nicholson-Smith (Oxford: Basil Blackwell, 1991; orig. pub. in French, 1974); Michel de Certeau, *The Practice of Everyday Life*, trans. Steven Rendall (Berkeley, CA: University of California Press, 1984). For a critique of these theorists, see Casey, *Fate of Place*, 285–330; also, from the perspective of early modern drama, see Lloyd Edward Kermode, "Experiencing the Space and Place of Early Modern Theater," *Journal of Medieval and Early Modern Studies* 43, no. 1 (Winter 2013): 1–24.

[12] Berger, "The Renaissance Imagination: Second World and Green World," and "The Ecology of Mind: The Concept of Period Imagination—An Outline Sketch," in *Second World and Green World*, 1–109. For the "second world," Berger invokes Meyer Abrams' term "heterocosm" (14); see M. H. Abrams, *The Mirror and the Lamp: Romantic Theory and the Critical Tradition* (New York: Norton [1953] 1958), 35 and *passim*.

[13] John Patrick Lynch, "Introduction," in Berger, *Second World*, xv–xxiii, on xviii.

[14] For *MA*, I treat Sicily as effectively a part of Italy. Sites for the other comedies include Ephesus (*CE*), Athens (*MND*), Windsor (*MW*), France (*LLL, AYL, AW*), and Vienna (*MM*).

[15] For example, Shakespeare mentions a nonexistent salt-water river between Verona and Milan, and hills in Mantua in *Two Gentlemen*; he locates Padua in Lombardy rather than the Veneto in *Shrew*; in *All's Well*, he sends Helen from Roussillon, France to St. James Compostela in Spain by way of Florence; and in *Merchant*, his Venetian ships range inaccurately as far as Mexico.

Some locales are lightly sketched. Messina in *Much Ado* lacks characterizing physical features almost entirely, as does Milan in *Two Gentlemen*. Although a patina of factuality was typically sufficient to Shakespeare, certain places do receive more detailing than others. Venice in *The Merchant of Venice* blossoms forth as atypically realistic: The city lies near Padua and its law school; gondolas and traghettos (or "traject[s]" [3.4.54]) ply its canals; the government extends cosmopolitan hospitality to foreign merchants; gabardine-clad Jewish moneylenders await the latest business news on the Rialto, where banking transactions for shipping expeditions historically took place; golden ducats are the coin of the realm; and even the play's overall sense of "hazarding" befits this great port of international trade that thrived on sea ventures.[16] Elizabethans attached special value to Venice because of its republicanism, expansive sea trade, openness to outsiders, religious tolerance, resistance to the Papacy, and courtesans (thousands, according to William Thomas). It was one of the Italian locales most visited by Shakespeare's countrymen.

For young Englishmen of means, Italy was a focus of what would eventually become known as 'the grand tour,' that finishing school of worldly education;[17] understandably so, since Italy stood as the birthplace of humanist letters and the fountainhead of sophistication and manners. The Italophilic William Thomas celebrates it as the international destination for pleasure and study.[18] (Thomas's *History of Italy*, published in 1549, was the first history in English to treat of contemporary Italy; the next year he produced the first Italian grammar book in English, *Principal Rules of Italian Grammar*). Italian Renaissance literature and treatises—Petrarch, Boccaccio, Castiglione, Ariosto, Machiavelli—were being translated into English and were strongly influencing Tudor writers. In drama,

---

[16] Shakespeare's knowledge of Venice aligns with the description in Gasparo Contarini's *The Commonwealth and Government of Venice*, trans. Lewis Lukenor (London, 1599); see Drakakis, *MV*, 5; also Gillies, *Geography of Difference*, 123–4. Aspects of *Merchant* reflect specific Italian sources, including Boccaccio's *Decameron* (c. 1351) and Giovanni Fiorentino's *Il pecorone* (Milan, 1558; available to Shakespeare only in Italian). *Merchant* does not mention the Jewish Ghetto, and it is unclear whether Shakespeare knew of its existence. It is not noted in either William Thomas's important *The History of Italy* (London, 1549) or in Lukenor. Shaul Bassi, however, argues that "the Ghetto is presupposed in *The Merchant of Venice*" as the basis of the play's exclusionary practices; *Shakespeare's Italy and Italy's Shakespeare: Place, "Race", Politics* (New York: Palgrave Macmillan, 2016), 150.

[17] See, among others, Edward Chaney, *The Evolution of the Grand Tour: Anglo-Italian Cultural Relations Since the Renaissance*, rev. edn. (Abingdon: Routledge, 2000); and Sara Warneke, *Images of the Educational Traveller in Early Modern England* (Leiden: Brill, 1995).

[18] Thomas's suggestive phrase is, "vnder pretence of studie" (sig. A1v). Andrew Hadfield describes Thomas's *History* as "undoubtedly the central influence on English perceptions of Italy" during the sixteenth century; "Shakespeare and Republican Venice," in *Visions of Venice in Shakespeare*, ed. Laura Tosi and Shaul Bassi (Farnham, Surrey: Ashgate, 2011), 67–82, on 68. Hadfield argues that Shakespeare's *Merchant* was influenced by Thomas's *History*. For a case study of Englishmen attending Italian universities, see Jonathan Woolfson, *Padua and the Tudors: English Students in Italy, 1485–1503* (Toronto: University of Toronto Press, 1998). For a helpful overview of Tudor England's growing knowledge of Italy, see the Introduction in *The History of Italy (1549) by William Thomas*, ed. George B. Parks (Ithaca, NY: Cornell University Press, 1963).

at least three Italian cinquecento comedies had received English adaptations by 1600;[19] other examples were undoubtedly known. Between 1579 and 1595, the London printer John Wolfe "issued twenty-five texts in Italian, fourteen in Latin written by Italian authors, and five English translations from Italian," summarizes Michael Wyatt.[20] This English fascination with Italy infected Shakespeare. He apparently learned Italian (perhaps under the influence of John Florio) in the mid-1590s, and he read sources in Italian for plays such as *The Merchant of Venice* and *Much Ado About Nothing*.[21] For Shakespeare and his countrymen, "[t]he idea of Italy," as Wyatt puts it, "took on a life of its own" (7).

Imaginative life in Shakespeare's comic Italy is essentially urban. Places consist largely of piazzas and campos (city squares, marts, undifferentiated public venues), houses, gardens, and occasional streets;[22] when Shakespearean comedy becomes pastoral it often feels English. The fictional city is cosmopolitan (particularly so in *The Merchant of Venice*), and includes foreigners and Italians from other cities. It is located primarily in the north (Venice, Verona, Milan, Padua, Florence), the single exception being *Much Ado*'s featureless Sicilian Messina. In this generic Italian city dwell prosperous merchants, aristocrats, some outsiders, and various servants; its elite characters include fathers, eligible daughters, and youthful suitors (but few mothers). Anachronistically, the speeches of the lower-class characters—such as Lance, Speed, Grumio, Launcelet,[23] and Dogberry—place them in England.[24] Real-world political conflicts between city-states or between a region and its foreign overlord recede from view. In *The Taming of the Shrew*, the Paduan interdict against Mantuans is only a hoax, and in *Much Ado*, Don John's defeated insurrection has no consequences, while the deep historical problems of the Spanish occupation of Italian Sicily, which form the play's background, turn virtually invisible, even though they figure importantly in the source material and in the analog Italian comedy, Giambattista della Porta's *Gli duoi fratelli rivali* (c.1590). When conflict arises between the Sicilian governor Leonato and his overlord, the Spanish Prince of Aragon, it never takes a political turn or makes bitter recourse to national stereotypes. Even an Italian comedy as

---

[19] Those include John Jefferey's (?) manuscript comedy *The Bugbears* (c. 1566), based on Anton Francesco Grazzini's *La spiritata* (c. 1561); George Gascoigne's *Supposes* (1566), adapted from Ludovico Ariosto's influential *I suppositi* (1509); and Anthony Munday's *Fedele and Fortunio* (1584), drawn from Luigi Pasqualigo's play, *Il fedele* (1576).

[20] Michael Wyatt, *The Italian Encounter with Tudor England: A Cultural Politics of Translation* (Cambridge: Cambridge University Press, 2005), 196.

[21] On Shakespeare's knowledge of Italian, see Jason Lawrence, *"Who the Devil Taught Thee So Much Italian?": Italian Language Learning and Literary Imitation in Early Modern England* (Manchester: Manchester University Press, 2005), 118–76. On the Italian community in London, see Wyatt, *Italian Encounter*.

[22] Jack D'Amico, *Shakespeare and Italy: The City and the Stage* (Gainesville, FL: University Press of Florida, 2001), e.g., 3.

[23] On "Launcelet," see Chapter 1, n. 3.

[24] D'Amico makes this point variously; see, e.g., 5, 59, 63, 66–7, 95, 131.

politically charged as *The Merchant of Venice* retains a conceptual dimension: What is justice, what mercy? There is something abstract, even mysteriously unreal, about this Italy.

One might wonder, then, why does Shakespeare make this so-lightly realized locale the metaphoric home of his comedy? To answer, let us consider two complementary characteristics as perceived by outsiders: Italy's contradictions and its openness to change and transformation, values that Shakespeare appropriates and heightens.

"a paradise inhabited by devils"

In the Elizabethan imagination, Italy was a vivid but precarious land of extreme contradictions, from internecine strife and personal vice to nascent utopianism. In Shakespeare's time, it existed as a group of wealthy and intensely competitive city-states jealous of their local identities and autonomy but also periodically overrun by Turks, Spanish, and French. One of the sub-themes of Italian cinquecento comedy, from Cardinal Bibbiena's *La calandra* (1512) to Alessandro Piccolomini's *L'alessandro* (1543) to della Porta's *Gli duoi fratelli rivali*, is the displacement of people—because of invasion, piracy, internecine conflict, and war—transmogrified into comedy. Italian comedies, like Shakespeare's, are full of travelers, many of them so by force. Elizabethans conceived of Italy as divided between qualitative extremes, a paradoxical combination of enlightenment and monstrosity, idealism and upheaval.[25] If the contradictions of human behavior are at the heart of comedy; then Italy's presumed moral dichotomies served Shakespeare's purposes well. On the positive side, Italy was perceived as the birthplace of humanist learning, the cradle of fine arts, the training-ground for the cultivation of manners, the center of cosmopolitanism, and the home of glittering wealth, elegant women, and "marvelous" sites (variations of *marvel* occur repeatedly in Thomas's *History*). On the negative side, it was perceived as the seat of demonic Catholicism (with the Pope as Antichrist), unmanly foppishness, labyrinthine political treachery, sensational violence (as in Nashe's *The Unfortunate Traveler* [1594]), and sexual lasciviousness and transgression (as also in Nashe). It could resemble, as Sir Henry Wotton said famously about Florence in 1592, "a paradise inhabited by devils."[26] This Italy's corrosive influence is famously reviled in Roger Ascham's *The Schoolmaster* (1570), Nashe's *The*

---

[25] Jonathan Bate, "The Elizabethans in Italy," in *Travel and Drama in Shakespeare's Time*, ed. Jean-Pierre Marquerlot and Michèle Willems (Cambridge: Cambridge University Press, 1996), 55–75.

[26] Logan Pearsall Smith, ed., *The Life and Letters of Sir Henry Wotton*, vol. 1 of 2 (Oxford: Clarendon Press, 1907), 281; noted in Bate, "Elizabethans in Italy," 56.

Unfortunate Traveler, and numerous other works[27]; likewise on stage, as in *The Jew of Malta* (*c.*1589), the Italianate Machiavel made for a figure of monstrosity.

Yet Italy's equal power to civilize emerges in writings such as Thomas's *History* or Castiglione's influential *The Courtier* (trans. Sir Thomas Hoby, 1561).[28] Thomas's work offers abundant information, but it also feels gossipy and selective and reads like a fiction. Thomas emphasizes the ill effects of tyrannical government, but he also attends to the endearing civility, customs, manners, and style of Italian living. Italy is a country of "pleasure" (sig. A2r), gustatory delight, and cultivated hospitality, helping to make it "the infinite resorte of all nacions" (sig. A2v); for commerce, it is "the principall place of recourse of all nacions" (sig. A2v). Through it flows the exotic merchandise of the East, and there one meets "Iewes, Turkes, Grekes, Moores and other easterly merchauntes" (sig. A2r). Thomas celebrates Italy's commercial goods, its wine and food (especially the fruit), and even its temperate weather. In Thomas's surveys of regional violence, the struggle for liberty and against tyranny emerges as a key through-line. He praises the justice and piety of Cosimo di Medici and the fidelity to friendship (at great personal risk) of Duke Frederick of Parma. He notes the public-minded street-planning in Ferrara, the respect for public oratory in Florence, the striking freedom of speech allowed to women in Genoa. Likewise, the importance of civic "liberty" forms a recurrent idea in Thomas's *History*. Within the narrative's record of turmoil, glimpses appear of an Italian communal harmony that seems apt for Shakespearean comedy. This Italy demands a complex response. Of Italian morals, Thomas remarks:

> For wheras temperance, modestie, and other ciuile vertues excell in the numbre of the Italian nobilitee, more than in the nobilitee of any other nacion that I knowe: so vndoubtedly the fleshely appetite with vnnaturall heate and other thynges in theim that be vicious, dooe passe all the termes of reason or honestie.
>
> (sig. A4v)

Perceiving a double dimension to Italy, Thomas cultivates a double perspective, one that reflects the humanist value of thinking *in utramque partem*, on both sides of the question. On the customs of Venice, Thomas cites a stranger's criticism of

---

[27] On the potentially corrupting influence of Italy as represented in books, see Michael J. Redmond, *Shakespeare, Politics, and Italy: Intertextuality on the Jacobean Stage* (Farnham, Surrey: Ashgate, 2009), 29–46.

[28] On the dueling images of Italy, see, among others, George B. Parks, "The Decline and Fall of the English Renaissance Admiration of Italy," *Huntington Library Quarterly* 31, no. 4 (August 1968): 341–57; Murray J. Levith, *Shakespeare's Italian Settings and Plays* (New York: St. Martin's Press, 1989), 1–11; Manfred Pfister, "Shakespeare and Italy, or, the Law of Diminishing Returns," in *Shakespeare's Italy: Functions of Italian Locations in Renaissance Drama*, ed. Michele Marrapodi, A. J. Hoenselaars, Marcello Cappuzzo, and L. Falzon Santucci (Manchester: Manchester University Press, 1993), 295–305, on 298; Bate, "Elizabethans in Italy,"; and especially D'Amico, *Shakespeare and Italy*, 1–20.

its citizens' covetousness and niggardliness, followed by a Venetian speaker's rebuttal: "If I be spare of liuyng, it is because my common wealth alloweth no pompe, and measure is holesome" (sig. Y4r). In the Venetian's view, parsimoniousness turns out to be communalism by another name.

Such works perhaps encouraged Shakespeare to imagine Italy as the quintessential fictive place where one must observe with "parted eye / When everything seems double" (*MND* 4.2.187–8). Shakespeare's comedies often toy with the possibility of tragedy, more so than do those of his peers; for that purpose, the dark volatility of Italy, its latent capacity for the monstrous, seems germane. Yet the comedies still emphasize the positive (more so the early comedies, less so the late ones). In an oft-cited essay, Mario Praz notes that Shakespeare largely avoids "the usual horrors and thrills" of Italy that other dramatists employ, preferring instead its "pure and noble" aspects.[29] According to Levith, Machiavellianism may leave its traces, as in Don John's cruel duplicity in *Much Ado* and Claudio's vicious pride,[30] but Shakespeare's comic depiction of Italy is largely favorable—arguably more so than for the Elizabethan public in general.

"transform me then"

Jack D'Amico argues convincingly that "Shakespeare's Italy was a society uniquely open to exchange and transformation," yet one familiar enough to be suggestive for the author's own urban world; "[t]hrough Italy ... Shakespeare could imaginatively project the promise and danger of a more open society" than that of his homeland.[31] The "openness," the relative social freedom, of the Italy-inflected comic world shows in the prominence and relative independence of its women: Julia and Sylvia, Katherine and Bianca, Portia and Jessica, Beatrice, Helen.[32] These females move about their worlds unimpeded, even if sometimes in disguise; they speak up with wit and intelligence more than equal to the men's; they are knowledgeable, pragmatic, and sensible. Italian sixteenth-century comedy contains certain empowered, even bold female characters, such as Lelia in *Gl' ingannati* (1531); likewise, that sourcebook of manners, *The Courtier* (1528), has the organizing force of Lady Elisabetta Gonzaga and the wit of the Lady Emilia Pia; and an earlier inspiration comes in Boccaccio's enterprising and persevering women in *The Decameron* (*c.*1353). But Shakespeare's empowered women surpass their continental exemplars in their initiative and their impact on the action—as if Shakespeare had taken a premise of Italian literature and extended its implications.

[29] Mario Praz, "Shakespeare and Italy," in *The Flaming Heart* (New York: Norton, 1958), 146–67, on 148.

[30] Levith, *Italian Settings*, 78.   [31] D'Amico, *Shakespeare and Italy*, 1.

[32] Two of Shakespeare's first three comedies are set in Italy (*TGV* and *TS*), while *The Comedy of Errors*'s Ephesus is Italianate in everything but name.

Shakespeare's Italianate women create the profile for those related female comic characters, such as Rosalind, who inhabit other venues.

Italy's literary image of openness for women sorts well with its reputation for cultivating transformative worldly experience and for learning. For Shakespearean comic characters, those two values can shear apart humorously; protagonists set out to study and to learn, but often with surprising results. Valentine will venture from Verona to Milan so that he might begin to "see the wonders of the world abroad" (*TGV* 1.1.6). Likewise, Proteus's father worries that his son "cannot be a perfect man / Not being tried and tutored in the world" (1.3.20–1); their Milanese adventure will be the refining fire for their values and sensibilities. Lucentio, having left Pisa and Florence behind, expresses his enthusiasm at arriving in "fair Padua, nursery of arts," where he will study the philosophy of "[v]irtue" as the source of "happiness" (*TS* 1.1.2, 18, 19). In response Tranio argues, "[n]o profit grows where is no pleasure ta'en" (39), the play proceeding to question the motivation for, and the process of, learning. Padua, *Shrew*'s opening locale, contained one of the oldest and greatest universities in Europe, a beacon to outsiders, including the English; Italy as a whole was replete with other such renowned institutions. Thus, Italian courts and cities provide Shakespeare with the apt setting for a fundamental trope of his comedies, the theme of education— usually treated ironically. In many of the early comedies, the action critiques conventional learning, as male would-be students—Proteus, Valentine, Lucentio, Narvarre and his friends—reject the study of books in favor of the study of women (sometimes citing book-wisdom to justify their abdication). Conversely, the collapse of the woefully inadequate male world—be it academic, courtly, military, or rhetorical—before the more complex and captivating world of women consti-tutes an Italianate backbone of Shakespearean comedy. Magical transformation arrives in unexpected form. Lucentio in *Shrew* emphasizes the enchanting power of Bianca over him. He suddenly feels "the effect of love-in-idleness" (the magical aphrodisiac of *A Midsummer Night's Dream* [1.1.150]), such that he instantly "burn[s]," "pine[s]," and "perish[es]" for Bianca (154). He likens himself extrava-gantly to Jove transformed to woo Europa (167–9), while for him Bianca is all sweet "sacred[ness]" (175); Tranio fears that Lucentio has fallen into a "trance" (176). In the pursuit of Italian education, the source of metamorphosis turns out to be, not book-learning, but the wild magic of romantic desire.

Italy's free-spiritedness helps to underwrite the possibility of comic enchant-ment and personal transformation, building out the Ovidian sense of metamor-phosis that so interested Shakespeare.[33] The widespread image of Italy as a land of

---

[33] On Shakespeare and Ovid, see, among others, William C. Carroll, *The Metamorphoses of Shakespearean Comedy* (Princeton, NJ: Princeton University Press, 1985); Jonathan Bate, *Shakespeare and Ovid* (Oxford: Clarendon Press, 1994), esp. 118–70; and Sean Keilen, "Shakespeare and Ovid," in *A Handbook to the Reception of Ovid*, ed. John F. Miller and Carole E. Newlands (London: Wiley-Blackwell, 2014), 232–45.

the artful performance of social roles, of *sprezzatura*, as in Castiglione's *The Courtier* and Sidney's *Defense of Poesy* (1595), deepens the sense of transformability or instability in the Italian character.[34] In Shakespeare's unreal, 'conceptual' Italy, sudden moments of serious, transformative insight can rock characters, recognition arriving with the force of metamorphosis. Early in the comic oeuvre, Proteus will be psychologically floored when he recognizes Julia in the final act of *Two Gentlemen*; at the far end of the canon, Bertram, having passed through Italy, will eventually have his own transformation, albeit belated and qualified.

Comic metamorphosis in Shakespeare draws resonance not only from Ovid but also from the Protestant interest in a transformative newness of life (as in St. Paul's New Testament Letter to the Romans). Such metamorphosis is personal—but not exactly private, not a lone encounter with a burning bush on the road to Damascus. Sometimes, as with Proteus and Lucentio, it entails a sense of competition, perhaps envy or jealously, even "mimetic desire."[35] At other times, it turns more communal and Catholic-tinged. The "sympathized one day's error" that the (necessarily Catholic) Abbess describes in *The Comedy of Errors* identifies an apparently providential occurrence shared by all the main characters, who seem equally to have drunk from "Circe's cup" (5.1.397, 271). A similar, unsettling instance of "minds transfigured so together" occurs in *A Midsummer Night's Dream* (5.1.24). Catholic communal spiritualism colors the visionary wisdom of Friar Francis in *Much Ado*, particularly his sense, after the broken nuptials, that Claudio's image of Hero will effect a transformation, as if she came to him like a visitant from the other world, preciously appareled and "[m]ore moving delicate and full of life / ... / Than when she lived" (4.1.228–30). While comic transformation may arrive in a flash of recognition, it typically proceeds from a participatory social experience. Herein lies one of the secrets of Italy for Shakespeare: It facilitates a combination of English Protestant and Ovidian individual transformation, but within the social context of an intense, mysterious, quasi-Catholic communalism.

Yet the magical transformational potential of this Italy entails a dark side, for its inhabitants possess a plasticity that can yield to monstrous and destructive impulses. In Milan, Proteus's desire for Sylvia alters him instantaneously into a mini-Machiavel, ready to betray his best friend and, in his thoughts, to kill off his formerly beloved Julia; Shylock devolves, from rage and frustration, into a merciless version of the beast that the racist Venetians already believe him to be; Claudio in his violent anger needlessly shames Hero in public; Beatrice, in response, importunes Benedick to "kill Claudio" and "would eat his heart in the marketplace" (*MA*, 4.1.288, 305); anger-filled Orsino is ready to murder Cesario-Viola,

---

[34] Bate, "Elizabethans in Italy," 61–3.
[35] On imitative desire in Shakespeare, see René Girard, *A Theater of Envy: William Shakespeare* (Oxford: Oxford University Press, 1991).

the thing he loves; Helen in Florence, decides suddenly, despite her pledge to the contrary, to force herself on Bertram through trickery. Italian openness of expression and fluidity of being allow characters to elevate or to compromise themselves (with Helen it is unclear which). Indeed, in *Much Ado*, powerful passions and the clear field of play that an 'open' society gives them, as in the "merry war" between Beatrice and Benedick (1.1.58), threaten at multiple moments to send the comedy hopelessly off the rails.

As part of its Otherness and even its quasi-Catholicism, Shakespeare's Italy always retains an aura of spiritual or magical values, of enchantment. Comic characters will metaphorically return from the dead, as do Julia, Hero, and Helen, while Katherine rises transformed (for better or worse) from the carnivalesque purgatory of Petruccio's household (on this topic, see Chapter 5). The same theme plays out subtly in *The Merchant of Venice*, where Portia herself functions as a kind of revenant. At the end of *The Comedy of Errors*, magic or an intervening providential grace remain active possible explanations, despite the Duke's rationalist sorting out of identities and personal histories; so too in *Dream*. A residual Catholic numinosity lingers over Shakespeare's Italian and other comedies, so that Italy as a place of humanistic enlightenment and pseudo-Protestant transformation intermingles with Italy as the heir of Ovidian magic and the breeding ground of Catholic sorcery.

Criticism and the Dialectics of Comic Geography

Like Italy's rationalism and magic, a principle of opposing values typically organizes a comedy's internal geography.[36] In perhaps the most influential theory of place and movement in Shakespearean comedy, Northrop Frye, using *The Two Gentlemen of Verona* as a prototype, argues that "the action of the comedy begins in a world represented as a normal world, moves into the green world, goes into a metamorphosis there in which the comic resolution is achieved, and returns to the normal world."[37] In Frye's view, Shakespeare adopts John Lyly and Robert

---

[36] The plays can be roughly grouped by their uses of place for peregrination or intrusion. Certain ones require the protagonists to journey from the city or court to a wood, forest, or retreat and typically back again; those include *Two Gentlemen*, *Dream*, *Merchant*, and *As You Like It*. Others are launched by an outsider or outsiders who intrude upon a specific locale; these are *Errors*, *Shrew*, *Love's Labour's Lost*, *Merry Wives of Windsor*, *Much Ado*, and *Twelfth Night*. But such distinctions are not hard and fast: In *Shrew*, for example, the protagonists also peregrinate; *Merchant* entails Portia's intrusion into Venice; and in *Much Ado* characters make recourse to the orchard as an alternative site, just as *Merry Wives*'s characters do with Windsor Forest. In *Errors* and *Twelfth Night*, furthermore, some protagonists regard the locale as normal while others find it enchanted or mad: the same place, opposite conceptions.

[37] Northrop Frye, "The Argument of Comedy," in *Theories of Comedy*, ed. Paul Lauter (Garden City, NY: Doubleday, 1961), 450–60, on 454; reprinted from *English Institute Essays 1948*, ed. D. A. Robertson (New York: Columbia University Press, 1949), 58–73. Alexander Leggatt refers to

Greene's model of romantic comedy but transforms it by crystalizing in it a "green world" that bespeaks medieval, festive folk ritual and that celebrates life and spring over death and winter. Frye's magical green world is a quasi-dream world symbolizing summer, resurrection, abundance, matriarchy, and nostalgic utopianism. Shakespeare's innovation of the green world makes his comedies original in their form, veering away from the legacy of Roman New Comedy, whose heir was Jonson.[38] Stanley Cavell sees its modern afterlife in the Hollywood comedies of the 1930s and 1940s.[39] C. L. Barber follows Frye but emphasizes comedy's aura of holiday and sets out an influential psychological formula for festive transformation: "from release to clarification."[40] For François Laroque, certain comic motifs can express aspects of specific Elizabethan festival days. He argues, for example, that in *A Midsummer Night's Dream*, Shakespeare associates "the popular May Day festival with a disordering of the senses and a loss of consciousness" related to potentially "ridiculous" erotic events.[41] Phebe Jensen likewise explores comic festivity, emphasizing its religious and spiritual dimension.[42] In a later essay, Laroque frames differently the dichotomy of Shakespeare's comic topographies: "real places" versus "dream-like backgrounds"[43] (although "real," like Frye's "normal," might merit qualification). Angela Locatelli sees in Shakespearean geography a sharply drawn "double axis" of "information and utopia, social criticism and idealisation, . . . description and prescription."[44] A few critics have invoked Michel Foucault's notion of "heterotopias" to describe alternative sites in

Frye's "still-influential analysis of Shakespearean comedy"; *English Stage Comedy: 1490–1990: Five Centuries of a Genre* (London: Routledge, 1998), 75. See also Northrop Frye, *Anatomy of Criticism: Four Essays* (Princeton, NJ: Princeton University Press, 1957), esp. 163–86.

[38] Notwithstanding, Raphael Lyne sees some Shakespearean debt to Plautus in the use of comic space; "Shakespeare, Plautus, and the Discovery of New Comic Space," in *Shakespeare and the Classics*, ed. Charles Martindale and A. B. Taylor (Cambridge: Cambridge University Press, 2004), 122–38.

[39] Stanley Cavell, *Pursuits of Happiness: The Hollywood Comedy of Remarriage* (Cambridge, MA: Harvard University Press, 1981), 1.

[40] C. L. Barber, *Shakespeare's Festive Comedy: A Study of Dramatic Form and its Relation to Social Custom* (Princeton, NJ: Princeton University Press, 1959), see 3–15. For a critique of Frye and Barber, see François Laroque, *Shakespeare's Festive World: Elizabethan Seasonal Entertainment and the Professional Stage*, trans. Janet Lloyd (Cambridge: Cambridge University Press, 1991), 192–6.

[41] Laroque, *Festive World*, 216.

[42] Phebe Jensen, *Religion and Revelry in Shakespeare's Festive World* (Cambridge: Cambridge University Press, 2008). From a more sociological perspective, see also Robert Weimann, *Shakespeare and the Popular Tradition of the Theater: Studies in the Social Dimension of Dramatic Form and Function*, ed. Robert Schwartz (Baltimore, MD: Johns Hopkins University Press, 1978; orig. pub. in German, 1967); and, although not about Shakespeare, Mikhail Bakhtin, *Rabelais and His World*, trans. Helen Iswolsky (Bloomington, IN: Indiana University Press, 1984; orig. pub. in Russian, 1965).

[43] François Laroque, "Shakespeare's Imaginary Geography," in *Shakespeare and Renaissance Europe*, ed. Andrew Hadfield and Paul Hammond (London: Thomson Learning, 2005), 193–219, on 193.

[44] Angela Locatelli, "The Fictional World of *Romeo and Juliet*: Cultural Connotations of an Italian Setting," in *Shakespeare's Italy: Functions of Italian Locations in Renaissance Drama*, ed. Michele Marrapodi, A. J. Hoenselaars, Marcello Cappuzzo, and L. Falzon Santucci (Manchester: Manchester University Press, 1993), 69–86, on 72.

the comedies.[45] John Gillies reads *The Merchant of Venice* in terms of "a primal drama of identity, difference and transgression."[46] Here Antonio stands for the tight, interlocking communal values of an Aristotelian city-state, and Shylock represents the threatening outsider from a hated race (at least for Antonio), the Jews, a species of barbarian. "More than just a 'Jew', Shylock is a 'stranger', an 'alien' and an 'infidel,'" says Gillies (128). The two characters represent the geographic center and the margin (the third place, Belmont, falls away in this discussion). Yet, argues Gillies, Shakespeare shows enormous ambivalence about those dichotomies by humanizing Shylock and likening Antonio to him in various ways (3, 122–37).[47]

Frye's argument that the comedies employ dichotomously organized worlds thus filters through virtually all commentary on Shakespeare's comic places. Notwithstanding, Harry Berger, Jr. offers useful refinements to Frye's dichotomy. As we have noted, the world of a fiction can be deemed a "second world" in contrast to the world of actuality in which readers and spectators live. If a second world is "normal," to recall Frye's adjective, it's normativity is that of an aesthetic realm, one "explicitly fictional, artificial, and hypothetical," with its own values and protocols, its own "gestalt," placed at one remove from the actual or real world.[48] The Venice of *The Merchant of Venice* and the Ilyria of *Twelfth Night* do not compose mirror images of existing actualities. Yet *Merchant*'s Venice still stands closer to quotidian reality than does Belmont, and the Ilyria in Orsino's mind hews closer to normalcy than the one in Sebastian's.[49] In Berger's system, then, Frye's green world becomes an idealized, pastoral, utopian fantasy, one of "clarity and simplicity" recollective of a golden world, within an already fictional one—a construct of the mind now twice removed from actuality compared to the

---

[45] E.g., Laurel Moffatt, "The Woods as Heterotopia in *A Midsummer Night's Dream*," *Studia Neophilologia* 76, no. 2 (2004): 182–7. Peter G. Platt applies "heterotopia" to Venice but concentrates on *Othello*; "'The Meruailouse Site': Shakespeare, Venice, Paradoxical Stages," *Renaissance Quarterly* 54, no. 1 (Spring 2001): 121–54, esp. 123–4. Heterotopias (from hetero-topia as "other-where") are real places that appear set off as "counter sites" where a culture's other real sites are "simultaneously represented, contested, and inverted"; they create a displacing mirror effect, as with cemeteries, reflecting in a way that is both real and unreal and that confers destabilizing potential; Foucault, "Utopias and Heterotopias," 46–9.

[46] Gillies, *Geography of Difference*, 12.

[47] Similarly, Elliot Krieger argues that the juxtaposed worlds of Shakespeare's comedies are "part of the same continuous representation of reality—single nature's double name"; *A Marxist Study of Shakespeare's Comedies* (London: Macmillan, 1979), 2, see 1–7.

[48] Berger, *Second World*, 16; "The second world is the playground, laboratory, theater, or battlefield of the mind, a model or construct the mind creates, a time of place it clears in order to withdraw from the actual environment" (11–12); "Frye does not clearly distinguish the actual normal world from the fictional 'world represented as a normal world'" (13). Frye's model may hint that the 'green world' is to the 'normal' play-world what the theatrical comedy is to the spectator's everyday world; Berger implicitly challenges any such view.

[49] Berger's concept of the second world contains a certain awkwardness, in that it is used to refer to the world of the artifact—for example, that of *The Merchant of Venice*—but it can also be applied more narrowly to a domain within that world—for example, Venice as opposed to Belmont—so that one needs a flexible sense of reference.

second world (14). Berger identifies two additional qualities of the green world: first, that it is itself capable of "change"; second, that it is "ambiguous" and, once its functions are fulfilled, even "inadequate" (36).[50] The green world poses the danger, according to Berger, of becoming an escapist hideaway, a land of lotus eaters. Berger's approach, stressing the green world as fundamentally imagined, removed, and unnatural, warns against embracing it naïvely.

According to Lisa Hopkin, the "'green world'" remains "the exemplary locus of the encounter in the world of Shakespearean comedy," even for a political perspective such as hers.[51] Frye's green world figures especially in present-day ecological critiques of Shakespeare, for which comedy emerges as a crucial genre. Steve Mentz declares that Frye's green-world model "has proved foundational for thinking about the relationship between the natural world and comic form," even as it is variously reconfigured.[52] Modifying Joseph W. Meeker's argument that comedy—as the genre that favors community, accommodation, adaptation, and muddling-through—comports better than does tragedy with ecological values,[53] Mentz warns that an idealized green world can promote deceptive notions of homeostasis and harmony in nature, against which he advocates a corrective ecocriticism attuned to "change and disruption in natural systems" (250). Mentz's paradigm is "blue oceanic disorder," which he finds lurking in the interstices of Shakespeare's comedies (250). Mentz endorses Berger's vision of the green world as dynamic and "ambiguous"—although the danger resides in the mind for Berger and in the natural world for Mentz (252).[54] Thus reconceptualized and critiqued, the green world along with the second world have proven to be durable models for investigating the function of place in Shakespearean comedy.

In attempting to outline those worlds within the plays, however, one may find that a large, somewhat unruly, flock of adjectives starts to take wing. Each locus of value calls forth a Wittgensteinian family of descriptors rather than any set, essential, and defining features. Thus, at the second-world pole, we have attributes that evoke nouns and adjectives such as prosaic, workaday, established, centered, predictable (with associated terms such as law, hierarchy, reason, patriarchy, and

---

[50] "Those who wish to remain, who cannot or will not be discharged, are presented as in some way deficient" (Berger, *Second World*, 36), a comment that weighs against characters such as Jaques. In that regard, the "negative aspect" of the green world "projects the urge of the paralyzed will to give up, escape, work magic" (36).

[51] Lisa Hopkins, "Comedies of the Green World: *A Midsummer Night's Dream, As You Like It*, and *Twelfth Night*," in *The Oxford Handbook of Shakespearean Comedy*, ed. Heather Hirschfeld (Oxford: Oxford University Press, 2018), 520–36, on 520.

[52] Steve Mentz, "Green Comedy: Shakespeare and Ecology," in Hirschfeld, *Oxford Handbook, op. cit.*, 250–62, on 250. See also Steve Mentz, *At the Bottom of Shakespeare's Ocean* (New York: Continuum, 2009).

[53] Joseph W. Meeker, *The Comedy of Survival: Studies in Literary Ecology* (New York: Scribner's, 1972).

[54] See also William N. West, *As If: Essays in* As You Like It (Goletta, CA: Punctum Books, 2016) 47–52.

state authority). Conversely, at the green-world end, we have enchantment, allegory, marginality, play, holiday (with associated values such as inversion, matriarchy, passion, permeability, and metamorphosis). Altogether, they suggest variations on the differences between reason and fantasy, as in Alma's representatively Renaissance tripartite division of the mind (*The Faerie Queene*, 2.9.48–54), or, psychologically, the super-ego in contest with the id. Perhaps we might use 'regulative' versus 'protean' to stand for the two general categories. Regulative locales display custom, consistency, and logocentrism, while protean ones suggest mutability, multiplicity, and magic. Of course, as Gillies warns, we might assume that an opposition reveals an ultimate truth only to find it exposed as a penultimate falsehood. Antitheses may turn out to have characteristics in common, while the very act of seeing the world dualistically may overlook other important categories.

The Regulative, the Protean, and Their Discontents

Seemingly exclusionary oppositions can share qualities and overlap: In *Merchant*, racism, materialism, and patriarchy, for example, touch not only the center but also the margin; and not only Venice, with its citizens and aliens, but also Belmont. Or they can exchange qualities: Arden Forest exhibits more civility and less violence than does Duke Frederick's court. Likewise, as we shall see, each kind of locale can contain its own inconsistencies, instabilities, and dangers, and each undergoes comic critique. Emphasis on such dichotomies tends, unfortunately, to marginalize the problem comedies, where the regulative world dominates and the protean world loses much of its oppositional distinctiveness (in *Measure for Measure*, the protean world is the prison, which might be considered heterotopian; in *All's Well* it is Florence and its martial field, a peculiar variation on the pastoral).

The regulative world is typically that of the civilized city or court, while the protean world makes its home in bordering nature: woods, forests, outskirts, and orchards. In Shakespeare's comedies, the civilized center is exposed as calcified, closed off, or distorted in specific ways—far from ideal or "normal." The patriarchy in *A Midsummer Night's Dream* stifles youthful love, as it also does in *The Two Gentlemen of Verona*, and elsewhere. In *As You Like It*, proper relations within families have succumbed to envy and paranoid authoritarianism (showing the precariousness of the primogenitorial system). Similarly, the equilibrium of *The Merry Wives of Windsor* is thrown off-kilter by male sexual jealousy and parental rigidity. Tyranny in law and lust drive the Viennese governor Angelo in *Measure for Measure*. In *Merchant*'s Venice, commerce, law, and religio-ethnic exclusiveness operate with cruel agency. Characters in *The Taming of the Shrew* forge marriage contracts on the assumption of conventional female stereotypes that the action blows sky-high. *Love's Labour's Lost* and *Much Ado About Nothing* present male worlds—one of monastic scholarship, the other of pseudo-military aggressiveness—that fail to accommodate or comprehend women or even the male characters' full range of feelings. In *The Comedy of Errors*, Ephesus offers an environment of troubled marriage and humdrum commerce, with no place for the quasi-magic recursions that will afflict (or save) it. Sites of regulation fail according to an Aristotelian ethic, for the city (or court or home) has lost its moderation and equilibrium and suffered a perversion of its proper values.

Social or political breakdown of sufficient depth can make the possibility of healing from within unlikely or unachievable. Some corruptions derive, at least on the surface, from individual characters, such as the autocrat Duke Frederick. Some reveal the bias and blindness of a class or group, as with the gallants of *Much Ado About Nothing*. Some reflect pervasive, but increasingly questionable, cultural practices, such as the father's tyrannical power in *A Midsummer Night's Dream*. Worse, others seem resiliently systemic, as in the early-modern capitalism of Venice. Consequently, the outcasts of *As You Like It* can be easily restored by Duke Frederick's abrupt forest conversion, while the social problems that linger at the end of *The Merchant of Venice* threaten to persist.

In these plays social and political problems are confronted not from within, through reform, or revolution inside the pre-exiting system, but from without, by a change of venue (or a changed way of perceiving) that constitutes a reorientation of social relations and individual psyches and a new venture into imaginative possibility—not unlike theater itself. For how does one change the world? By hurling one's intellectual and physical energies against the corrupt power structure? Yes, sometimes—but neither Brutus, nor Hamlet, nor Coriolanus leaves a better world behind him. The comedies dream differently, even fantastically, of transformation. Yet one must avoid stating the case too optimistically or categorically, for different plays entertain different conjectured futures. In the protean world, characters will be altered, but whether the power of their metamorphoses can truly reform the regulative world often remains in question. Shakespearean comedy sometimes sets up such strong second world and green world polarities, furthermore, that their far distance from each other can potentially defeat the possibility of moral reconciliation. That difficulty helps to explain why Shakespeare's problem comedies contain less obvious, more diminished protean worlds than do the early plays, for the values of the alternative environment have come to appear fragile or evanescent against the intransigence of a city such as Vienna or even a character such as Bertram. We find ourselves once more at the crux of Renaissance comedy, which often raises social problems greater than any individual play can solve and which offers not pat answers but provocations to emotional awareness and thinking. In that respect, the dialectic of regulative and protean places goes far to illuminate the conceptual tensions within Shakespearean comedy and, even more, to illuminate how much politics in the comedies becomes alchemized into the dialectics of place.

In contrast to the regulative world, the protean enclave exists at the edge of, or a remove from, the city and court. It can be the Forest of Arden in *As You Like It*, or the Athenian Wood in *A Midsummer Night's Dream*, or the wood outside Milan in *The Two Gentlemen of Verona*, or Windsor Forest in *The Merry Wives of Windsor*. The "orchard" or "garden" in *Much Ado About Nothing* serves the same purpose (1.2.9, 5.1.175; we shall return to the orchard), as does the field outside the court in *Love's Labour's Lost*. In *The Merchant of Venice*, Belmont ("beautiful mountain") constitutes the metaphoric protean (or golden) world, as profuse in riches as Venice is cash-strapped. In *The Taming of the Shrew*, the world of transformation might be identified as Petruccio's country estate near Verona, or sometimes that in-between place, the road running from Verona to Padua. In the larger context of Christopher Sly's "flattering dream or worthless fancy" (Induction 1.43), however, the green world is the play-within-the-play itself (setting up parallels for *Shrew*'s actual spectators). An equally complicated pattern is evident in *The Comedy of Errors* and *Twelfth Night* where everyday worlds are disrupted by the intrusions of strangers. In the former play, the "normal" world and the fantasy world are the same, for Ephesus, viewed from different perspectives, appears to be either bourgeois or supernatural. In the latter play, Viola brings her transgressiveness into a place that is already a little mad, as in the melancholy of Olivia's upstairs and the misrule of Sir Toby's downstairs. Like Ephesus, Illyria—suggesting illusion, lyricism, Elysium, and delirium[55]—functions as its own protean world.

In Tudor and Elizabethan drama (and especially in romance plays), places can have magical powers but with less a sense of systematic differentiation by locale than in Shakespearean comedy. *Gammer Gurton's Needle* (*c*.1553), an important early Tudor farce, evokes a sense of unpredictable possibility by shrouding a familiar place with a new sense of magic and mystery. The anonymous *Rare Triumphs of Love and Fortune* (pub. 1589) employs the forest as implicitly a locale of magical possibility and of opportunity, where problems created within the court might potentially be addressed; but the oppositions in the play arise not so much between places as between the goddesses Love and Fortune. In George Peele's comic romance *The Old Wives' Tale* (1590), a story narrated by Madge, the old woman, suddenly takes over the whole play, so that it turns into a scene for conjuring, magical events, spirits of the dead, and a mysterious head rising from a well; but those properties and the dreamscape in which they occur exist not for

---

[55] Laroque, "Imaginary Geography," 211. For a different kind of argument, that Shakespeare's choice of the location had to do with "the region's concrete historical and geopolitical associations," see Elizabeth Pentland, "Beyond the 'Lyric' in Illyricum: Some Early Modern Backgrounds to *Twelfth Night*," in Twelfth Night: *New Critical Essays*, ed. James Schiffer (London: Routledge, 2011), 149–66, on 149.

thematic contrast but for their own sake. The comedic, magical, and protean possibilities of the forest are best realized, among Shakespeare's predecessors, by John Lyly. His *Gallathea* (c.1584) sends its sacrificial maidens, comic pages, charlatans, nymphs, and goddesses into a wood where they mix and intersect like characters in an Italian city but where the possibilities of enchantment are also considerably heightened. Shakespeare surely learned from Lyly's use of place. Perhaps most suggestive for a comedy such as *As You Like It* were the various generically hybrid Robin Hood plays extant in Shakespeare's time, plays such as Anthony Munday's paired works *The Downfall* and *The Death of Robert Earl of Huntington*, both composed presumably in 1598. In those plays, Robin, hiding in Sherwood Forest, afflicts the nobility, aids the poor, and expresses egalitarian values. Yet none of the earlier comedies thinks so systematically as do Shakespeare's about oppositions such as regulative and protean locales. And none evoke the green world as such a manifestation of the imagination as do Shakespeare's comedies.

For those plays, in contrast to earlier works, proteanism brings into comedy cultural and human values that unfold fan-like one from another: resurrection, magic, metamorphosis, youth, sexuality, love, femininity, spring, and nostalgia for the utopianism of the Golden Age—characteristics again clustering family-like. Here fairies might cast enchantments, or a bloodthirsty duke might encounter "an old religious man" and instantly abandon all worldly ambitions (*AYL*, 5.4.158). The comedies express a politics of fecundity against the regulative restraints of legalism or patriarchal tyranny. Such locales are, as a whole, sites of wish-fulfillment—conscious and unconscious, and not always flattering. Belmont, as Walter Cohen observes, constitutes an anti-capitalist fantasy-site where wealth drops like manna and one finds relief from the crushing anxieties of the mercantile world, yet it also embraces materialism and social exclusion (see Chapter 6).[56] In *A Midsummer Night's Dream*, the lush wetness and darkness of the Athenian Wood drenches it in the sexuality blocked in Athens, yet the wood gives expression, as well, to shadowy, repressed desires of quasi-masochism and sexual violence. The protean world can be limited or even threatening—an interesting place to visit, but one might not want to live there.

But what about a site such as the orchard or garden in *Much Ado About Nothing*, which exudes only a whiff of greenness? What has it to do with fantasy or desire? The orchard exists close to the glittering court, as a peripheral place for private conversation or solitary withdrawal, away from the more formal, communal spaces in Leonato's Messinian palazzo. Antonio hints at its atmosphere in the phrase, "the thick-pleached alley in mine orchard" (with "thick-pleached" meaning "lined by closely woven intertwined branches" [1.2.8–9, 1.2.8n.], presumably

---

[56] Walter Cohen, "*The Merchant of Venice* and the Possibilities of Historical Criticism," *English Literary History* 49, no. 4 (Winter 1982): 765–89.

identical with the "arbour" to which Benedick later retires [3.2.34]). Metaphorically, this densely interwoven orchard signals shroudedness, complexity, and intrigue, although those colorations are brushed in only lightly. The orchard is where Claudio and Don Pedro are twice misheard planning the courtship of Hero;[57] where Benedick and Beatrice are separately tricked into believing that each loves the other; and where, less remarked, Don John brings Don Pedro and Claudio to witness the duplicitous and catastrophic window scene. (The "orchard" is mentioned five times, from 1.2 to 5.1, so that it is persistently, if subtly, brought to consciousness; "garden," "arbour," and "bower" each occur once, and the place is also likened to the Garden of Eden [5.1.174–5].) The orchard is a site of intimate conversation, eavesdropping, deception, self-reflection, and transformation (for better or worse). Benedick goes there to read and contemplate, while his beguilers follow ostensibly to appreciate the "still" evening and to enhance its "harmony" with music (3.3.36, 37). In such an orchard, characters become unusually vulnerable to suggestion and their emotions can spring wildly to life. The place lacks the psychological depths of the Athenian Woods; rather, it lies very close to Messina's social surface and thereby illustrates how easily (and willingly) characters in the social world can go astray or be misled (by others, themselves) in an unguarded moment, their protean potential ignited in this place suggestive of greenness. The orchard approaches Foucault's heterotopia, as a reflection, a revelation of the character of the regulative world, and yet it remains enough apart to offer the possibility of change.

The Magic of Arden Forest

At the opposite extreme from *Much Ado*'s orchard lies Shakespeare's most complexly protean locale, the Forest of Arden in *As You Like It*. The play organizes itself in terms of place. "Know you where you are, sir?" asks the enraged Oliver of Orlando (1.1.38), asserting his primogenitorial identity in terms of property ownership.[58] Likewise, the malignant Duke Frederick dominates his world by dispossessing his brother, forcing him into exilic vagabondage in Arden Forest. The political issues of the play, too, map themselves by locale. As critics have pointed out, the play's depiction of the forest casts intermittent light on Elizabethan rural political and economic problems of hunger, poverty, vagrancy, enclosure, exploitive land-ownership, and even hunting.[59] Those

---

[57] There is some confusion here, for Antonio reports the conversation as overheard in his "orchard" (1.2.9), while Borachio describes hearing it while he was perfuming "a musty room" (1.3.55).

[58] On primogeniture in the play, see Louis Adrian Montrose, "'The Place of a Brother' in *As You Like It*: Social Process and Comic Form," *Shakespeare Quarterly* 32, no. 1 (Spring 1981): 28–54.

[59] For a valuable review of criticism on those matters, see Andrew Barnaby. "The Political Conscious of Shakespeare's *As You Like It*," *Studies in English Literature* 36, no. 2 (Spring 1996): 373–95. On political-ecological issues, see Randall Martin, *Shakespeare and Ecology* (Oxford: Oxford University Press, 2015), 56–77.

troubles fester at the edge of the romantic action: Even though they provide "an almost subliminal source of conflict," they never "swamp" the play.[60] The forest instead evokes nostalgia for a prelapsarian golden world of "liberty" (1.3.135) where men "live like the old Robin Hood" (1.1.110–11) in communitarian brotherhood, free from political strife, and in harmony with nature.[61] Arden combines an overarching pastoralism with the popular pre-Reformation festivity of the merry men in Sherwood Forest[62] (the specifically English countryside coloring the protean world). No "perils" from the "envious court" exist there, says Duke Senior; instead, the forest's cold winds "'feelingly persuade me what I am'" (2.1.4, 11). Yet the sweet adversity of the forest always registers as imagined and somewhat forced. As Alexander Leggatt notes, the different characters who come to Arden actually "find in it reflections of themselves"; furthermore, the forest world is "touched with thoughts and images" of the court world, even as the court world is touched by it.[63] Mirroring back, Berger-like, the minds of its inhabitants, the forest is not truly *sui generis*. Nor is the forest the place of simple truth that Duke Senior claims, for his men's sentimental pastoralism, brotherly utopianism, and anthropomorphizing of creatures are exaggerated so much as to seem self-parodying. The forest's liberties, such as the liberty to love in the springtime of youth, are utterly consuming and simultaneously a little ridiculous, as Rosalind so vibrantly shows.[64]

To its inhabitants and observers, the forest gives back the power—really, the experience—of multiple perspectives, wound to the highest pitch, a way of being transported to the fullest of one's passions and of embracing, too, the probable absurdity of the experience, as itself part of the ardency. Personal metamorphosis can occur not only because the forest affords liberty but also because it engenders an open welcoming of paradox (as Touchstone implies). Characters adopt different views of the forest and experience their changes differently, William West points out.[65] In the spirit of multiple perspectives, *As You Like It* also repeatedly calls attention to the theatricality of events in Arden, to its constructed, disguise-happy, posturing, self-absorbed play-world.[66] In Arden, we know love to be true because it turns out to be much like going to a play.

Arden Forest becomes finally an elusive, changeable-taffeta place, weaving realistic details into its essential fantasticality. As Arden editor Juliet Dusinberre notes, it is detailed with life-like "great oak trees, running brooks, green pastures,

[60] James Shapiro, *A Year in the Life of William Shakespeare: 1599* (New York: HarperCollins, 2005), 245.
[61] Robert N. Watson argues that the play showcases a late Renaissance and Protestant desire to return to origins and essences but that it treats that unattainable goal wryly; *Back to Nature: The Green and the Real in the Late Renaissance* (Philadelphia, PA: University of Pennsylvania Press, 2008), 77–107.
[62] See Jensen, *Religion and Revelry*, 117–48.
[63] Leggatt, *Stage Comedy*, 80.
[64] See, e.g., Barber, *Festive Comedy*, 222–39.
[65] West, *As If*, 46–52.
[66] Leggatt, *Stage Comedy*, 80–1.

banks of willows, flowers, birds, sheep and deer."[67] Old shepherds, young shepherds, foresters, goat-girls, and priests populate it, along with a band of cave-
dwelling outcast lords. Yet the flora extends, less credibly, to palm-trees and a "tuft
of olives" (3.5.76), and the fauna includes not only great snakes but also lions (a
lioness proves easy to defeat in hand-to-paw combat). Despite its details, Arden
Forest always feels more abstract than localized. And it changes before our eyes.
When we first enter there, in Act Two, the forest is wintry, cold, dense, and
dangerous; Orlando attacks Duke Senior's encampment as if expecting to confront
the kinds of outlaws Valentine meets in *Two Gentlemen*. Act Two, argues Ruth
Nevo, piles up "disjunctive contraries," including court and country, wisdom and
folly, and other dichotomies, creating "attitudes of indecision" or "quasi-
dilemma," with everybody "talking philosophically."[68] All dither, little momentum. Yet season, place, and possibility shift miraculously in Act Three. In modern
productions, sunny springtime always reigns there, the trees glistening brightly
with green leaves and love sonnets. The dark woods have given way to pleasant
cornfields, cultivated acres of rye, and sheepcotes, where two young exiles live "in
the purlieus" (or forest outskirts) (4.3.75).[69] Feeble old Adam is displaced by the
able Corin, and even he is pushed aside by the more youthful and energetic Silvius
and William. As West concludes, the forest is "unplaceable";[70] it exists not as a
location but as a prismatic spectrum of colors. Indeed, the more one progresses
into Arden Forest, the less realistic it becomes and the more it exerts a magical,
idealizing pull, yet always a bit preposterously.

The forest has an "ambiguous" aspect, to return to Berger's and Mentz's term,
but not exactly because it entails escapist fantasies or oceanic threats. Rather, the
forest's ambiguity inheres in its incapacity to satisfy the very emotions that it
arouses, and in that respect it might be paradigmatic of the green world. In Arden
Forest, desires and longings skyrocket, concupiscence thrives, and passions soar to
a fever pitch, but the place endlessly defers their fulfillment. Rosalind experiences
ecstasy over Orlando, proclaiming to Celia, "that thou didst know how many
fathom deep I am in love! But it cannot be sounded" (4.1.193–4). Orlando, like his
namesake, is virtually mad with love: "Run, run, Orlando, carve on every tree /
The fair, the chaste and unexpressive she!" (3.2.9–10). Here everyone falls in love
"'at first sight'" (3.5.82). Arden's elevated passions recall the effect of the woods in
A Midsummer Night's Dream or even the orchard in *Much Ado*. Yet Arden Forest

[67] Dusinberre, *AYL*, 51.
[68] Ruth Nevo, "Existence in Arden," in *William Shakespeare's* As You Like It, ed. Harold Bloom
(Broomall, PA: Chelsea House Publishing, 2004), 21–37, on 25, 27; orig. pub. in Nevo, *Comic
Transformations in Shakespeare* (New York: Methuen, 1980).
[69] Martin identifies the woods where Duke Senior lives, pastures where Corin grazes sheep,
cultivated corn and rye fields, interconnecting streams and rivers, and adjoining human domains
such as Oliver's estate; *Shakespeare and Ecology*, 17–18. Notwithstanding, the play does not etch such
distinctions sharply.
[70] West, *As If*, 46.

fills out the green-world model, for here characters also suffer love's deferrals. Phoebe becomes instantly enraptured with Rosalind-as-Ganymede but is destined for disappointment. Silvius, besotted with love for Phoebe, serves her slavishly even though he recognizes his hopelessness. Rosalind turns prickly over Orlando's impunctuality: "An you serve me such another trick, never come in my sight more!" (4.1.36–7). Orlando, his emotions set ablaze by Rosalind's theater of unconsummated wooing, concludes famously and emblematically, "I can live no longer by thinking" (5.2.49). Even poor William suffers the loss of his courtship of Audrey, brow-beaten out of it by Touchstone. Low-grade irritations and disruptions reach other characters. Celia seems peculiarly annoyed by Rosalind's amorous play: "You have simply misused our sex in your love-prate!" (4.1.189–90). Touchstone wants Sir Oliver Mar-Text to marry Audrey to him hurriedly but oddly abandons the priest and his offices on a sudden impulse (after Jaques disparages Sir Oliver's services for the very reason that Touchstone prefers them). The one character who lives by thinking, Jaques, remains a melancholic, having "gained nothing" from his worldly observations; his melancholy travels and observations have merely wrapped him "in a most humourous sadness" (4.1.17). Desire and, surprisingly, its disappointment serve as the coordinates of Arden Forest. In that place, you can never quite get what you want, and you remain a little unsettled, even irritated, transformed and ready but with nowhere to go. If Arden provides satisfaction, it will only arrive in some imagined future, perhaps fittingly so for a locale that seems conjured forth by the hypothetical "as if."[71] Satisfaction will come finally when characters, at play's end, conclude their sojourn and leave the forest metaphorically (even though some will literally stay). The ambiguity of Arden Forest forms a part of its mystery.

Whence comes all that magical pull, that capacity to transform, to arouse and defer, to obscure even "the polarity of real and ideal"?[72] One might answer that Arden Forest is presided over by its own magical and ineluctable spirit, a genius of the place. That spirit manifests itself in Rosalind, of course, the improvisational, fantastically imaginative "trickster / heroine," as if from folklore, who can call the gods down from the heavens.[73] The magical spirit is further manifested in the figure of Ganymede's "old religious uncle," himself also "a great magician / Obscured in the circle of this forest" (3.2.332, 5.4.33–4), as if the forest itself were alive with prestidigitation. Indeed, the magician-hermit not only casts ghostly spells in the background but finally becomes fully materialized, born out of Rosalind's imagination into the authentic "old religious man" whom Duke Frederick meets and whose conversation converts the vengeful Duke "from his

---

[71] West, *As If*, 46.   [72] Dusinberre, *AYL*, 51.
[73] For "trickster / heroine," see Nevo, "Existence," 22; Maurice A. Hunt argues that the god Hymen itself (not some character acting the part) appears in the ending; *Shakespeare's* As You Like It (New York: Palgrave Macmillan, 2008), 41–7.

enterprise and from the world" (5.4.158, 160)[74] (see Chapter 4 on the comic device of 'manifestation'). Historically, Arden Forest was associated with pilgrimage, penance, and conversion, notes Dusinberre, values captured and elaborated by Shakespeare.[75] Not only is the forest a place of magic and "conversion" (4.3.135)—for Duke Frederick, for Oliver, for Orlando in saving Oliver—it also "surrounds all who enter it with images of pilgrimage" (96). The forest, too, is peculiarly animate. It " 'feeling persuade [s]' " Duke Senior of who he is; it harbors "tongues in trees, books in the running brooks, / Sermons in stones, and good in everything" (2.1.11, 16–17). It even listens: "let the forest judge," says Touchstone to Rosalind (3.2.119). Spirit pervades.

Arden Forest has gone from being a frigid, desperate, holding pen of social maladies to a magic circle of conversion and impatient wonder: "O wonderful, wonderful and most wonderful, and yet again wonderful" (3.2.186–7). In its range, it represents the protean multiplicity of perspectives that its inhabitants ideally achieve. In such a place, at its extreme, one might imagine the goddess Hymen really appearing, as Maurice Hunt argues. The values of the forest remain those slightly naïve utopian ones that characters state so abundantly: brotherhood, neighborliness, hospitality, generosity, honesty, simplicity, and contentment (even though social ranks have not been entirely abandoned)—all of those irradiated by love, playfulness, and joyous exuberance—but with their consummation still held in abeyance. In such a protean place, identities can be discovered, clarified, developed, and transformed, even though their fulfillment requires removal from the forest. The finale of As You Like It occurs at such a psychic distance from the play's earlier allusions to dispossession, poverty, and hunger that perhaps one can be forgiven for suspecting that the virtues of the magical forest might struggle to cure the ills of society. Nevertheless, one must start from somewhere.

Geography and Agency

The critical models of transformative comic geography return us to the question of whether a place itself can have causal power. In comedy, some things can occur only in a given locale: You must go to the Athenian Wood, for example, to find "love-in-idleness" (Dream, 2.1.168). As we have seen with Arden Forest, certain places radiate psychological, transformational, and even magical powers that are associated only with them. Those associations reflect the human inclination to behave as if objects or places possessed essences.[76] But what then of human

---

[74] See Dusinberre, AYL, 95.   [75] Dusinberre, AYL, 96, 4.3.135n.

[76] On what psychologists consider the instinctive and universal characteristic of humans to treat things (here locales) and people as if they had hidden, invisible essences, see Paul Bloom, How Pleasure Works: The New Science of Why We Like What We Like (New York: Norton, 2010).

agency? Are the denizens of comedy simply acted upon by external forces? The evidence is mixed, and the answer can vary with one's perspective. Laroque teases out one aura- and language-centered way that Shakespearean comic transformation might work: "Under the influence of festivity, words begin to bubble and fizz like a fermentation"; language becomes playful, intoxicated, and "stumble[s] in unexpected directions,"[77] so that a wit-game can open up a character's consciousness. In this atmosphere, the outpouring of verbal dexterity corresponds to "the dawning of a new awareness" (196). For Laroque, causal power resides more in festivity than in place *per se*: "Festivity... produces an intoxication endowed with the power of metamorphosis" (198). If bubbling wit in Shakespearean comedy is not always an expression of place, conversely not all comic transformations— Demetrius's for example—are prompted by verbal ingenuity.

Let us map out some possibilities for the power of place to effect transformation. At the negative end, in the late comedies the magic of place decreases. *All's Well's* locale of potential change is faraway Florence and its field of honor. There a game of deception—as embarrassing as it is humorous—publicly exposes the truth about Parolles. In Florence, Helen reverses herself dubiously and reinvents her intentions, while Bertram learns about Parolles's dishonorableness but discovers nothing about his own. Only when Helen metaphorically returns from the dead at the French court will Bertram finally undergo a seeming conversion. This comedy disturbs in part because of the limited efficacy of its protean places.

In some comedies, more positively, the festive locale operates as a condition for transformation but not as the direct cause. In *The Taming of the Shrew*, Petruccio needs the freedom of his remote home to work his device for subduing Katherine, that device itself being a form of aggressive, almost abusive, festivity. The topsy-turvydom of his household makes it an appropriate staging-ground, but the relationship between place and transformation is mainly opportunistic. The orchard in *Much Ado* possesses affective powers not obvious but insidious. It functions, as we have noted, as the retreat for intimacy and music, where characters are vulnerable to suggestion and deception because the locale itself puts them in a receptive mood, with guards down. Here place facilitates, almost causes, the change associated with a freeing of perspective. If the orchard is the place of conspiracy, as between Claudio and Don Pedro to woo Hero, it is also the place of complicity, the unacknowledgeable complicity of Benedick with his deceivers, and of Beatrice with hers, the tricksters fabricating and the gulls willing to believe extravagant fantasies. It is also the place where feelings and desires are heightened. Altogether, the orchard allows the lovers to act. What may surprise about the orchard is the scale of transformational power that it unleashes in comparison to the slightness of its difference from other spaces in the play, for only in the

---

[77] Laroque, *Festive World*, 195.

orchard can Benedick and Beatrice instantly reverse themselves, burst into passion, and embrace the concept of love and the specific love objects that, before, they had obdurately dismissed. This surprise of scale fits with a play whose protagonists are often given to overreactions. In *The Two Gentlemen of Verona*, place has even more causal power. Proteus turns would-be rapist in the forest, but there, too, the Duke, on the merest pretext, gives over his resistance to Valentine as a suitor, and the unreliable outlaws are suddenly rehabilitated as "men endued with worthy qualities," "reformed, civil, full of good" (5.4.151, 154). Metamorphosis here relates to locale and equally to a change in perspective.

Finally, place might sometimes be itself the product of characters' desires.[78] In *As You Like It*, characters remark on properties of Arden Forest that, as we have noted, often reflect their perspectives or obsessions, as if place and selfhood were reacting chemically with each other. Even more, the forest comes to assert a magical power, one that takes possession of—or radiates from—a character, Rosalind. We can think of the wood in *A Midsummer Night's Dream* as called forth by the sexual desires of the young lovers. They not only dream in the wood, but the wood itself is their dream manifested. It is dewy and moist, full of snakes, lions, and bestiality, always somewhat preternatural and expressive of the mental images of its sleeping characters. If so, then desire might exercise some agency over place, and not just vice versa. A similar claim might be made about Windsor Forest in *Merry Wives*. It functions as the place of symbolic exorcism, where child-fairies pinch Falstaff black and blue, but it also may give expression to the unspeakable sexual fantasies of the chaste wives, Mistresses Page and Ford, for it is there that the mythical pagan woodsman, Herne the Hunter, displays his great horns and lurks about his immense oak tree (see Chapter 4). The etiology of place varies as Shakespeare explores different comic possibilities. It is striking, however, that in some of his most popular comedies, such as *Dream*, locale operates powerfully, as if the idea of generically blessed, magical places had trans-historic appeal. The comedies use the idea of locale—proto-scientific or enchanted, regulative and protean—to lay out the problem of social and personal metamorphosis. What could have prompted that tactic? Perhaps, thought Shakespeare, in the place of the theater, we are happy to consider the transformational potential of place within a drama.

The Comedies' Other Places

By way of conclusion, let us acknowledge other places in Shakespeare's comedies not captured by the dualisms that we have been considering. One of those is the

---

[78] See Carroll, *Metamorphoses*.

world off-stage. The capacity of comic characters to evoke in a few verbal brushstrokes an active world just behind the *frons scenae* helps to give the comedies' sense of place concreteness and definition. Thus, in *The Comedy of Errors*, when Ephesian Dromio urges the baffled Syracusan Antipholus to hasten home because "The capon burns, the pig falls from the spit; / The clock hath strucken twelve upon the bell; / My mistress made it one upon my cheek" (1.2.44–6), he calls into existence the domestic life out of which Adriana will step in the next scene. Much later, when the Goldsmith has Antipholus of Ephesus arrested for debt, he will be accompanied by a merchant "bound / To Persia" (4.1.3–4) and in need of cash. To pay his debt, Antipholus will send Dromio home with the instruction that "in the desk / That's covered o'er with Turkish tapestry, / There is a purse of ducats" (103–5). Bustling mealtime preparations, trade by sea voyage to the exotic east, Turkish coverlets in luxury homes, purses filled with ducats: Such strategic details call exotic worlds into imaginative being. Another imminent place is London. There is some truth in the familiar claim that Shakespeare's comic cities and centers—Ephesus, Milan, Athens, Venice, Vienna, and the like—intermittently evoke London, the unnamed place that hovers in the background of the comedies. London life may be alluded to critically or satirically, as when Dromio of Syracuse riffs in 4.2 and 4.3 about the horrors of arrest for debt, or when Pompey in *Measure for Measure* confronts the audience with the houses of prostitution that were a feature of the Thames's south bank. But more often, London becomes less delimited as a place than newly invested with magical possibilities. In Shakespeare's comedies, the more developed the place is, the more opaque it becomes. In this regard, the abstract, allegory-friendly openness of the Elizabethan stage—so different from Sebastiano Serlio's architecturally detailed, prototypical city of Renaissance Italian comedy—found its perfect realization in Shakespeare's wide-ranging, magical geographies.

4

The Manifestation of Desire

(Be Careful What You Wish For)

... since we were still at that age when
one believes one creates what one names

Marcel Proust
Swan's Way

Perhaps you have fantasized that you had telepathic powers (who has not?), powers that would bring you wealth, or make others fall in love with you, or even turn you magically into the head of state (what great things you would do!). In those moments, you were probably experiencing your life as a comedy. A whole subgenre of modern film comedies is premised on wish-fulfilling magic—'magical thinking'[1]—such as reading the minds of others, exchanging lives with someone else, becoming invisible, controlling the future, or time-traveling to the past to correct a romantic mistake. Shakespeare's great predecessor, John Lyly, used such effects prominently, as in *Gallathea*, where Venus agrees to fulfill the romantic love between two girls by performing an immediate, supernatural sex-change operation on one of them. There a girl's desire has the power to move a god to alter her body. Shakespeare's comedies, too, are infused with magical thinking, which can have a disarming, childlike power, as the epigraph from Proust suggests. We might call one form of it 'manifestation,' by which term I mean the capacity of a character's desires, thoughts, and words to bring forth external material effects, activity in the mental world generating quanta in the physical. We have just noticed, in the previous chapter, an example in the way Rosalind's imagined magician-uncle, as a fictive spirit of the forest, seems to come literally to life in the holy hermit who converts Duke Frederick.

Critics have occasionally broached the idea of manifestation, if not always invoking the term. Rosalie Colie, for example, employs "unmetaphoring" to indicate the way that something verbal may acquire a concrete form; Margaret W. Ferguson says that Hamlet's language has the "curious effect of *materializing* the word"; while Patricia Parker applies the term, "manifestation," to the appear-

---

[1] On the argument that magical thinking can function as a complement to rational and scientific thinking, see Eugene Subbotsky, *Magic and the Mind: Mechanisms, Functions, and Development of Magical Thinking and Behavior* (Oxford: Oxford University Press, 2010).

Shakespeare and the Comedy of Enchantment. Kent Cartwright, Oxford University Press. © Kent Cartwright 2021.
DOI: 10.1093/oso/9780198868897.003.0005

ance of the chain in *The Comedy of Errors*.[2] Relatedly, Judith Anderson uses "literalism" to distinguish metaphors that "cross into reality," and Henry Turner approaches the idea in his discussion of "*metaphormosis*."[3] These variations on 'manifestation' are suggestive, but the notion has not had comprehensive treatment. The term draws our focus to Shakespeare's comedies: While the device functions differently in different genres, it sorts especially well with comedy's strain of fantasticality. Let us, first, introduce some examples and explain manifestation in detail; second, outline its connection to Renaissance thought (especially about magic) and its usefulness as a concept; third, scrutinize its operation in a number of plays, including the manifestation of an object in *A Midsummer Night's Dream* and of a personage in *The Merry Wives of Windsor*; and, fourth, outline certain of its literary contexts. A latent but insufficiently recognized generic possibility emerges in the device of manifestation: It enhances the moral dimension of comedy, challenges notions of dramatic causation, adds dynamism and psychic depth to comic experience, and celebrates—amusingly and disturbingly—the uncanny power of desire and imagination.

Telepathic Entrances and the Concept of Manifestation

Consider entrances. In Renaissance comedy, off-stage characters often enter a scene, by convention, just at the moment when those onstage require them. That practice descends from Roman theater, as in Terence, where an unanticipated character might pop into the fifth act 'catastrophe' in the nick of time, with the right information needed to resolve the impasse. Donatus, the fourth-century commentator on comedy whose work typically accompanied Renaissance editions of Terence, refers to this character as the "'*persona ad catastropham machinata*'" (i.e., the character contrived or devised for the catastrophe).[4] In Shakespeare, the *persona machinata* of Marcadé in *Love's Labour's Lost* can serve as an example.

---

[2] Rosalie L. Colie, *Shakespeare's Living Art* (Princeton, NJ: Princeton University Press, 1974), 145; Margaret W. Ferguson, "*Hamlet*: Letters and Spirits," in *Shakespeare and the Question of Theory*, ed. Geoffrey H. Hartman and Patricia A. Parker (New York: Methuen, 1985), 291–307, on 291; Patricia Parker, *Shakespeare from the Margins: Language, Culture, Context* (Chicago, IL: University of Chicago Press, 1996), 71.

[3] Judith H. Anderson, *Words That Matter: Linguistic Perception in Renaissance English* (Stanford, CA: Stanford University Press, 1996), 143; Henry S. Turner, *Shakespeare's Double Helix* (London: Continuum, 2007), 92. The notion of manifestation echoes the Renaissance interest in the relationship between the linguistic and the material; see Catherine Richardson, *Shakespeare and Material Culture* (Oxford: Oxford University Press, 2011), 164–96. The phenomena under consideration here are not transformations or metamorphoses of the self but projections of it; on metamorphosis, see William C. Carroll, *The Metamorphosis of Shakespearean Comedy* (Princeton, NJ: Princeton University Press, 1985).

[4] T. W. Baldwin, *Shakspere's Five-Act Structure* (Urbana, IL: University of Illinois Press, 1947), 40. On Donatus's structural analysis of Terence's *Andria*, see Baldwin, *Five-Act*, 28–52. See also Donatus, "On Comedy," trans. S. G. Nugent, in *Classical and Medieval Literary Criticism: Translations and*

Unheard of until his late entrance, Marcadé brings the news of the French king's death, and, in modern productions, always wears black and looks solemn. His very name may signify "the *danse macabre*."[5] Marcadé's entrance constitutes the play's "great dramatic moment" to which "all that goes before it ... leads up."[6] Not only will his demeanor accord with his news but both elements magnify and make almost visible, as if by conjuration, the aura of dissonance and failure that hangs over the last action, centered on the court ladies' rejection of the love offers of the men. Rosaline refuses Berowne now and will accept him later only after he spends a year staring into the face of death. Marcadé's entrance, then, is both shocking and mysteriously apt. If Shakespeare makes salient atmosphere out of an entrance such as Marcadé's, he might well extend that principle to entrances elsewhere in a play, giving what had been conventional a new psychological twist, as if arrivals were not happenstance but events called forth, telepathically and uncannily, by the wishes, fears, or comments of characters onstage.

Such manifested entrances dot the comedies. In *The Comedy of Errors*, for example, Antipholus of Syracuse, distressed by the seeming witchcraft of Ephesus, especially of its women, implores, "Some blessed power deliver us from hence!" (4.3.45). His answer makes entrance immediately in the figure of the Courtesan, whom Antipholus and his Dromio take as the "devil" or "devil's dam" because of her flame-colored clothing (51, 53). "Blessed" or devilish, the Courtesan's arrival responds comically to Antipholus's conflicted fears and desires about women. He has already expressed attraction yet also repulsion towards Adriana, just as he has towards his love-interest, Luciana, who alternates in his imagination as a "dear creature" or a "siren" (3.2.33, 47). The Courtesan functions here as a real character and as a comic projection, the female both alluring and fiendish, called forth by Antipholus's fears.

In *Love's Labour's Lost*, the courtiers swear not to see or converse with women during three years of hermetic study, but no sooner have they taken oath than Berowne reminds them of the impending arrival of a delegation of ladies from the French court, the women manifested, as with humorous reflexivity, by the actual, if repressed or "quite forgot," desires of the men (1.1.139). Orsino, towards the end of the first scene of *Twelfth Night*, likens love music to the sweet scent that "breathes upon a bank of violets" (1.1.6). Keir Elam, the Arden editor, calls the line "a possible 'hidden' and prophetic allusion to Viola" (who is herself associated with music) (1.3.6n.); even more, we might say, it confers some oblique agency on

---

Interpretations, ed. Alex Preminger, O. B. Hardison, Jr., and Kevin Kerrane (New York: Frederick Ungar, 1974), 305–9; and Evanthius, "On Drama," trans. O. B. Hardison, in *Classical and Medieval Literary Criticism*, ed. Preminger et al., 301–5.

    [5] Woudhuysen, *LLL*, 109, n. 10. William C. Carroll sees in the name a pun on "mars Arcadia" as a synonym for death; he also associates Marcadé with Mercury; Carroll, ed., *Love's Labour's Lost* (Cambridge: Cambridge University Press, 2009), 5.2.690n.

    [6] G. R. Hibbard, ed., *Love's Labour's Lost* (Oxford: Clarendon Press, 1990), 10.

Orsino's fantasies in effecting Viola's entrance immediately thereafter. In the last scene of *The Merchant of Venice*, Lorenzo asks the musicians to play in a manner that will "[w]ith sweetest touches pierce your mistress' ear, / And draw her home with music," imitating the power of Orpheus (5.1.67–8). In an efficient sense, Portia is making her own way home already, but in a more teleological sense, Lorenzo's beckoning of her through music—the dream of harmony—seems to summon Portia to Belmont.

The concept of manifestation in those examples foregrounds the power of characters' thoughts, words, feelings, and desires. Desire, especially, drives comedy, even more than it does tragedy—comic desire in all its permutations: lust, impulse, wish, fantasy, hope, dream, longing, dominant humor, obsession, passion, fear (desire's negative twin), and especially romantic and sexual desire. According to Donatus, "Comedy is a [form of] drama containing the various designs of public and private individuals' desires."[7] Desires and words give rise to manifestations, which are more than just metaphors, symbols, or representations; rather, they constitute preternatural effects. Manifestations are cousins to early modern personifications, but they are not abstract beings with indicative names; they do not fit into an allegorical landscape;[8] and they come, as it were, disguised as something else. They are objects and figures suited for the quasi-realism of New Comedy.

The claim that desires, thoughts, and words can have active power in comedy may sound surprising.[9] Shakespeare's plays are full, after all, of romantic lovers whose longings have rendered them passive and melancholy, as immobilized as Patience on a monument. But comic desires can also have a more predictive and assertive dimension, somewhat analogous to, and typically in concert with, the power of imagination. That power is the subject of Michel de Montaigne's essay, "Of the Force of the Imagination," which begins, "*A strong imagination begetteth chance*, say the learned clearks."[10] For Montaigne, imagination has a voluntary as

---

[7] Quoted from Donatus, "The Fragment Containing *On Comedy and Tragedy*," in *Plato to Congreve*, vol. 1 of 4, *Sources of Dramatic Theory*, ed. Michael J. Sidnell (Cambridge: Cambridge University Press, 1991), 79–83, on 79. Of course, tragic protagonists are often moved by desires, such as ambition, and tragedies feature conflicting desires among characters; yet tragedy can also involve resistance to desire, withdrawal, and ambivalence (as with Hamlet), and it has a special interest, greater than comedy's, in the power of self-conscious will. History plays also foreground desire, but typically of a specific political kind, the desire for kingship.

[8] For a recent study of personification as an expression of a character's will, see Andrew Escobedo, *Volition's Face: Personification and the Will in Renaissance Literature* (Notre Dame, IN: University of Notre Dame Press, 2017).

[9] For a recent study of desire and its agency, see Gillian Beth Knoll, *Conceiving Desire in Lyly and Shakespeare: Metaphor, Cognition and Eros* (Edinburgh: University of Edinburgh Press, 2020).

[10] Michel de Montaigne, *Essays*, trans. John Florio (London, [1603] 1613), 40; Early English Books On-line: https://eebo.chadwyck.com. For "*begetteth chance*," Donald M. Frame has "*creates the event*"; Michel de Montaigne, *The Complete Essays*, trans. Donald M. Frame (Stanford, CA: Stanford University Press, 1958), 68. Montaigne observes that "by experience wee see women to transferre divers markes of their fantasies, vnto children they beare in their wombes: witness she that brought foorth a Blacke-a-more. There was also presented vnto *Charles* king of *Bohemia*, an Emperour, a young

well as an involuntary force.[11] He recalls an elderly man who seeks his (Montaigne's) youthful company so that by imbibing the writer's vigor with his own senses and imagination the old man might re-energize himself. As John Lyons puts it, for Montaigne, "imagination...is more powerful than physical causes."[12] That power of imagination can be observed not only in humans but also in beasts, as with "partriges and hares that grow white by the snow vpon mountaines" and "*Jacobs* sheep."[13] Montaigne shares that last example with *The Merchant of Venice*, where Shylock relates how Jacob induced Laban's ewes to give birth to "parti-coloured lambs" by holding up before their eyes, at the time of conceiving, parti-colored branches (1.3.84; see 73–86). The mind can reproduce its internal images as qualities in the real world. Such power, under the sway of desire, becomes a subtext in Shakespeare's comedies.

Magical efficacy fascinated late sixteenth-century dramatists and thinkers, helping to account for manifestation in Shakespeare. Italian late cinquecento comedy and English comedy of the 1580s and 1590s feature plays rich with magicians, conjurors, witches, and concerns about magic.[14] English dramas include *The Old Wives' Tale, Endymion, Dr. Faustus, Friar Bacon and Friar Bungay, John of Bordeaux*, and *The Comedy of Errors*, among many others. Renaissance thinkers, among them Marsilio Ficino (*Three Books of Life* [1489]), Heinrich Cornelius Agrippa (*Three Books of Occult Philosophy* [1533]), and Giordano Bruno (especially *On Magic* and *A General Account of Bonding* [1588]), sought the natural, spiritual, and philosophical foundations for magic.[15] These influential theorists explored magic as an aspect of natural science, seeing different kinds of causation operant in the world: for example, the material, efficient causation expressed when one object, such as a ball, strikes a second,

girle, borne about *Pisa*, all shagd and hairy over and over, which her mother said, to have beene conceived so, by reason of an image of Saint *Iohn Baptist*, that was so painted, & hung over her bed" (Florio trans., 45). Among other commentators, Agrippa describes similar effects; see Henry Cornelius Agrippa, *Three Books of Occult Philosophy*, trans. James Freake, ed. Donald Tyson (St. Paul, MN: Llewellyn Publications, 1995; orig. pub. in Latin, 1533), 204–5. See also Wes Williams, *Monsters and their Meanings in Early Modern Culture: Mighty Magic* (Oxford: Oxford University Press, 2011).

[11] John D. Lyons, *Before Imagination: Embodied Thought from Montaigne to Rousseau* (Stanford, CA: Stanford University Press, 2005), 48, see 32–60.

[12] Lyons, *Before Imagination*, 47.   [13] Montaigne, "Of Imagination," Florio trans., 45.

[14] On magic in late sixteenth-century Italian comedy, see Louise George Clubb, *Italian Drama in Shakespeare's Time* (New Haven, CT: Yale University Press, 1989), 59–60.

[15] See, for example, Marsilio Ficino, *Three Books on Life*, trans. and ed. Carol V. Kaske and John R. Clark (Tempe, AZ: Medieval and Renaissance Texts and Studies, Arizona State University, [1989] 1998) (see especially Book Three); *Heinrich Cornelius Agrippa,* Three Books of Occult Philosophy; *and Giordano Bruno,* Cause, Principle and Unity; *Essays on Magic*, trans. and ed. Robert De Lucca (Cause) and Richard J. Blackwell (*Magic*) (Cambridge: Cambridge University Press, 1998). For studies on Renaissance magic, see Ioan P. Couliano, *Eros and Magic in the Renaissance*, trans. Margaret Cook (Chicago, IL: University of Chicago Press, 1987; orig. pub. in French, 1984); Brian P. Copenhaver, *Magic in Western Culture: From Antiquity to the Enlightenment* (Cambridge: Cambridge University Press, 2015); D. P. Walker, *Spiritual and Demonic Magic from Ficino to Campanella* (University Park, PA: Pennsylvania State University Press, [1958] 2000); and Frances A. Yates, *Giordano Bruno and the Hermetic Tradition* (London: Routledge and Kegan Paul, 1964).

forcing a reaction; and a different, spiritual causation by which an object attracts ontologically similar objects to it and repulses dissimilar ones, the theory of sympathy and antipathy.[16] The Renaissance believed in the "pervasive power of hidden operations," especially those "antipathies and sympathies that compelled both bonds and animosities among an unpredictable mix" of elements, including humans, as Mary Floyd-Wilson states.[17] According to recent Renaissance historians, notes Floyd-Wilson, "belief in spirits, demons, and occult qualities was commonplace."[18] The Renaissance, that is, embraced theories, seen as scientific, according to which everything in nature was linked by attraction or repulsion, and bodies and minds might work long-distance effects. The world was networked together by a "World-soul" (in Ficino's phrase) that infused all things; consequently, even "things which are at a distance from one [an]other" communicated by means of a vapor-like universal spirit, a pneuma, that derives from the "World-soul."[19] That essence constitutes the pathway of communication that allows animate creatures to transmit thoughts and desires telepathically, to infect things and people with their natures, or to exert influences, as the moon controls the tides through sympathy. The World-soul gives the magus "generative power."[20] The magus's knowledge enables him magically to attract, summon, or manipulate objects at a distance. In Ficino's view, a human soul under certain conditions could exercise "telepathy, telekinesis, levitation and other paranormal abilities."[21] Judith Anderson, whose concept of "literalism" (akin to manifestation), focuses on language, cites Ficino's notion that "magic is a materializing of language," and she offers the example of Lancelot Andrewes' treatment of "hope as a thing."[22] Ficino, Agrippa, and Bruno give detailed attention to the etiology by which form projects into matter a variety of types, shapes, and materials. As Agrippa summarizes it, "Natural magic... is that which contemplates the powers of all natural and celestial things, and searching curiously into their sympathy, doth produce occult powers in nature into public view... that from thence arise wonderful miracles."[23] Magic constructs a theory of causation by which ideas have sufficient potency to come to life in the material world. Shakespeare appropriates this theory for comical ends: While the magus figure illustrates how the individual acquires power through magic, manifestations will

[16] See Ernst Cassirer, *The Individual and the Cosmos in Renaissance Philosophy*, trans. Mario Domandi (Mineola, NY: Dover Publications, [1963] 2000), 117–18; see also Seth Lobis, *The Virtue of Sympathy: Magic, Philosophy, and Literature in Seventeenth-Century England* (New Haven, CT: Yale University Press, 2015), 1–35.

[17] Floyd-Wilson, *Occult Knowledge, Science, and Gender on the Shakespearean Stage* (Cambridge: Cambridge University Press, 2013), 1, see 1–27.

[18] Floyd-Wilson, *Occult Knowledge*, 2.   [19] Ficino, *Three Books*, 243.

[20] Ficino, *Three Books*, 243, 257; see Copenhaver, *Magic*, esp. 55–156, 231–71.

[21] Copenhaver, *Magic*, 269.   [22] Anderson, *Words*, 143, 144.

[23] Agrippa, *Three Books*, 690.

show everyday characters exercising a wayward agency of which they are blithely unaware.

From a literary rather than a theoretical perspective, we might also note Shakespeare's indebtedness to Ovid's interest in magical transformations. In *The Metamorphosis*, will and desire seem capable of permeating borders, between the living and the inanimate, for example, and between one character and another, much as the Renaissance theorists argue. According to Charles Segal, magic in *The Metamorphosis* "helps depict the irrational and demonic force of the passions."[24] Shakespeare's allusion to Orpheus in Lorenzo's call for music to draw Portia home suggests that the comedies' telepathic effects might sometimes take inspiration from Ovidian myths.[25] In Ovid, for example, Pygmalion falls in love with the marble statue of his own making, and Venus, in sympathy, gives it life.[26] Shakespeare refers to the Pygmalion myth in *Measure for Measure* (3.1.313–14) and refashions it in the awakening of Hermione's statue in *The Winter's Tale*. Such are the values that become empowered by Renaissance theorists of magic.

The Values of Manifestation

If the idea of manifestation sorts well with Renaissance thinking about imagination and magic, it resonates, too, with recent theorizing about comedy. We can sketch out four general values. First, at the most mundane level, manifestations have moral force. To the extent that a manifested entity makes visible and ridiculous a character's passions or obsessions, as the Courtesan does for Antipholus, it affords a humorously ethical perspective, one even potentially reformative. Thus, manifestation casts a satirical eye on character and action, in the spirit of Terence or of Italian cinquecento comedy, but with an innovative twist. For many readers in Shakespeare's time, the moral implications of drama and literature mattered, as they do to some in our own time: New understanding about how such meanings are formulated is always relevant.

Second, manifestation shifts our understanding of how causation can work in comedy, as our comments on sympathy suggest. Causation constitutes an especially important topic for comic drama (perhaps even more so than for other modes such as prose narrative or poetry). New Comedy, for example, typically presents runaway confusions that must be solved by tracking actions back to their

[24] Charles Segal, "Black and White Magic in Ovid's *Metamorphosis*: Passion, Love, and Art," *Arion: A Journal of Humanities and the Classics*, 3rd series, 9, no. 3 (Winter 2002): 1–34, on 6.
[25] Shakespeare several times alludes to the power of "Orpheus' lute" to move inanimate objects, to "soften steel and stones" (*The Two Gentlemen of Verona*, 3.2.77–8)—in effect, to animate them.
[26] Ovid, *Metamorphoses, Books IX–XV*, trans. Frank Justus Miller; rev. G. P. Goold (Cambridge, MA: Harvard University Press, 1984), 10.270–94.

causal origins. Thus, the concept of manifestation puts in tension two types of agency: one, the familiar, Aristotelian efficient causality of physical entities acting upon each other;[27] the other, a less obvious, stranger symbolic and psychic agency—manifestation—in which events take their form according to the blueprint of desire.[28] While the first dominates most comic actions, the other emerges intermittently like a path of light flickering in the shadows. Manifestation, then, exposes a second layer of meaning working alongside the quotidian; it doubles comic causation, and in that regard it contributes to the quality of doubling and multiplication that characterizes comedy generally (see Chapter 2).[29] Thus, manifestation helps us to recognize the subtle fantasticality that so often defines a comic world (see Chapter 3)—a value that can be missed by overly realistic readings— further distinguishing comedy as a genre. By hinting at the magical and numinous, manifestation brings into a play's etiology an aura of mystery whose lingering after-effects insinuate themselves into one's memory and residual life.[30]

Third, the notion of desires manifested adds dynamism to comedy.[31] When we postulate that an object can be summoned by wishes and thoughts, rather than just represent them, the relationship between vehicle and tenor alters from conceptual to functional and active. Manifestation shortens the distance between word and thing, self and world, and in that regard, comic character becomes supercharged and complex. The claim that language can morph into physicality occurs anecdotally in Shakespeare, as when Feste speaks to Viola of his sister: "Why, sir, her name's a word, and to dally with that word might make my sister wanton" (*Twelfth Night*, 3.1.19). Manifestation offers one way to conceptualize the wantonness of words. The concept even bears some affinity to modern language theory. George Lakoff and Mark Johnson, discussing the metaphoric dimension of causation in everyday language, provide instances in which "a mental or emotional state is viewed as causing an act or event," such as, "He became a mathematician *out of* a passion for order"; the passion is here the "container" from

[27] In Aristotle, the material cause of the bronze statue is the bronze itself; the efficient cause, the skill of the artisan; the formal cause, the idea or image in the artisan's mind; and the final or teleological cause, the ends that the statute serves, such as giving pleasure or honoring a person or god.

[28] For the purposes of this discussion, I am treating agency and causation as synonymous; agency captures the latter term's sense of an active doer. With manifestation, however, the manifesting character is typically unaware of his or her efficacy.

[29] That sense of dual, overlapping agencies can be compared to the Renaissance intersection of natural magic and natural science; on that intersection, see Floyd-Wilson, *Occult Knowledge*, 3–6. For a discussion of doubling in comic plotting, see Matthew Bevis, *Comedy: A Very Short Introduction* (Oxford: Oxford University Press, 2013), 49–62.

[30] For a recent study of mystery in prose fiction, see Maud Casey, *The Art of Mystery: The Search for Questions* (Minneapolis, MN: Greywolf Press, 2018).

[31] Manifestation can cast light on the dynamics of comic interludes in tragedy: Just when Hamlet's thoughts turn to the dusty fate of princes, the gravedigger appears, sod-filled skull in hand, a comic projection with revelatory power.

which becoming a mathematician emerges.[32] Manifestations concretize that kind of linguistic formulation and make visible the energy of thought.

Fourth—now from a perspective opposite to that of everyday morality— manifestation celebrates outsized human desires and fantasies, thus offering another indice for defining comedy. Manifestations—the love drops in *A Midsummer Night's Dream* or the Witch of Brainford in *The Merry Wives of Windsor*, as we shall see—constitute sources of delight in themselves. Although the neatness of a comic ending can create wonder and admiration, the exuberant amusement that audiences find in the middle parts of a comedy derives, as Alenka Zupančič points out, from the hilarious spiraling out of control of obsessions and errors (which we do not really want to end).[33] The pleasure of comic manifest- ations arises less from their ethics and more from the delirious anarchy that they release into the play-world. In Zupančič's argument, a comic figure not only slips and falls on a banana peel but also resumes striding down the street as if nothing had happened, full of indefatigable Dogberrian self-confidence (like a cartoon character never injured by his pratfalls).[34] That wondrous irrepressibility—the presumption of human indestructibility, and thus the defiance of mortal limitations—distinguishes comedy, she argues. Manifestations, as they show the fecundity of certain characters' imaginations—their funny, slightly monstrous, unconscious drive to multiply themselves in the form of objects or beings—fill out Zupančič's picture of comic larger-than-lifeness.

Dynamism appears in a further regard. Henri Bergson famously contended that comedy occurs when we see a human behaving as a thing, the organic subsumed by the reflexive or mechanical; but, Zupančič adds, that connection also reveals that humans can really be a little like things.[35] The inanimate thingness that, for Bergson, requires immediate correction, expresses, she argues, its own vitality, "something vivid at the very core of inelasticity" (115), so that the comic is revealed not in the falseness of one pole set dichotomously against another but in the impossible but inalienable interconnectedness between the two. That rela- tionship introduces a new, additional quality, a surplus, that, for Zupančič, goes to the core of comedy.[36] In this fourth value, manifestation, beyond whatever moral message it possesses, advances our apprehension of comedy's mysterious double- ness, the recognition that we are potentially both ourselves and something more.

One might object that what I am describing as manifestation is nothing more than the playwright's artistry, the Courtesan in *The Comedy of Errors*, for example,

---

[32] George Lakoff and Mark Johnson, *Metaphors We Live By* (Chicago, IL: University of Chicago Press, 1980), 75, see 69–76.

[33] Alenka Zupančič, *The Odd One In: On Comedy* (Cambridge, MA: MIT Press, 2008), 130, see 128–47.

[34] Zupančič, *Odd One*, 22–3.   [35] Zupančič, *Odd One*, 111–26.

[36] Broadly speaking, Zupančič's discussion of the relationship between object and person may recall Bruno Latour's treatment of "quasi-objects"; Bruno Latour, *We Have Never Been Modern*, trans. Catherine Porter (Cambridge, MA: Harvard University Press, 1993; orig. pub. in French, 1991), e.g., 51–5.

called forth not by Antipholus's conflicted fantasies but by Shakespeare's skill at apposite placement. First, of course, that kind of argument might be aimed against many aspects of dramatic atmosphere and action. The objection works best when the reader or spectator stands away from the play-world as a detached observer; it works less well in describing one's immersion in a fictional world. Second, the objection misses the special nature of the comic world itself, which is neither quite *locus* nor quite *platea*. In the Forest of Arden, when Jaques departs to avoid having to listen to "blank verse" (*AYL*, 4.1.28–9), he is identifying something that is an aspect of both the dramaturgy and the play-world; his quip is more than merely meta-dramatic commentary. Likewise, in the Athenian woods of *A Midsummer Night's Dream*, when a character enters to exactly the same spot where another has just fallen asleep, the action not only demonstrates the playwright's skillful stage management but also realizes one of the uncanny valences of the locale, as Bart van Es observes.[37] In a famous essay, G. R. Elliott writes about the "weirdness" and "eeriness" of *The Comedy of Errors*, which derives partly from the way scenes echo and parallel each other; for example, the second scene subtly recalls the first, such that Antipholus of Syracuse's presence and manner in 2.1 are "felt to be *fathered by Aegeon's*" in 1.1.[38] Elliott links the uncanniness of those elements to the atmosphere of magic in Ephesus. Here, as with manifestation, Shakespeare's artistry can be read back into qualities of the comic world itself. Third, for Protestant theologians and Renaissance writers and readers, accidents and coincidences beg for metaphysical explanations (as discussed in Chapter 2). Such events could be signs of the wondrous, as Michael Witmore argues: "Strictly speaking, there are no accidents in a providential world."[39] The accidental, then, becomes a submerged sign of divine will, "a spontaneous form of revelation,"[40] its very indirectness according with new protocols for Baconian experimentation. Additionally, "accidents become associated with theatrical display," Witmore concludes (4), so that poetic understanding and providential disclosure, the aesthetic and the real, overlap. In such a system, one might well read 'artistic' juxtapositions, such as Antipholus and the Courtesan, as signs of the enchanted world.

Fundamentally, manifestation evokes, and revels in, the human desire to remake the world in the image of the self. Shakespeare's comedies critique human desires but, more interestingly, they appreciate and celebrate desire's

---

[37] "The forest seems infinitely large and at the same time infinitely congested"; Bart van Es, *Shakespeare's Comedies: A Very Short Introduction* (Oxford: Oxford University Press, 2016), 22. As van Es also points out, it is the forest in *AYL* that makes instant transformations of character credible (27–8); the atmosphere of comic place, that is, solves a plot problem.

[38] G. R. Elliott, "Weirdness in *The Comedy of Errors*," in *The Comedy of Errors: Critical Essays*, ed. Robert Miola (New York: Routledge, 2001), 57–70, on 61; reprinted from *The University of Toronto Quarterly* 9, no. 1 (October 1939): 95–106.

[39] Michael Witmore, *The Culture of Accidents: Unexpected Knowledges in Early Modern England* (Stanford, CA: Stanford University Press, 2001), 2, see esp. 1–16. Witmore treats coincidences as a subset of accidents.

[40] Witmore, *Culture of Accidents*, 3.

transformative power. Our longings are fatuously grotesque yet also magnificently human, simultaneously ridiculous and enchanted—and delightful in both regards. They are, like jokes, "a counter-intuitive celebration of...false beliefs."[41] Thus, whereas tragedies punish desires, comedies embrace them. Manifestation can crystallize our sense of characters and values, elicit amusement, and help us to understand the paradoxical double vision at the center of comedy. It summons forth a realm of preternatural causes and numinous possibilities, the world of comedy, which enlarges the spirit. To the extent that manifestation creates its effects in a subliminal way, just below our threshold of overt recognition, it will also produce that persistent but soft-focused sense of something more, a psychic resonance, a memorability.

Comic manifestation can apply to simple occurrences, such as when a character enters telepathically, as we have seen, in response to other characters; or it can apply to distant and complex effects, such as when thoughts and desires call forth objects or even other characters, as if ushering them into being.

Manifested Objects

A stage property can "take on a life of its own," according to Andrew Sofer, who points to Shakespeare's use of "fetishized" or even "uncanny" objects.[42] Yet that stage life is not so alien from everyday life, for as psychologist Paul Bloom points out, individuals often treat objects as if they had a numinous, hidden "essence";[43] such a belief helps to explain why people pay extraordinary prices for objects associated with famous people—Judy Garland's ruby slippers from *The Wizard of Oz*, for example—as if the object came imbued with the celebrity's magic. In Shakespearean comedies, particular objects often have a mystical association with particular characters. Rings given by women to their lovers, for example, always come impregnated with sacred power, so as to be inalienable from the closed circuit of the romantic couple. The physical "band" possesses magically the adhesive properties of the human "bond." When Proteus in *Two Gentlemen of Verona*, or Bassanio in *The Merchant of Venice*, or Bertram in *All's Well that Ends Well* would bestow the beloved's ring on someone else, it is—can only be—handed over, with charmed inevitability, to the giver herself. At work in these tokens of love is sympathetic magic. *The Comedy of Errors* provides, by contrast, an object

---

[41] Bevis, *Comedy*, 51.

[42] Andrew Sofer, *The Stage Life of Props* (Ann Arbor, MI: University Michigan Press, 2003), 14, 17, 20. According to Italo Calvino, "the moment an object appears in a narrative, it is charged with a special force and becomes like the pole of a magnetic field"; "in a narrative any object is always magical"; *Six Memos for the Next Millennium*, trans. Geoffrey Brock (Cambridge, MA: Harvard University Press, 1988), 33.

[43] Paul Bloom, *How Pleasure Works: The New Science of Why We Like What We Like* (New York: W. W. Norton, 2010), 1–23.

that must go astray. The Duke's introduction of "dilation or delay" into the action (through the postponement of Egeon's execution) becomes subsequently "material[ized]," argues Patricia Parker, in the form of the chain or necklace that circulates, misdirected, among characters.[44] Or, we might say, the propensity of characters to misunderstand each other and to misconceive events in a serial, self-perpetuating way calls forth the chain—something more than a metaphor—passed errantly among linked characters. The chain manifests a collective longing for, and fear of, human connection, both sympathy and antipathy.

In *Twelfth Night*, Sir Toby and his co-conspirators drop the ambiguous love letter, presumably from Olivia, in the path of Malvolio, who enters the scene fantasizing about love-making with his mistress: "'Tis but fortune, all is fortune. Maria once told me she did affect me" (2.5.21–2). With Malvolio, the concept of "fortune" entails the possibility that the world can bend to one's wishes (to the wishes of the Chosen), and his fantasy of Olivia's affecting of him restates his fervent desire for her, but with their positions reversed in wish-fulfillment. As Lionel Trilling observed long ago, "Malvolio's daydreams ... present themselves to him as reality."[45] Sir Toby and his fellows, of course, are the agents who plant the letter; but in an uncanny sense, Malvolio's desires express a deeper agency transmitted through the ether, for the letter arrives as an immediate, comically mystical response to his love-vision, in the form of an enigma ripe to be crushed into a meaning that will verify his intuition of actuality. For Malvolio, the letter converts his spoken fantasies into written narrative, seemingly authentic, objectively outside himself. It fulfills the determinism of fictional desire.

Even a false claim can make an object come true. In the gulling-of-Benedick scene in *Much Ado About Nothing*, Leonato declares duplicitously that Beatrice has been composing love letters to Benedick, an awkward lie improvised by the conspirators that they then extend into a subject of badinage:

CLAUDIO 'Tis true indeed, so your daughter says. "Shall I," says she,

"that have so oft encountered him with scorn, write to him that I love him?"

LEONATO This she says now, when she is beginning to write to him; for

she'll be up twenty times a night, and there will she sit in her smock till she have writ a sheet of paper. My daughter tells us all.

. . . .

LEONATO O, she tore the letter into a thousand halfpence, railed at

---

[44] Parker, *Margins*, 71.
[45] Lionel Trilling, "Manners, Morals, and The Novel," in *The Liberal Imagination* (New York: Viking Books, 1950), 199–215, on 204.

herself that she should be so immodest to write to one that she knew would flout her. "I measure him," says she, "by my own spirit; for I should flout him, if he writ to me—yea, though I love him I should."   (2.3.126–44)

But this notable fabrication materializes hilariously into fact, when in the last act Hero—the "daughter" indicated in the previous dialogue—suddenly produces a "paper" "Writ in my cousin's hand, stolen from her pocket, / Containing her affection unto Benedick" (5.4.86, 89–90). This stolen object provides the exact and necessary evidence, from the very witness magically identified by the conspirators, to prove to Benedick and even to Beatrice herself that she loves him. The paper appears manifested by the conspirators' well-intended make-believe, just as they have ignited the romance between the two. They have, after all, undertaken to make themselves "the only love-gods" (2.1.357), and the paper that these gods have magically summoned works, in turn, to confirm—arguably even manifest—the pair's love.

Yet sometimes objects can involve a preternatural boomerang effect. Antipholus of Ephesus calls for a "rope's end" with which to thrash his wife and her servants for locking him out of his house (CE 4.1.16). But the rope's end never reaches its intended destination. Rather, it recoils with a vengeance on Antipholus himself in the form of Dr. Pinch's constraining ropes, which will bind Antipholus for a madman and prevent his lashing of Adriana. Adriana seeks to get Antipholus home with her, and for that purpose she employs as her agent the conjuror Pinch. The punitive wish of the would-be wife-persecutor is manifested against him as the restraint and abjection at her hands that he apparently fears.

In A Midsummer Night's Dream, the manifested object is the "love juice" (3.2.37). In that comedy, reality mirrors states of mind, and characters even undertake comically to refashion themselves as things: the moon, a wall. Although the "liquor" falls magically out of fairyland into the lovers' eyes (2.1.178), it also results from human psychic agency. The love juice manifests Helena's longing for Demetrius, and it materializes her conception of love as dotage. It derives, we are told, from the mythological immunity of "the imperial votaress," Queen Elizabeth, to Cupid's "fiery" arrow (2.1.163, 161). According to Oberon, Cupid's "shaft" failed of its mark, saw its fire "[q]uenched in the chaste beams of the watery moon," and fell to earth, striking "a little western flower," whose juice is the play's love "charm" (161, 162, 166, 183). Critics typically refer to the drops and their magic as "Oberon's," and thus sometimes judge the flower-magic to be as much an "instrument" of "patriarchal order," as Stephen Orgel puts it, as a force for liberation from it.[46]

---

[46] Stephen Orgel, Imagining Shakespeare: A History of Texts and Visions (Houndmills, Basingstoke: Palgrave, 2003), 89. Orgel further identifies the flower as "the agent of indiscriminate lust" and of "the libido as a free radical" (89). Cupid's unsuccessful arrow has been associated, too, with Leicester's last unsuccessful effort to win Elizabeth in marriage. The love juice is overdetermined; the present discussion aims to admit Helena into the circle of causes.

But a different perspective emerges when we consider the love juice as a feminine manifestation. Cupid's phallic shaft caused the flower, in effect, to bleed.[47] The flower had been "milk-white," but, when impaled, turns "purple with love's wound" (167), evoking obvious vaginal associations.[48] The bleeding represents an eroticized fantasy about the loss of virginity less suited to Oberon than to a mooning Athenian maiden such as Helena, and it recalls Ovid's complicated coital image in the Pyramus and Thisbe story.[49] The flower in question, the wild pansy (*viola tricolor*) is called "love-in-idleness" by "maidens" (168); it was also known as heart's ease[50] (a reference to "love-in-idleness" also occurs in *TS* 1.1.150). The wild pansy, so feminized and fantasized, reputedly possessed aphrodisiac powers. Hence, the blossoming of love-in-idleness releases female sexual passion into the world.[51] Such pansies occur at another famous moment in Shakespeare, when mad Ophelia gives Laertes "pansies: that's for thoughts" (i.e., *pensées*) (*Ham*, 4.2.178). Read back into *A Midsummer Night's Dream*, that association suggests imagination, here imaginings not of death but of its double, sexual consummation. The character to whose thoughts the love juice hews closest is Helena. Hyppolita and Titania (before she is charmed) show little sexual desire; the love juice fits neither. Rather, it is Helena's erotic desire that the play stresses, while it also downplays Hermia's. Hermia mocks male pretentions to love (see 1.1.168–78) and insists repeatedly that Lysander "[l]ie further off" (2.2.48). Helena, by contrast, makes herself vulnerable to sexual misuse, even rape. She offers to be Demetrius's "spaniel" (2.1.203), and when Demetrius threatens to "do thee mischief in the wood," Helena embraces his mischief-making, offering punningly "[t]o die upon the hand I love so well" (2.1.237, 244).

The verbal link between Helena and the love juice is "dotage": that image connects Helena's view of desire to the operations of the drops. The juice from petals of the pansy is squeezed into the eye, where it transforms the sight so as to make its victim dote upon "the next live creature that it sees" (2.1.172). Helena,

---

[47] Cf. the anemone in *Venus and Adonis*, 1165–76.

[48] The association of virginity with a flower occurs elsewhere in Shakespeare, as in Diana's response to Bertram in *All's Well That Ends Well*: "But when you have our roses, / You barely leave our thorns to prick ourselves / And mock us with our bareness" (4.2.18–20). On the flower as connoting virginity in Shakespeare, see Gordon Williams, *A Glossary of Shakespeare's Sexual Language* (London: Athlone Press, 1997), 128–9.

[49] Ovid, *Metamorphoses, Books I–VIII*, trans. Frank Justus Miller; rev. G. P. Goold, 3rd edn. (Cambridge, MA: Harvard University Press, 1977), 5.55–92.

[50] Harold F. Brooks, ed., *A Midsummer Night's Dream* (London: Methuen, 1979), 2.1.168n; Peter Holland, ed., *A Midsummer Night's Dream* (Oxford: Oxford University Press, 1994), 2.1.168n., 2.1.170–2n.

[51] In Orgel's formulation, Queen Elizabeth's preserved virginity "releas[es] into the play's world an embodiment of unbridled and arbitrary sexual passion" (*Imagining*, 86). Jan H. Blits indirectly links the potion to femininity when he observes that "Oberon's account of the love juice recalls much of Titania's account of the Indian boy and mother"; *The Soul of Athens: Shakespeare's* A Midsummer Night's Dream (Lanham, MD: Lexington Books, 2003), 67. In a source text, Gil Polo's *Diana enamorada* (1564), the Lady Felicia uses her herbal magic to cause Syrenus to renew his love for Diana; Judith M. Kennedy, ed., *A Critical Edition of Yong's Translation of George of Montemayor's* Diana *and Gil Polo's* Enamoured Diana (Oxford: Clarendon Press, 1968), 375.

more than any other character, conceives of love as sight transformed by imagination, *pensées*. While *Dream*, as a whole, represents love as a magical force that causes its victims to dote, the play's most marked dotage is that of Helena, who "dotes" for love of Demetrius, "[d]evoutly dotes, dotes in idolatry" (1.1.108, 109). Doting means being "out of one's wits" and suffering impairment of one's intellect (*OED* dote v. 1–2);[52] it entails an enraptured, disabling desire, even a failure of discrimination. To link love's dotage with devotion and "idolatry" is to imagine the lover's mind as possessed by a pseudo-religious, magical power that dominates sight. Radiating from Helena, "dote," "doting," and "dotage" will organize the play's sense of love.

Helena makes clear that she dotes on Demetrius, even to folly: "And as he errs, doting on Hermia's eyes, / So I, admiring of his qualities" (1.1.230–1). She would learn the "art" by which Hermia "sway[s] the motion of Demetrius' heart" (192–3).[53] In Helena's description, the art of physical allurement posits love as working by magical manipulation and preternatural possession, with Hermia as the sorceress and dotage as the effect. Helena longs to transform herself into her friend: She would catch Hermia's "favour ... my eye [should catch] your eye, / My tongue should catch your tongue's sweet melody" (1.1.186–9). She would, that is, have herself magically metamorphosed, "to [Hermia] translated" (191).[54] Helena's fantasy of inhabiting her rival's body pushes her tactics towards necromantic possession. Ultimately, Helena wishes to exercise love's power to induce dotage through mastery over the beloved, whose "mind," once "beguiled," can "transpose" anything it sees to its liking (1.1.234, 239, 233)—exactly the effect of the love juice. Helena's language serves as description, prophecy, and agent.

The play orchestrates the audience's sympathies in Helena's favor. We are her confidants, share her suffering, admire her intensity and moxie. In that sense, it is inaccurate to say that the lovers are interchangeable or that it matters little who ends up with whom. That objection is reinforced when we consider the love juice as manifested by Helena. The juice is associated extraneously with Elizabeth, and it bears no specific or necessary connection to the quarrel between Oberon and Titania. Its relation to them is arbitrary, and Oberon uses it as merely one method out of many possibilities for gaining control of the changeling boy. Indeed, as Blits observes, the love juice deployed against Titania makes little sense: Why would her embarrassment about falling in love with the next creature that she sees impel her

---

[52] *OED: Oxford English Dictionary* on-line, see http://www.oed.com.

[53] "Sway" means "cause to go or move, drive" (*OED* sway v. 1c), implying determinative power, while "motions" identifies "capacit[ies] for movement" (*OED* motion n. 3a, b). Shakespeare sometimes uses "motion" in association with puppetry; see *OED* motion n. 8b; *The Two Gentlemen of Verona*, 2.1.87 and *Measure for Measure* 3.1.374. The idea of puppetry will return when Helena later calls Hermia a "puppet" (3.2.288), apparently in reference to her stature but perhaps also with a larger resonance.

[54] Puck's later makeover of Bottom into an ass, of course, will demonstrate the meaning of "translated" (see 3.1.115), a usage that may reflect negatively on Helena's earlier desire.

to yield up the boy to Oberon?[55] While Elizabeth and Oberon may be the efficient agents of the love liquor, they are not its only cause.

The juice stands, rather, as the objective manifestation of Helena's description of love's properties and as the comic but sympathetic response of the cosmos to her longing for Demetrius: "The juice of it, on sleeping eyelids laid, / Will make or man or woman madly dote / Upon the next live creature that it sees" (2.1.170–2). The love juice, says Blits, is "the reification of desire aroused entirely by the imagination."[56] The drops work during dreaming by transforming the mind, which then dominates sight and creates dotage—just as Helena had described the workings of love.[57] They fulfill Helena's request for the art to beguile, and they manifest her desire magically to possess Hermia's power of allurement, to absorb Hermia into herself. The love juice confirms the image, associated with Helena, of love as magical dotage, and it bottles up the bewitching love-power that she envisions. The love drops occur as a female metonymy, the "purple" of "love's wound," reflecting Helena's desire for consummation (2.1.167).[58] The drops also make concrete the metaphor for love voiced by Theseus: More happy than celibacy is marriage, which is epitomized by "the rose distilled," the flower represented as feminized "essence" crushed into perfume, into female love juice (1.1.76).[59] The drops manifest the power of female desire.[60] So let us call it, not Oberon's love liquor alone, but also Helena's.[61]

Helena's love juice recalls Alenka Zupančič's interest in the doubleness of comedy when played out in objects: Comedies often include, she argues,

the surprising appearance of a (small) other: in the form of a double or in the form of a surplus comic object that could be defined (in comedies of error) as "error incorporated." This surplus comic object is not simply this or that object

[55] Blits, *Soul*, 68.   [56] Blits, *Soul*, 67.

[57] Shakespeare's probable sources for the love drops include Lyly's *Euphues*; Ovid's *Metamorphosis*; and, perhaps less directly, Montemayor's *Diana* and *Diana enamorada* and Spenser's *Faerie Queene*, Book 2; see Brooks, *Midsummer*, lxxxi–lxxxii.

[58] The love drops stand for the "end of virginity celebrated in one pleasing moment of aesthetic intensity"; Hugh Grady, *Shakespeare and Impure Aesthetics* (Cambridge: Cambridge University Press, 2009), 87.

[59] The metaphor is obviously vaginal. On the "rose distilled" as "the essence of the maiden's swiftly passing beauty," see R. A. Foakes, ed., *A Midsummer Night's Dream*, updated edn. (Cambridge: Cambridge University Press, [1985] 2003) 1.1.76n. A curious, proleptic magic works elsewhere in the opening scene, since Hermia's jocular suggestion of Lysander's possible oath-breaking (see 1.1.173–6) will come to pass later in the play, rather like Beatrice's love letter.

[60] Wendy Wall discusses early modern syrup, often made from violets or roses, as associated with the power of female healing and eroticism; she likewise elucidates syrup's association with poetry's erotic juices that join lovers and, relatedly, with the erosion of "rationality" and "masculine will"; "Just a Spoonful of Sugar: Syrup and Domesticity in Early Modern England," *Modern Philology* 104, no. 2 (November 2006): 149–72, on 167, see also 158–61.

[61] Shakespeare will apparently allude to *Dream*'s Helena when he later creates another mistress of magical herbal remedies, Helen (or Helena) of *All's Well That Ends Well*. Likewise, if *Dream* was written after *Romeo and Juliet* (as seems likely), its love drops might be understood as the comic response to Juliet's sleeping potion and Romeo's vial of poison.

that we see in the play but, rather, something like an objective surplus of error which sticks to different protagonists at different moments, implicating them in all sorts of comic situations; or the protagonists keep handing it on to each other like a hot potato.[62]

In *Dream*, that supercharged object is the love liquid. Not only is Helena obsessed but her obsession also engenders a magical object whose use leads to, in turn, a potentially uncontrollable surplus of dotage organizing the comic errors. As a manifestation of Helena, then, the love drops (similar to the necklace in *Errors*) encapsulates the "surplus" that splashes over other characters, helps to generate misperception and confusion, and introduces the complex pleasure of watching humankind's monstrously comic obsessions.

Seeing an aspect of *Dream*'s action as launched by Helena's desire affects our understanding of the play. It emphasizes, for example, the importance of Helena's ultimate surrendering of her pursuit of Demetrius and her intended embarking on a return to Athens: "To Athens will I bear my folly back, / And follow you no further" (3.2.315–16; see also 431–4). Helena must give over her wish to possess Hermia's beguiling art and body parts and to induce dotage in Demetrius—her folly—before the action can move towards resolution. She must, in effect, foreswear her dream (perhaps our comic dream, too) that desire has transformative power. Paradoxically, when she does so, Demetrius can awake in new remembrance of his formerly betrothed love, rejecting the "sickness" of pursuing Hermia and rediscovering himself in "health," returned to his "natural taste" (4.1.172–3) for Helena—the feminized liquid charm now implicitly reconstituted as medication.[63]

In the present reading, then, it matters that the right Jill find the right Jack, and in the right way. Identities confused in the beginning are sorted and distinguished through the action, while the movement of the juice among the lovers—manifested, allowed to create mayhem, finally redirected—tells the story of overflowing desire in little. There are other, less normative implications, too. If Helena's desire functions as one cause of the love juice's introduction, then wishes and fantasies in the human sphere can have a kind of co-agency in the fairy realm. Action in the fairy world takes its form, in part, from longing in the human one, so that the two domains become less static mirrors and more sympathetic or cooperative (or reflexively silly) orders. The desiring imagination—in Theseus phrase, "shaping fantasies" (5.1.5)—can have real effects. The Duke's famous speech about the power of the imagination to body forth "The forms of things

---

[62] Zupančič, *Odd One*, 92.

[63] On female syrups as medicinal, see Wall, "Spoonful." From one perspective, it could be argued that the play works to defuse the threat of female desire; from another, that, with Demetrius remaining enchanted, desire has ultimately worked its effects beyond anyone's knowledge or final intention.

unknown" (15) is essentially right. Helena's longing, so disturbing for its apparent submissiveness, has re-emerged as uncannily active—and she as the central protagonist of the story. Her longing bespeaks female agency that, if potentially "unbridled and arbitrary,"[64] can also resolve into comically right and joyous relationships.

Characters Called Forth

Characters, or character-qualities, can also be manifested. According to Philip Davis, thought in a Shakespearean play constitutes a "verbally powerful" matrix.[65] Indeed, as we have seen, characters can change according to the fantasies of others: Bottom becomes the ass of Puck's conceiving (Chapter 1); Shylock turns into the villain that his enemies had already assumed him to be; and Julia becomes the shadow that Proteus imagines her to be when he forsakes her (Chapter 5). Davis, for his part, gives the example of Leontes's certainty about Hermione's guilt (in *The Winter's Tale*, 3.2), which "virtually stands there alongside of the innocent Hermione on stage, like another character coming out of one mind and trying to embody itself in its near likeness" (88). Something similar, argues Davis, happens with Isabella in *Measure for Measure*. "[S]weet Isabel, take my part; / ... Isabel! / Sweet Isabel, . . . / O Isabel, Will you not lend a knee?" cries Marianna in seeking to save Angelo's life (5.1.428–40). "[L]anguage call[s] this Isabella into being," especially, it seems, through the incantatory reiteration of her name, so that Isabella, by consenting, accepts transformation into the implied figure of Mercy.[66] Marianna coaxes and conjures a new Isabella into existence. That sense of manifestation accords with the last scene of *Measure*, where characters appear to be layered with multiple identities. It also accords with a play in which objects morph into characters—lusty Pudding, Master Shoetie, "wild Halfcan that stabbed Pots" (4.3.17–18)—or characters are on the verge of becoming personifications, as Escalus tells Angelo that "he is indeed justice" (3.1.511). A second subjectivity, it seems, may be called forth out of a character.

Reiteration of a concrete adjective creates humorous pseudo-life in *Much Ado About Nothing*. When Borachio, overheard by the Watch, asks, "what a deformed thief this fashion is?" (3.3.120), the First Watch angrily picks up the image, "I know that Deformed. 'A has been a vile thief this seven year" (121–2). "Deformed" comes further into life as Borachio refers again to that "deformed thief" fashion (126), and the First Watchman, exulting in the possibility of apprehending Deformed, adds descriptive detail ("'a wears a lock" like a courtier [163]). The

---

[64] Orgel, *Imagining*, 86.
[65] Philip Davis, *Shakespeare Thinking* (London: Continuum, 2007), 88.
[66] Davis, *Thinking*, 88.

Second Watchman now insists that the malefactors be made to bring forth Deformed. This virtual Deformed constitutes the fantastical embodiment of the watchmen's fear of thieves. Their anxieties manifest Deformed into shadow-life and make urgent the arrest of Borachio and Conrad, so that manifestation contributes to the action. Indeed, for Kiernan Ryan, Deformed is an "uncanny, disembodied figure" who "materializes out of a misunderstanding" and comes to stand for the ghostly nature of existence in *Much Ado*.[67]

Other manifestations can inject uncanny poignancy and invite sympathy. *Twelfth Night* provides an example in Viola's expressions of hope and desire for Sebastian's return. Viola's dressing in imitation of Sebastian makes his semblance an active presence in the play, as if partially embodied. The effect generates a desire in Olivia that, along with Viola's desire, helps to materialize Sebastian. Those acts of memorializing and cumulative longing call Sebastian back from the sea, make him manifest through the power of desire. Sebastian enters, at one level, as a surprise and, at a deeper level, a fulfillment—and through both a source of delight. The situation recalls that of Malvolio's letter. Although in a quotidian sense Sebastian returns because Antonio has rescued him, in another, more mysterious sense, he answers—indeed, in the logic of comedy, must answer— the call of yearning.

More uncanny comic effects occur in *The Comedy of Errors* and *The Merry Wives of Windsor*. Dr. Pinch in *Errors* possesses a capacity to unnerve other characters to the extent that they react with notable excess.[68] In 4.4, Pinch, at Adriana's instruction, binds and carries off her husband, Antipholus of Ephesus, as a madman. Pinch appears in only that scene and speaks just a dozen lines, yet he leaves an impression. Later, Ephesian Antipholus will express an outsized and extravagant personal revulsion towards Pinch:

> ...a hungry, lean-faced villain,
> A mere anatomy, a mountebank,
> A threadbare juggler and a fortune-teller,
> A needy, hollow-eyed, sharp-looking wretch,
> A living dead man. This pernicious slave...
>
> (5.1.238–42)

Nothing about the action requires or explains Antipholus's disgust for, and his detailed description of, the loathsome, shabby, zombie-like conjurer. Pinch is summoned by Adriana, of course, but he is also a traveler from the psychic domain. When Dromio of Syracuse had worried that Adriana and Luciana were

---

[67] Kiernan Ryan, *Shakespeare's Comedies* (Houndmills, Basingstoke: Palgrave Macmillan, 2009), 165.
[68] The following discussion draws from ideas in the Introduction to Cartwright, *CE*, e.g., 3–4, 16, 20, 30–1, 35.

spirits from "fairy land," he imagined with horror that they would "pinch us black and blue" (2.2.195, 198). Dromio's fear of being pinched helps to call forth the subsequent figment-figure of Dr. Pinch, whose tight-binding ropes might be said to squeeze the Syracusans black and blue, actualizing their fears.[69]

A deeper cause arises from the brother, Antipholus of Syracuse. Early in the play, after his bewildering encounter with Dromio of Ephesus, he expressed a full-blown fear of Ephesian enchantment:

> They say this town is full of cozenage—
> As, nimble jugglers that deceive the eye,
> Dark-working sorcerers that change the mind,
> Soul-killing witches that deform the body,
> Disguised cheaters, prating mountebanks
> And many such—like liberties of sin.
>
> (1.2.97–102)

Antipholus's fantastical landscape of "jugglers," "cheaters," and "mountebanks," all capable of taking control of one's body, calls forth the completing, representative figure, Dr. Pinch (with certain descriptive terms even migrating from the speech of Syracusan Antipholus to that later of Ephesian Antipholus). The Syracusan's intense fear of magic will turn subsequently into an obverse longing, since Antipholus will show himself eager to be enchanted, "[t]ransform[ed]," and possessed by the "siren" Luciana (3.2.40, 47). The idea of demonic possession inspires both repulsion and desire (antipathy and sympathy). In the uncanny psychological economy of *Errors*, the Ephesian brother's disgust for Dr. Pinch expresses the dread felt by each of the Syracusans, with the conjurer summoned forth like a nightmare from their fraught and fearful psyches. Pinch haunts the play because he encapsulates comically its bugbear of the id, both psychogenically powerful and a bit abject, the form of the characters' comic obsessions. As such, Pinch serves as an index to the larger problems of misinterpretation in *Errors*.

Merry Wives also traffics in uncanny excesses. The play emphasizes Master Ford's abhorrence for the old woman of Brainford,[70] although Ford provides no explanation for his attitude. When he learns of her presence in his house, Ford flies into a violent rage against the old woman (the would-be seducer Falstaff in disguise): "A witch, a quean, an old cozening quean! Have I not forbid her my house?... She works by charms, by spells, by the figure, and such daubery as this

---

[69] In *The Tempest*, Caliban both fears and defies the pinches of Prospero's spirits; other characters are pinched, too, for their sins, including Sebastian, who suffers strong "inward pinches" for contemplating fratricide (5.1.77). Thoughts seem to activate pinches.

[70] Melchiori reads "Brentford" (4.2.72), an emendation introduced by Capell in 1776; The first quarto (1602) and the First Folio (1623) texts both read "Brainford" throughout. On the "witch's origin in Ford's brain," see Carroll, *Metamorphosis*, 188–90, to which the present remarks are indebted.

is, beyond our element: we know nothing.—Come down, you witch, you hag you! Come down, I say!" (4.2.162–9). When "she" appears, literally called forth by Ford, he sets upon her with sustained ranting and beating: "I'll prat her! [*Beats him.*] Out of my door, you witch, you rag, you baggage, you polecat, you runnion, out, out! I'll conjure you, I'll fortune-tell you!" (174–6). The incident adds to Falstaff's humiliation and bafflement, of course, but Ford's violence seems strangely extreme and unmotivated, and his anxiety about witchcraft bizarrely out of context and inordinate—impressions often heightened in theatrical performance.

The excess and emotional intensity in Ford's behavior argue that the fat woman comes laden with psychological meaning, functioning as a kind of surplus. Ford's irrational fear of her divining constitutes a repudiation of a truth about himself: that she is the avatar of his own magical thinking. The Brainford woman's power of charms and spells virtually allegorize the capacity of his own psyche to body forth the bogeyman he fears. Ford has, in a sense, conjured the witch himself. Falstaff as the fat woman is a comic manifestation of the jealousy in Ford's mind, and it is no accident that Shakespeare gives her the punning name "Brain-ford." His / her power to charm reflects the self-bewitching quality of Ford's obsession; her flaccid corpulence measures the size and substance of Ford's delusion; and her asexuality, age, and even cowardice hint at something insecure, epicene, or insufficient behind Ford's rage. Beyond the ethical perspective it may provide, the manifestation also generates our amoral fascination with, and pleasure in, the monstrous power of anxiety and imagination.

The old Brainford woman serves as the manifestation of Master Ford's jealous and fearful imagination; Ford had, after all, promised to show his henchmen a "monster" (3.2.73). That Ford manifests the old woman is made clear, of course, by the fact that Ford's alter ego, Master Brook, has requested Falstaff's attempt on the wife ("Brook" functions as the subconscious flowing forth of what "Ford" keeps in restraint). The play underlines variously the power of Ford's delusions: His wife accuses him of having "crotchets in [his] head" (2.1.139–40), and his horn-madness causes him to fantasize irrationally about her: "Then she plots, then she ruminates, then she devises... God be praised for my jealousy!" (2.2.289–93). Whether a blessed visitation or not, that jealousy calls forth its physical correlative in the unspeakable monster of Ford's imaginings.[71] The manifested witch of Brainford will continue to have effects in the play: According to Falstaff, she will confirm to Master Slender's page that it was Nim who cozened Slender of his chain. Likewise, Falstaff avers that the "wise woman" "hath taught me more wit than ever I learnt before in my life" (4.5.57, 58–9). The Brainford woman, that is, takes on a comic afterlife, a bit like that of the foul thief Deformed.

---

[71] Falstaff himself offers a version of this same effect when, in the Herne's oak episode, he notes that, among other things, the "guiltiness of [his] mind" (5.5.123) made him believe that the fairies were real even though he doubted it.

The revelatory power of excess, as suggested by Ford's frantic behavior, can be glimpsed elsewhere in *Merry Wives*. The plot of the Fords and Pages to humiliate Falstaff at Herne's oak, reconceiving him variously as a devil and monster, betrays a superfluous punishing of the knight that makes evident certain comic qualities in the conspirators. Falstaff is demonized for his attempted adulterous deception of husband with wife, yet Master and Mistress Page are blind to their own bad faith in undertaking to deceive each other by means of competing, semi-illicit, elopement plots for their daughter Anne. And whence comes the heated need of the wives to humiliate and physically punish Falstaff yet again with their climactic plot—in which Falstaff is to be terrified, pinched, burned, and publicly mocked—when the point has already been sufficiently and repeatedly won? One might wonder whether the wives harbor some unspoken Fordish fantasy, some deeply repressed desire, that calls forth the image of the shadowy, stag-like night-hunter Herne, the mythical "woodman," lurking in mating time around the sacred oak (5.5.27). The term "woodman" occurs in *Measure for Measure* as a hunter of women (4.3.158), and later in *Merry Wives* whoring will be referred to as "late-walking" (5.5.143). Herne perhaps operates as a fantasy-figure, again a little like Deformed, taking the shape of, and manifested by, desires in the wives that simply cannot be acknowledged but must be ridiculed, making their excess in vengeance a means of releasing (and perhaps controlling) energies in themselves more than it is a means of exposing Falstaff. The deception at Herne's oak functions as not only a social exorcism but also, for its perpetrators, a psychological one. For all its flaccidness, perhaps Ford's jealousy had some intuitive foundation.

Literary Contexts: Early Drama and Romance

No playwright before Shakespeare had discovered the dramatic richness of manifestation, even though it appears occasionally. Its multiple inspirations include literary traditions, of which we will consider two: first, the simple but suggestive matter of desire regarding stage entrances in early drama, coupled with the broader wish-fulfillment patterns of John Lyly's comedies; and, second, the influence of prose romance, with an example from Book 2 of Spenser's *The Faerie Queene*. Because manifestation as a device for comic drama has not been previously specified, it may be helpful to give attention to its antecedents and kindred effects.

Early Drama

Let us return to the matter of stage entrances. "The catastrophe is a nuptial," remarks Boyet in *Love's Labour's Lost*, speaking wittily of narrative form (4.1.75–6). The term "catastrophe," as we have noted, refers to Donatian criticism of Roman comedy, which often employs the entrance of an outsider late in the play. Thus, in Terence's *Andria* (the first Roman comedy translated into English), Simo appears with news that radically reorders relationships and makes possible the play's denouement of unions and reunions (a young woman turns out to be the lost daughter of a wealthy citizen). This familiar Terentian and Plautine plot twist also figures recurrently in cinquecento Italian comedy, modeled along Roman lines.[72] Sixteenth-century *commedia erudita* typically proceeds by means of fast-changing urban street scenes that convey the impression of characters ceaselessly coming and going, who thus cause little surprise by entering when thought of or needed by others. As with Roman comedy, the Italian urban stage set (such as the one surviving in the Vicenza's Teatro Olympico, built in 1584) creates a *mise en scène* of dense houses and intersecting streets in a lively city center where one might reasonably meet one's neighbor at any moment. Romanesque or Italianate early English comedies such as *Gammer Gurton's Needle* (c.1553), *Ralph Roister Doister* (c.1553), and *Supposes* (1566) reflect similar settings. But where Shakespeare's continental predecessors had a theatrical *frons scenae* meant to evoke a busy city crossroads, the bare and abstract Elizabethan stage requires a further act of the imagination—or facilitates more mysterious intuitions about why characters enter or behave as they do.[73] The realism of the *locus* in Italian comedy puts telepathic entrances out of bounds. But the unlocalized Elizabethan stage is always vulnerable to imaginative intrusion and psychic causation.[74]

Relevant here is not only Roman drama but also the tradition of English morality plays. In the medieval morality play *Mankind*, when Mercy addresses the audience about saving the corn and burning the chaff (43),[75] the reference calls forth Mischief, who associates himself with chaff (50; "chaff" will later be applied to Mankind in his fallen condition). "Why come ye hither, brother? Ye were not desired," asks Mercy (53). Mercy has been talking about spiritual food and about the need to be preserved from the devil, calling on his audience to bear in mind "this premeditation" (44). Mischief arrives not only as the self-appointed defender

---

[72] For an example of the last-act "catastrophe" in Italian comedy, see Alessandro Piccolomini's *L' alessandro*, written in Siena, 1543. *L' alessandro* even calls attention to the absurdity of the catastrophe, making clear that the recognition of the device's artificiality was already a part of stage history. For a later example (among many), see Giambattista della Porta's *La sorella* (*The Sister*), written in Naples, c. 1591–8.

[73] On the difference between the Italian fixed space and the Elizabethan fluid space in relation to *Twelfth Night*, see Charlotte Presser, "Intertextual Transformations: The *Novella* as Mediator between Italian and English Renaissance Drama," in *Shakespeare, Italy, and Intertextuality*, ed. Michele Marrapodi (Manchester: Manchester University Press, 2004), 107–17.

[74] I do not see manifestation as a regular feature of city comedy, but one exception might be *The Alchemist*'s introduction of the Faery Queen as the satiric manifestation and fulfillment of Dapper's desires.

[75] Citations of *Mankind* will refer to Douglas Bruster and Erik Rasmussen, eds., *Everyman and Mankind* (London: Methuen, 2009).

of chaff but also as exactly the force that Mercy had been instructing the audience to think about avoiding, as if to "premeditate" about keeping oneself from mischief by not thinking about it is perversely to call Mischief forth. Mischief arrives a bit like Dr. Pinch.[76]

In early plays, then, dramaturgical convention often dictates that characters enter a scene just at the moment that they are needed. But, as we have suggested, sometimes that practice might create additional effects aligned with a play's atmosphere and thematics. Indeed, as with some of the moralities, certain human-istically inflected plays of the sixteenth century employ entrances whose appos-ition seems preternatural. *Mankind*'s obverse telepathy, for example, functions frequently in John Skelton's *Magnificence* (*c.*1516): Felicity's insistence that reason must keep will "under subjection" (19) calls forth the oppositional Liberty; Liberty's claim for "free liberty" as the pathway to "pleasure" (78, 79) draws the regulating Measure onto the stage; and Magnificence's paean to "just measure" (249) generates Measure's antagonist, Fancy; and on it goes.[77] Such entrances turn the on-stage speakers' assertions into wishful thinking—and perhaps expose unconscious desires. More conventionally, in Nicholas Udall's Romanesque farce *Ralph Roister Doister*, characters enter repeatedly at exactly the moment that they are wanted: "I will seek him out—but lo! he commeth this way," says MerryGreek of Roister Doister at the end of the first scene.[78] Entrance after entrance in *Roister Doister* functions by the same formula: No sooner is a desire to meet a character announced than he or she is spotted approaching. Such foregrounding of the intersection of character's desires and dramaturgical devices—almost a metadramatic joke in *Ralph Roister Doister*—may not have passed unnoticed by a playwright as keen as Shakespeare. Illustratively, in *Lusty Juventus* (*c.*1542), Hypocrisie says, as Juventus enters, "You are the last man, / Which I talked on" (534–5), as if drawing his prospective victim to him,[79] while, in

---

[76] Most entrances in medieval plays are not telepathic, but Corpus Christi plays do often traffic in answered prayers. In the N-Town "Shearmen and Taylor's Pageant," for example, the three kings ask for divine guidance to get them to the scene of Christ's nativity: "I wot not where I am," says III Rex, who prays to the "Kyng of kyngis" for a "gyde" (583, 584). The heavens answer instantly: "A! yondur I se a sight, be-semyng all afar / . . . / Asse me thynke, a chyld peryng in a stare" (586–8). Similarly, in the N-Town's "Weavers' Pageant," after the aged Semeon prays that his "wholle desyre" (289) is to see Christ at his temple, he hears during sleep the dream-like "solam noyse" of responding angels (300). The intensity of his godly desire creates the condition for the angels' answer (see 307–8). Plays quoted from Hardin Craig, ed., *The Coventry Corpus Christi Plays*, The English Text Society (London: Kegan Paul, 1902). One might think of manifestation as the secularizing of answered prayers.

[77] Cited from John Skelton, *Magnyfycence*, ed. Paula Neuss (Manchester: Manchester University Press, 1980).

[78] Citations of *Ralph Roister Doister* are from Charles Whitworth, ed. *Three Sixteenth-Century Comedies:* Gammer Gurton's Needle, Roister Doister, The Old Wives Tale (Tonbridge, Kent: Ernest Benn, 1984).

[79] R. Wever, *An Enterlude Called Lusty Juventus*, ed. Helen Scarborough Thomas (New York: Garland, 1982).

The Merchant of Venice, Shylock quips to the just arrived Antonio, with premonitory phrasing, "Your worship was the last man in our mouths" (1.3.56).

For exploring the power of desire beyond the suggestive matter of entrances, no plays influenced Shakespeare as much as those of John Lyly. The fulfillment of fantastical desires is Lyly's subject: a man who loves the moon; two girls who long for each other; a king who would have his touch turn objects into gold.[80] In *Gallathea* (*c.*1584), the wood functions as does the city *mise en scène* of an Italian urban comedy, for gods, pages, artisans, citizens, and masquerading maidens roam through it, encountering each other incessantly as they pursue their disparate ends.[81] While telepathic entrances recede as a feature of this locale, the magnetic and transformative power of desire, especially erotic desire, colors everything. Gallathea and Phyllida become enamored with the awkward, blushing male-femaleness that they perceive in the other and experience in themselves (before they have even spoken to each other; see 2.1 and 2.4). Each girl sees in her counterpart the very image that she conceives of herself; the two are, in a sense, manifestations of each other. Lyly thus explores the complexity of erotic desire as simultaneously solipsistic and other-centered. In their love-duets, Gallathea and Phyllida's suspicions about the other's identicalness of sex lead them to test their reciprocal desire through verbal thrust yet also to exercise psychological deferral (3.2, 4.4), the self refusing to acknowledge the truth that it already knows.

Ultimately, fantastical desires in *Gallathea* have the capacity to effect material changes. The mutual devotion of the maidens is such that Venus (partly to sort out a conflict among the gods) agrees to transform one of the virgins into a man. Indeed, extravagant wish-fulfillment is the stock-in-trade of Lylyan comedy, and *Gallathea*'s apprentices, in their pursuit of one vain-gloriously deluded master after another, give voice to the irrepressible (although here defeated) human desire for god-like transformation. Not surprisingly, these plays are populated with gods, witches, and would-be alchemists and astrologers. With fantastical desire as his main subject, Lyly moves well beyond Italian drama, for Italian *commedia erudita* was too cynically anti-romantic and too reductive in its treatment of sex to allow desire to swell into a force with almost magical power.

Prose Romance

Besides Tudor comedy, another tradition established an important model for manifestation, that of medieval and Renaissance romances, the sort of centuries-old works that Shakespeare likely read in childhood and that remained popular in

---

[80]   On erotic desire in Lyly in relation to figuration and imagination, see Knoll, *Conceiving Desire*.
[81]   On *Gallathea*, see Kent Cartwright, *Theatre and Humanism: English Drama in the Sixteenth Century* (Cambridge: Cambridge University Press, 1999), 167–93.

Elizabethan England.[82] A device similar to manifestation constitutes a fundamental narrative strategy in romance, from Malory to Spenser.[83] A helpful example occurs in *The Faerie Queene*, Book 2, Canto 4. There Guyon encounters the vengeful lover Phedon who, betrayed into murdering his beloved, Claribell, has taken in response the life of Philemon, the treacherous friend who had convinced him that Claribell was betraying him sexually. Likewise, Phedon is attempting now to kill Pryene, the woman who had assisted Philemon. He tells Guyon how his enraged pursuit of her has been interrupted by a "mad man": "As I her, so he me pursewd apace"; "I breathing yre, / ... my heat kindled his cruel fyre" (*FQ* 2.4.32).[84] The "mad man" who chased, captured, bound, beat, and gored Phedon is Furor, who has just been conquered by the knight of temperance, Sir Guyon. Furor obviously personifies Phedon's own "yre," his giving of himself over to a consuming rage that has produced an ongoing murderous violence. Phedon's furor calls forth Furor, who constitutes the objective correlative to Phedon's actions and thoughts and who makes visible their self-destructive implications.

Yet inside the allegory of Phedon's-wrath-as-Furor resides a deeper manifestation. Phedon has been betrayed by his intimate friend, Philemon (less a name than a synonym for friend): "Our selues in league of vowed loue we knit" (2.4.18). In the language of friendship, Philemon is Phedon's "other self." That mutuality hints that Phedon's certainty about Claribell's guilt derives, as Paul Alpers argues, as much from within himself as from the external facts of deception. The seed of jealousy, once either generated from the self or planted from without, festers in Phedon's "engreeued mind," "Till that the truth thereof I did outwrest" (2.4.23). The role of betrayer, as Alpers puts it, "is not simply the office of an external agent ... [T]he friend's role is produced by the energies of the hero's own mind, and the false friend becomes inextricably a part of himself."[85] After murdering Claribell, Phedon contemplates suicide (2.4.3) but instead kills Philemon and attempts to kill Pyrene. For Phedon, "agon[ized]" by "griefe and furie" (2.4.33), suicide and murder become like each other.

---

[82] See Helen Cooper, *Shakespeare's Medieval World* (London: Bloomsbury, 2010), 170–203.

[83] For a recent study of the English medieval and romance tradition much interested in the functioning of desire, see Helen Cooper, *The English Romance in Time* (Oxford: Oxford University Press, 2004), especially "Landscapes of Desire and Fear" (77–86), which analyzes the landscapes of various romances in terms of the desires, fears, and state of mind of the questing knight. *A Midsummer Night's Dream* has as a source for Oberon and the fairies the romance *Huon of Bordeaux*, translated sometime before 1533, itself turned into a play for the 1593–4 season; see Geoffrey Bullough, ed., *Narrative and Dramatic Sources of Shakespeare*, vol. 1 of 8, *Early Comedies, Poems, Romeo and Juliet* (London: Routledge, 1957), 370–1.

[84] Cited from Edmund Spenser, *The Works of Edmund Spenser: A Variorum Edition*, vol. 2 of 8, ed. Edwin Greenlaw; gen. eds. Edwin Greenlaw, Charles Grosvenor Osgood, and Frederick Morgan Padelford (Baltimore, MD: Johns Hopkins Press, 1933).

[85] Paul J. Alpers, *The Poetry of* The Faerie Queene (Columbia, MO: University of Missouri Press, 1982), 61. For a theorizing of the kind of effect under consideration, see Harry Berger, Jr., "Displacing Autophobia in *Faerie Queene* I: Ethics, Gender, and Oppositional Reading in the Spenserian Text," *English Literary Renaissance* 28, no. 2 (Spring 1998): 163–82.

Thus, Furor embodies not just outward wrath but also the inexplicable perversity within the self that would destroy exactly what it presumes to love, that would destroy even oneself. Phedon's "internal psychological action becomes an event in the poem."[86] The Palmer's comment on the "fearefull" power of unbridled affections (2.4.34) recognizes, as Alpers argues, that those affections "have an independent energy of their own" (67). Such "independent energy" might mean that our fears, angers, and desires once fully unleashed have the power to multiply and contaminate the world with their likenesses. The psyche turns not only fearsome but also unpredictable and opaque.[87]

Besides being a complex allegory, Furor is also a real monster with iron teeth, burning eyes, "long lockes, colour like copper wire," and a "tawny beard," who fights wildly like a bull and who cannot be subdued with a sword (2.4.7).[88] Such realistic materializations populate the landscape of The Faerie Queene.[89] Furor expresses the violently willful psyche that has consumed Phedon. He represents not only the figuration of Phedon's particular self-destructive wrath but also the possibility of a realistic Furor in the world at large.[90] In Shakespearean materialization, the Spenserian reflexive and allegorized opponent becomes less generalizable and more opaque, while the sense of the manifested figure's independent existence grows. Master Ford's overblown and epicene jealousy takes the form of the witch of Brainford; she is not the form of all jealousy but rather the shape that it generates in Ford. In Shakespearean comedy, furthermore, the monstrous manifestation inspires not just revulsion but also a kind of indulgent wonder.

* * * *

For manifestation, then, two of Shakespeare's literary building blocks were early English drama and medieval–Renaissance romance. More expansive than the entrance devices of old comedy, less overt and universalized than the allegory of the narrative romances, Shakespearean manifestation introduces into comedy a level of causation that is characterological, metaphoric, and enigmatic. It adds a

---

[86] Alpers, Poetry, 66.

[87] On psychological allegory in Spenser, see also A. C. Hamilton, The Structure of Allegory in The Faerie Queene (Oxford: Clarendon Press, 1961); Rosamund Tuve, Allegorical Imagery: Some Mediaeval Books and Their Posterity (Princeton, NJ: Princeton University Press, 1966); Kathleen Williams, Spenser's Faerie Queene: The World of Glass (London: Routledge and Kegan Paul, 1966); C. S. Lewis, Spenser's Images of Life (Cambridge: Cambridge University Press, 1967); John Erskine Hankins, Source and Meaning in Spenser's Allegory: A Study of The Faerie Queene (Oxford: Clarendon Press, 1971); and Felicity Hughes, "Psychological Allegory in The Faerie Queene, III.xi–xii," Review of English Studies 29 (1978): 129–46.

[88] On that aspect of The Faerie Queene, see Susanne L. Wofford, "The Faerie Queene, Books I–III," in The Cambridge Companion to Spenser, ed. Andrew Hadfield (Cambridge: Cambridge University Press, 2001), 106–23.

[89] As Wofford puts it, "To learn to read Spenser's poem is to learn that everything—a person in the story, a place, a house, a tree or a giant—can represent an aspect of the hero or heroine's own psyche" ("Books I–III," 116).

[90] I am here borrowing from Wofford on Sans Foy, "Books I–III," 117, see 116–19.

memorable mysteriousness largely absent even in the great Italian comedies of the age. Manifestations evoke a kind of ethical realism and, perhaps more interestingly, a fascinated awe for the perverse powers of the human psyche—the kind of awe that readers have historically attached to a character such as Falstaff. The device generates a Zupančičian admiration for the immensity and monstrousness of human presumption, shining light on a quality that comedy is suited to recognize. Manifestation exposes and celebrates the determination of humans to behave like "contemplative idiot[s]," as Sir Toby says of the about-to-be-gulled Malvolio (*Twelfth Night*, 2.5.17), living as if the world were a materialization of our fantasies. It gives to thoughts, feelings, fears, and desires an enchanted causal power. We may extol the forays of wit and the bright surfaces of Shakespeare's comedies, but manifestation takes us into their depths, their moments of uncanniness, helping to explain the plays' staying power. Manifestation anticipates the forms of wish-fulfillment that Shakespeare will explore in the late romances, where desires and fears are potentially more disastrous than delightful and where dramatic resolutions turn more spiritual than ethical. With manifestation, Shakespeare recognizes an under-explored possibility in earlier drama and develops it into a vibrant comic device.

5

The Return from the Dead

> It is quite true that the past *haunts* us; it is the past's function to
> haunt us.
>
> Hannah Arendt
"Home to Roost"

"To fake dying or death and to come to life 'miraculously' is a frequent, favorite
motif of comedies," observes the philosopher Agnes Heller, and that motif
recurs because "comedy presents being toward life."[1] Despite Heller's claim,
Shakespearean scholarship has given far less attention to revenants in the comedies than to the resurrection figures and ghosts in the histories, tragedies, and late
romances.[2] Yet comedies from *The Two Gentlemen of Verona* to *Measure for
Measure* showcase protagonists—Julia, Portia, Hero, Sebastian, Claudio, and
Helen, among others—who are thought to be, or who figuratively are, dead,
only to be climactically rejuvenated. These metaphoric revivifications catapult
their plays into structural and emotional completion and instance Renaissance
drama's capacity for, according to Stephen Greenblatt, raising, managing, and
releasing anxiety.[3] The trope also expresses important affective and thematic
concerns of Shakespearean comedy, including the tensions between imagination
and rationality, and wonder and skepticism. It puts at issue, too, the countervailing
pulls of individualism and communalism, since returns from the dead illuminate
the uncanny interconnectedness among comic characters and their mysterious
capacity to act distantly upon each other. It refuses, as William Faulkner might

---

[1] Agnes Heller, *The Immortal Comedy: The Comic Phenomenon in Art, Literature, and Life*
(Lanham, MD: Lexington Books, 2005), 38. Anthropologically and mythically, the resurrection of the
sacrificial god has long been considered fundamental to comedy; see the classic study by Frances
Macdonald Cornford, *The Origins of Attic Comedy* (London: Edward Arnold, [1934] 2014). As Wylie
Sypher puts it, "Comedy is essentially...a triumph over mortality by some absurd faith in rebirth,
restoration, and salvation"; "The Meaning of Comedy," in *Comedy*: An Essay on Comedy *by George
Meredith;* Laughter *by Henri Bergson;* Introduction and Appendix, "The Meanings of Comedy," *by
Wylie Sypher,* ed. Wylie Sypher (New York: Doubleday, 1956), 220, see esp. 214–26.
[2] On tragic ghosts, see, for example, Catherine Belsey, "Shakespeare's Sad Tale for Winter: *Hamlet*
and the Tradition of Fireside Ghost Stories," *Shakespeare Quarterly* 6, no. 1 (Spring 2010): 1–27; and
Stephen Greenblatt, *Hamlet in Purgatory* (Princeton, NJ: Princeton University Press, 2001). On
resurrection in the late romances, see, among others, Sarah Beckwith, *Shakespeare and the Grammar
of Forgiveness* (Ithaca, NY: Cornell University Press, 2011).
[3] Stephen Greenblatt, "Martial Law in the Land of Cockaigne," *Shakespearean Negotiations: The
Circulation of Social Energy in Renaissance England* (Berkeley, CA: University of California Press,
1988), 129–64.

Shakespeare and the Comedy of Enchantment. Kent Cartwright, Oxford University Press. © Kent Cartwright 2021.
DOI: 10.1093/oso/9780198868897.003.0006

put it, to let the past be past; it reveals how the past "haunts us," as the chapter epigraph suggests. If Shakespearean comedy anchors itself in present life, as Heller might say, it can yet facilitate a less-recognized encounter between newer early modern and older medieval world views, between the present and the irrepressible past.[4] "In medieval England it was fully accepted that dead men might sometimes return to haunt the living," observes Keith Thomas.[5] In Shakespeare's world, however, the Reformation banished ghosts and revenants. For Protestants, pre-sumably, no unsettled shades from Purgatory wandered the night, calling out to their kinsmen for intercessory prayer, warning of the pains of the other world, or troubling the thoughts of the living—except that the idea of the return from the dead retained a powerful half-life in Elizabethan culture and Shakespearean comedy.[6] Nothing so refuses to give up the ghost as a revenant.

The Comic Business of Death

Shakespeare's comic business often oddly commences with death or the threat of death, a practice that infuses emotional power into the motif of the return from the dead. Examples abound: Condemnation to death confronts the world-weary Egeon; the decease of Petruccio's father sends his son to seek a wife in Padua; execution or living death in a nunnery threaten Hermia; the deceased grand-father's bequest to Anne Page prompts rival stratagems for matching her in marriage: the dead hand of the father rules Portia; the passing away of Oliver and Orlando's father affords the elder son impunity in seeking the life of the younger; her brother's inconsolable death has sent Olivia into prolonged grief, while Viola fears that her own brother has drowned; beheading is to be Claudio's penalty for making Julia pregnant; and Helen's father and her guardian have both died, while the King faces a potentially fatal illness. Death's imminence figures in the opening of Shakespeare's comedies so often as to be characteristic, a practice absent in Jonson or earlier Elizabethan playwrights. We might say that death or its threat in the comedies creates a psychological displacement, a new set of circumstances, that functions as counterpart to the physical displacement or exile that characters often suffer (see Chapter 3). It signals profound loss and demands a response.

[4] Heller, *Immortal Comedy*, 13.
[5] Keith Thomas, *Religion and the Decline of Magic: Studies in Popular Beliefs in Sixteenth- and Seventeenth-Century England* (London: Penguin Books, [1971] 1991), 701.
[6] It also retains a trace in magic treatises; Agrippa devotes a chapter to "Of the Reviving of the Dead"; he cites numerous examples from ancient authorities, although he favors the argument that the individuals in question were only seeming dead, having fallen into a stupor (that might last months and years); Heinrich Cornelius Agrippa, *Three Books of Occult Philosophy*, trans. James Freake, ed. Donald Tyson (St. Paul, MN: Llewellyn Publications, 1995; orig. pub. in Latin, 1550), 181–5.

Death not only launches but also haunts the action of many of the comedies, just as, in some productions of *The Comedy of Errors*, Egeon can be glimpsed wandering in the background through Ephesus. Valentine faces banishment or execution. Falstaff fears murder at the hand of Master Ford, while Doctor Caius challenges Sir Hugh to a comic duel to the death ("I will cut his troat in de park" [*MW* 1.4.101]). Antonio comes to the brink of death from Shylock's ready knife. "Kill Claudio," demands Beatrice famously—she who had promised to eat all of Benedick's war killings—and a potentially deadly challenge ensues. Rosalind and Orlando flee from death threats to Arden Forest. Violence slowly invades Ilyria to the point where Orsino threatens to murder Viola. The executioner's axe hangs over the prison action of *Measure for Measure*. Helen risks death by torture if she cannot cure the King. To be sure, the theme of death registers with different tonalities and emphases in those plays, but it recurs with a frequency that suggests a pattern. As Simon Palfrey and Emma Smith put it, "[d]eath provides a formal frame" for the comedies, all of them undertaking, in a sense, to "'move wild laughter'" in the "'throat of death.'"[7] Death or its threat seems calculated to induce in audiences a surge of relief and completion in those late moments when characters metaphorically return from the dead. More than just a nifty surprise, then, the return motif typically fulfills a profound desire for life against the threat of death lodged deeply in the action. We see here some of the predicates in Shakespearean comedy for the emotional power of the wondrous and the miraculous.

Perhaps more often than criticism has recognized, metaphoric revivifications shape both the comic action and the endings. Julia is treated as dead by Proteus in *The Gentlemen of Verona* but comes alive in the denouement. Petruccio in *The Taming of the Shrew* promises to "kill" Kate with "kindness" (4.1.197), so that, by the end, she has become for Baptista "another daughter,...changed as she had never been" (5.2.120–1).[8] Egeon in *The Comedy of Errors*, takes on, as we have noted, the affect of a wandering shade, and the presumed-dead mother, Emilia, makes a rabbit-out-of-the-hat appearance in the finale.[9] Portia at the beginning of the *Merchant of Venice* is confined figuratively like an effigy buried in a coffin, to be brought alive by the winning suitor. Hero is resurrected metaphorically in *Much Ado About Nothing* with a shock to Claudio rather like that of a real resurrection. Falstaff's adventures with Mistress Ford turn him figuratively into a comic revenant. Sebastian appears as if risen out of the sea in *Twelfth Night*, with all the disruptive force of a divine intervention. Claudio in *Measure for Measure* is

---

[7] Simon Palfrey and Emma Smith, *Shakespeare's Dead* (Oxford: Bodleian Library, 2016), 48, 71.

[8] One of Norton's glosses for that last phrase is "as if she had never existed before"; Stephen Greenblatt, et al., eds, *The Norton Shakespeare*. 3rd edn. (New York: W. W. Norton, 2015); see also Northrop Frye, *A Natural Perspective* (New York: Columbia University Press, 1965), 84.

[9] The mother's return in *Errors* looks forward to the motif in the late romances, such as *The Winter's Tale*.

restored from reported death by the Duke, himself something of a returning Christ-figure; Mariana returns from figurative death, and Angelo from prospective death. Helen in *All's Well That Ends Well* brings the King back from near expiration and dramatically returns herself from alleged death. And at the edge of those plays lurks Falstaff, who, like the medieval Vice, springs back to life near the climax of *Henry IV, Part 1*. If comedy is "being toward[s] life," as Heller asserts, then one of its conditions is the reminder of death, deepening the emotional force of comedy's triumphs.

Dramatic and Critical Contexts

Medieval, Elizabethan, and continental drama provide context for the revenant motif in Shakespeare's comedies. Christ's resurrection constitutes, of course, a climactic event in Cycle theater, sometimes associated visually with a sudden brightness, as in the Chester "Resurrection" play.[10] Alexandra Johnston notes that "[t]he Easter or 'Resurrection' Plays have the longest history of any vernacular biblical plays from the medieval and early modern period" (5), so that any invoking of the resurrection motif in Elizabethan theater would appeal to cultural memory. The motif threads through Tudor and Elizabethan drama. Of many possible examples, the eponymous comic hero Ralph Roister Doister revives himself after enacting his own mock requiem mass; the ghost of the unburied Jack in George Peele's *Old Wives Tales* (1590) figures prominently in the play's action; the title character of Lyly's *Endymion* (1588) is awoken from a spell-induced twenty-years' sleep as if from the dead; and in the opening of Robert Greene's *The Scottish History of James IV* (*c.*1590), the character Bohan rises in the first scene out of a tomb. Cinquecento Italian comedy regularly employs not only the imagery of revivification but also characters who are presumed to have perished only to appear climactically at the end. Instances include Bernardo Dovizi da Bibbiena, *La calandria* (Urbino, *c.*1513); Niocolo Machiavelli, *La mandragola* (Florence, *c.*1518); the Academy of the Intronati, *Gl' ingannati* (Siena, 1531); Annibal Caro, *Gli straccioni* (Rome, 1543); and Giambattista Della Porta, *Gli duoi fratelli rivali* (Naples?, *c.*1590). One of the first Italian cinquecento comedies, *La calandria*, involves an elaborately developed ruse by the servant Fessenio to train the rich, old fool Calandro in how to die and come back alive in order to hide himself in a casket to be taken to an assignation with the presumed maiden Santilla; the return motif parodies Calandro's apparent erotic

---

[10] On the medieval dramatizing of Christ's resurrection, see Elizabeth Williamson, "Things Newly Performed: The Resurrection Tradition in Shakespeare's Plays," in *Shakespeare and Religious Change*, ed. Kenneth J. E. Graham and Philip D. Collington (Houndmills, Basingstoke: Palgrave, 2009), 110–32, on 114–19; on the history of the English resurrection play, see Alexandra Johnston, "The Emerging Pattern of the Easter Play in England," *Medieval English Theatre* 20 (1998): 3–23 (cited in Williamson).

fantasy of would-be rejuvenation. Meanwhile Santilla and Lidio are twins separated by war who each discover that the other is alive. The motif of return derives from the Roman comedies of Plautus and Terence, but in many of the Italian plays, it takes on contemporary urgency because of the separation of Italian families (as with Santilla and Lidio) by regional violence, such as the Turks' coastal incursions into the peninsula (similarly, the Punic wars divided families in Plautus and Terence) or the 1527 sack of Rome. The Italian comic motif of return from the dead appears in some of the plays translated from Italian into English in the Elizabethan era. John Jefferey's (?) *The Bugbears* (c.1566), a translation of Antonio Francesco Grazzini's *La spiritata* (1561)—and a play that makes references to *La calandria*—involves the metaphoric return from the dead of the female love interest, who has been reported as sick throughout. In a hilarious bit in Anthony Munday's *Fedele and Fortunio* (1585), an adaptation of Luigi Pasqualigo's *Il fedele* (Venice, 1576), the *miles gloriosus*, Captain Crackstone, rises shockingly from his hiding place in a tomb when tapers are thrown into it at the end of a scene of magical incantation. The return from the dead was already a stock device in sixteenth-century comedy (and other literature[11]) when Shakespeare gave it new and more significant treatment.

The revenant motif in Shakespeare's comedies has long been noted in passing by Shakespeare scholars, but it has gained particular attention only of late. A pattern of mythic renewal, from winter to spring, marks Northrop Frye's influential view of comedy: "The mythical or primitive basis of comedy is a movement toward the rebirth and renewal of the powers of nature."[12] Frye's interest in revenants focuses on the sense that a character "really dies and comes back to life," but his brief comments in that regard are limited to Hero, Katharine, Portia, and Helen (84), and his study does not consider how the death-and-return motif plays out through a comedy. Frye folds the revenant's return, moreover, within a strongly registered vision of the harmonizing power of nature. The present study, by contrast, entertains a quality of mystery in the comedies that resists being rationalized within a system of harmony. Another influential study, by Alexander Leggatt, also touches on the resurrection motif, and in a manner that seems representative for much criticism.[13] *Shakespeare's Comedy of Love* notices magic and miracle in the plays and attends intermittently to characters who

---

[11] Revivification also constitutes a familiar motif of early chivalric romances: "a return from an encounter with death—a symbolic resurrection," as Helen Cooper puts it; *The English Romance in Time: Transforming Motifs from Geoffrey of Monmouth to the Death of Shakespeare* (Oxford: Oxford University Press, 2004), 10. The motif occurs in Malory's *Morte d'Arthur* (1485) and, closer to Shakespeare's time, in Sidney's *Arcadia* (1590), where Duke Basilius, believed dead, revives climactically to solve otherwise intractable problems. Return also figures in the romance tradition represented by the Apollonius of Tyre legend, a source for *Pericles*, which Shakespeare apparently knew when he was writing *The Comedy of Errors*.

[12] Northrop Frye, *A Natural Perspective: The Development of Shakespearean Comedy and Romance* (New York: Columbia University Press, 1965), 119.

[13] Alexander Leggatt, *Shakespeare's Comedy of Love* (London: Methuen, 1974).

metaphorically return from the dead, focusing typically on the denouements. In general, Leggatt sees an "intersection" and "interweaving" of "the fantastic and the everyday" (18), the comedies "linking the miracle of the ending with the normal processes of life" (16, on *Errors*), a picture of coherence and harmony that excludes any lasting thematic or emotional disturbance from the revenant. Some recent criticism has enlarged the discussion of this motif. Sarah Beckwith focuses on the resurrection trope as it structures final recognition scenes, especially in *Measure for Measure* and the late romances, where those who are supposedly dead confront—and forgive—those who have harmed or metaphorically killed them.[14] Drawing power from the Gospel narratives, such scenes are concerned with recollection, as opposed to forgetting: "The 'resurrected' characters burst into the present as reminders of an ineradicable past that must be confronted" (129). (On forgiveness in the comedies and its effect on the past, see Chapter 6.) If, as Katharine Goodland argues, history and memory can be said to pull in opposite directions—the first, more early modern, seeing the present as a break with the past; the second, more medieval, seeing the present as a continuation of the past— then, for Beckwith, the Christian paradigm of resurrection refuses historical forgetting.[15] For Sean Benson, who studies the resurrection trope in recognition scenes from five Shakespearean comedies, the stories of the presumed-dead characters hover between the mundane and the quasi-miraculous, more than metaphoric but less than theological.[16] Shakespeare develops a figure, that is, who resists assimilation into a familiar paradigm. Differently, Kiernan Ryan finds in Helen's resurrection in the recognition scene of *All's Well That Ends Well* evidence not for Christian doctrine or quasi-religious mystery but for "the revolutionary spirit of utopian hope" (38).[17] These arguments take the resurrection motif as crucial but diverge in assessments of its effect: deeply Christian, not quite miraculous, futuristic. The present analysis will be close in spirit to those treatments, especially Benson's, though it will differ from them, first, by unearthing more examples, and, second, by focusing not only on last scenes but also on the revenant motif as it functions throughout a play, thus emphasizing how important Shakespeare's border-crossers are to the shape of the comedies.

[14] Sarah Beckwith, *Shakespeare and the Grammar of Forgiveness* (Ithaca, NY: Cornell University Press, 2011), see esp. chapters 3 and 6.

[15] Katharine Goodland, *Female Mourning in Medieval and Renaissance Drama: From* The Raising of Lazarus *to* King Lear (Aldershot: Ashgate, 2005), 2–4; Goodland draws upon work by Beckwith.

[16] Sean Benson, *Shakespearean Resurrection: The Art of Almost Raising the Dead* (Pittsburgh, PA: Duquesne University Press, 2009), see esp. 35–76. Benson focuses on *The Comedy of Errors, Much Ado About Nothing, Twelfth Night, All's Well That Ends Well,* and *Measure for Measure.* On the relationship between the return motif and female hysteria, see Kaara L. Peterson, "Shakespearean Revivifications: Early Modern Undead," *Shakespeare Studies* 32 (Madison, NJ: Fairleigh Dickinson University Press, 2004), 240–66.

[17] Kiernan Ryan, "'Where hope is coldest': *All's Well That Ends Well,*" in *Spiritual Shakespeares,* ed. Ewan Fernie (London: Routledge, 2005), 28–49. See also Kiernan Ryan, *Shakespeare's Comedies* (Houndmills, Basingstoke: Palgrave Macmillan, 2009).

The Value of the Motif: Three Questions and a Little History

Let us pose three questions. First, what brings characters back from metaphorical or presumed deaths? Second, what difference does a return from the dead make? Third, what does the return motif tell us about Shakespearean comedy and even comedy in general? To the first question, one answer is that in the comedies, the presumed-dead re-appear because they are longed for so much by the living. Thoughts, feelings, and desires can have telepathic and magnetic power (see Chapter 4); in that respect, revenants illustrate the power of survivors' prayers towards those dead and believed to be in Purgatory. The Gospel of John's raising-of-Lazarus story, although it glorifies God, stresses Jesus's love for Martha, Mary, and Lazarus, and it calls repeated attention to the love, grief, and longing of all those bereaved. "Lord, if thou haddest been here, my brother had not been dead," says Mary, restating Martha's earlier assertion (John 11:32, The Geneva Bible). The narrative continues: "When Iesus therefore sawe her wepe, & the Iewes *also* wepe which came with her, he groned in the spirit, & was troubled in him self" (33); "Iesus wept" (35); "Then said the Iewes, Beholde, how he loued him" (36). In this influential story, the deep personal love for Lazarus, felt not only by his sisters Mary and Martha and by other sympathizers but also keenly by his friend Jesus, seems a condition for resurrection. What is conditional there becomes instrumental in Shakespearean comedy.

Second, concerning the difference that a return from the dead makes, several answers offer themselves. For one, revivification can confer on those who symbolically return an enlarged vividness or vitality, a dimension not typically taken up in criticism. Thus, the possibility for new life enters the play with the revenant. That possibility helps us to understand how returning can be influenced, as argued above, by thoughts and desires, and thus how early moderns understood the ontology of death. In the medieval Catholic world view, a visitation from someone dead can offer a kind of communion, effected by the prayers of the bereaved extended to the departed.[18] In this spiritual economy, the desire of the living calls forth the revenant, who returns to give thanks for intercessory prayers or to comfort those left behind. "[A] recurrent motif in treatments of Purgatory," writes Eamon Duffy, "is the centrality of both natural and supernatural bonding between the living and the dead" (348). For Duffy, that bond of love is exemplified in a story from *The Golden Legend* in which a mother unable to pray for herself on her deathbed is saved from damnation by the intervening prayers of her son; later, in thanks, the soul of the mother appears to him "'bryght and schynyng as the sone thonkynge hym of her delyveraunce'" (353). Likewise, according to

---

[18] See Stephen Greenblatt, *Hamlet in Purgatory* (Princeton, NJ: Princeton University Press, 2001), 40–5; on Purgatory and its relation to the living, see Eamon Duffy, *The Stripping of the Altars: Traditional Religion in England c. 1400–1580* (New Haven, CT: Yale University Press, 1992), 338–78.

sixteenth-century Swiss Protestant theologian Ludwig Lavater, souls delivered from Purgatory were said by Catholics to show themselves afterwards "in greate lyght and glorie."[19] Radiance marks the revenant. The key to this energizing is the psychic communion between those remaining and those remembered, captured by the Elizabeth Catholic priest William Allen, who envisions the living faithful on earth crying out for help from heaven and the souls of the dead—"happily promoted to the joy of Christ's blessed kingdom"—"perpetually pray[ing]" for "their . . . fellows beneath."[20]

Just that peculiar medieval and Catholic economy—with its emphasis on the spiritual contact between those living and those dead, and on the luminosity of spiritual return—touches Shakespeare's comedies. Here death turns into adumbrated presence. Rather than receding from memory, the revenant haunts the survivors, demands attention: After the reported death of Helen in All's Well, for example, the Countess and the King insist again and again that her memory must be put aside—but doing so proves impossible, their repeated declarations only bringing back the sense of her aura.[21] Indeed, Shakespeare's comic characters sometimes become more real by seeming to have died; their revived existences, bathed in the numinous, take on a vividness and charisma greater than they previously possessed. Stephen Greenblatt gets at this effect when he argues that the ghost in Hamlet is "amazingly disturbing and vivid."[22] Shakespeare's revenants can be brimming with life. Such powerful ideas shift our attention away from conventional formulas about comedy (e.g., that it ends with a marriage) and towards its deep emotional wellsprings. Yet, as we shall see in the case of Hero, Shakespeare insists on complexity, employing the motif but also sometimes putting its effects in doubt.

As a related difference made by the theme of revivification, returns often emphasize the bondedness and interconnectedness of characters to each other. Consider the example of Angelo in Measure for Measure. (The idea of return or remission from death saturates this play, touching the characters of Claudio, Marianna, Angelo, Barnardine, Lucio, and even the Duke and Isabella.) When

[19] Ludwig Lavater, Of Ghosts and Spirits Walking by Night, trans. R. H. [Robert Harrison] [London, 1572], ed. J. Dover Wilson and May Yardley (Oxford: Oxford University Press, 1929), 72. Although Lavater rejects the idea of Purgatory, he accepts as true "that spirits do often appeare," those being "good or euill Angels" (53, 98). Lavater's book, published in Latin in Leiden in 1569, was quickly translated into German, French, Spanish, Italian, and English. It constitutes "[t]he fullest and most influential work on angels and ghosts in the sixteenth century"; Bruce Gordon, "Malevolent Ghosts and Ministering Angels: Apparitions and Pastoral Care in the Swiss Reformation," in The Place of the Dead: Death and Remembrance in Late Medieval and Early Modern Europe, ed. Bruce Gordon and Peter Marshall (Cambridge: Cambridge University Press, 2000), 87–109, on 95.

[20] William Allen, A Defense and Declaration of the Catholic Church's Doctrine, Touching Purgatory (Antwerp: by John Latius, 1565), 133r; for Allen's passionate discussion of the unity between the living and the dead, see 132r to 137r. Allen treats biblical instances and the general possibility of return from the dead on 110v to 111r.

[21] Shakespeare will return to this powerful effect in A Winter's Tale.

[22] Greenblatt, Hamlet in Purgatory, 4.

Marianna importunes Isabella to help beg the Duke to forgive Angelo, the Duke rejoins in shock: "Should she kneel down in mercy to this fact, / Her brother's ghost his paved bed would break / And take her hence in horror" (5.1.432–4). The dead, he suggests, are listening nearby and are capable of recoiling emotionally and intervening punitively in the actions of the living, as if the two realms and their beings were bonded. In her subsequent plea for Angelo, Isabella brings Claudio imaginatively back to life but identifies him with Angelo: "Look, if it please you, on this man condemned / As if my brother lived" (442–3). Isabella's hypothesis materializes into fact, and as the Duke reveals Claudio living, he also observes Angelo: "By this Lord Angelo perceives he's safe— / Methinks I see a quickening in his eye" (494–95). The "quickening" of Angelo's eye proclaims that he, too, is coming back to life along with Claudio from his own prospective death. It declares again his bondedness to Claudio, now as much in revivification as in potential death, as if they were interchangeable with, substitutable for, one another. Indeed, revivification always pulls a character back into human connect-edness, into dense new interpersonal relations, and into the creation of comedy's climactic new community.

Behind those revelations of interconnectedness lies a sense of community more medieval—or imagined as medieval—than modern. To be sure, medieval com-munities could be highly hierarchical, status conscious, and competitive. As Peter Womack points out in regards to the medieval *urbus* portrayed in the N-Town Passion Plays, it was not "'communal' in an egalitarian or collectivist sense, but was minutely graded, horizontally and vertically, by occupation, seniority, gender, wealth, and civic position."[23] According to Keith Wrightson, among historians "the prevailing view is that in medieval society neighborliness was less a real, existing, state of harmonious social relations than an ideal."[24] On the other hand, Wrightson argues, historians have demonstrated "the enduring significance of a variety of forms of cooperation and mutuality" in medieval and early modern England, with communities highly dependent on trust, honesty, and neighborli-ness (21). Beyond practical, social, and economic bonds, religious bonds worked to fashion a profound and profoundly shared sacramental identity, deeply etched through church services and strictures, a central one being the importance of communal fellow-feeling and charity.[25] Medieval Britons also participated in an amazing series of religious holidays and related customs that saturated the entire

---

[23] Peter Womack, "Imagining Communities: Theatres and the English Nation in the Sixteenth Century," in *Culture and History 1350–1600: Essays on English Communities, Identities and Writing*, ed. David Aers (Detroit, MI: Wayne State University Press, 1992), 91–146, on 102.

[24] Keith Wrightson, "'Decline of Neighborliness' Revised," in *Local Identities in Medieval and Early Modern England*, ed. Norman L. Jones and Daniel Woolf (Houndmills, Basingstoke: Palgrave Macmillan, 2007), 19–49, on 20. Wrightson's essay helpfully details the debate among historians about medieval and early modern "neighborliness."

[25] See Wrightson, "'Decline,'" 32–3.

liturgical year and that involved extensive shared and ritualized activities.[26] Such activities, including the N-town plays, sought to forge a sense of communal oneness in Christ, an ideal, perhaps, but a compelling one.

Finally, to return to *Measure for Measure* for an additional difference created by the revenant motif, the precarious situation of Angelo and others in the denouement makes clear that comic lives entail alternative possibilities, arguably more so than do tragic lives. Marianna returns from such an alternative life. For Hero in *Much Ado*, if her reputation cannot be redeemed, she will be shipped off to wear out a solitary, invisible existence "[i]n some reclusive and religious life, / Out of all eyes, tongues, minds and injuries" (4.1.242–3). Viola's situation illuminates that sense of potentially dire alternatives. When "Cesario" tells the story of his sister's undivulged love (that is, Viola's own), Orsino responds, "And what's her history?" to which Viola answers, "A blank... / She sat like Patience on a monument, / Smiling at grief" (*TN* 2.4.110–13). The suffering lover becomes, in effect, a marmoreal effigy on a burial monument. The possibility of death and especially of living death in these examples suggests that, in comedy, lives entail alternative futures (rather than the absolute destinies of tragedies) and that figurative return from death means the triumph of one possibility over another.

That sense of alternative destinies points towards a correlative contribution of the return motif: Its own effect is ultimately unpredictable; the vision of new life brings with it the risk of something anticlimactic, possibly a little deflating. Will Barnardine reform? Will Angelo be reborn morally into harmonious union with Marianna? To that, Angelo says nothing, just as Isabella makes no verbal response to the Duke's marriage offer. (Lucio, for his part, would rather be whipped and hanged than forgiven and forced to marry a prostitute.) An incident in a lower key in *The Merchant of Venice* plays with the unpredictability of comic revivification. When Launcelet sees his sandblind father approaching,[27] he decides to deceive him in order to "raises the waters"; that is, to make the old father cry (*MV* 2.2.44). (The episode recalls Greenblatt's discussion of early modern drama's obsession with representing, provoking, and releasing anxiety.) Launcelet incites Old Gobbo's grief by insisting that his son is dead (whether or not Gobbo weeps is

---

[26] Ronald Hutton, *The Rise and Fall of Merry England: The Ritual Year 1400–1700* (Oxford: Oxford University Press, 1994). Hutton outlines the ritual year (4–48), which included: Christmas eve and morning; the Twelve Days of Christmas and Epiphany; Plough Sunday and Monday; the feast of the Purification of the Virgin and the recognition of Christ as the Messiah; Candlemas; Saint Valentine's Day; Shrovetide; Ash Wednesday and Lent; Passiontide culminating in Easter and followed by Hocktide; St. George's Eve and Day; May Day and its subsequent and extensive May games; Ascension and Rogation Days; Whitsuntide; Midsummer and the Feast of Corpus Christi; St. Peter's Eve; Lammas; Martinmas; the long period of Advent; All Saints' Day (with its prayers for souls in Purgatory); and St. Nicholas Day. Communal activities included revels, feasts, seasonal drinks and foods, fastings, watches, decorations, processions, mummings, games, plays, costumes, and more, all with extensive, traditional features.

[27] On "Launcelet," see Chapter 1, n. 3.

left open),[28] but the clown is less successful in disabusing Gobbo of the ruse, for the old man remains perplexed, not quite believing that his son is really living or that the person before him is he. Launcelet fails to produce convulsive relief from distress; instead, ironically, he has difficulty bringing himself back to life for his father.

Third, what does the motif of figurative return tell us about Shakespearean comedy? In addition to the points suggested above, it illustrates, reassuringly, the indestructibility of the comic persona. Falstaff returns metaphorically from death in *The Merry Wives of Windsor* (as he does in *Henry IV, Part 1*). He has been carried out of Mistress Ford's house, secreted away in a laundry buck-basket, a kind of fantastical coffin, "like a barrow of butcher's offal," and dumped in the river, where he "had been drowned, but that the shore was shelvy and shallow" (3.5.4–5, 13–14). Yet Falstaff, despite his brush with metaphoric and literal death, rebounds to pursue his would-be seduction of Mistress Ford with unfazed enthusiasm. With Bottom, the motif brings a glimpse of new life. Consider Bottom's first return from figurative death, after his "bottomless" dream (a second comes after Pyramus' suicide), when Bottom wakes up from his alternative existence in Titania's fairy-world (see also Chapter 1). The awakening constitutes, according to J. Dennis Huston, "Bottom's dramatic resurrection from a formless mass to a vitally formed personality."[29] He returns from metaphoric death with a comically mystical vision cobbled from St. Paul's first Letter to the Corinthians; he utters aphorisms about love and truth keeping little company; and imperturbably, as Sukanta Chaudhuri puts it, he "assimilates the supernatural to the mundane."[30] Bottom's indestructible sense of self seems to qualify him alone for ethereal interactions and sublime visions. When a comic character slips on a banana peel, argues Alenka Zupančič, more is at work than a human's ideal self-conception being undermined by material reality; rather, the character becomes more "vivid and palpable" as he carries on unfazed—"vivid and palpable" because the character's humanness shows forth not simply in his vulnerability to brute materiality but also in his absurd but touching presumption of invulnerability, as if the recovery crystallized a paradox in the human condition as much as did the fall.[31] The motif of the return from the dead heightens the comic mystery and poignancy of our belief in our own continuance.

Return addresses comedy in other ways. The recovery of what is lost—a sibling or parent, a social standing, a way of life—constitutes a basic thematic and structural device of comedy (which the late romances will develop). As we shall emphasize in the last section of this chapter, that sense of recovery—or perhaps of

[28] I follow Q2's "Gobbo" rather than Arden's "Giobbe."
[29] J. Dennis Huston, *Shakespeare's Comedies of Play* (New York: Columbia University Press, 1981), 101.
[30] Chaudhuri, *MND*, 91.
[31] Alenka Zupančič, *The Odd One In: On Comedy* (Cambridge, MA: MIT Press, 2008), 30.

perpetuation—applies to values that we might think of as medieval that are kept alive in the comedies. On the level of character and action, the experience of recovery, expressed through revivification, takes on an aura of the potentially miraculous, deepening the motif's emotional power. Egeon, condemned to execution, is a kind of walking dead-man, aged and wraith-like, while his redemption coincides with the recovery of his long-lost wife and sons. Although the wonder and efficaciousness of the return might be put in question, Shakespeare seems nonetheless intent on exploring the theater as a reincarnational site,[32] as he does as early as the *Henry VI* plays. Talbot can come alive in the histories for a while, but comedy offers the form where Shakespeare first experiments fully with theater as a place of resurrection.

Zombies in Action and Comic New Life

We have been looking at the values associated with the return motif. Next let us examine that motif in particular moments in various plays, not only as they illustrate its values in action but especially as they show the return motif working through the play and leading to a new sense of vividness. In *The Two Gentlemen of Verona*, to begin, the heroine Julia must suffer metaphoric life-in-death and then experience revivification.[33] Proteus loves Julia, but when he goes off to Milan to join his friend Valentine, he becomes madly infatuated with Valentine's beloved, Silvia. As Proteus burns for Silvia, he simultaneously consigns the unknowing Julia to ashes, "[e]ven as one heat another heat expels" (2.4.189). His love for Julia is melted, he says, "like a waxen image 'gainst a fire" (198). Proteus, that is, burns the image of Julia from his mind as if it were an effigy (or a religious martyr). He proclaims his "remembrance" of Julia to be now "quite forgotten" (191, 192) and asserts later, "I will forget that Julia is alive," only "[r]emembering that my love to her is dead" (2.6.27, 28). (Of course, by speaking self-contradictorily of a remembrance as something forgotten, Proteus hints that the image of Julia still retains a hold on his imagination.) To suffer the razing of one's picture or the melting of one's likeness, to be forgotten as if dead, is to undergo figurative death. In the late Middle Ages, as Duffy argues, the souls of the Purgatorial dead depended for their deliverance upon the remembrances of the living. Proteus makes "remembering"

---

[32] The image of theater as a reincarnational site points, almost inevitably, to the profound power of that motif in the late romances. In *The Winter's Tale*, of course, Hermione will famously return from the dead, as will Thaisa in *Pericles*, while deceased characters such as Antigonus and Mamillius in *The Winter's Tale* might be said, after their demise, to haunt the action. The late plays invest extraordinary emotion, meaning, and redemptive authority in a motif first developed in detail in the comedies.

[33] The motif is introduced by Shakespeare; it was absent from a principal source-text, Jorge de Montmayor's *Diana enamorada* (Valencia, 1542); see Geoffrey Bullough, ed., *Narrative and Dramatic Sources of Shakespeare*, vol. 1 of 8, *Early Comedies, Poems, Romeo and Juliet* (London: Routledge and Kegan Paul, 1957), 205–6.

Julia into a form of death-dealing—although his memory of her will not stay buried.

Julia follows after Proteus, ignorant and full of high spirits and love-longings, but she will soon enough feel like the zombie of Proteus's imagination. Julia enters a Milanese inn moments before she will overhear Proteus talking to Silvia. As she converses with the innkeeper in the evening semi-darkness, she already reveals a curious melancholy, enough so that the innkeeper notices and asks, "why is it?" (4.2.27). Why should she be melancholy when she has not yet learned of Proteus's metaphoric murdering of her? Julia has fallen in spirits, as if she had already emotionally intuited Proteus's rejection, manifested it; she will now even stand in the shadows, emblematic of a new shadow existence. That change in Julia has commenced because Proteus has consigned her to darkness and the grave. Such causation is not physical but psychic; like much in comedy, it proposes an inter-subjective etiology whereby a character responds mentally and emotionally to someone else even at a distance. With the disguised Julia listening from the shadowy margins, Proteus attests to Silvia that once he "did love a lady, / But she is dead" (4.2.102–3), strategically and self-servingly killing off Julia once again. Overhearing, she confirms her now-ghosted condition, describing herself as "but a shadow" (124).[34] That image stands as a signature of her new state, for later she again refers to herself as a "shadow," with cheeks "starved" and face darkened to "black" from the loss of Proteus's love (4.4.195, 152, 154). Overhearing Proteus figuratively end her life, Julia now resembles the shade in which she stands.

So, what is it like for Julia to be the walking dead? Paradoxically, life in the shadows begins to give her a fuller emotional reality than that of her naïve, impulsive, and transparent earlier self.[35] Despite suffering from Proteus's betrayal, Julia now discovers her feelings of pity as love's new reality: "Because I love him, I must pity him" (4.4.94). Shadow-Julia likewise evokes pity herself. The Host has offered one instance; another comes from Silvia, who, after hearing the story of the betrayed Julia's "sorrow" (145), is so touched with sympathy that she gives money to Julia-as-page in remembrance of his mistress. Although Julia sees herself as diminished in material self-"substance" (199), she nonetheless has increased in emotional depth and affect; she has become more vivid. The disguised Julia, observes William C. Carroll, acquires a "self-consciousness" that is "new on the stage," for she now speaks on two levels and with two voices, "Julia" herself and "Sebastian" herself-as-page.[36] She thus takes on a complex stage position and an increased charisma. The play, that is, draws the spectators close to Julia in the shadows and makes her paradoxically more life-like, more real to them.

---

[34] The source material involves a love triangle resolved by the death of one of the two women: See Carroll, TGV, 42.

[35] Alexander Leggatt analyzes Julia's maturing sense of self while she is in disguise; Love, 35–7.

[36] Carroll, TGV, 49.

The ending enacts Julia's death-in-life status. When Valentine idiotically gives "All that was [his] in Silvia" to Proteus (5.4.83), Julia-as-Sebastian faints. Thus, in a climactic moment, Julia's collapsed and enervated body makes almost literal her murdered condition.[37] Oppositely, when Julia is revived from her lethargy, she reveals her true identity with a sudden fervor and unpredictable boldness: "Behold . . . / O Proteus . . . Be thou ashamed . . ." (100–4), she commands insistently. As Proteus perceives the beauty that he had once beheld "in Silvia's face" now "[m]ore fresh in Julia's" (113, 114), he is shocked into a life-altering transformation. Michael Shapiro argues that Julia's speech, if forcefully and energetically acted, can, as Carroll puts it, "dazzle Proteus with Julia's presence and convince spectators" that he has emotionally rediscovered her.[38] Thus, the stage moment achieves its full theatrical potential when Julia is conceived as bursting vividly into life. That transformation seems to be what the blushing Proteus (see 103) recognizes when he finds Julia's animated beauty now "more fresh" than Silvia's. His sudden rehabilitation into Julia's constant lover hints that, indeed, he had retained some quiescent desire for her all along: "Bear witness, heaven," he says, "I have my wish forever" (118).

Proteus's dormant love helps to draw Julia forward in the play and to call her back from the dead. Likewise, Silvia's sympathy for Julia—"I weep myself to think upon thy words," she says of Julia's plight (4.4.173)—aids in keeping Julia's memory alive and her return imminent (see also 5.4.45–9). The last scene subtly maintains the sympathetic connection established earlier between Silvia and Julia: At the crucial moment when Julia swoons, "O me unhappy!" (84), she repeats the word, "unhappy," invoked and reiterated moments before by Silvia (28, 31), the emotion moving between them. Thus, Julia revivifies through a community of caring. Proteus's ring adds a further talismanic power. Julia-as-Sebastian attempts to explain away her swoon as merely a sudden shock at not having delivered Proteus's ring to Silvia (that ring being the one given previously by Julia to Proteus), but, instead of producing it now, she brings forth the ring that Proteus had bestowed upon her as a love-token. Accidentally, purposefully, or providentially? The ring symbolizes Proteus's love for Julia, and, arguably, it also operates now with more than metaphoric force, manifesting Proteus's desire for her and helping Julia to rise from her swoon. In such ways, the recognition scene invests emotional power in the trope of Julia's return from zombie-hood. That trope creates a symbolic narrative that deepens the truth of the quotidian narrative, the vividness of Julia's physical presence generated by the return metaphor. In one of his earliest comedies, Shakespeare already experiments with the mystery of

---

[37] Some critics have wondered whether Julia's faint might be faked, a strategic ruse to capture attention and change the dynamics of the situation; see, for example, Leggatt, *Love*, 37. A calculated faint, however, would reduce the emotional impact of the return motif.

[38] Carroll, *TGV*, 5.4.100–8n; Michael Shapiro, *Gender in Play on the Shakespearean Stage* (Ann Arbor, MI: University of Michigan Press, 1994), 80n.

revivification by creating a prototypical revenant who returns from the land of shadows with heightened reality.

Portia in *The Merchant of Venice* offers another figure who metaphorically returns from the dead.[39] The play is rife with images of death and return, touching not only Portia but others, too. Jessica regards Shylock's house as "hell," and later her death is willed by Shylock: "I would my daughter were dead at my foot" (2.3.2; 3.1.80). Yet Jessica will figuratively return from death to new life with Lorenzo, who even provides spiritual succour: "I shall be saved by my husband," Jessica declares to Launcelet (3.5.17). Antonio, by the time of the trial, seems to have lost his desire to live; subsequently he will come back from near death. Lorenzo accepts the inheritance from Shylock as relief from starvation. Even Launcelet cruelly convinces his blind father of his death for the pleasure of rejuvenating the old man's spirits by resurrecting himself. Portia makes the most distinct metaphoric revenant. Critics such as Harry Berger Jr., Janet Adelman, and Kenneth Gross have associated the casket scenes with death and the heroine with an enchantress figure, sometimes alluding to Sigmund Freud's 1913 essay "The Theme of the Three Caskets," but criticism has been less quick to recognize Portia as a figurative returner from the dead.[40] Portia's "casket" constitutes both a jewel-case and a coffin (1.2.88);[41] it is her emblem, standing for her doubleness, "the will of a living daughter curbed by the will of a dead father" (1.2.23–4). During the scene of Morocco's choice, the audience learns that one of the three caskets contains Portia's "heavenly picture" (2.7.48). That "picture" transforms metonymically into the lady herself: "Is't like that lead contains *her*? ... / Or ... in silver *she*'s immured" (49–52, emphasis added), asks Morocco of the caskets. Selecting the

[39] The following comments on *MV* and Portia draw upon Kent Cartwright, "The Return from the Dead in *The Merchant of Venice*," in *Visions of Venice in Shakespeare*, ed. Laura Tosi and Shaul Bassi (Farnham: Ashgate, 2011), 167–83, on 168 and 171–4.

[40] Harry Berger Jr., "Marriage and Mercifixion in *The Merchant of Venice*: The Casket Scene Revisited," *Shakespeare Quarterly* 32, no. 2 (Summer 1981): 155–62; Janet Adelman, *Blood Relations: Christian and Jew in* The Merchant of Venice (Chicago, IL: University of Chicago Press, 2008), 130; Kenneth Gross, *Shylock is Shakespeare* (Chicago, IL: University of Chicago Press, 2006), 29–42. Bassanio's image of being tangled in Portia's hair evokes the figure of Medea, as critics note; later Jessica's effect on Lorenzo will be compared more generously to Medea's reviving of Aeson.

[41] "The golden casket approximates a coffin," observes Grace Tiffany, "Names in The Merchant of Venice," in The Merchant of Venice: *New Critical Essays*, ed. John W. Mahon and Ellen MacLeod Mahon (New York: Routledge, 2002), 353–68, on 360. Shakespeare substitutes "casket" for the term "vessel," which occurs in the Elizabethan translation of his source, the *Gesta Romanorum*. For Elizabethans, "casket" meant primarily a small jewel-box; The *Oxford English Dictionary* treats the emergence of "casket" as a synonym for "coffin" as a mid-nineteenth-century American innovation (casket *n.* 3). Yet Shakespeare uses it ironically as a container of the dead: "They found him dead ... / An empty casket, where the jewel of life ... was robbed and ta'en away" (*King John*, 5.1.40–1; cited in the *OED* 2a); see Cartwright, "Return," 171. Freud associates the leaden casket with death, but transformed into a symbol of love (exemplifying reaction-formation), an argument that adds psycho-logical context to that of returning from the dead; Sigmund Freud, "The Theme of the Three Caskets" (1913), trans. C. J. M. Hubback, in *Character and Culture*, vol. 9 of 9, *The Collected Papers of Sigmund Freud*, ed. Philip Rieff (New York: Collier Books, 1963), 67–79. Modern critics often read the casket scene in terms of patriarchy, marriage economics, gender, trickery, and power; see, for example, Berger, "Marriage and Mercifixion."

golden chest, Morocco imagines that "an angel in a golden bed / Lies all within" (58–9). In the choosing scenes, then, Portia is envisioned as a corpse buried in a casket, a living dead person, and a heavenly angel waiting to be reborn into erotic life with the right suitor.

Thus, when Bassanio approaches his choice, Portia cries out to him, "Live thou, I live" (3.2.61). Portia sees herself as hovering on the brink of life or death, and her sense of endangerment will heighten her emotional catharsis. She must endure a divided existence: Morocco had referred to her as both "mortal breathing saint" and inanimate "shrine" (2.7.40).[42] Such imagery fashions Portia as both alive and dead. Trapped in her present existence, she must stand to the side, passive, waiting for release, from the dead hand of her father, into fullness of life. Portia's dualistic status now turns uncanny as Bassanio makes his choice and opens the leaden casket to discover Portia's picture. Bassanio's specific terms for the portrait—"counterfeit" and "shadow" (3.2.115, 128)—suggest that hidden within the casket lies the lady's uncanny double. And, indeed, Portia's simulacrum now comes strangely to life, for to Bassanio the portrait's eyes seem to move and its lips to part with "sugar breath," as if the picture could, in its vividness, entrap hearts and rob men's sight: "What demigod / Hath come so near creation?" (119, 115–16). Intense with desire, Bassanio perceives the depiction in the casket as her. The doubling of Portia as both picture and self represents her as an object, a shrine, or a portrait that is capable of coming alive. Thus, in a form of reciprocity that seems slightly magical, Bassanio describes a vivification in the "shadow" that is also enacted simultaneously in the "substance" (127), for as the portrait appears alive to Bassanio, Portia experiences herself likewise as coming into new life. She feels a sudden infusion of energy and vitality, so extreme as to be threatening: "O, love," she says, "be moderate, allay thy ecstasy, / . . . scant this excess. / I feel too much thy blessing: make it less / For fear I surfeit" (111–14). Portia's apostrophe even has a suggestively sexual quality—"ecstasy," "rain thy joy," "I feel too much thy bless-ing" (111, 112, 113)—as if she were suffused with love or even penetrated by its god. The casket opened, the picture awakened, Portia herself can now come erotically, dangerously to life, drawn forth by Bassanio's vitalizing desire. Such reciprocity constitutes one more of the play's many bonds. Likewise, Portia's uncanny revivification confirms on her the charmed, preternatural power needful for her subsequent actions.

---

[42] In the Middle Ages, the graves of saints were thought to have "thaumaturgical powers" and were capable of inspiring revelations and dream-apparitions; Jean-Claude Schmitt, *Ghosts in the Middle Ages: The Living and the Dead in Medieval Society*, trans. Teresa Lavender Fagan (Chicago, IL: University of Chicago Press, 1998; orig. pub. in French, 1994), 11. Some hint of that power seems to operate in this scene.

New Life and Its Doubts

Much Ado About Nothing offers a signal example of desire calling the revenant back to new life—but here change becomes open to doubt. Hero, at her wedding, is accused of adultery by her fiancée Claudio, who leaves her for dead after she falls into a swoon. In the aftermath, Friar Francis deduces Hero's innocence from her responses and begins to turn her into a spiritualized being: "I have marked / A thousand blushing apparitions / To start into her face, a thousand innocent shames / In angel whiteness beat away those blushes" (4.1.158–61). Hero's face, like the soul of a medieval Everyman, has become the site for contending forces of apparitions and angels. The Friar spiritualizes Hero's features and allegorizes her predicament as much as he anatomizes her. The process continues as he predicts Claudio's reaction to the news of her demise:

> When he shall hear she died upon his words,
> Th'idea of her life shall sweetly creep
> Into his study of imagination,
> And every lovely organ of her life
> Shall come apparelled in more precious habit,
> More moving, delicate and full of life,
> Into the eye and prospect of his soul
> Than when she lived indeed.[43]

(223–30)

"Come, lady, die to live" (253), says the Friar to Hero moments later, evoking an image of distinctly Christian resurrection.

Does Hero in mock death become "[m]ore moving-delicate, and full of life"? Maybe so, but maybe not. Imagined dead, Hero begins to assume a presence and emotional power greater than she previously had in life. She will haunt Claudio's mind and fascinate others, even generating passionate excess. When Hero's father, Leonato, and her uncle, Antonio, challenge Claudio, they emphasize the intensity of their love for Hero, her almost prelapsarian innocence, and the shocking cruelty of Claudio's calumny: "Thou hast so wronged my innocent child and me / ... I say thou has belied mine innocent child. / Thy slander hath gone through and through her heart"; "God knows, I loved my niece, / And she is dead, slandered to death by villains" (5.1.63–8, 87–8).[44] Hero's story is here dramatized and romanticized. The accusers' sense of conviction is so great that some critics have even wondered

---

[43] Editors see the phrase, "organs of her life," as applying not only to her body but also, more abstractly, to her whole being and aura. See e.g., *Much Ado About Nothing*, ed. F. H. Mares (Cambridge: Cambridge University Press, 1988), 4.1.219n.

[44] On "innocent child" and "innocent," see also 248, 266. While Leonato and Antonio emphasize Hero's innocence, they simultaneously be-monster her accusers; see 89–91.

whether Antonio really does believe that his niece is dead. Giambattista della Porta based his late sixteenth-century comedy *Gli duoi fratelli rivali* ("The Two Rival Brothers") on the same Bandello story as did Shakespeare for *Much Ado*.[45] In della Porta's version, the father does not know that his daughter is alive, believing her to have died in what turns out to have been only a deep faint, and he speaks with a passionate suffering comparable to Leonato and Antonio's. Leonato and Antonio express an authenticity of outrage and grief that treats Hero as the more arousing and compelling for being imagined dead. The presumed-dead "child," now a kind of hovering angel of innocence, brings the charged vitality of the spirit-world into the living world.

Given Friar Francis's prophecy and the father and uncle's responses, one can hypothesize that Hero re-emerges, like Julia and Portia, with the new energies of the revenant. Hero's reappearance is preceded by a scene of epitaph and song at her tomb, as if to reinforce her otherworldly aura, invoke her presence, and, implicitly, show the desire needed for her return. Claudio, shocked into recognizing his wrongful traducing of Hero, has reversed his estimation: "Sweet Hero! Now thy image doth appear / In the rare semblance that I loved it first" (5.1.241–2).[46] His rite of music and song at Hero's tomb sets the conditions for her revivification. Claudio's epitaph of "woe" celebrates Hero's *"fame which never dies"* and imagines the maiden *"Liv[ing] in death with glorious fame"* (5.3.33, 6, 8). Hero now enjoys a reverence that she could not command previously. In the spirit of return, the choric song calls upon "[g]raves [to] yawn and yield your dead," who will apparently join in the mourning (19). Life-in-death is the scene's theme, as Claudio in grief envisions the dead Hero's imminent presence and new, transcendent glory. The mourners "sound" music, sing a "solemn hymn," and circle "[r]ound about [Hero's] tomb" (11, 15): Such ceremony has spiritual efficacy. Marsilio Ficino, one of the first Renaissance theorists of the relationship between music and spirit, argues that "musical sound, more than anything else perceived by the senses, conveys, as if animated, the emotions and thoughts of the singer's or player's soul to the listeners' souls; thus it preeminently corresponds with the soul."[47] Claudio's music of the soul, constituted by thought and feeling, "as if animated," helps to call Hero back from the dead.

But does the returned Hero live up to the Friar's prophecy? When Hero is finally revealed in the last scene, Claudio cries, "Another Hero!," and, differently, Don Pedro reacts in wonder, "Hero that is dead!" (5.4.62, 65). For Claudio, Hero is a simulacrum; for Don Pedro, a ghost: Both reactions register not only shock but

---

[45] See Giambattista della Porta, *Gli duoi fratelli rivali / The Two Rival Brothers*, ed. and trans., Louise George Clubb (Berkeley, CA: University of California Press, 1980).

[46] Cf. Claudio: "In mine eye, she is the sweetest lady that ever I looked on" (1.1.177–8).

[47] From Ficino's commentary on Plato's *Timaeus*, quoted from D. P. Walker, *Spiritual and Demonic Magic from Ficino to Campanella* (University Park, PA: Pennsylvania State University Press, [1958] 2000), 9.

also doubt. Hero herself enigmatically reformulates their responses: "One Hero died defiled, but I do live" (63). Her declaration suggests that she has not so much returned to life as died and been born anew in the prelapsarian innocence that her father and uncle imagined—or that she has arisen as an unsullied double to replace the original. The dialogue, as Benson notes, now lingers temporarily in the confusion set off by "the suggestion that [Hero] is both living and dead,"[48] and the spectator or reader is left for a moment to wonder about her condition. Noting the onlookers' "amazement," the Friar, sounding strangely literal, promises, "I'll tell you largely of fair Hero's death, / Meantime, let wonder seem familiar" (67, 69–70).[49] Wonder and amazement are important aspects of the ending, as often in Shakespeare's comedies. Those reactions are possible here because, arguably, the spiritualized Hero, sanctified, energized, and enlarged in death, is now reborn with a new aura, putatively "[m]ore moving, delicate and full of life" than she was before her pseudo-death. Conceived thus, the trope of resurrection adumbrates and informs this scene, lifting it beyond what we normally think of as romantic comedy.

Yet Hero's triumphant moment of wonder is disappointingly, painfully brief; attention skitters away quickly to the different yet extended wonder of Beatrice and Benedick's uncertain love. The notion, furthermore, that Hero returns with brilliant new life is only inferential; no character restates, even in paraphrase, what the Friar had prophesied, although Shakespeare with a few pen-strokes could have established Hero's new vividness. Perhaps he intuited that she had been too superficially sketched to become transformed to the same degree as a character such as Julia. Or perhaps he wished to leave the meaning to the actors to determine, even to do so in performance. An openness about the moment of wonder may enhance its enigma and activate the audience's imagination—and its own desires. Comedy, more than tragedy, engages audiences and readers in its fantasies,[50] such that they can develop desires on behalf of the characters (the

---

[48] Benson, *Shakespearean Resurrection*, 46; see *MA* 5.4.60–71.

[49] In the source tale from Bandello, the onlookers are filled with "utmost wonder and great delight"; the Claudio-figure, Sir Timbreo, turns virtually bathetic at the revelation of the true identity of Hero's counterpart, Fenicia: "he threw his arms around Fenicia, kissing her a thousand times, filled with infinite joy and gazing on her endlessly, unable to take his eyes from her; and all the time he wept gently"; and Fenicia, for her part, behaves with a mercy and forgiveness almost more than heavenly toward Sir Girondo, her traducer; see Geoffrey Bullough, ed., *Narrative and Dramatic Sources of Shakespeare*, vol. 2 of 8, *The Comedies, 1597–1603* (London: Routledge and Kegan Paul, 1958), 130. Della Porta's *Two Rival Brothers* greatly lengthens the experience of wonder in the denouement; see 5.3.103–5.4.17. In typical fashion, Don Ignazio, her beloved, discovering that Carizia is alive after all, exclaims: "But, ah me, I feel as if I were going to faint for boundless joy! My heart's spirits, released from my body through conduits distended by the heat of happiness, seem to fly away . . ." (5.4.25–7). For a recent study interested in *Much Ado*, Hero's return, and "the role of the spectral 'revenant' as a model" for studies of literary sources, see Susanne L. Wofford, "Veiled Revenants and the Risks of Hospitality: Euripides's *Alcestis*, Bandello, and Shakespeare's *Much Ado About Nothing*," in *Rethinking Shakespeare Source Study: Audiences, Authors, and Digital Technologies*, ed. Dennis Austin Britton and Melissa Walter (New York: Routledge, 2018), 90–123, on 95.

[50] See, e.g., the discussion of fantasy and desire in Chapter 4.

counterpart of identification with characters in the tragedies). Shakespearean comedy typically incites such desires (as for Beatrice and Benedick) and allows audiences to project them into the play. In that case, the hopes of spectators and readers for Claudio's reformation and Hero's new life would empower their experiences, but it might leave their expectations under-fulfilled. Such a technique makes room for anti-romantic as well as romantic views of the play.[51] Or perhaps Shakespeare wanted audiences to feel an unsettling distance between the Friar's fantasy and the reality of Hero's return, as if the dream of new life were a possibility that cannot be fully achieved—or, at least, in this particular world, among these particular sensibilities. In all of these cases, audiences are allowed to invest in, and yet to question, Hero's return from the dead.

Return and Desire

So far, we have been emphasizing the newness of life of the character who comes back from the dead, with some noticing of the instrumental desire expressed by lovers, family, friends, and even audiences that facilitates the return. The example of Sebastian in *Twelfth Night* underscores the efficacy of the desires of others in drawing back the presumed dead. Here desire functions imitatively and telepathically. Viola, disguised as a boy and mourning for her brother lost at sea,[52] serves as a love-ambassador from Orsino to Olivia and becomes the object of Olivia's sudden infatuation. Viola's name refers not only to the sweet-smelling violet flower but also to a musical instrument, presumably the viola da gamba.[53] A viola makes music, of course, when the vibrations of its strings are amplified by its chamber, which produces a resonantly mellow, even melancholy sound, made the more complex by the instrument's six strings (as opposed to the cello's four). Correspondingly, the character Viola possesses a special responsiveness to others, a sympathy that reciprocally draws them to her. Apropos of the melodic richness that her name connotes, Viola claims that she can speak "in many sorts of music" (1.2.55). The reverberations of the musical viola are a form of echo, with which the character Viola is also associated: Listening to music with Orsino, she says, "It gives a very echo to the seat / Where love is throned" (2.4.21–2), the deep

---

[51] Hero's return also facilitates, and stands in symbolic kinship with, the renewal of the love bond between Beatrice and Benedick, itself perhaps something of a revivification.

[52] "By contrasting Illyria with Elysium, land of the happy dead," Steve Mentz observes, "Viola emphasizes that she hovers between life in a new land and death beneath the waves"; *At the Bottom of Shakespeare's Ocean* (New York: Continuum, 2009), 52.

[53] This musical instrument is inferred from Sir Toby's reference to the "viol-de-gamboys" (1.3.23–4), in the Renaissance, the viola da braccio also existed but did not gain dominance until later.

chamber of the heart.[54] These associations converge when Viola-as-Cesario describes to Olivia how, if she were to suffer love for Olivia as her master does, she would

> Make me a willow cabin at your gate
> And call upon my soul within the house;
> Write loyal cantons of contemned love
> And sing them loud even in the dead of night;
> Hallow your name to the reverberate hills
> And make the babbling gossip of the air
> Cry out, 'Olivia!' O, you should not rest
> Between the elements of air and earth
> But you should pity me.
>
> (1.5.260–8)

Call, sing, hallow, make the air cry out: What Viola's declaratives promise is an homage of poetic sound and music delivered here in rising crescendo, until, as with *Much Ado*'s Claudio, the hovering spirit of Olivia must respond sympathetically to the petitioner.[55] Viola's speech also recalls Ficino's argument that song has a special ability to communicate with the soul. The chamber of a viola da gamba amplifies sound by making the air vibrate around it, and that is exactly what Viola imagines herself as doing. Viola would haunt Olivia by singing her name in "the dead of night," as if love could invade and challenge the realm of death. Viola's "willow cabin" plays upon the association of willows with the death-dealing grief of unrequited love, hinted by Feste (2.4.52), imagined vividly elsewhere in Desdemona's song of the maid Barbary who died, forsaken of love, singing "willow." Likewise, the speech alludes to the nymph Echo who, when refused love by Narcissus, faded into the sound of her voice. To "hallow [someone's] name to the reverberate hills" is to call love back from the dead, turning the "willow cabin" into a kind of medieval chantry chapel.[56]

But who is Viola being here, and whom is she calling into life? Viola can adapt herself masterfully to a role or part, and the part that she ostensibly plays in the willow-cabin speech is the agent of Orsino's desire for Olivia. Yet perhaps we should not call that desire Orsino's entirely, for Orsino quite lacks a capacity for the haunting and irresistible longing to which Viola gives voice. Likewise, the desire, as an expression of Viola herself, exceeds its ostensible object, for she

---

[54] On Viola's relationship to Echo, see D. J. Palmer, "'Twelfth Night' and the Myth of Echo and Narcissus," *Shakespeare Survey* 32 (Cambridge: Cambridge University Press, 1979), 73–8, esp. 75–6.

[55] Olivia's response, "You might do much" (268), and the possible half-line that ends Viola's speech suggest a pause after it that would allow its resonance and effect to settle in. Here, as with the "echo" speech to Orsino, Viola's lines stand forth from the narrative and take on a special power.

[56] With a possible pun on "hallow" as to shout or to bless; Elam, *TN*, 1.5.264n.

harbors no romantic interest in Olivia. Viola is giving some expression to her own feelings for Orsino surely, but her image of a hallowing sentinel hardly corresponds to her actions towards him. Her speech seems open to further possibilities. Viola will acknowledge later that she has kept the memory of her possibly dead brother alive by "imitat[ing]" him, especially by dressing herself after the "fashion, colour, ornament" of his apparel so that, as she puts it, he is "[y]et living in my glass" (3.4.380, 379, 377). In the guise of the mysterious, echoed spirit of her brother, she enchants Olivia—indeed, calls Olivia herself back from the pseudo-death of excessive mourning. Inspired by her imitation of Sebastian, Viola imagines romantic desire for Olivia; in a sense, she becomes her desiring brother, Sebastian, and in that role, by the power of her own voice and vision, conjures Olivia's love for him and even his own, later-realized love for Olivia into being. If so, Viola's imagining has prophetic and inter-subjective power.[57]

But the image of the watchman calling out into the night for what is lost fits Viola herself, her heart crying out for the perhaps-drowned brother whose memory she keeps alive through impersonation. Indeed, the willow, as a symbol, is associated not just with unrequited romantic love but with the grief and lament of the exile bereft of homeland and of what she loves: "By the riuers of Babel we sat, and there we wept, when we remembred Zion. / We hanged our harpes upō the willows in the middes thereof" (Psalm 137, 1–2, quoted from the Geneva Bible; it is the Bible's perhaps most famous psalm of exile). And what spirits could rest, but they should pity Viola? Not by accident, then, in the very next scene, Sebastian emerges as from the sea, pulled toward the courts of Illyria (see Chapter 2). The memory that reverberates in Viola, the love that she embodies and that she impersonates, and even the desire for her that she generates from others, all establish together an inexorable magic that draws her lost brother back from shipwreck and the sea. In a realistic sense, of course, Sebastian's life is saved by Antonio, but in another, figurative and mysterious sense, Sebastian can return from the dead in part because Viola has already recreated his image and echoed him to the reverberate hills. Her desire calls back the revenant. Viola's "willow cabin" speech expresses such a surplus of complex desire—love for Orsino, empathy for Olivia's imagined lover, longing for her brother—that its elements would be difficult to comprehend in a moment of spectatorship. Yet it is hauntingly memorable. It makes for one of those events that invite post-performance or readerly contemplation.

Given Viola's speech, it is fitting that Sebastian returns in 2.1 as the instantaneous object of infatuation. Viola, Olivia, Antonio, Orsino: Desire for Sebastian seems to have a strange multiplying power, the equivalent of Julia's radiance. Sebastian's first scene establishes his magnetism. As he departs from Antonio,

---

[57] The incident subtly develops an idea hinted in *The Comedy of Errors*, that the feelings of one twin can be transferred telepathically to the other; see Cartwright, *CE*, 16.

Sebastian exhibits the active principle that balances Viola's early passivity (see 2.1.1–3; see also Chapter 2). And in an echo of unconscious reciprocity towards her, he emphasizes his love and "remembrance" for the presumably drowned Viola (29). He almost weeps at Antonio's kindness (see 36–8). Sebastian is so vibrant with feeling and a related beauty that Antonio cannot help but "love" and "adore" him (32, 43). From his encounter with Olivia, Sebastian feels "enwrap [ed]" in "wonder" (4.3.3). He finds his senses quickened: "This is the air, that is the glorious sun; / The pearl she gave me, I do feel't and see't" (1–2). He has become so responsive to the moment that he is willing instantly to marry Olivia—who has herself acquired an emotional urgency (perhaps from the scale and physicality of Sebastian's presence, as opposed to Viola's). Sebastian the revenant experiences himself as charmed with new life.

Returning in the Late Comedies

Rather than coming to rest with *Twelfth Night*'s celebration of telepathic desire and of return from death into new life, we might do well to complicate that picture with an example from the late comedies, Helen in *All's Well That Ends Well*.[58] Helen's function differs from the schema that we have been discussing because she is both avatar of desire and revenant.[59] (Overall, *All's Well* is thick with references to death and renewal.) Helen's stratagems call Bertram back from self-exile and moral self-degradation but not back from the dead. She does, of course, retrieve the King from near-death with her inherited, enigmatically divine skills as a medical healer ("sanctified / By th' luckiest stars in heaven" [1.3.242–3]). Yet it is Helen herself, who, abhorred by Bertram, turns wandering pilgrim and is reported dead. Indeed, her very magic, as G. K. Hunter points out, is "clearly associated" with "the dead and departed."[60] In a sense, Helen's agency—the force of her desire, persistence, and transformative herbalism—exists anachronistically as a remnant from a deceased world. Helen embodies a longing, expressed on behalf of the play, for the return of something that has passed or may be passing. "[T]here is no living, none, / If Bertram be away," says Helen in longing despair over Bertram's departure (1.1.84–5). The assertion may be overstatement, but

---

[58] On the resurrection motif, especially in the recognition scene of *All's Well*, see Benson, *Shakespearean Resurrection*, 58–68. For a recent discussion of the tension between the religious and the secular in the play, see Helen Wilcox, "Shakespeare's Miracle Play? Religion in *All's Well That Ends Well*," in All's Well That Ends Well: *New Critical Essays*, ed. Gary Waller (New York: Routledge, 2007), 140–54.

[59] To apply different models, Helen can also be viewed, as Steven Mentz argues, as the active, ingenious heroine of the novella tradition or the suffering heroine dependent on Providence of the romance tradition; "Revising Sources: Novella, Romance, and the Meanings of Fiction in *All's Well That Ends Well*," in *New Critical Essays*, ed. Waller, *op. cit.*, 57–70.

[60] G. K. Hunter, ed., *All's Well That Ends Well* (London: Methuen, 1959), xxxvi.

perhaps not, since she will later put her life on the line to win Bertram, and, in any case, her association with "the dead and departed" makes the claim emotionally unsettling.

From early on, Helen inspires awestruck comment from character after character: She "hath amazed me," says Lafew to the King (2.1.82), and the King himself hears in her "some blessed spirit" (173). Although Helen will be reported as having died a pilgrim at St. James Compostela (see 4.3.45–51), the sense of her wondrousness will only increase thereafter. The Countess remembers her as "the most virtuous gentlewoman" ever created by nature (4.5.9), and Lafew recalls her "astonish[ing]" beauty, her captivating speech, and her "dear perfection" (5.3.16, 18). Helen in memory makes true the Friar's perspective in *Much Ado* when he predicts that Claudio will rediscover the dead Hero as "[m]ore moving, delicate and full of life... [t]han when she lived indeed." Characters just cannot forget Helen: "Praising what is lost / Makes the remembrance dear," says the King (19–20). They cannot forget her even when they try: Planning to marry Bertram to Lafew's daughter, the King consigns Helen to "oblivion" like "incensing relics" (24, 25), forbids "one word more" about her (38), and presses Bertram, when he declares his unacknowledged love for Helen, to "forget her" (67).[61] Like Proteus's image of Julia in *Two Gentlemen*, the memory of Helen cannot be exorcised. Helen illustrates the quasi-Catholic state of the dead in the comedies, for they seem to hover near to the living, luminous and ghostly—"incensing." It is poetically just that such a spirit become manifest, for the haunted characters of the court seem to cry out for Helen's presence even as they would relinquish her.

For Louise George Clubb, Helen constitutes a prime example of the "woman as wonder" found in late cinquecento Italian tragi-comedy.[62] The constancy of the wonder-woman reveals her spiritualism and symbolic power; she possesses "an extra-fabular reality that is invoked not by an obvious allegory but as an image of a truth physically unseen" (68).[63] Clubb finds antecedents and analogues for Helen in a host of late sixteenth-century Italian tragi-comedies where the metaphor of revivification infuses the wonder-woman with transcendent grace. Clubb locates the Counter-Reformation content of those plays in a spiritualism that operates outside the allegorizing of medieval drama (71). On the other hand, Clubb appreciates "the universalist and neomedieval trend" in Counter-Reformation

---

[61] As Garrett A. Sullivan, Jr. puts it, this scene's "reconfigured relationships...are haunted by that which must be forgotten in order for them to come into being"; "'Be this sweet Helen's knell, and now forget her': Forgetting, Memory, and Identity in *All's Well That Ends Well*," *Shakespeare Quarterly* 50, no. 1 (Spring 1999): 51–73, on 67.

[62] See Louise George Clubb, *Italian Drama in Shakespeare's Time* (New Haven, CT: Yale University Press, 1989), 65–89. See also Michele Marrapodi, "The 'Woman as Wonder' Trope: From *Commedia Grave* to Shakespeare's *Pericles* and the Last Plays," in *Shakespeare and Renaissance Literary Theories: Anglo-Italian Transactions*, ed. Michele Marrapodi (Farnham: Ashgate, 2011), 175–99.

[63] Clubb includes Helen and Isabella as wonder-women but excludes Julia, Rosalind, and Viola (see *Italian Drama*, 67).

thought (70). Indeed, one cannot entirely distinguish the spiritualism of the woman-as-wonder from allegory, since her providential grace and the attendant motif of return from the dead unavoidably invoke Christian allegory.[64]

Helen represents the dead who have never quite departed. The inability of others to stop remembering her, even when commanded, testifies to their emotional engagement with her living image, an engagement expressive of their desire and love, ultimately of their spiritual need. But if Helen is not quite departed, neither is she quite reborn into newness of life; her almost hyperbolically mystical aura is antecedent to her return, while her return itself is surprisingly cryptic, emotionally reserved, and anti-climactic. According to Hunter, Helen cannot be saved by the power of nostalgia; rather, she must first embrace self-sacrifice and accept herself as rejected and despised, as in some sense dead, in order to achieve a "fuller life";[65] she offers, perhaps, a version of Hero. Behind that view stands a model of the protagonist who learns to suppress the self in favor of connecting with others. But that model might be juxtaposed to another way of describing Helen, for it is not clear what she has learned, if anything, by the play's end. Her success relies on good-will (towards Diana and the Widow) and constancy in love (towards Bertram) combined with active opportunism and smarts—a combination of grace and moxie, Castiglione plus Machiavelli, a bit like Portia. We might say that circumstances now call forth a fuller version of her, the pragmatic new woman now twinned with wonder-woman. In some ways, All's Well ponders equivocally a receding age when miracles were possible, turning the question of how comedy engages with the past into a formal problem.

That question of how to understand and place Helen is highlighted by the comedy's contrasts to its Italian analogue play, Girolamo Bargagli's La pellegrina ("The Female Pilgrim"), c.1568, drawn from the same tale in Giovanni Boccaccio's Decameron.[66] Drusilla, Bargagli's pilgrim, "bears a strong generic resemblance to Helena," states Clubb (77). But Drusilla is far more saintly, sexually pure, passive, and self-sacrificing (a bit like Patience on a monument) than her counterpart. When she at last is reunited with her geographically separated husband, who thinks she is dead and whom Drusilla thinks loves another woman, the

---

[64] Chaucer's Patient Griselda (a model for Helen), for example, while offering opaque allegory, manifests an affective and preternatural constancy akin to that of Clubb's woman-as-wonder. The emotional depth of late medieval spirituality is attested to by studies such as Theresa M. Coletti's *Mary Magdalene and the Drama of Saints: Theater, Gender, and Religion in Late Medieval England* (Philadelphia, PA: University of Pennsylvania Press, 2011).

[65] Hunter, *AW*, xxxvii.

[66] On Boccaccio as a source for *All's Well*, see Gossett and Wilcox, *AW*, 7–9. On the relationship of *La pellegrina* and its heroine Drusilla to *All's Well* and Helen, see Clubb, *Italian Drama*, 77–80, 82. The comments above are drawn from Kent Cartwright, "Secularity Meets Wonder Woman in *All's Well That Ends Well*," in *Sacred and Secular Transactions in the Age of Shakespeare*, ed. Katherine Steele Brokaw and Jay Zysk (Evanston, IL: Northwestern University Press, 2019), 49–67, on 58–62.

scene gushes with sustained Counter-Reformation sentimentalism and floridity of language.[67] Among other things, Drusilla says to her beloved, Lucrezio: "I was dead because I was deprived of you" (5.7, 145), as the return motif plays variously through the scene. Thus, *La pellegrina* and *All's Well* take very different approaches to their adaptation of the same scene, as *All's Well* may be drawn towards wonder but declines to commit to it fully. Combining the "incensing relics" of the past with an earthier and more pragmatic early modern selfhood, the play seeks to flesh out in Helen an ambivalent, enchanting but new kind of heroine.

Secular Spiritualism and Medieval Remnants

Exploring the return from the dead in Shakespearean comedy illuminates two current and important topics: first, the early stirrings of England's gradual transformation from a sectarian towards a more secular culture; and, second, the afterlife of medieval values in a world of emerging early modernity. These two topics, secularization and residualism, share an interest in the adaptive persistence of old values in a changing culture. Concerning the first topic, secularization, Henry VIII's assertion of state authority over religion, and humanism's appreciation of secular values (e.g., lived experience, individual expression, civic virtue) mark a drifting away from the otherworldliness of scholastic Catholicism and towards a gradual questioning of received truths.[68] The Reformation, according to Brian Cummings, marks a world "poised between" the two psychic conditions, "clarity of faith and the melancholy of skepticism," phrases that evoke the slow, affective experience of religious change.[69] Yet Catholicism left a system of affects in England that lingered beyond the break with Rome. To consider in Shakespeare issues such as residual habits of thought, sacramental communal experience, feelings of wonder, and a generalized sense of the sacred is to look in secular literature for values derived from religious experience, even if detachable from a creed, as in the example of *All's Well*.[70] At work is a secular spiritualism (or cultural Catholicism) rather than a precisely theological one.

---

[67] See Girolamo Bargagli, *The Female Pilgrim (La pellegrina)*, trans. Bruno Ferraro (Ottawa, Canada: Dovehouse Editions, 1988), Act 5, scene 7.

[68] These elements were already present in the Middle Ages. Kellie Robertson demonstrates how late medieval poetry grappled with the tensions between Aristotelian science and theological views of God's power; *Nature Speaks: Medieval Literature and Aristotelian Philosophy* (Philadelphia, PA: University of Pennsylvania Press, 2017).

[69] Brian Cummings, *The Literary Culture of the Reformation: Grammar and Grace* (Oxford: Oxford University Press, 2002), 5.

[70] On habits of thought, see Anthony B. Dawson and Paul Yachnin, *The Culture of Playgoing in Shakespeare's England: A Collaborative Debate* (Cambridge: Cambridge University Press, 2001); also Debora Kuller Shuger, *Habits of Thought in the English Renaissance: Religion, Politics, and the*

Those concerns lead into the second topic, the afterlife of medieval values in early modernity. The revenant metaphor shines a light on aspects of Shakespeare's comic oeuvre somewhat incongruent with what we think of as 'early modern.' That term emphasizes rationality, empiricism, incipient science, proto-capitalism, state formation, Protestantism, and subjectivity.[71] Its most fertile grounds for discussion in Shakespeare have been the tragedies and histories, less so the comedies where the early modern paradigm has brought attention to domestic economy, marriage, gender, sexuality, race and Otherness. Alongside those, certain features of the comedies that we might associate with medievalism turn out to have a continuing, albeit mutating, cultural life.[72] Providential, magical, and communal habits of perception and thought, for example—values close to comedy—were alive and well in Shakespeare's time.[73] In the case of Providentialism, as Alexandra Walsham shows, the belief in a dynamic and active deity that intervened regularly (and miraculously) in human affairs served as a mainstream Protestant credo in early modern England.[74] There, such ideas were "residual" (to invoke Raymond Williams's term) in the sense of deriving from a cultural life that antedates "emergent" early modernism, while being profoundly current and lively.[75]

Dominant Culture (Berkeley, CA: University of California Press, 1990). On wonder, see, among others, T. G. Bishop, *Shakespeare and the Theatre of Wonder* (Cambridge: Cambridge University Press, 1996) and Lorraine Daston and Katherine Park, *Wonders and the Order of Nature, 1150–1750* (New York: Zone Books, 1998). On Shakespeare and religious change, see among others, Fernie, *Spiritual Shakespeares* (according to Fernie, "Shakespeare's is the drama of the *possibility* of spirituality" [7]) and Graham and Collington, *Shakespeare and Religious Change*.

[71] Recent criticism, however, has complicated some of the givens of the early modern *episteme*, especially the view of the subject as a unified and autonomous agent; see, for example, Cynthia Marshall, *The Shattering of the Self: Violence, Subjectivity, and Early Modern Texts* (Baltimore, MD: The Johns Hopkins University Press, 2002); and Nancy Selleck, *The Interpersonal Idiom in Shakespeare, Donne, and Early Modern Culture* (Houndmills, Basingstoke: Palgrave, 2008), 6.

[72] For a recent argument for medieval values in Shakespeare, see Helen Cooper, *Shakespeare and the Medieval World* (London: Bloomsbury, 2010). A body of critical literature, too extensive for critique here, has developed on the relationship between the medieval and the early modern in Shakespeare. For a helpful review, see Lucy Munro, "Shakespeare and the Uses of the Past: Critical Approaches and Current Debates." *Shakespeare* 7, no. 1 (April 2011): 102–25; for one example, see Ruth Morse, Helen Cooper, and Peter Holland, eds., *Medieval Shakespeare: Pasts and Presents* (Cambridge: Cambridge University Press, 2013). As Munro observes, "the past can be a number of things. It can be historical, mythical or fictional; it may be a site of memory, subjectivity or nostalgia; . . . the past may even turn out to be simultaneously the present, or even the future. Its configuration may also vary according to the genre in which the play is written, or according to the formal requirements within it" ("Uses of the Past," 105). For a concise and suggestive discussion of the "premodern" in chronological, moral, and dialogic relationship to the "modern," see Sarah Beckwith and James Simpson, "Premodern Shakespeare," *Journal of Medieval and Early Modern Studies* 40, no. 1 (Winter 2010): 1–5, esp. 1–2. It is not clear that Shakespeare distinguished the Middle Ages as an historical period different from his own; see Deanne Williams, "Shakespearean Medievalism and the Limits of Periodization," *Shakespeare Compass* 8, no. 6 (June 2011): 390–403.

[73] Likewise, the Counter-Reformation Council of Trent (1545–63) strongly affirmed certain medieval tenets—for example, the belief in purgatory, the veneration of saints and of relics, the efficacy of indulgences—and with those doctrines sanctioned a revival of religious emotionalism.

[74] Alexandra Walsham, *Providence in Early Modern England* (Oxford: Oxford University Press, 1999).

[75] Raymond Williams, *Marxism and Literature* (Oxford: Oxford University Press, 1977), esp. "Dominant, Residual, and Emergent," 121–7.

Sixteenth-century England was still, to an extent, medieval, a fact that entertains recursive aspects of Shakespearean comic form. Medieval mysticism, magic, and festivity can work as a counterforce, or offer a resistant narrative, to a more familiar early modern logic and set of values.

To the extent that the medieval persists in the comedies, it does so less as an historical model than as an imaginary, as, in Jean-Paul Sartre's sense of that term, a "mélange of past impression and recent knowledge."[76] The past undergoes a transformation, perhaps into something shadowy, or strange and incensing, or humorous, with its contours showing just a little above the water. Overall, in the comedies, the residual elements refuse to be reconciled to strict rational explanations; they constitute a mysterious left-over or surplus. The medieval imaginary, then, operates in tension with early modernism, just as in *Twelfth Night* the idea of telepathic causation works in tension with materialistic causation. Its gift to the present is in the relevance of its alterity, of enchantment.

Comedy embraces rationality; it relies, for example, upon our awareness of disproportion and folly, upon our mental perception to activate laughter, upon our acceptance of logical solutions to the riddles of the plot; comedy puts the audience "in the position of the *raisonneur*."[77] But Shakespeare's comedies also employ emotionally resonant cultural narratives, such as the return from the dead, that develop deeply, long before the denouement. Such elements reveal a substratum of psychic power and mysterious etiology. Yet it is perhaps that sense of the enigmatic—the emotional penumbra that survives the rationality of the ending—that draws us back, again and again, to the comedies, as if we, too, were Sebastians hallowed and raised from the shipwreck of our lives. Though comedy often tells a story of disenchantment, Shakespeare insinuates into his works a residual counternarrative of re-enchantment. There can be something a little self-conscious and humorous about it, and, indeed, rationalist norms largely prevail, but not without a disturbing remainder of wonder and doubt. The uneven sense of the familiar and the foreign, of the rational and the enigmatic, of the early modern and the medieval, creates its own uncanniness. The dead return in Shakespearean comedy because they have never quite gone away.

---

[76] Jean-Paul Sartre, *The Imaginary: A Phenomenological Psychology of the Imagination*, trans. Jonathan Webber (New York: Routledge, 2004; orig. pub. in French, 1940), 90.

[77] Heller, *Immortal Comedy*, 40.

6

Ending and Wondering

[P]oetry...is capable of saving us.

I. A. Richards
Poetries and Sciences

In the last chapter we have discussed the weight of the past on Shakespeare's comedies, but the past need not be a hopeless burden. The endings of Shakespeare's comedies also negotiate the future, turn antecedent events opaque, and make a wondrous, intervening forgiveness possible. In that regard, comedy hints at the redemptive power that I. A. Richards sees in literature. Yet a Shakespearean comedy arrives at a resting place, not a full resolution. The denouement's unraveling of problems creates enough delight to allow audiences comfortably to exit the theater or close the book, but the comedies can also leave some characters hanging and some questions unanswered, provoking an afterlife of auditorial doubt and wondering.[1] Endings give emotional satisfaction while rendering our sympathies or insights uneasy: How do we feel finally about Shylock? What do Beatrice and Benedick really come to understand? How can cads like Claudio be forgiven? Plays that presumably trade in providential finality emerge as rich in opportunities for speculation about facts and implications. Such tensions reflect, in part, the way that comedy as a genre raises global problems—about, say, ethnic, gender, or generational relations—but offers only local and contingent solutions, turning endings dialectical. A forensic agent, the "duke," fits

---

[1] Paul Prescott emphasizes the way that Shakespeare's endings do not quite end and thus invite continued post-production talk by the audience; "Endings," in *Shakespeare and the Making of Theatre*, ed. Stuart Hampton-Reeves and Bridget Escolme (Houndmills, Basingstoke: Palgrave, 2012), 50–68, esp. 59–60. Douglas L. Peterson sees two notions of effect operating together in Shakespeare's comic endings, one about recreation (the Ludic) and the other about "extraordinary actions which arouse wonder, admiration, and reflection" (the Ideal); "Beginnings and Endings: Structure and Mimesis in Shakespeare's Comedies," in *Entering the Maze: Shakespeare's Art of Beginning*, ed. Robert F. Willson, Jr. (New York: Peter Lang, 1995), 37–54, on 41. For an inventory of inconsistencies or unresolved elements in Shakespeare's comedies, see Kristian Smidt, *Unconformities in Shakespeare's Early Comedies* (Houndmills, Basingstoke: Macmillan 1986); and *Unconformities in Shakespeare's Later Comedies* (New York: Palgrave Macmillan, 1993). June Schleuter observes that only with drama have definitions of kinds "rested their case on the ending"; thus, a form such as comedy asserts a certain tyranny (marriage) over its conclusion; June Schleuter, *Dramatic Closure: Reading the End* (Madison, NJ: Fairleigh Dickinson University Press, 1995), 37. Narrative trajectory and generic closure, then, might be at odds. Ejner Jensen argues that criticism gives too much attention to the comedies' endings; *Shakespeare and the Ends of Comedy* (Bloomington, IN: Indiana University Press, 1991). To Jensen, Shakespeare's art is one of "local effects" rather than teleological closure (xi).

Shakespeare and the Comedy of Enchantment. Kent Cartwright, Oxford University Press. © Kent Cartwright 2021.
DOI: 10.1093/oso/9780198868897.003.0007

together the puzzle pieces and exudes generosity of spirit, yet without sweeping away the denouement's sprinkling of contradictions, enigmas, and possibilities. Experientially, we are left not knowing whether we should believe in what we are made to hope for. The wondering induced by such endings is the fairy dust that prompts notions of alternative pasts and futures. Shakespeare's presumed conclusions actually create openings for further thinking, which might range from ironic suspicion to utopian optimism.

Whereas previous chapters have focused on comic devices or tropes, this one concentrates on the endings' affective strategies (exclusion, delusion, and forgiveness) and their intellectual force, their sense of wonder and wondering as the final distillation of the comedy of enchantment. Of course, each of the comedies' denouements presents its special problems; here I select only representative plays in order to discuss their endings' dialectics. The chapter contains five main parts. The first acknowledges the tension of harmony and dissonance in the comic conclusions, a problem recognized by critics from the formalist to the political. To establish context, the second section surveys the influential theory and practice of endings in Italian Renaissance comedy. The third section, about exclusion, applies the preceding perspectives to questions raised by the figurative death of Shylock, his omission from the last act of *The Merchant of Venice*, and his residual influence on the new world of Belmont. The fourth section, about delusion, questions just what Benedick and Beatrice, along with the audience, really come to recognize about the couple's falling in love in *Much Ado About Nothing*. That knowledge remains more tentative than they or we might think. The final section, on forgiveness, argues that in certain of the comedies, wonder precedes, and creates the conditions for, forgiveness; that sequence—reversed in late romances such as *The Winter's Tale*—illustrates comedy's potential for radical unpredictability, a quality upon which modern philosophy throws light. Comedy can help us learn to forgive.

These sections all imagine spectators and readers leaving a play in a state of wonder and yet questioning. Comic conclusions often withhold crucial information or raise vast issues while offering only partial, sometimes sleight-of-hand solutions. They leave us with the great humanist dilemma identified by political critics, the challenge of addressing systemic, even global problems simply by changing the human heart. Notwithstanding, changing the heart might be a good thing, and where better to undertake it—since change must begin somewhere—than through the dramatic literature by which individuals collectively think and feel about culture. Comedy's instability and openness, its capacity for wonder and wondering, herald its greatest gift, the possibility of new beginnings.

Harmony and Dissonance

The perception of harmony—the pleasing musical effect from simultaneous notes and rhythms—involves hearers' subjective judgments, thus differences in interpretations. In Renaissance music, the rise of polyvocal harmony prompted debates that were pertinent to drama. As Joseph Ortiz points out, some Elizabethan commentators "condemned" the development of early modern polyphony, in contrast to Protestant plainsong, for "having too many voices," "too many musical parts."[2] But this "complex, intricate harmony" (24) had its uses. "For late medieval and early modern musical theorists, the idea of 'harmony' suggests concord and resolution," argues Katherine Steele Brokaw: "[T]he most beautiful harmonies follow discordant sounds."[3] That notion of musical harmony "translates to the social and political sphere" (3). By "staging harmony," Brokaw concludes, Tudor drama uses music as a device to encourage understanding and tolerance.

The problem of harmony and discord features in present-day criticism of Shakespeare's comic endings. For mid-twentieth-century critics, comic conclusions typically produce harmony, manifesting a "unity" without uniformity that "balances a variety of moods, conflicting with and to some degree neutralizing each other."[4] About the final scene of *The Merchant of Venice*, C. L. Barber summarizes: "No other comedy, until the late romances, ends with so full an expression of harmony."[5] But for some formalist critics, the content of the comedies conflicts with their form. According to Anne Barton, Shakespeare's comedies persistently confront the opposing claims of romanticism and realism; in *As You Like It*, a classical balance is struck, but in *All's Well* and *Measure for Measure*, "realism collides painfully with romance" and "belittles" "the laws of comedy."[6] The latter plays' dissonant endings amount to "confessions of the inadequacy of comedy resolutions" (112). In Pauline Kiernan's view, the problems of realism in the comic endings are a means by which Shakespeare demonstrates the inadequacy of a mimetic concept of drama.[7] Thus, in the finale of *Love's*

---

[2] Joseph M. Ortiz, *Shakespeare and the Politics of Music* (Ithaca, NY: Cornell University Press, 2011), 24. Ortiz cites Thomas Becon as arguing that polyphonic church music was a "'confused noise of voices'" (24); that is, as Ortiz says, "it voices too many meanings at the same time" (25). For its detractors, polyphonic complexity and intricacy challenged the ancient notion of a universal heavenly harmony based on a Pythagorean theory of proportion (88–103).

[3] Katherine Steele Brokaw, *Music and Religious Change in Early Modern English Drama* (Ithaca, NY: Cornell University Press, 2016), 3.

[4] Northrop Frye, *A Natural Perspective: The Development of Shakespearean Comedy and Romance* (New York: Columbia University Press, 1965), 50, 48.

[5] C. L. Barber, *Shakespeare's Festive Comedy: A Study of Dramatic Form and Its Relation to Social Custom* (Princeton, NJ: Princeton University Press, 1959), 187.

[6] Anne Barton, "*As You Like It* and *Twelfth Night*: Shakespeare's 'sense of an ending' (1972)," in *Essays Mainly Shakespearean* (Cambridge: Cambridge University Press, 1994), 91–112, on 112.

[7] Pauline Kiernan, *Shakespeare's Theory of Drama* (Cambridge: Cambridge University Press, 1996), 98–116. See also Ben Wiebracht, "'The vile conclusion': Crises of Resolution in Shakespeare's Love Plots," *Shakespeare* 12, no. 3 (June 2016): 241–59.

Labour's Lost, the ladies punish the gentlemen for mistakenly "believing that life can be imitated by art" (106). In the background of these and related approaches stands Frank Kermode's *The Sense of an Ending*, which argues that humans, inevitably born *in media res*, struggle, through myth, religion, and literature, to find meaning by understanding their lives in the context of a larger, elusive Apocalyptic pattern.[8] Comedy addresses in its own pragmatic ways the tensions aroused by content and pattern, the desire for consonance and the fact of dissonance.

For recent political critics, the "faultlines" in comedy (and other forms) expose the failed strategies—one being a forced harmony—of the dominant ideological orders to establish their interests as facts of nature. Arden editor John Drakakis's treatment of the ending of *The Merchant of Venice* illustrates that approach. With the outsider Shylock left behind, and with his daughter Jessica now a nascent Christian, the last, golden-world scene attempts to reinstate the behavioral standards of the prevailing, ethnically homogenous Venetians and to obfuscate the inhumanity in their prior actions. Drakakis sympathizes with "the plight of Shylock," focuses on the play's antisemitic elements, and sees *Merchant* "as Shylock's tragedy" (110).[9] Here, the fifth act's palliatives of music talk and ring tricks cannot overcome the fourth act's exposure of false piety. With *Merchant*, the form of comedy fails: The denouement generates a "discomfort" that "exceeds the capacity of the genre to contain" (111–12).[10] We are not enchanted. The emphasis on "harmony" in *Merchant*'s ending—made thematic in Lorenzo's music speech—becomes an unsuccessful device to "contain," modulate, and divert attention from those subversive Shylockian energies that cannot be easily forgotten. The normative comic ending becomes, then, an attempt at political suppression, and aesthetics becomes hegemonic politics in disguise.

The two lines of arguments outlined above diverge, for where the formalist sees a "complex, intricate" polyphony that appreciates generic limits, the political critic finds bad faith. The matter is more than a squabble among the clerisy, for competing perceptions of harmony and dissonance bear on our understanding of literature itself.[11]

---

[8] Frank Kermode, *The Sense of an Ending: Studies in the Theory of Fiction* (Oxford: Oxford University Press, [1967] 2000).

[9] Drakakis rebuts Lawrence Danson's reading in *The Harmonies of* The Merchant of Venice (New Haven, CT: Yale University Press, 1978).

[10] Drakakis repeatedly uses *contain*, evoking the New Historicist model of "subversion and containment," developed by Stephen Greenblatt, in which the dominant ideology encourages subversive behavior in order to release and manage its energies and to convert them to its own uses; see Stephen Greenblatt, "Invisible Bullets," in *Shakespearean Negotiations: The Circulation of Social Energy in Renaissance England* (Berkeley, CA: University of California Press, 1988), 21–65.

[11] For a seminal study that sees the tension as central not only to literature but also to the brain's processing of information, see Paul B. Armstrong, *How Literature Plays with the Brain: The Neuroscience of Literature and Art* (Baltimore, MD: Johns Hopkins University Press, 2013), especially chapters 1 and 2.

The two ensuing sections make two claims. First, the qualities of enchantment, wonder, and wondering in the comedies need not be allied exclusively with harmony or dissonance. Consider Italian dramatic theory. It pays tribute to a nexus of affects—surprise, delight, pleasure, joy, and wonder—felt by characters and spectators, affects that express narrative immersion and enchantment. Those values, however, do not rule out the possibility of contradictions, unresolved problems, and loose ends related to their larger social questions. In both theory and practice, Renaissance comedy loves surprise solutions and worries little about discontinuities. Such freedom allows for affective power to arise from the dynamic interplay of harmony and dissonance, creating absorbing satisfactions along with tantalizing intricacies and doubts.

Second, the complementary interplay of harmony and dissonance possible in wonder finds illustration in the denouement of *The Merchant of Venice*. Although physically absent, Shylock nonetheless broods in spirit over the ending. Jessica and Antonio each stand for alternative, conjectural responses to the unresolved problem of the alien, responses that acknowledge the audience's residual sympathy for Shylock and that activate wondering. The effect encompasses both hypothetical harmony and lingering dissonance. The denouement's wondering—sparked by juxtapositions and contrasts and kindled by close observation[12]—induces its own auditorial fascination for the ending's complexity. Such enchantment operates not prescriptively but interrogatively and speculatively.

Comic Endings in Renaissance Theory and Practice

Regarding comic effects, Renaissance Italian theorists focus not on unity or harmony but on the delight achieved through surprise. In the sixteenth century, Italian comic theory and practice were built on the foundation, adapted and expanded, of Roman forms and models.[13] Writers about comedy looked to medieval commentaries on Terence, especially *On Comedy and Tragedy*, written by the fourth-century AD Roman grammarian Aelius Donatus, and *On Drama*, probably authored by Evanthius of Constantinople.[14] Here comic theory follows

---

[12] Lorna Hutson describes Shakespeare's interest in "arousing strong feelings," including comic ones, "by emphasizing characters' partial, uneven, and often merely conjectural knowledge of one another's thoughts and hidden actions"; *The Invention of Suspicion: Law and Mimesis in Shakespeare and Renaissance Drama* (Oxford: Oxford University Press, 2007), 105.

[13] Among many sources, see Richard Andrews, *Scripts and Scenarios: The Performance of Comedy in Renaissance England* (Cambridge: Cambridge University Press, 1993).

[14] For Donatus, see *A Fragment on Comedy and Tragedy*, trans. George Miltz, in *Theories of Comedy*, ed. Paul Lauter (Garden City, NY: Anchor Books, 1964), 27–32, on 30. Donatus influentially quotes Cicero's definition of comedy as "an imitation of life, a mirror of custom, and an image of truth" (26). For Evanthius, see "On Drama," trans. O. B. Hardison, Jr., in *Classical and Medieval Literary Criticism: Translations and Interpretations*, ed. Alex Preminger, O. B. Hardison, Jr., and Kevin Kerrane (New York: Frederick Ungar Publishing, 1974), 301–3.

the lines of Aristotle's *Poetics* (even though the rediscovered *Poetics* was not published until 1508[15]). Donatus established protasis, epitasis, and catastrophe as comedy's main divisions (after the prologue), divisions largely followed by Renaissance commentators. The protasis is the "unfold[ing]" of "part of the argument," with another part "kept back" to maintain the audience's "expectation"; the epitasis is the "increase and advance of the disturbance," "the tangling of the maze"; and the catastrophe is the change to "a pleasant outcome" "made clear to all" through the revelation of error, of "what has happened."[16] Thus, a chief goal of comedy, announced in a foundational document, is to create the shock of surprise—signified by the audience's laughter.

Italian sixteenth-century theorizing about comedy touches repeatedly on that affective dimension. Treatises analyze the ridiculous, described as a deformity of mind or an ugliness that, while not hurtful, is inapt, disproportionate, or incongruous. Vincenzo Maggi (or Madius), in a 1550 work, recognizes that not all comic incongruities produce laughter and concludes that the ridiculous, to be risible, must entail surprise and wonder.[17] A host of other Italian theorists— Giovanni Trissino, Francesco Robortello, Antonio Minturno, Julius Caesar Scaliger, Ludovico Castelvetro—explore the pleasure of comedy in related terms. Trissino (writing c.1543-50) emphasizes the "pleasant feeling" that comedy produces by "jokes and laughter," and the "surprising reversals and recognitions" that give characters "tranquility and unhoped-for pleasure."[18] Francesco Robortello's important *On Comedy* (1548), the first treatise directly influenced by translations of Aristotle's *Poetics*, discusses how in comedy "[i]t is necessary to intermingle," among the characters' troubles and distresses, "accidental events as bring unexpected joy, or grief, or wonder."[19] Julius Caesar Scaliger describes the catastrophe of comedy as "the transformation of the intrigue...into a calmness not anticipated."[20] Antonio Minturno's *The Art of Poetry* (1563) underscores the importance in comedy of surprises that go beyond expectation; moreover, from the "unexpected event" some "remarkable mutation will follow," "against all our expectations and with the greatest pleasure."[21] Castelvetro gives attention to

[15] See Daniel Javitch, "The Assimilation of Aristotle's *Poetics* in Sixteenth-Century Italy," in *The Cambridge History of Literary Criticism*, vol. 3 of 9, *The Renaissance*, ed. Glyn P. Norton (Cambridge: Cambridge University Press, 1999), 53-65.

[16] Donatus, *Fragment*, 30.

[17] See Vincenzo Maggi (Madius), from *On the Ridiculous* (1550), trans. George Miltz, in Lauter, *Theories of Comedy, op. cit.*, 64-73.

[18] Giovanni Georgio Trissino, "from Poetics, Division VI (c. 1543-50)," trans. Anita Grossvogel, rev. Paul Lauter, in Lauter, *Theories of Comedy, op. cit.*, 42-7, on 43.

[19] Franciscus Robortellus, *On Comedy* (1548), trans. Marvin T. Herrick, in Marvin T. Herrick, *Comic Theory in the Sixteenth Century* (Urbana, IL: University of Illinois Press, 1964), 227-39, on 231.

[20] Julius Caesar Scaliger, *Poetices libri septem [Poetics]* (1561), trans. C. J. McDonough, in *Plato to Congreve*, vol. 1 of 4, *Sources of Dramatic Theory*, ed. Michael J. Sidnell (Cambridge: Cambridge University Press, 1991), 99-110, on 102.

[21] Antonio Sebastiano Minturno, from *The Art of Poetry* (1563), trans. Anita Grossvogel, rev. Paul Lauter, in Lauter, *Theories of Comedy, op. cit.*, 74-86, on 85.

comic deceptions that produce the experience of the ridiculous.[22] In 1585, Antonio Riccoboni summarized Italian theories of laughter in a manner that anticipates Freud: Comic laughter "is a sign of joy, and...the mind makes it through a dilation of the heart from the liberation of the spirits, which cannot be held in once the image of the joyful thing conquers."[23]

Surprise, wonder, pleasure, laughter, calm, joy: Such are the key terms, ones of affect, that recur in Italian discussions of comedy. The theorists do not envision anything in the comic ending that resembles the complex system of balances and compensations that has been understood as modern aesthetic harmony; rather, they see the conclusion of comedy as achieving, through reversal, surprise, and laughter, an experience of unpredictable delight—for characters and, implicitly or explicitly, for audiences. Likewise, in England, Nicholas Udall, in his often-cited c.1550 prologue to *Ralph Roister Doister*, takes up a related sense of an affective "mirth" as a key feature of comedy: "mirth prolongeth life,...causeth health; /... recreates our spirits,...voideth pensiveness; / [and] increaseth amity" (The Prologue, 8–10).[24] In mirth, Udall envisions the health benefits of comic joy and pleasure in a form not inconsistent with Riccoboni's sense of the comic "liberation of spirits."

Italian commentaries devote little or no attention to the question of whether the denouement ties up all plot elements or addresses their social contradictions. Trissino, to be sure, sees the reversals and recognitions of comedy as leading to marriage, peace-making, and tranquility (43); such terms are as close as theorists come to "harmony." Two decades later, Minturno mentions—in representative language—that Greek and Roman comedy "reduce the troubles and difficulties and all the serious and annoying things to a serene and happy outcome...in order to bring pleasure" (80), but his analysis centers on how pleasure is produced by surprise. For Renaissance theorists, comedy aims to achieve pleasurable wonder and "liberation of spirits" through surprise-producing incongruities, an effect not easily captured by modern notions of either formalist harmony or political dissonance. In practice, endings feed on incongruities. In *Merchant*, Lorenzo's lyrical celebration of the pacifying power of music will be followed shortly by the discordant squabbles erupting between Portia and Bassanio, and Nerissa and Gratiano. Such sequential incongruities generate auditorial surprise; their recognition prompts laughter and amusement. Italian conceptualizations simply do not

---

[22] Lodovico Castelvetro, from *Commentary on Aristotle's "Poetics"* (1570), trans. Andrew Bongiorno, in Lauter, *Theories of Comedy, op. cit.*, 87–97. See also Lodovico Castelvetro, *Castelvetro on the Art of Poetry*, trans. Andrew Bongiorno (Binghamton, NY: Medieval and Renaissance Texts and Studies, 1984).

[23] Antonio Roccoboni, from *The Comic Art* (1585), trans. George Miltz, in Lauter, *Theories of Comedy, op. cit.*, 98–107, on 106.

[24] Nicholas Udall, *Roister Doister*, in *Three Sixteenth-Century Comedies*: Gammer Gurton's Needle, Roister Doister, The Old Wife's Tale, ed. Charles Walters Whitworth (London: Ernest Benn Limited, 1984).

envision thematic harmony or political dissonance as goals of the comic denouement. Renaissance comic theory, with its love for the surprise of incongruity,
tacitly embraces contradictions and loose ends.

Likewise, Renaissance comedies themselves resolve some problems but willingly leave others in suspension. In essence, comic endings open a gap between
global problems that appear intractable and local solutions that depend on
contingency and opportunity. That gap, an incompleteness arguably inherent in
comic form, offers a space for imagination and conjecture. The trendsetter of
Italian comedy was Ariosto's *I suppositi*, premiered at Ferrara in 1509 and adapted
influentially into English in 1566 by George Gascoigne as *Supposes*. Shakespeare's
The Taming of the Shrew takes its "lock-out" scene from *Supposes*. Although the
mix-ups in *I suppositi* are caused by the rebellious sexual passion of the young
lovers and by the deceptions that they and their servants practice, the ending
largely reverts to patriarchal order. The last scenes give the disruptive young male
lover only one line, "Oh, Father!";[25] the doddering male blocking figure suddenly
becomes a wise elder statesman; while the wily servant Dulippo is absent from the
ending. The large structural problem of disruptive, youthful desire in conflict with
patriarchal restraint has been acknowledged during the play's action, but it is
simply set aside by a surprise circumstantial solution and a subsequent moment of
festive goodwill. Youthful, rebellious love implicitly wins out.

Cardinal Bibbiena's seminal *La calandra* (Urbino, 1513) focuses on two identical twins driven from their home and separated by war. Unknown to each other,
the young woman, Santilla, assumes the disguise of a male, and her brother, Lidio,
of a female. While Santilla is trying to avoid a forced marriage, Lidio uses his
disguise to gain access to, and sleep with, a married woman. In the end, Lidio
agrees to marry a bride he has never met (the woman intended for Santilla), so
that he can continue his affair, which is never publicly revealed. The play raises
issues of dislocation by war, marital betrayal, and illicit sexual intrigue, but simply
passes over them in the end.

The important Sienese comedy *Gl' ingannati* was staged in 1533, and it, or a
1592 version by Curzio Gonzaga, figures as a possible source-text for
Shakespeare's *Twelfth Night*.[26] Like *La calandra*, the play features identical twins
going about in disguise. The female lead character, Lelia, engages in aggressive,
potentially shameful behavior for a woman, and has a famous on-stage, same-sex
kiss. Her male beloved's nearly murderous action is never challenged; the blocking
figure gains no wisdom and is given no substitute love-interest; the conflict
between the servant girl and the braggart soldier is left feeling incomplete; and
the community of characters does not reunite at the end. Lelia gets her man, and

---

[25] Bernardo Dovizi da Bibbiena, *The Pretenders / I suppositi*, in *Renaissance Comedy: The Italian
Masters*, vol. 2 of 2, ed. Donald Beecher (Toronto: University of Toronto Press, 2007), 21–100, on 94.
[26] See Elam, *TN*, 61–4.

her rebellious female behavior is rewarded. As Douglas Radcliff-Umstead puts it, "A spontaneous, impetuous, even insolent spirit dominates the play."[27]

Finally, in this brief tour of endings in Italian cinquecento comedy, Giambattista della Porta's *Gli duoi fratelli rivali* (*c.*1590) stands out, in part because it is an analogue play for Shakespeare's *Much Ado About Nothing*. The melodramatic plot revolves around the competition of two brothers for the same woman. The brothers' emotions towards each other shuttle between fraternal affection, defensive suspicion, and outright hatred—yet, in the end, all is forgiven, and their seemingly unsalvageable camaraderie is restored, much as the heroine is discovered not dead but alive after all. The extremes of anger aroused in the action feel utterly inconsistent with the peaceful ending, but as long as every Jack has his Jill, the play is content to live with its contradictions. The point that emerges from these examples (others could be added) is that comedy, in the influential Renaissance Italian tradition, often presents large-scale problems but offers only small-scale and incomplete solutions, leaving some issues and plot-threads dangling. The actions come to rest in a moment of pleasurable surprise, but the endings do not pretend that all problems have disappeared; rather, they offer selective, pragmatic answers, situation by situation. The seeds of a large-scale solution may be planted within the local one—and modern critics see Italian Renaissance comedy as a forum for dissecting broad social conflicts and contradictions—but any grand arbitration is left for another day.

In England, the comic playwright John Lyly, writing in the 1580s, established the stage genre of romantic comedy and greatly influenced Shakespeare's comic art. In *The Merchant of Venice*'s denouement, Shakespeare apparently alludes to a Lyly play. As Portia returns with Nerissa to Belmont, she sees Jessica and Lorenzo sleeping on the grass: "Peace! How the moon sleeps with Endymion / And would not be waked" (5.1.109–10).[28] Portia's description brings to mind Lyly's dramatic comedy *Endymion* (*c.*1588; pub. 1591), which, like other Lyly plays, focuses on impossible love-longing. Relevant to *Merchant*, it contains a debate about the claims of friendship versus the rival claims of love, in which Eumenides, the best friend of Endymion, decides to sacrifice his own love-desires to help bring Endymion back from a twenty-year sleep. That decision provides the opportunity for Endymion to obtain his love-wishes—and for Eumenides, his—so that friendship and love become interdependent. The ending resolves all the play's love-disputes, but it treats underlying conflicts capriciously. Endymion has suffered painful aging from his twenty years of unrequited love for Cynthia, but those effects are simply reversed by Cynthia's shining of her anti-aging, goddess

---

[27] Douglas Radcliff-Umstead, *The Birth of Modern Comedy in Renaissance Italy* (Chicago: University of Chicago Press, 1969), 200.
[28] The eighteenth-century editor Edmund Capell first conjectured, correctly I think, that the moon–Endymion allusion refers to Jessica and Lorenzo.

moonlight on him. The ending also glosses over Endymion's deception of the beautiful Tellus, the source of most of the play's problems. Tellus's bitter, decades-long hatred of Endymion and her employment of sorcery against him are forgiven as if they were no more than bad judgment. Cynthia solves another problem by turning an enchanted tree back into a woman. The anger, cruelty, and melancholy that the play evokes are side-stepped by the overt contrivances of the denouement's moon-magic and love-knots. In that respect, *Endymion* is typical of Lyly's comedies—and a forerunner of the more complex *Merchant of Venice*.[29] Renaissance comedies raise more problems, and deeper problems, than they can possibly solve. Their nonce endings are always pragmatically devised, the hallmark of comedy. It would strike the wrong note to fault these plays for glossing over social problems, or to treat them as wistfully recognizing the limitations of comic form, since those dilemmas give Renaissance comedy its underlying premise. Such comedy lays open the gap between the global and the local, which becomes a space for engagement and speculation.

Exclusion in the Ending of *The Merchant of Venice*

In the last act of *The Merchant of Venice*, the space for wondering is filled by the question of what reconciliation is possible after the raw hostilities of the trial scene.[30] Here Antonio and Jessica each emerge as a response to that question, asking us to consider them not in isolation but in their relatedness. Every comedic denouement, of course, implicitly imagines a future. In *The Merchant of Venice*, that matter acquires urgency because the character at the play's emotional hub has just been symbolically killed off, rendered unavailable for integration into a newly constituted comic community.[31] In Plautus or Terence, even the corrupt panderers are brought back within the circle of society, but, in Shakespeare, exclusion becomes sometimes the fate of the anti-comic character—the evil Don John in *Much Ado About Nothing*, the cynic Jaques in *As You Like It*, the unreconcilable Malvolio in *Twelfth Night*—as if by such disbarments Shakespeare were saying

---

[29] *Endymion* and *Merchant* also differ. Janette Dillon contrasts the nuanced parallelisms in Lyly's plays with the sharper, tonally distinct, and even parodic juxtapositions that Shakespeare employs; "Shakespeare and the Traditions of English Stage Comedy," in *A Companion to Shakespeare's Works*, vol. 3 of 3, ed. Richard Dutton and Jean E. Howard (Malden, MA: Blackwell Publishing, 2003), 4–22. Dillon writes about *Gallathea* and *As You Like It*, but her comments apply to the playwrights' differences generally.

[30] Concerning the trial scene, I take David Margolies's position, that spectators or readers are left torn between a rational desire that Shylock's attempt fail and an emotional desire that he triumph; *Shakespeare's Irrational Endings: The Problem Plays* (Houndmills, Basingstoke: Palgrave, 2012), 86–111, on 102–3.

[31] Shakespeare enjoys undermining comic closure in additional ways, as with the unfulfilled romance of *Love's Labour's Lost* or the sudden transformations and rushed closure of *All's Well That Ends Well*.

that inclusiveness has its limits. But seldom do excluded characters dominate the action and define their play's ethical and emotional conflicts as does Shylock, and seldom does a character's irreconcilability take on the scale of Shylock's.[32] In *The Merchant of Venice*, then, Shakespeare sets the stakes unusually high, making us wonder about what future the figures of this playworld can have. As David Margolies puts it, the play "ends in unions the happiness of which, if not completely in doubt, feels uncertain."[33] That uncertainty applies not only to the marriages but also to specific individuals, especially Jessica and Antonio as apparent outsiders.[34] Here Shakespeare complicates the reintegration of the comic community, pitting consonance against dissonance, and experiments with forms of incompletion as means to entangle and fascinate spectators.[35]

Shakespeare's approach recalls that of Italian sixteenth-century comedies, which, as we have suggested, often leave loose ends, keep secrets, and sometimes exclude characters from reconciliation. Let us add to our earlier inventory a relevant, final Italian example, Aretino's *La cortigiana* (1525), featuring the venomous servant-trickster Rosso whose exclusion from the denouement puts Shylock's in relief. Among other acts of gratuitous cruelty, Rosso defrauds and betrays a poor Jewish pedlar, Romanello, causing his false arrest, imprisonment, and whipping. Towards the play's end, Rosso describes at length how his own master mistreats his servants by feeding them food that is virtually filth. Rosso's accusations share something with Shylock's against the Venetians for their treatment of slaves. Because Rosso's own cruelty and his hatred for his master put him beyond reclamation or reconciliation, Aretino has him sneak away and thus bars him from the comic ending. Rosso, not unlike Shylock, is hardened in animosity, incapable of self-knowledge; consequently, he is denied redemption. He just disappears.

Not quite so for Shylock. Observers of modern productions of *Merchant* testify to how powerful his ghostly "absent presence" can feel.[36] He is the numinous shade of the departed that haunts the ending, the revenant who cannot return but

---

[32] Kenneth Gross sees Shylock as "*what cannot be named or measured or converted*," paradoxically an open wound and a "closed, blank cliché"; *Shylock Is Shakespeare* (Chicago, IL: University of Chicago Press, 2006), 18, 6. Such terms put Shylock beyond strictly the social problem of the Jew.

[33] Margolies, *Irrational Endings*, 86.

[34] On inclusion, exclusion, and social status in *MV*'s last act, see Richard A. Levin, *Love and Society in Shakespearean Comedy: A Study of Dramatic Form and Content* (Newark, DE: University of Delaware Press, 1985), 78–85.

[35] Jean E. Howard argues that if comic conventions require differentiating among sets of "characters, locales, and motives," then *The Merchant of Venice* makes those conventions difficult to maintain; "The Difficulties of Closure: An Approach to the Problematic in Shakespearean Comedy," in *Comedy from Shakespeare to Sheridan: Change and Continuity in the English and European Dramatic Traditions*, ed. A. R. Braunmuller and J. C. Bulman (Cranbury, NJ: Associated University Presses, 1986), 113–28, on 123. But, in *MV*, I would argue, comic conventions function as the fine instrument for demonstrating that ethnic, racial, or religious categories do not equate to moral ones, thus sharpening the notion of the moral.

[36] Gross, *Shylock*, 108.

refuses to go away. According to Patrick J. Sullivan, writing about Laurence Olivier's 1974 production, the attempted lyricism of Lorenzo's fifth act "music speech" and Jessica's response reveal only "how we have never really returned with emotional fullness to Belmont. The courtroom and its memories have cast a shroud" over the ending.[37] Sullivan attests to the finale's potential, perhaps inevitable, effect. After all, as Margolies demonstrates, Shylock is the most "real" character in the play;[38] thus, as Kenneth Gross observes, "it is not likely he will go out of our minds... [H]e hovers in a kind of limbo" (108). Yet the ending also includes Shylockian substitutes, for Antonio and Jessica, as we will see, operate as peculiar factors for the Jew.[39] And just as Shylock, the spirit of anti-comedy, might be—today, must be—subliminally present, the comic spirit of Portia, imagined as light emerging from darkness, hovers, too, in juxtaposition, having absorbed, argues William C. Carroll, qualities from the trial scene's male characters "while transcending their limitations."[40] Whatever moral calibrations we wish to apply to these figures, the denouement evokes strikingly complex and mysterious shadow-relations.

We might think of Antonio and Jessica both as echoes, or displacements, of Shylock, who assist in making him metaphorically present in Act Five. Antonio and Jessica allow the denouement to hint at alternative endings, alternative futures, for the Other, different from the quasi-tragedy of Act Four. Antonio's situation imagines the anti-comic figure's accommodation; Jessica, the alien's assimilation. Such intimations of different possibilities are characteristic of Shakespeare's experiments with dramatic conventions; they are particularly pertinent to comedy, where metamorphosis and radical shifts in perspective inhere in the form. Some critics argue, convincingly, I think, that Antonio's melancholy is constitutional, not caused, and thus it cannot be explained or remedied.[41] It is hardly a humour in the conventional sense, for it is never linked to any physiological imbalance. As *Merchant*'s opening makes clear, Antonio's melancholy arises not from the torments of love or from anxiety over his merchandizing ventures. When Antonio announces, "In sooth, I know not why I am so sad" (1.1.1), he stakes out his position as an un-diagnosable and incurable melancholic, and thus a figure inherently resistant to the reformative effects of Shakespearean comedy, such as self-understanding and personal transformation. Although

[37] Patrick J. Sullivan, "The National Theatre's *Merchant of Venice*," *Educational Theatre Journal* 26, no. 1 (March 1974): 31–44, on 43.

[38] Margolies, *Irrational Endings*, 91–3.

[39] There are other echoes of Shylock. Robert Ornstein points out that, in accusing Bassanio about the ring, Portia "pretends to be more literal-minded than Shylock," an echo of the trial scene; *Shakespeare's Comedies: From Roman Farce to Romance Mystery* (Newark, DE: University of Delaware Press, 1986), 115.

[40] William C. Carroll, *The Metamorphoses of Shakespearean Comedy* (Princeton, NJ: Princeton University Press, 1985), 123.

[41] J. F. Bernard, "*The Merchant of Venice* and Shakespeare's Sense of Humour(s)," *Renaissance Studies* 28, no. 5 (November 2014): 643–58.

melancholics are not necessarily antisemites, Antonio's particular melancholy is akin to his antisemitism, which presents itself as a fixed ideological hatred, one that precedes moral rationalization and that Antonio expresses by spitting on Shylock and spurning him like a dog.[42] Ideology occurs here as a world view that is prior to, and in excess of, the evidence; it is beyond reason, and it cannot lead to the individual's change. Such ideology shines a light on those characters in *Merchant* who are rigid, self-isolated, and little capable of positive growth. For Antonio, melancholy is ideology's emotional counterpart.

For his part, Shylock owns a range of dark feelings—hatred, envy, sadness, sorrow, vengefulness—richer and more complex than Antonio's. Yet, as in his animosity towards Christians and especially towards the merchant, Shylock expresses a loneness and inelasticity similar to Antonio's. If Shylock develops at all in *Merchant*, he develops step by step into an embodiment or emblem of hatred that, by his own description, has moved beyond explanation. "Which is the merchant here, and which the Jew?" (4.1.170): To see an affinity between Antonio and Shylock is, certainly, to side-step our recognition that one of these two is the beneficiary of practices of social and economic exclusion while the other is the victim; but each of them, whether from a fixed antisemitism or of "a lodged hate and a certain loathing" (4.1.59), exemplifies an anti-comic being condemned to live within the confines of his own painful world view.[43]

If Shylock is physically absent from *Merchant*'s last act, then, his ideological and emotional stand-in, Antonio, is present. Drakakis cites Jean-François Lyotard's argument that society can never include, exclude, or quite assimilate the figure of the Jew.[44] And so it is, too, with Antonio.[45] He finishes the play *in* Belmont, but he is never *of* Belmont; he is tinted with moon-glow but denied its romance, restored to wealth but robbed of agency and reduced to a new condition of bondage as guarantor of Bassanio's marital truth. Belmont accommodates Antonio but does not assimilate him—and in performance he is sometimes left at the end standing onstage alone. Neither the terms "harmony" nor "dissonance" rightly describes his situation, for it is mixed and nuanced. Antonio's estrangement from, but containment within, the final community of comedy expresses the subtlety of Renaissance comic form.

---

[42] On the perception of Jewishness as threatening to the Elizabethan mentality, see James Shapiro, *Shakespeare and the Jews* (New York: Columbia University Press, [1996] 2016). See also Janet Adelman, *Blood Relations: Christian and Jew in* The Merchant of Venice (Chicago, IL: University of Chicago Press, 2008).

[43] In a complex cultural, religious, and psychoanalytic reading, Adelman develops linkages between Antonio and Shylock; *Blood Relations*, 99–133.

[44] Drakakis, *MV*, 27–8.

[45] By the end of the play, according to Gary Rosenfeld, Antonio has become a figure much diminished from that of the martyr and one out of sync with Belmont; "Deconstructing the Christian Merchant: Antonio and *The Merchant of Venice*," *Shofar* 20, no. 2 (Winter 2002): 28–51. Rosenfeld discusses Antonio as a merchant, but Antonio's homosexuality or extreme homosociality would also underscore his apartness.

Shylock's ghost also lives in Jessica, a character more plastic than Antonio. When Jessica says to Lorenzo, "I am never merry when I hear sweet music" (5.1.69), and Lorenzo answers, "The man that hath no music in himself... / Is fit for treasons, stratagems and spoils" (83–5), he alludes unmistakably to Shylock, who had warned Jessica to shut the casements against "the drum / And the vile squealing of the wry-necked fife" (2.5.28–9). But does Jessica too have no music in her? Is she Shylock's factor, the Jewish misfit and Other projected into Belmont despite its exclusionary politics?[46] That position is, in effect, the one taken by Launcelet Gobbo.[47] According to Launcelet, Jessica's only "bastard" hope for Christian salvation is that she might be illegitimate and thus "not the Jew's daughter" (3.5.11, 10). Launcelet's argument—that Jessica bears the damnable stigma of her father and that, by inference, she is also the Jewish alien disrupting the harmonies of Belmont—is implicitly the attitude adopted by those theatrical productions (following Olivier's) that conclude with Jessica isolated and alone onstage.

But the play suggests a quite different possibility, albeit one that some may find not altogether pleasing: that of Jewish assimilation. Critics such as James Shapiro and M. Lindsay Kaplan argue from cultural history that her femaleness makes Jessica more assimilable than Shylock, thereby turning gender into the determinative factor.[48] But the play expresses little obvious interest in whether or not Jewish identity is marked by physiological inscription (e.g., circumcision) or descends exclusively through one sex (e.g., the male).[49] Within the action, from Launcelet's plebeian standpoint, the key distinction about Jews is that they are non-eaters of pork. Thus, the evil of converting Jews is that "[t]his making of Christians will raise the price of hogs" (3.5.21–2). Jessica expands on Launcelet's position when she complains to Lorenzo that the clown "says you are no good member of the commonwealth, for in converting Jews to Christians you raise the price of pork" (30–3). Launcelet largely obliterates differences in religious denominations and

---

[46] Shaul Bassi sets Jessica against contradictory historical images of the Jewish woman as unruly and as passively beautiful; "Jessica, Sarra, Ruth: Jewish Women in Shakespeare's Venice," in The Merchant of Venice: The State of Play, ed. M. Lindsay Kaplan (London: Bloomsbury, 2020), 173–93.

[47] On "Launcelet," see Chapter 1, n. 3; on "Gobbo," see Chapter 5, n. 28.

[48] Shapiro, Shakespeare and the Jews, 120; M. Lindsay Kaplan, "Jessica's Mother: Medieval Constructions of the Jewish Race and Gender in The Merchant of Venice," Shakespeare Quarterly 58, no. 1 (Spring 2007): 1–30. Kaplan is responding in part to Adelman's view of Jessica as fundamentally alien in Blood Relations, 66–98. Likewise, for Bassi, Jessica remains "the potential vehicle of ineffable Jewish identify," "Jessica, Sarra," 181, see 180–3. For a discussion of the different positions, for and against, on Jessica's assimilability, see Suzanne Tartamella, "Jessica's Silence and the Feminine Pyrrhonic in Shakespeare's The Merchant of Venice," Renaissance Drama 48, no. 1 (Spring 2020): 83–101, on 92–6. Tartamella concludes astutely that "the arguments on both sides of the question of Jessica's conversion and assimilation cannot be definitively answered by the play—or even by the cultural context" (96). While the play entertains the possibility of assimilation, it remains only that.

[49] Notwithstanding, Shapiro (Shakespeare and the Jews), Adelman (Blood Relations), and others interpret Shylock's prospective cutting of Antonio, "in what part of" Antonio's "body pleaseth" Shylock (MV 1.3.143), as a symbolic circumcision.

cultures by reducing them to the economics of food consumption and the prospects for financial inconvenience (more visions of the future). Audiences laugh, but such reductiveness has the advantage of imposing a new perspective and shifting the grounds of thinking away from virulent antisemitism.

To Launcelet's charge that Jessica is damned because of her parentage, she retorts, "I shall be saved by my husband; he hath made me a Christian!" (17–18). A cynical response might be that Jessica's profligate squandering of her father's wealth provides ample evidence that Lorenzo has indeed "made [her] a Christian." Yet even before her elopement, Jessica had claimed that though she was "a daughter to [Shylock's] blood," she was not a daughter "to his manners" (2.3.18, 19), and she had promised to end the "strife" of divided loyalties by "[b]ecom[ing] a Christian" and Lorenzo's "loving wife" (20, 21). Here religious affiliation becomes part, not of the commonwealth's economy, but of a more domestic one. The Jessica and Lorenzo whom we meet at Belmont seem nothing like the earlier reported wastrels who exchanged Leah's ring for a monkey. They behave with modesty and decorous respect towards Portia, and the departing Portia does not hesitate to "commit into [Lorenzo's] hands / The husbandry and manage of [her] house" (3.4.24–5). Jessica and Lorenzo thus become identified with Portia and Bassanio. "I wish your ladyship all heart's content," says Jessica in parting; "I thank you for your wish, and am well pleased / To wish it back on you. Fare you well, Jessica," responds Portia (42, 43–4). Actress Elena Pellone, rehearsing this scene as Nerissa, reports that the exchange gave her "goose bumps": "*Not infidel. Them recognising each other. A small moment...a jewel of Shakespearean connection.*"[50]

When we encounter Lorenzo and Jessica again at the beginning of Act Five, they are entrusted by Shakespeare with the task of resetting the play's mood: "The moon shines bright," says Lorenzo, "In such a night as this..." (5.1.1)—and the two proceed to banter about lovers—Troilus, Thisbe, Dido, Medea—whose passions brought them to grief. The classical legends that the two invoke may be tragic, yet the present relationship between Jessica and Lorenzo seems playful: Numerous critics see a tension here, as if the dark allusions were hinting at one possible, but not necessary, future for this marriage. For now, the two match wits equitably, and Jessica even wins a round, if her reference to Medea's rejuvenating of Aeson with enchanted herbs can be taken as a joke about her own rejuvenation of Lorenzo. The dialogue puts something further at stake when Jessica says, "I am never merry when I hear sweet music." Lorenzo takes her remark not as a repudiation of music but an affirmation of its power. Jessica is not "merry," he says, because her "spirits are attentive" (70), transformed from their restless condition into a focused listening by "the sweet power of music" (79), as if, in

---

[50] E. M. Pellone, "Shylock's Ghosts," unpublished essay (2019), discussing Pellone's experience with the 2016 production of *The Merchant of Venice* in the Jewish Ghetto of Venice.

another version of the future, music (or poetry) could have metamorphic power.[51] While some critics emphasize the praise of harmony in this exchange,[52] we might note its claim for the possibilities of concentrated attentiveness—of the sort, if not so hushed and breathless, that Shakespeare may wish upon his own audience regarding the denouement. Indeed, Suzanne Tartamella sees in Jessica an attitude of "moral awareness" yet suspended judgment that "the audience is invited to mirror."[53] Jessica becomes the playgoers' potential stand-in. As suggested in the Introduction, in the spirit of Jane Bennett, this absorbed and focused wondering makes for a form of enchantment.

The picture of Jessica at Belmont sketched here differs from that of the Jew-as-Other. Her presence offers presumptive evidence that the sins of the father are not laid upon the daughter; that the garment of religion can be worn lightly; that marriage and music are transformational; and that the figure of the alien can perhaps be assimilated into a comic community.[54] Such a message of assimilationism might seem naïve to some observers and objectionable to others: fair enough. Perhaps critics such as Drakakis would see it as a projection "of a fantasy world that can never quite satisfy desire or shake itself free from quotidian concerns" (61). But the assimilationist dream is surely no more sentimental than, say, the restorative ending of *Romeo and Juliet*, which registers no doubts that the self-sacrifice of the titular characters will cause the Montagues and Capulets to give over generations of feuding; that is certainly a "fantasy" ending oblivious "to quotidian concerns." The test of realism seems wrong in both cases, for our interest centers on possibility. In *Merchant*, the assimilationist vision hints that playfully fond relationships at an intimate human scale are capable of releasing individuals from the death-grip of ideology.

Thus, the last phase of *The Merchant of Venice* offers three possible responses to the problem of Shylock poised in relation to each other: first, the figurative destruction of him in the quasi-tragic ending of Act Four; second, the uneasy accommodation given to his factor, the melancholy ideologue Antonio; and, third, his Christian assimilation imagined in the malleable persona of Jessica. In response to the kind of thinking discussed by Jean-François Lyotard, that the Jew as a cultural Other "cannot be" "expelled," integrated," or "converted,"[55] Shakespeare offers the hypothetical modeling of all three possibilities. Thus, the climactic efforts to create a comic community address implicitly the problem of Shylock, albeit in symbolic form. The ending offers a comic closure that is only provisional, creating uncertainties and hypotheses about the futures of these

---

[51] On Shakespeare's use of music, especially with reference to this scene, see (among others), David Lindley, *Shakespeare and Music* (London: Bloomsbury, 2006), 1–49.

[52] See, for example, Danson, *Harmonies*, 187.   [53] Tartamella, "Jessica's Silence," 97.

[54] For a darker, less assimilationist interpretation, see Adelman, *Blood Relations*, 96–8.

[55] Jean-François Lyotard, *Heidegger and "the jews"*, trans. Andreas Michael and Mark S. Roberts (Minneapolis, MN: University of Minnesota Press, 1990), 22; (Drakakis cites these remarks, *MV*, 28).

couples, yet in doing so it offers an invitation to further thought—to a reflection not abstract but tinged deeply by the play's emotional intensity, a wondering born in the charmed circle of dramatic effects. Belmont becomes something more than the home of smug Venetian values; by means of Jessica and Antonio's awkward presence there, it becomes a place where we are invited to wonder. Although Renaissance comedy tends to relocate its problems from the societal level to that of the personal, it also makes its endings sufficiently open and provocative to prompt further ruminations and conjectures—and even auditorial desires on behalf of its characters, a lingering enthrallment. Consequently, instead of unearthing the fragility of genre, one might recognize a stance of pragmatism; and instead of seeing a failure of comic form, we might discover the model of its possibility. *Merchant*'s ending emerges as an intricate machine that arouses subtly juxtaposed and incompletely resolved emotions, a play of consonance and dissonance, that both absorbs and provokes its "attentive spirits" with wondering.

Delusion in *Much Ado About Nothing*

Yet sometimes even our most attentive spirits will have trouble understanding the final facts of a denouement, thus introducing a different kind of wondering. In the case of *Much Ado About Nothing*, the ending arrives at a truth of feelings that seems, paradoxically, to go beyond the truth of evidence. Critics such as Lorna Hutson have argued that Renaissance comic denouements showcase empirical and rationally coherent explanations that clarify the confusions of the action (see Introduction). Yet for those rationalists Beatrice and Benedick, arriving at the disenchanted, demystified truth proves surprisingly difficult, partly because love has overwhelmed them as a transforming "miracle" (5.3.91), not as a last step in a causal chain, and partly because the truths that all the protagonists perceive are incomplete or distorted by self-interest. As a play proceeds, an audience's knowledge, argues Claire McEachern, typically exceeds that of individual characters; consequently, by the end, we, as audiences, feel a "desire" for characters to come to know what we know, confirming our "intuitions" about events.[56] But in *Much Ado*, the protagonists' knowledge never catches up to ours, nor is ours certain. Beatrice and Benedick, the lodestones of our emotional interest, achieve a love that feels right, yet we might still wonder how, or even whether, it really happened, as if the process were a little mysterious or magical.

By the end, do Beatrice and Benedick truly love each other, or have they—and we—only been deluded into thinking so? One does not find such issues in *Much Ado*'s Italian analogue plays, Giambattista della Porta's *Gli duoi fratelli rivali*

---

[56] Claire McEachern, *Believing in Shakespeare: Studies in Longing* (Cambridge: Cambridge University Press, 2018), 142, see 157–67.

("The Two Rival Brothers") (c.1590) and Luigi Pasqualigo's *Il fedele* (1576), the latter published in an adapted translation, Anthony Munday's *Fedele and Fortunio* (1585). *Duoi fratelli* showcases love's gyroscopic passions, and *Fedele* its cruelty and obsessiveness, but both lack *Much Ado*'s epistemological interest. Unwarranted credulity and self-deception make for familiar human problems.[57] When Dogberry brings Borachio and Conrad before the Sexton, he asks, "Is our whole dissembly appeared?" (4.2.1). Dogberry's conflation of "assembly" and "dissemble" suggests inadvertently that when people come together in a group they almost necessarily masquerade and misrepresent—the side-effects of social intercourse. *Much Ado*, more than most of Shakespeare's comedies, explores the mesmerizing power of human deception. In the public world of Messina, strong feelings, such as anger or pain, can be expressed only indirectly or euphemistically; conversation requires a degree of dissimulation. Conventions of polite speech displace aggression into raillery and jesting: "Is Signor Mountanto returned from the wars or no," asks Beatrice in the first scene (1.1.28–9). Here and elsewhere her opaque drollery not only distances her from her own aggressiveness but also draws us in, charms us into wondering, scrutinizing her speech for meaning. "I wonder that you will still be talking, Signor Benedick," deadpans Beatrice later in the scene, "nobody marks you" (110–11).[58] Nobody except us, marking both characters and trying to sort out this curious relationship.

Enraged Affection, Horrible Love

The two lovers' friends would shock and magically transform Beatrice and Benedick's minds with the "miracle" of love (5.3.91). Claudio calls beauty a "witch" capable of casting "charms" that subvert one's beliefs, while Don Pedro accuses Benedick of having been "ever an obstinate heretic in despite of beauty" (2.1.164–5; 1.1.219–20). By tricking the "merry war[riors]" to fall in love (1.1.58), Don Pedro, Leonato, and their fellow intriguers will snatch Cupid's "glory" and make themselves "the only love-gods" (2.1.356–7). Through the rhetorical spell woven by these nouveau deities, Beatrice and Benedick will each presumably fall to love's enchantments. Benedick's eavesdropping scene occurs in the "orchard" (2.3.4), *Much Ado*'s subtle version of the green world (see Chapter 3), the place where one's guard drops, apprehension melts away, and change becomes possible. The scene's emphasis on "noting" and "wonder[ing]" invites the audience to

---

[57] The well-known impact of Pyrrhonian skepticism on Renaissance epistemology is beyond the scope of this discussion; for a recent study of the problem of knowing in the period, see Katherine Eggert, *Disknowledge: Literature, Alchemy, and the End of Humanism in Renaissance England* (Philadelphia, PA: University of Pennsylvania Press, 2015).

[58] Variants of "wonder" occur nine times in the play, frequently in the sense of doubting, speculating, being baffled for explanation.

respond similarly, especially regarding the power of love (52–5, 8, 97). While the conspirators employ images of fowling ("stalk on"), fishing ("hook"), and disease ("infection") to describe their ruse (94, 110, 122), notions of love as enchantment also sift through the scene. The "still[ness]" of the evening, perfect for music, feels "hushed on purpose to grace harmony," remarks Claudio (36–7).[59] The music-softened orchard invites magic, and, fittingly, the mystery of love's transformational power saturates Benedick's thoughts: "I do much wonder..." (8); "May I be so converted...?" (21); "I will not be sworn but love may transform me to an oyster" (22–3). Variants of "convert" and "transform" recur in the play in relation to the experience love, displaying both the play's "imagery of metamorphosis"[60] and its aura of quasi-religious enchantment. Those ideas stand out palpably here: Benedick mocks the notion of the singer's soul being "ravished" by love music (56) until he himself succumbs to the same spell.

With Benedick overhearing, Don Pedro, Claudio, and Leonato claim that Beatrice "dote[s] on Signor Benedick, whom she hath in all outward behaviours seemed ever to abhor" (98–9). "Dote" and "dotage" occur in the scene four times (98, 165, 204, 209). The *Oxford English Dictionary* defines doting as exhibiting an extravagant, excessive affection (dote *v.* 2a–b), and other entries associate it with derangement or madness (1a, c). It expresses symptoms that might be associated with enchantment, and the word and its variants recall Helena's transformed state in *A Midsummer Night's Dream* (see Chapter 4). According to the deceivers' verbal conjurations, Beatrice is in "ecstasy" (149), which the *OED* identifies with rapture and transport (ecstasy *n.* 4a) (the entry's examples suggest being elevated, dissolved, or overwhelmed ["thrown into ecstasies"]). In the conspirators' story, Beatrice, torn between her secret passion and her public scorn for Benedick, falls on her knees, weeps, beats her heart, and cries contradictorily, "'O sweet Benedick! God give me patience!'" (146–7). This comically over-the-top counterfeit persona keeps true to Beatrice's passionate nature. Thus, her alleged, paradoxical "enraged affection" for Benedick sounds authentic (102–3), with her subsequent harshness towards him becoming corroboration.

How happily charmed Benedick is by this semblance! He rationalizes away the possibility of a "gull[ing]" because "the white-bearded fellow speaks it" (2.3.119–20); likewise: "This can be no trick. The conference was sadly borne; they have the truth of this from Hero" (213–15). "I will be horribly in love with her," he concludes (226–7), his terms reformulating unconsciously Beatrice's supposed "enraged affection." A similar reversal will overwhelm Beatrice. The effect on Benedick of the tricksters' device recalls that of the love potion sprinkled in Demetrius's eyes; Benedick mutates almost instantaneously into a lover

---

[59] Claudio's line echoes distantly Lorenzo's opening lines of the last scene of *The Merchant of Venice*.

[60] McEachern, *MA*, 52.

impervious to reason and blind to evidence, now bursting with the very emotions that he had dismissed. Rhetoric, of course, had a long and controversial association with magic.[61] Here that association underscores the outsized transmutational power of the rhetorical ploy. Likewise, Benedick's metamorphosis delivers outsized pleasure to the audience, perhaps because, especially in romantic comedy, love tends to be rather like magic.

But audiences will not be completely surprised by either Benedick's "horribl[e]" love or Beatrice's "enraged affection." Other forces may be at work besides rhetorical magic, for, at multiple points, the dialogue hints at a prior relationship between the two characters. The Joss Whedon film of *Much Ado* (2012) even begins with an interpolated scene in which Benedick sneaks guiltily away from Beatrice's bed, as if from some awkward one-night stand. In the play's opening scene, Beatrice alludes enigmatically to Benedick's having "set up his bills here in Messina and challenged Cupid to the flight" (1.1.36–7); she accuses him of "always end[ing] with a jade's trick" (138); and she will observe later that Benedick had once "lent" his "heart" to her but that when she "gave him" hers in return, he played with "false dice" (2.1.255–7). Beatrice glances consistently, concludes Joost Daalder, at a previous love relationship in which Benedick won her heart and then betrayed her affection.[62] Actress Karen Martin-Cotton, playing Beatrice in a 2016 production, discusses how Beatrice's various speeches point to a prior relationship, so that when the play begins, "I am still in love with him ... [e]ven if I think he's an impossible person."[63] But we never learn precisely what happened. Beatrice speaks only metaphorically and elliptically, consistent with Messina's world of verbal artificiality, where the deepest feelings can never be fully acknowledged or expressed.

Love as Reciprocal and Mysterious

For audiences, part of the delight of Beatrice and Benedick derives from the sense that this perfectly matched pair is discovering what we have known, that they are already actually, or at least latently, in love.[64] But critics have not always been so receptive. Stephen Greenblatt, in an argument that editor Claire McEachern calls "unusually cynical," ash-cans the notion of a prior love and sees the couple's union

[61] See, for example, John O. Ward, "Magic and Rhetoric from Antiquity to the Renaissance: Some Ruminations," *Rhetorica* 6, no. 1 (Winter 1988): 57–118, e.g., 66.

[62] Joost Daalder, "The 'Pre-History of Beatrice and Benedick in *Much Ado About Nothing*," *English Studies* 85, no. 6 (December 2004): 520–7.

[63] Michael Don Bahr, "Acting Shakespeare: A Roundtable Discussion with Artists from the Utah Shakespeare Festival's 2016 Production of *Much Ado About Nothing*," *Journal of the Wooden O* 16, no. 1–7 (2018): 38–55, on 45.

[64] Richard Henze, "Deception in *Much Ado About Nothing*," *Studies in English Literature* 11, no. 2 (Spring 1971): 187–201, on 189.

as the effect of "social manipulation."[65] Jean Howard, in order to argue that *Much Ado* reinforces patriarchal power structures, insists likewise that the love between Beatrice and Benedick is socially constructed; several other critics endorse that view.[66] But such assertions have trouble explaining the ambience created by the couple, which urges a pre-existing affinity: The way that Beatrice and Benedick keep talking about each other, the way that one mentions the other unnecessarily in conversation, the way that they react so strongly to each other, the way that they so suddenly and overwhelmingly fall in love—all these argue for an emotional engagement well beyond the terms of a "merry war."[67] They are at the tips of each other's tongues and the edges of each other's feelings. As actress Maggie Steed puts it, Beatrice's "first words in the play are asking for Benedick and she refers to him constantly"; around him she is "very excited, firing on all cylinders."[68] The play gives approval, furthermore, to the idea that love can exist *in potentia*. When Claudio reveals to Don Pedro his seemingly abrupt love of Hero, he explains that he had "liked" her on first meeting but was then too preoccupied with war "to drive liking to the name of love" (1.1.280–1). Now his former "war-thoughts" have ceded their place to "soft and delicate desires" (282–4). Claudio's earlier attraction to Hero was firewood ready to be fanned consciously into full-blown love once those impeding war-thoughts were dampened. Love here seems both of the heart and of the mind. Claudio's description constitutes a diagnostics of Benedick and Beatrice—although their minds keep missing the evidence of their feelings, the Messinian condition.

But with how much certainty do we know that Beatrice and Benedick "latently" or "actually" love each other? In a play that straightforwardly confronts the problem of drawing false inferences from external evidence, do we have sufficient grounds for being absolutely, positively, completely sure? After all, unlike the characters, only spectators and readers know, or conjecture, that the love between Beatrice and Benedick has a prior existence and is not a counterfeit manufactured by the conspirators. Leonato, Don Pedro, Claudio, and even Hero apparently believe that they have truly invented the couple's love. As the three men exit the deception scene, Claudio says, "If he do not dote on her upon this, I will never trust my expectation" (2.3.204–5), and Don Pedro replies, "The sport will be when they hold one an opinion of the other's dotage, and no such matter" (208–10). In the parallel deception of Beatrice, Hero concludes, "Some Cupid kills with arrows,

[65] Stephen Greenblatt et al., eds., *The Norton Shakespeare*, 3rd edn. (New York: W. W. Norton, 2015), 528; McEachern, *MA*, 52.

[66] Jean E. Howard, *The Stage and Social Struggle in Early Modern England* (New York: Routledge, 1994), 65–7. For a similar view, see Nova Myhill, "Spectatorship in/of *Much Ado About Nothing*," *Studies in English Literature* 39, no. 2 (Spring 1999): 291–311.

[67] As Margolies observes, the play goes to great length to show Beatrice and Benedick as "counterparts; their flyting is as integrated as a dance and suggests intimacy"; *Irrational Endings*, 50.

[68] Maggie Steed, "Beatrice," in *Players of Shakespeare*, vol. 3 of 3, ed. Russell Jackson and Robert Smallwood (Cambridge: Cambridge University Press, 1993), 42–51, on 47.

some with traps" (3.1.106). The conspirators have no idea whatsoever that Beatrice and Benedick might be already, or potentially, in love.

For their part, Beatrice and Benedick each explain loving the other as a necessary act of reciprocation. "Love me?" Benedick ponders, "Why, it must be requited"; "If I do not take pity of her I am a villain" (2.3.216–17, 252–3). Likewise, Beatrice concludes, "Benedick, love on, I will requite thee" (3.1.111). (Beatrice also speaks of "recompense" in the last scene [5.4.83].) From one angle, their love seems like a reflection bouncing inside a hall of mirrors ("I love you because you love me . . ."). But from another angle, the lovers' reciprocity crystalizes a new kind of almost magical awareness awakened in their relationship—something that might resonate with a modern audience beyond the back-and-forth circuitry of a gift-giving culture. According to Derek Gottlieb, Benedick and Beatrice move from the notion that love can be confirmed by applying predetermined, tick-box criteria, to an altered stance in relation to the world, a tectonic shift from disengagement and avoidance to engagement, from love based on causation to love based on acknowledgment: "[r]esponsiveness, reception, and conversion."[69] That shift empowers Benedick's alogical leap: "Love me? Why, it *must* be requited" (emphasis added). Actor Ben Livingston, playing Benedick in the 2016 Utah production, fastened on the power of "Love me?" as a "watershed moment" that "cracks [Benedick's] heart open" and overthrows his resistance to engage-ment, to love.[70] The acknowledgment of love entails reciprocity—and reciprocity, love's imperative, flips on its head Beatrice and Benedick's prior bond of antag-onism, harnessing and re-routing its energy. For Martin Buber, the reciprocity of the "I–You" relationship describes our deepest engagement with the other, when we stop treating him or her as an object to be experienced; rather, we now respond with our whole beings to the other in the spirit of reciprocity: "[R]elation is reciprocity."[71] Here, the I and the You are open to, and act upon, each other— as Beatrice and Benedick have been doing in unacknowledged ways—and quo-tidian causality evaporates as an explanation.[72] Reciprocity, for Buber, is "myster [ious]" (68), and it arrives not as something conventionally caused but as "a force that flashes, strikes, . . . a volcanic motion without continuity" (72). No surprise, then, that both Benedick and Beatrice in the gulling scenes experience an over-whelming, almost unaccountable, sense of transformation, as their relationship inverts from oppositional to reciprocal. If engagement with the other is reci-procity, a mutual acting upon, it becomes what Buber calls an "encounter"

[69] Derek Gottlieb, *Skepticism and Belonging in Shakespearean Comedy* (New York: Routledge, 2016), 68–80, on 72.
[70] Bahr, "Acting Shakespeare," 46.
[71] Martin Buber, *I and Thou*, trans. Walter Kauffmann (New York: Charles Scribners' Sons, 1970; orig. pub. in German, 1923), 58, 67.
[72] "Here I and You confront each other freely in a reciprocity that is not involved in or tainted by any causality"; Buber, *I and Thou*, 100.

(62)—and perhaps Buber's view reveals something about the radical potential in a comic 'encounter.'[73]

Not Knowing

At the end of a Shakespearean comedy, characters typically learn those crucial pieces of information that had been withheld from them, so that their knowledge comes to match that of the audience, as McEachern argues.[74] Such revelations fulfill the terms of the Aristotelian denouement, applied in the Renaissance to comedy as well as to tragedy. But sometimes characters are left in an ambiguous state, as with Demetrius in *A Midsummer Night's Dream*, who will always see Helena through the film of the eye potion, its magic having restored his desire.

Two such key effects hang over the ending of *Much Ado*: a gap and a muddle. The gap pertains to Beatrice and Benedick's ignorance, in that the gullings are never fully revealed to them. Leonato hints to Benedick about the conspiracy, when he declares that Benedick's "eye of love" was "had from me, / From Claudio and the prince" (5.4.24–6). In reply, Benedick says only, "Your answer, sir, is enigmatical" (27); that is, indecipherable, as indeed it is, since Leonato does not explain that the conspirators fabricated, rather than reported, their evidence of Beatrice's love. Claudio and Don Pedro had earlier told Benedick tauntingly that they knew, or had learned, of his presence in the garden, but they never disclaim the Beatrician semblance they had counterfeited. In the denouement, Benedick and Beatrice each declare fairly that the other's love has been "swor[n]" to by their friends (76, 80). Thus, we face an impasse: testimony by friends versus the principals' demurrals that they love "no more than reason" (5.4.74, 77), that evidentiary stalemate broken by the friends' producing the respective love letters. The solution depends upon the gullings' trickery remaining hidden from the lovers.

That gap in knowledge creates a muddle not only for the characters but also for the audience, which must sift the evidence, as when the lovers almost break off:

BENEDICK

They swore that you were almost sick for me.

---

[73] Relatedly, Marta Strasnicky astutely observes that "the connection between Beatrice and Benedick enables... a reformation of patriarchal gender relations" because "it posits mutuality of charity... as the keystone of a just society"; "Shakespeare and the Government of Comedy: *Much Ado About Nothing*," *Shakespeare Studies 22* (Madison, NJ: Fairleigh Dickinson University Press, 1994), 141–71, on 161. On the comic 'encounter' see the present Introduction.

[74] McEachern, *Believing in Shakespeare.*

BEATRICE

They swore that you were well-nigh dead for me.

BENEDICK

'Tis no such matter. Then you do not love me?

BEATRICE

No truly, but in friendly recompense.

(5.4.80–3)

Does this exchange disabuse Beatrice and Benedick of the impression that one is sick from, and the other dying for, love? Maybe, but doubtfully. The two, after all, have been famously anti-romantic in public. As Gottlieb points out, they had already confessed their mutual love profoundly in private, so that the danger here consists not in the intrusion of new information but in the temptation for the two to revert to a stance of disengagement.[75] The text never develops any sudden disillusionment, and it offers only the slightest opportunity for actors to express it physically, for the friends intervene immediately to forestall the possibility of disenchantment and to right the lovers' course. A too-full exposure of the truth, they fear, would put the wedding of this skittish couple in jeopardy. And convincing the lovers requires only a modest effort. The conspirators never explain, nor do the lovers ever inquire into, their obscure hints of involvement, so that the couple's prior, convulsive love-awakenings remain as undiluted as a love potion. Beatrice and Benedick embrace their love while being ignorant of the facts of it. Likewise, the conspirators bask in the conviction that they are the only love gods without ever recognizing the profound current of emotion already alive between the witty pair. These are surely limited and self-interested authority figures. Everybody in this ending seems deliriously happy and more than a little deluded.

And the audience? Centuries of playgoing suggest that theater audiences find the coming together of Beatrice and Benedick wholly fitting, perhaps the most delightful match in the comedies. Yet only spectators and readers know what the tricksters and the lovers do not, and only spectators and readers can imaginatively construct Beatrice and Benedick's responsiveness to each other and the hints of prior relationship as constituting the foundation for love and marriage, the gullings thus serving to "discover" and "animate a preexisting affinity."[76] Are we the true love gods? The play makes it difficult to erase wholly from memory the hint that Beatrice and Benedick might love each other "no more than reason." Audiences are kept comfortable with their surmises about the couple's infatuation while being prompted simultaneously to suspect those conclusions. One might conjecture that playgoers prefer that the two lovers remain ignorant rather than that any further revelations jeopardize the happy ending that spectators desire.

[75] Gottlieb, *Skepticism and Belonging*, 77.   [76] McEachern, *Believing in Shakespeare*, 165.

When the conspirators interject themselves to insist upon the couple's love, they are speaking not only as the voice of society within the play but also as the voice of the society attending to it. We do not wish to admit the possibility that Beatrice and Benedick are not really, or sufficiently, in love, preferring to remain potentially deceived rather than to put the matter to the test. If so, the play invites audiences to acknowledge the conventions of comic endings and their investment in fulfilling them. That kind of ending—love as both certain and doubtful—arguably makes for a richer and more meaningful ending than would either a sentimental or a disillusioned one. The "whole dissembly," the entire assembly of dissemblers, may ultimately include us. Such possibilities answer another problem in the ending, for the strangely truncated wonder of Hero's return from the dead has now been converted into the wondering attendant of Beatrice and Benedick's union, the latter perhaps exemplifying the kind of "complexity" that Jane Bennett finds enchanting (see Introduction). Benedick provides closure when he playfully reprises his earlier transformation and renounces mechanistic cause-mongering: "In brief, since I do purpose to marry, I will think nothing to any purpose that the world can say against it, ... for man is a giddy thing, and this is my conclusion" (103–7). Rather than parse former positions, Benedick embraces an existential truth; love is a "miracle"; so, we might say, "let wonder seem familiar" (91, 70).

The Problem of Forgiveness

In Shakespeare's comedies, wonder can invite forgiveness. Typically, discussions of Shakespearean forgiveness have emphasized the late romances,[77] but the subject is explored to special effect in the earlier comedies. Because Shakespeare's interest in forgiveness was decades-long and experimental, it probably responds to broad historical trends rather than to local events.[78] Sarah Beckwith has argued convincingly that the Reformation moved the issue of forgiveness out of the institutional formalism of the church, with its sacrament of penance, and into the ordinary language of human relations, where it became subject to the contingency and fragility of social dealings and where it required constant renegotiation and reformulation.[79] Such secularization vexes the questions of what merits forgiveness and how it is achieved. Those matters arouse more than antiquarian interest, because forgiveness persists today as a profoundly important personal and social

---

[77] For an example, see Sarah Beckwith, *Shakespeare and the Grammar of Forgiveness* (Ithaca, NY: Cornell University Press, 2011).

[78] Those trends would include: the pressure of debt in a cash-strapped, neo-capitalist society; the emergence of equity jurisprudence; and, differently, a Protestantism that makes divine forgiveness inscrutable. On early modern debt's affective dimension, see Theodore B. Leinwand, *Theatre, Finance and Society in Early Modern England* (Cambridge: Cambridge University Press, 1999).

[79] Beckwith, *Forgiveness*, 1–14; see also McEachern, *Believing in Shakespeare*.

value: What could be more necessary for the successful functioning of a family or a polity than forgiveness? Individuals, groups, or nations that cannot forgive bind themselves to tragedy. The comic attitude has something to teach us about how forgiveness is attained and what difference it makes.

I shall make two arguments, one having to do with forgiveness and wonder, the other with forgiveness and the gift. For the first argument, let us contrast the way that forgiveness is reached in the comedies as opposed to the late romances. In certain of the romances, forgiveness emerges out of suffering and the sinner's penance, with the conclusion's restored relationships generating awe from the participants. Thus, the late plays entertain a progression: Forgiveness leads to wonder. But various of Shakespeare's comedies reverse that pattern: Wonder leads to forgiveness rather than following it. In the comedies, forgiveness can operate mysteriously, beyond the boundaries of logical causality. For my second argument, let us consider the problem that some acts of forgiveness, however wondrous, seem insufficiently merited and wrong. Here Tudor Protestant theology fails to provide clear answers for the nuanced secular situations that Shakespearean comedy creates. How do we know what degree of shame the guilty party should suffer, or when contrition is sincere or sufficient? In such doubtful situations, forgiveness comes as a gift, an intervention, wondrous in itself, that frees both the individual and the community and thus advances comedy's utopian vision. Overall in the comedies, forgiveness occurs as something supra-rational, transcendent of the boundaries of logical causality.

Wondrous Forgiveness

In the conclusions of certain Shakespearean comedies, wonder brings characters to the brink of crisis. In *Twelfth Night*, Malvolio disrupts the scene of reconciliation, accusing Olivia of having done him a "notorious wrong" (5.1.323). Given the moment's precariousness, Fabian intercedes: "[L]et no quarrel nor no brawl to come / Taint the condition of this present hour, / Which I have wondered at" (350–2). At this magical time, he continues, let the "device" played upon Malvolio "rather pluck on laughter than revenge" (354, 360). Fabian's remarks identify both the extraordinary power and the potential limitations of the comic denouement. Comedy can create moments that feel enchanted, in which seeming impossibilities are made into probable facts that converge in mutually complementing ways to make sense out of what before had appeared fantastical, inducing a delighted sense of shock and wonder. But not necessarily for every character. Malvolio responds to the moment not with transformative laughter but with a stormy exit.

On the optimistic side, the disruptive shock of enchanted endings makes possible acts of generosity and forgiveness that are unprompted and alien to any prior logic of cause and effect. That is, the capacity for uncaused yet climactic events inheres in comic endings. The Renaissance Italian theorist of poetry Antonio Sebastiano Minturno describes the culminating actions in a comedy as "happening outside our expectation"[80]—yet some developments seem more than just unanticipated and surprising. Shakespearean comedy embraces outcomes that paradoxically exceed the action's own train of implications; more than being beyond expectation, they are beyond inference or logic. Here the comic ending produces a kind of surplus.

Such a view of the denouement conflicts with some theories of comedy. The philosopher Dmitri Nikulin has argued, for example, that comic action reflects "careful and consequential—'logical'—reasoning" and that its "fundamentally rational" structure essentially dramatizes philosophical thinking.[81] Likewise, Renaissance comedy, as Lorna Hutson analyzes it, involves the progressive demystification of events that had appeared to the characters as magical and enchanted; it initiates a new drive in drama towards rationality based on logical causality and a coherent narrative of prior occurrences that makes sense of the whole. There emerges in comedy, concludes Hutson, a "habit of sceptical, forensic enquiry into likelihood, or...the strategic exploitation...of 'suspicion'."[82] In *The Comedy of Errors*, she argues, the "vocabulary of sorcery and conjuring" is dispelled by the "legal vocabulary associated with attempts to verify and render probable accounts of the apparently impossible things that characters have seen and heard" (150). Sorcery and conjuring thus dissolve as expository accounts.

Or, perhaps, not quite. For one thing, in *The Comedy of Errors*, the Abbess lobs a bit of a hand grenade into the exclusively rationalist explanation when she insists upon describing the prior events as "this sympathized one day's error" (5.1.399), her adjective invoking a world of sympathetic magic where like or related agents can affect each other psychically. The Abbess's claim goes unchallenged, and for good reason, because it makes sense of certain experiences in *Errors*. Likewise, her closing speech twice calls up the image of "nativity," with its aura of religious numinosity and rebirth (406, 408). In *Errors*, that is, rationalism leads finally to the recognition of a reservoir of enchantment, a sense of wonder at the revelation of the impossible as amazingly true.

As the Duke in *Errors* first listens to the feuding characters, he thinks that they must have "drunk of Circe's cup" because their claims contradict each other; these people can only be "mated or stark mad" (269, 270, 281). Thus, the climactic appearance together of the Ephesian and Syracusan twins leaves the Duke astonished, groping for metaphysical answers: "One of these men is genius to the other,

---

[80] Lauter, *Theories of Comedy, op. cit.*, 84. While Minturno is stating a principle, he (like other theorists) has in mind the kinds of surprising revelations (as of a slave girl's actual birth) that reverse the social circumstances in Roman comedy. Shakespeare extends the range of wondrous events.

[81] Dmitri Nikulin, *Comedy, Seriously: A Philosophical Study* (New York: Palgrave Macmillan, 2014), ix, xi. On reason and wonder in comedy see the present Introduction.

[82] Hutson, *Suspicion*, 149.

/ . . . which is the natural man, / And which the spirit?" (333–5). Likewise, the reunited father Egeon invokes the language of wonder in exclaiming, "If I dream not" (353); Antipholus of Syracuse similarly doubts: "If this be not a dream I see and hear" (379). The scene's state of dream-like amazement continues for quite some time, since, from the Duke's moment of recognition to Ephesian Antipholus's offer of ducats to free Egeon (at 391), the denouement sustains its wonder for some forty-three lines. That prolonging of wonder departs from the Aristotelian model wherein, as Peter G. Platt describes it, "wonder was generated by a difficult problem and dissipated by a solution."[83] In contrast, this scene's wonder is generated by a solution and barely dissipated at all. Wonder is likewise famously prolonged in the ending of *Twelfth Night*.[84] It sustains what Platt sees as the alternative Renaissance model of a wonder that lingers on, as opposed to the Aristotelian wonder that quickly evaporates.[85] The staying power of wonder hints at its transformational potential.

The Duke in *Errors* illustrates such a transformation. In the opening scene, although he had expressed sympathy for the impoverished Egeon, unable to pay the penalty, he had insisted that he could not violate Ephesus's laws to save Egeon's life. But in the last act, in a key reversal, the Duke says to Ephesian Antipholus, "It shall not need. Thy father hath his life" (392). Given the play's terms, the Duke's about-face implies the sudden triumph of sympathy over law, an action that feels right yet also gratuitous. The Duke offers no explanation for his unpredictable repudiation of all that he has said before or for his precipitous elevation of personal feeling over legal obligation. This pardon resembles a gift, unrequested and unforeseeable. It also resembles an act of forgiveness, since the Duke must make a concession, soften his resolve, and embrace a shift in his own attitude, all with no obvious gain to himself. Where does that change come from? The Duke's pardon, I propose, arises from the benevolent wonder and laughter shared communally, the kind of fellowship that Fabian celebrates in *Twelfth Night*. It is stimulated by the character's recognition of impossible probability and perhaps by an intellectual humility inspired by the upending of quotidian reality. With characters projected into a state of wonder, opportunities emerge in human interactions that were unreachable before; among them, forgiveness. As Platt puts it, "the marvelous challenges and often alters ways of knowing and perceiving the world" (xv). Wonder, a condition of liminal suspension, breaks down mental boundaries and categories, supercharges the affective dimension, and creates an

---

[83] Peter G. Platt, *Reason Diminished: Shakespeare and the Marvelous* (Lincoln, NE: University of Nebraska Press, 1997), 2. Platt insists on the power of wonder in the Renaissance and traces an ongoing tension between reason and wonder. He draws particularly from Francesco Patrizi's discussion of wonder in *Della poetica*, which posits wonder as arising from, among other causes, "the surprising and unexpected" (Platt, xv). See also the present Introduction.

[84] Some later Shakespearean comedies, however, foreshorten the experience of wonder, as if Shakespeare were consciously playing with the model registered here.

[85] Platt, *Reason Diminished*, 1–18.

access to new possibilities. In *Errors*, furthermore, it operates publicly and touches everyone, a shared living dream, as when the lovers awake in *A Midsummer Night's Dream*. Every character in *Errors* is afforded a moment of amazed recognition, as the figurative microphone passes among them. The episode contains laughter, too, and recovered amity, as various offenses are cleared away. The denouement ends with the Abbess's celebratory "gossips' feast," the egalitarian invitation extended to all (407).[86]

Wonder functions here as a condition that makes pardon and forgiveness possible, although it does not function exactly as the cause; rather, it creates an aura, a charmed moment and space, a break from etiology, in which forgiveness becomes newly conceivable through its disruption of causality. It recalls the stop-time power of comic clowning (see Chapter 1). Yet wonder does not force or oblige one character to pardon or forgive another, as the example of Malvolio illustrates. Will everyone in *Errors'* denouement put aside forever his or her resentments? The playtext does not tell us. Although forgiveness crystalizes the spirit of the occasion, that spirit does not impose itself; it functions only as an invitation, an opening. Forgiveness, then, remains contingent and unpredictable, a potentiality only. What fascinates here is that the unraveling of the story's knot of errors first validates a cause-and-effect logic of empirical solutions—the Duke's sorting out of the Egeon family history—but finally, through wonder, leads to a profoundly different kind of anti-Aristotelian vision, something close to the workings not only of clown interludes but also of the green world, the glimpse of a radical "nativity" that might arise in a particular moment (we shall return to "nativity"). Although not every Shakespearean comedy follows exactly, or to the same degree, this pattern of 'wonder to forgiveness,' it can be discerned in other plays beyond *Errors*. We have already noted this process in *Twelfth Night* and *A Midsummer Night's Dream*. In *The Two Gentlemen of Verona*, wonder apparently produces the Duke's forgiveness of the outlaws; in *The Taming of the Shrew*, it conditions Vincentio's pardoning of Tranio; and in *All's Well*, it facilitates the forgiveness of Bertram. Such acts of forgiveness predicated on wonder evoke comedy's utopianism—as in *Errors'* "gossips' feast"—and deliver it as a realistic possibility back into the field of the everyday.

Unmerited Forgiveness

Celebrating wonder is all well and good, but does it not also tempt us to tolerate acts of forgiveness that violate our moral sense? Take the example of Claudio in

---

[86] The Duke will join the feast, he says, "with all my heart," 409); Shakespeare's comic endings often involve a lessening of hierarchical and social distinctions, reiterated here in the concluding exchange between the Dromios.

Much Ado About Nothing. His public repudiation and humiliation of Hero at the altar has seemed needlessly harsh to most audiences. Likewise, after he performs the conventional ritual of penance, his attitude towards his new bride sounds cavalier: "Which is the lady I must seize upon?"; "Sweet, let me see your face" (5.4.53, 55). Claudio's breezy manner gives little evidence of deep remorse or self-reckoning. For such reasons, spectators and readers often find his forgiveness facile and unmerited. That objection extends to other comic endings: Valentine's forgiveness of Proteus's attempted rape of Silvia in *The Two Gentlemen of Verona*; Isabella's forgiveness of Angelo's attempted murder in *Measure for Measure*; and the King and Helen's forgiveness of Bertram's attempted adultery and his false-hood in *All's Well That Ends Well*. It will help later to contrast those plays with the example of *Love's Labour's Lost*, which ends with the rejection of forgiveness.

A few critics have addressed the problem of unmerited forgiveness. R. G. Hunter, for example, sees Shakespeare as developing a "comedy of forgive-ness" that adapts the medieval theme of repentance and mercy.[87] For Hunter, comedy recognizes the "necessity" of pardon and "mutual forbearance" (93), so that not only characters but also audience members are meant to forgive misbe-havers such as Claudio (104–5). Similar ideas have been advanced by others.[88] Hunter justifies his argument by invoking Protestant theology and by giving credit to acts, such as Claudio's, of Thomistic contrition, confession, and satisfaction. For Hunter, the audience is obliged to forgive, following the models of God's infinite mercy and of Calvin's view of salvation through preordained grace. We are all fellow sinners and do not know who is destined for reprobation and who for election. Accordingly, Protestant playgoers in Shakespeare's day, Hunter con-cludes, would have accepted the pardoning of Claudio and his fellows on religious grounds.

But in the sixteenth century, Beckwith argues, forgiveness was moving outside the confessional structure of church ritual; it was present as a residual religious value but required secular renegotiation. That position is bolstered by the presence of forgiveness as an issue in the comedies; by the complexity of the cases they present; and by the demand they make for nuanced judgment. Some of Shakespeare's comic endings have left observers dissatisfied, wanting more by way of atonement. Generally, Shakespeare's comedies address the problem of unmerited pardon without relying upon church doctrine; rather, Shakespeare probes, and even creates, the conventions of comic and secular forgiveness. Thus, the examples of Proteus, Claudio, Angelo, and Bertram challenge the audience morally and affectively, asking us, how generous are we willing to be?

[87] R. G. Hunter, *Shakespeare and the Comedy of Forgiveness* (New York: Columbia University Press, 1965).
[88] See, for example, Michael D. Friedman, *"The World Must Be Peopled": Shakespeare's Comedies of Forgiveness* (Madison, NJ: Fairleigh Dickinson University Press, 2002).

Elizabethan church doctrine offers little help in addressing unmerited forgive-ness in the comedies' secular world. While the Tudor church prescribes how a sinner seeks forgiveness from God—confession, contrition, penance, and absolution—its formulations are less clear about how we forgive each other and about what the effects are of doing so. Let us take the example of the Elizabethan Homilies, since they place Church doctrine in the area of practical living. The "Homily on Good Works" commands individuals, for the sake of God, to "loue all men, speake well of all men, helpe and succour euery man, as you may, yea, euen your enemies that hate you, that speake euill of you, and that doe hurt you."[89] Notwithstanding, much of the homily's emphasis actually falls on duty, obedience, and contentment with one's station.[90] The homily on "Christian Love and Charity" discusses kindness and conceives of loving others as an extension of the love of God and an imitation of Christ's goodwill towards those who perse-cuted him: "[A]lthough our enemie deserue not to be forgiuen for his owne sake, yet we ought to forgiue him for GOD'S loue" (Part 2, par. 3). Yet that same homily then proceeds to limit the implications of its own pronouncement, for a second "office of charitie, is to rebuke, correct, and punish vice . . . like as a good Surgion cutteth away a rotten and festered member . . . that GOD and the common wealth may be lesse hurt and offended" (Part 2, par. 6). Such righteousness makes little room for the possibility of pardon.

The "Homily on the State of Matrimony" takes a more generous stance about the way marital partners should behave and about the effects of good self-governance. The husband must learn "to winke at some thinges," to "expounde" "gently . . . and to forbeare."[91] Such indulgence and tolerance are necessary to preserve concord and to retain the equanimity of heart necessary for prayer, which sustains humans in all things. Forbearing partners establish, for their neighbors, a good model and ensure, for themselves, "that all things shall prosper quietly" (par. 3). The Homilies' winking at faults seems confined, however, to the special case of marriage and constitutes only a modest notion of pardon. The "Homily on the Passion for Good Friday" does take up the Gospel passage (Matthew 18.21–35) best known regarding forgiveness. Jesus tells a parable in which a king forgives the large financial debt of a servant, but when that servant refuses to forgive the small debt of a fellow servant, the king changes his mind and imprisons the first debtor. The story's import undergoes a subtle reduction in the homily, which refers only to forgiving "small trespasses" by "neighbours" and

---

[89] "Homily on Good Works," in *Certain Sermons or Homilies* ([1547] 1562), ed. Ian Lancashire (Renaissance Electronic Texts, 1.1, University of Toronto, 1994), par. 1, https://onesearch.library.utoronto.ca/sites/default/files/ret/homilies/elizhom.html.

[90] "Homily on Good Works," "Third Part," par. 7. These values are discussed in detail in the "Homily on Christian Love and Charity," *Certain Sermons or Homilies, op. cit.*

[91] "Homily on the State of Matrimony," *The Second Tome of Homilies* (London, 1623), ed. Ian Lancashire (Renaissance Electronic Texts 1.1., University of Toronto, 1994), par. 2. https://onesearch.library.utoronto.ca/sites/default/files/ret/homilies/elizhom.html.

"Christian brother[s]." No other homily addresses this difficult parable.[92] Altogether, the Tudor Homilies feel limited; forgiveness there must be undertaken largely for "the sake of God," while homiletic strictures and qualifications offer little guidance for understanding the kind of secular, equivocally earned forgiveness and pardon that feature in the comedies. There, some characters simply get more, or easier, forgiveness than we feel they deserve; that humanistic problem exposes the difficulty that doctrine frequently has in addressing the intricacies of experience.

We might break out of this impasse by thinking less about parsing the wrong done by the perpetrators and more, first, about forgiveness as a gift, and, second, about the effects, individual and communal, of forgiving. Forgiveness, besides often being facilitated by wonder, has something wondrous and magically transformative about it. Present-day thinking can help us understand unearned forgiveness and the perplexing implication in Shakespeare that "all's well that ends well."

One way of overcoming a balance-sheet mentality about forgiveness is to consider it as a gift, not simply from grace but also from humans. William Demastes argues that comedy, more than other genres, embraces the notion of the gift, because it favors social well-being over individual accumulation.[93] Likewise, Sean Lawrence finds in Shakespeare's comedies examples of pure gifts.[94] Both oppose what Lawrence sees as an anthropological assumption that "has come to dominate the study of Renaissance drama" (xxiii): that gifts always function inside a system of exchange, responding to benefits given or anticipating future ones, so that the gift can never express pure generosity.[95] If forgiveness operates as an exchange-item, then, implicitly, it is reduced to a form of barter, a quid within a system of quid pro quo, nullifying the freeing power of wonder that we have outlined. Lawrence rebuts that argument by identifying pure gifts in *The Merchant of Venice* and *The Tempest*, gifts that are hidden and thus incapable of being acknowledged or paid back.[96] How we understand comic forgiveness, as exchanged or freely given, haunts our understanding of the genre, since acts of pardon, publicly made, both instigate and validate the creation of comedy's

---

[92] "Homily on the Passion of Good Friday," *Second Tome, op cit.* par. 8.

[93] William W. Demastes, *Comedy Matters: From Shakespeare to Stoppard* (New York: Palgrave Macmillan, 2008), 127–52.

[94] Sean Lawrence, *Forgiving the Gift: The Philosophy of Generosity In Shakespeare and Marlowe* (Pittsburgh, PA: Duquesne University Press, 2012); see also Beckwith, *Forgiveness*.

[95] See Lawrence, *Forgiving the Gift*, 3–39. Lawrence's helpful discussion of gift theory addresses works by Marcel Mauss, Emmanuel Levinas, Jacques Derrida, and Paul Ricoeur, among others. With Levinas, Lawrence affirms generosity as an irresistible response of the self to the call from the Other. Such thinking would also describe Buber's sense of reciprocity, which expresses a pure recognition of the Other, different from reciprocity-as-exchange. On Renaissance gift culture, see Felicity Heal, *The Power of Gifts: Gift Exchange in Early Modern England* (Oxford: Oxford University Press, 2014).

[96] Similarly, Demastes critiques Jacques Derrida's claim that a true gift is a logical impossibility; *Comedy Matters*, 127–52.

reconciled community at play's end.[97] Thus, Demastes insists that "[c]hallenging the rationalist" denial of pure giving "plays a crucially important part in the comic agenda" and promotes the radical values of the "living social organism" as opposed to "individualism" (130, 133).

In Shakespeare, forgiveness does sometimes happen as exchange, as in Portia's exacting a price for her pardon at the end of *The Merchant of Venice*. But forgiveness can also be bestowed freely and unconditionally, without involving trade, penalty, or even penance—as in the Duke's pardon in *Errors*, Theseus's reversal of the law's condemnation of Hermia in *A Midsummer Night's Dream*, and the instances cited of wondrous forgiveness. Likewise, Portia's restoration of Antonio's fortune comes as an unconditional gift.[98] In *Measure for Measure*, too, the Duke gratuitously forgives Juliet and Claudio their adultery and Lucio his slander. From a certain perspective, in *Much Ado*, Hero's return from the dead constitutes a gift to Claudio greater than any earned by his penance at her tomb. If forgiveness can arrive freely, as a gift, then it challenges an instrumental interpretation of giving in the comedies.

Unmerited forgiveness might be explored further for its effects. In a comedy, argues Nikulin, "the end explicitly suspends and changes the beginning" (94). How would a beginning change? In the view of philosophers such as Hannah Arendt and Emmanuel Levinas, forgiveness has the power to rewrite the past.[99] For Arendt, the unpredictable consequences of action can be ameliorated by forgiveness, which "break[s] the chain" "of revenge" (although certain acts may fall beyond the pale).[100] Forgiveness can redeem us from "the predicament of irreversibility—of being unable to undo what one has done."[101] "Without being forgiven, released from the consequences of what we have done," argues Arendt, "our capacity to act would, as it were, be confined to one single deed from which we could never recover" (237); thus, pardon works radically "to undo the deeds of the past" (237). Perhaps because secular forgiveness is social and pluralistic, conferred by others, it has the power to wipe away consensually what has gone before, as happens with Claudio and his fellows.

Levinas takes a point of view similar to Arendt's, asserting, even more strongly, how pardon rewrites the past: "The paradox of pardon lies in its retroaction; ... it represents an inversion of the natural order of things, the reversibility of time ... It permits the subject who had committed himself in a past instant to be as though

---

[97] See Frye, *Natural Perspective*, e.g., 78, 87–92.

[98] Ronald A. Sharp, "Gift Exchange and the Economics of Spirit in *The Merchant of Venice*," *Modern Philology* 83, no. 3 (February 1986): 250–65.

[99] Beckwith mentions Arendt's treatment of forgiveness in *The Human Condition* (*Forgiveness*, 1–2).

[100] Margaret Canovan, "Introduction" to Hannah Arendt, *The Human Condition* (Chicago, IL: University of Chicago Press, [1958] 1998), vii–xx, on xviii, xix.

[101] Hannah Arendt, *The Human Condition* (Chicago, IL: University of Chicago Press [1958] 1998), 237.

that instant had not past [*sic*] on, to be as though he had not committed himself
... [P]ardon acts upon the past, somehow repeats the event, purifying it ... The
difference [between pardon and innocence] ... permits the discerning in pardon of
a surplus of happiness, the strange happiness of reconciliation."[102] In that
"strange" "surplus of happiness," forgiveness takes on an almost magical wondrousness. Levinas's notion of forgiveness, moreover, expresses his view that the
past, present, and future of the self are made possible by the Other. As Rudolf
Bernet puts it, "the forgiveness that is granted me by the other (and which only the
other can grant) modifies my past to the point of transforming it into a past that
has never been present as such for me."[103] Likewise, Aaron T. Looney, analyzing
the philosophy of Vladimir Jankélévitch, calls forgiveness a "rupture" between
"the past and the future" that "allows something new to emerge"; thus it not only
"releases one from the burden of the past" but also allows one "perhaps even to
transform [the past's] meaning."[104] We are here well beyond the Elizabethan
Homilies. Two relevant ideas emerge from these philosophers. First, forgiveness
decisively, if irrationally, alters the past; the field of reason becomes flooded by a
very different energy, even a surplus. Second, forgiveness confirms one's depend-
ence on others for a sense of being. Shakespearean comedy invokes both effects—
but it does so in a way that also questions them.

The comedies that stress the problem of forgiveness suggest, like the philosophers cited above, that the gift of pardon wipes away the stigma of the past, even
transforms the past itself. When Proteus confesses his "shame and guilt,"
Valentine responds, "Then I am paid, / And once again I do receive thee honest"
(*TGV* 5.4.74, 78–9): once again "honest," as if Proteus's past were purified of his
intended rape of Silvia and betrayal of friendship. Isabella, believing her brother
dead, rewrites the past in order to forgive Angelo: "Look, if it please you, on this
condemned man / As if my brother lived" (*MM* 5.3.447–8); "as if" becomes the
enabling fiction that serves in the place of truth—serves as truth. In such plays, the
effect of forgiveness is to treat prior sins miraculously as if they had not happened;
the past becomes disempowered, null; it no longer exits—or, if it is recalled, it only
happens to make visible a magical surplus, Levinas's "surplus of happiness, the
strange happiness of reconciliation." These acts of unearned forgiveness express a
politics in Shakespeare's comedies far more radical than might appear and quite
different from forgiveness as an obligation to God. As Arendt argues, forgiveness
makes the future possible; it releases the transgressor from the death-grip of his
action and restores him to community and relationship. It throws an enchanted

---

[102] Emmanuel Levinas, *Totality and Infinity: An Essay on Exteriority*, trans. Alphonso Lingis (The
Hague: Martinus Nijhoff Publishers, 1979; orig. pub. in French, 1961), 283.
[103] Rudolf Bernet, "Levinas's Critique of Husserl," in *The Cambridge Companion to Levinas*, ed.
Simon Critchley and Robert Bernasconi (Cambridge: Cambridge University Press, 2004), 82–99, on 95.
[104] Aaron T. Looney, *Vladimir Jankélévitch: The Time for Forgiveness* (New York: Fordham
University Press, 2015), 1–2.

shroud over the past. In those ways, undeserved forgiveness broaches the kind of idealistic vision close to the heart of comedy. But it requires a shift in perspective to be morally palatable, a paradoxically self-conscious act of forgetting. Shakespeare never laves the dream of forgiveness with bathos or sentimentality; his endings may create the climate of awe, but they sketch his radical vision with only a few key phrases that seem meant to provoke a tremor of cognitive dissonance, leaving us—perhaps for the better—to wonder.

One dimension of forgiveness remains that philosophy can overlook: that its effects extend not only to the sinner but also to those sinned against. The comic denouement, as critics recognize, involves the recreation of a community, one of comedy's distinguishing values. The past must be wiped away not only for the offended but also for the innocent and their families, who are thereby released from humiliation or the need for revenge. Hero makes exactly that point when she explains to Claudio, "One Hero died defiled, but I do live"; she is thus indeed, as Claudio exclaims, "Another Hero," different, the tainted maiden vanished along with the transgression (*MA* 5.4.63–4, 62).[105] For "Another Hero," no retribution is required. Unmerited forgiveness for the guilty may be the condition necessary for the innocent to go forward. But these comedies do not flood their final scenes with sentiment in order to force an intellectual conclusion; rather, they incorporate our wondering. We face a beautiful Shakespearean dilemma obliging characters and audiences alike to choose between their past resentments and the possibility of a future.

A Comedy of Unforgiveness

For an example of harboring resentments, consider *Love's Labour's Lost*. In criticism, the weight of moral opprobrium has fallen on the King, Berowne, and their fellows, who are convicted of oath-breaking in pursuing the French ladies and of artificiality, even self-absorption, in their wooing. Because of their inconstancy and shallowness, so the argument goes, the traditional reconciliation of the comic ending fails, or at least is deferred until the men can prove themselves. Without whitewashing the men, one might also argue in the opposite direction, that the comic denouement collapses equally because the women refuse to forgive them. The Princess takes offense when the King denies accommodation at court to

---

[105] Hero's "legal" situation shows the importance, for the victim, of wiping away the past. As Barbara Kreps, discussing this play, observes, "Defamation can permanently alter identity: when a reputation is ruined, the community no longer recognizes the person as he or she existed for them before"; "Two-Sided Legal Narratives: Slander, Evidence, Proof, and Turnarounds in *Much Ado About Nothing*," in *Taking Exception to the Law: Materializing Injustice in Early Modern English Literature*, ed. Donald Beecher, Travis Decook, Andrew Wallace, and Grant Williams (Toronto: University of Toronto Press, 2015), 162–78, on 173.

her and her company, as her taunting sarcasm during their first meeting indicates (see 2.1.90–110). The women are quite capable of maliciousness towards the men, whom they recognize unmistakably as their "lovers" (5.2.58). Says Rosaline, "That same Berowne I'll torture ere I go. / O that I knew he were but in by th' week! / How I would make him fawn, and beg, and seek" (60–2). After humiliating the lords as Muscovites, the ladies determine to continue their mocking when the men return as themselves (see 300–7). To the lords' protestations of love, the Princess says that the ladies have received their letters and favors only as "pleasant jest and courtesy; / As bombast and as lining to the time" (774–5). While the nobles might be guilty of jejune attempts at wooing, their claim that their letters and looks "showed more than jest" (779) is confirmed by the women's intention, as Rosaline had put it, to capture the affections of the lovers and then to "torture" them.

Earlier in the scene, when the King properly invites the ladies into his court (see 5.2.339–56), the Princess's pique at having been refused court lodging hardens into dubious righteousness towards oath-breaking. It is difficult to see what principle the Princess is defending in her criticism: an oath to be inhospitable? Julia and Portia have strong grounds for condemning the faith-breaking of their beloveds, but such conditions hardly pertain here. The Princess and her ladies may have been slighted, but their persistence in disdain begins to reflect on them.[106] The women, that is, show themselves to be, in the end, anti-comic characters, somewhat in the spirit of Jaques.[107] They lack the present willingness to forgive—although they promise the men their loves after the wooers complete a year of self-abnegation (Berowne is condemned to smile at grievous suffering—in effect, to live inside tragedy). The lords may act like silly geese, but worse has been excused in other comedies, and at equally short notice. In other plays, too, the reformation of the men is made possible through the women's benevolence, not through its opposite; through community, not withdrawal. We might think of *Love's Labour's Lost* as a 'comedy of unforgiveness,' for it demonstrates what it means to withhold generosity and love. It is difficult to consider these prospective marriages promising. *Love's Labour's Lost* explores the problem of pardon from a fresh angle, manifesting its importance and underscoring the stakes in comedies such as *Two Gentlemen*, *Much Ado*, *Measure for Measure*, and *All's Well*.

No comic dramatist before Shakespeare treated forgiveness as so crucial yet so knotty. For comic theory, Shakespeare's model of both wonder and wondering

---

[106] Frye sees the women as caught up themselves in the "pervading spirit" of "excess of wit" and "intellectual pride"; *Natural Perspective*, 81, 80.

[107] The women might be compared to the nymphs Nisa, Celia, and Niobe in John Lyly's *Love's Metamorphosis* (c. 1590). At the conclusion, the nymphs are released from their prior transformations into stone, flower, and bird and are required by Cupid to marry the three foresters. The nymphs refuse, partly out of distrust of men and partly out of their anger at the foresters, whom they blame for their metamorphoses. Only after dire threats by Cupid do they yield, but with the intentions to bring, respectively, coldness, prickliness, and flightiness into their marriages, for which they, again, blame the men.

shows how the genre can think through a problem. In various of the comedies, the aura of wonder enables the act of forgiving. Forgiveness occurs as an awe-induced potential, following upon, yet separate from, the rationality of the plot, thus expressing the power of comic enchantment. It also mysteriously revises the past, making offenses disappear, to the benefit of both sinners and victims. It becomes, to recall Joshua Landy and Michael Saler's language cited in the Introduction, an "everyday miracle." In its irrationality, forgiveness makes possible what the Abbess in *Errors* calls "nativity"—a term akin to Hannah Arendt's notion of "natality," the unknowable, new opportunity inherent in an action,[108] "the miracle of beginning."[109] In Shakespeare's comedies forgiveness is unmerited, irrational, and, in perhaps a new sense, miraculous.

*   *   *   *   *

The plays considered above treat dilemmas relevant to comic endings: the exclusion of anti-comic characters from the reconstituted community of the denouement; the limit in what characters and their audiences might actually understand about the play's central human relationships; the finale's embrace of characters who appear unworthy of reconciliation. In each situation, logical and causal explanations give way to other forces: Shylock's exclusion in the last act leads to metaphoric exploration of the situation of the Other; the miracle of Benedick and Beatrice's love bursts forth as reciprocal but finally uncaused; forgiveness arrives by means of wonder's unpredictable power and expresses a miraculous recreation of the past and the possibilities of the present. These situations, each substantial but different, demand both immersion in the experience yet mental probing of the situation, a provocative dialectic of enchanted passion and critical thought that opens a horizon of reflection calibrated to last long after the book closes or the curtain falls.

---

[108] Arendt defines natality as "the new beginning inherent in birth [that] can make itself felt in the world only because the newcomer possesses the capacity of beginning something anew, that is, of acting"; *Human Condition*, 9.
[109] Canovan, "Introduction," xvii.

Afterword

I completed the manuscript for this book during the COVID-19 pandemic of Spring 2020. I happened to have been in Italy, where people spent almost three months in unusually restrictive "lockdown." Connected with the outside through digital publications and social media, Italy and the world responded to the pandemic not only with recognition and empathy regarding the unfolding tragedy but also with pervasive and inventive humor. Immediately after rules for "social distancing" were promulgated, an Italian cartoon appeared in which a man and a woman are chatting each other up while an official kneels between them measuring the distance. When handshakes and hugs were discouraged, comic videos popped up on YouTube with individuals touching elbows or shoes in dance-like choreography; indeed, YouTube became loaded with hilarious skits, send-ups, and funny talk-show bits related to the pandemic. My old roommate from college, who kept an e-mailing list for social and political jokes, used it for the pandemic almost every day. Comedy, of course, cannot remove sickness and death, as Berowne acknowledges, but it can help us endure, and, even more, it can provide the shift in perspective that allows us to engage with something in a new way, to reimagine it, just as a joke can alter the momentum and possibilities of a casual conversation or a committee meeting. Shifting into the comic moment requires us to put our political, social, economic, religious, or other differences aside. We just might come back from it having changed our attitudes, and we might find ourselves, later, in the wake of the moment of comic enchantment, thinking more deeply still about matters.

In the foregoing chapters, I have been arguing for the social and cultural significance, even profundity, of comedy, and in particular of Shakespeare's oeuvre. My goal has been to identify certain devices, strategies, and values that have not been fully recognized by previous criticism but that give the comedies emotional resonance, intellectual depth, uncanny power, and memorability. Those chapters also show the comedies to be dense with unexpected causal forces: the decisive interventions of fools and clowns; the pressure of structural double-ness; the transformative agency of place; the manifestations of wishes, fears, and thoughts; the power of longing and desire metaphorically to bring revenants back from the dead; the capacity of wonder to make forgiveness possible. The effects and devices discussed here bring a sense of the numinous to bear on everyday causation and humdrum rationality. The comedies energize us, too, with their communalism and utopian dreams. Nonetheless, although some of their

Shakespeare and the Comedy of Enchantment. Kent Cartwright, Oxford University Press. © Kent Cartwright 2021.
DOI: 10.1093/oso/9780198868897.003.0008

characters may be innocent, the plays themselves are never naïve. For all their magic, they always clear a space for doubt, wondering, and for an awareness of their own limits. In the logic of "subversion" and "containment," the comedies reveal the porousness of containment and the mysteriousness of subversion. They address social and cultural problems, sometimes directly, but more often obliquely, and they seldom provide other than provisional solutions to the ills that trouble them. Yet they bring us together. They will not resolve differences of political ideology, or heal the wounds of racial discrimination, or eliminate gender bias, or save us from the ecological crisis. But, in creating a means for seeing causes, experiences, and feelings differently, seeing things anew, they build the conditions for changed attitudes and actions. As Jane Bennett argues, enchantment is a "mood" that can be actively "cultivat[ed]" and that can facilitate ethical engagement.[1] Understood in that spirit, comedies irradiate the world with possibility and hope.

---

[1] Jane Bennett, *The Enchantment of Modern Life: Attachments, Crossings, and Ethics* (Princeton, NJ: Princeton University Press, 2001), 3–4.

Bibliography

With a few minor exceptions, this bibliography lists the works that I have cited critically or consulted. It does not, however, list editions for all the Tudor plays, Renaissance Italian comedies, or other period works mentioned in the text, unless they are quoted directly. For Italian comedy, I have found useful the following anthologies: Donald Beecher, ed., *Renaissance Comedy: The Italian Masters*, 2 vols. (Baltimore, MD: The Johns Hopkins University Press, 2008–2009); and Laura Giannetti and Guido Ruggerio, trans. and eds., *Five Comedies from the Italian Renaissance* (Baltimore, MD: The Johns Hopkins University Press, 2003).

PRIMARY SOURCES

Agrippa, Heinrich Cornelius. *Heinrich Cornelius Agrippa*, Three Books of Occult Philosophy; *and Giordano Bruno*, Cause, Principle and Unity; *Essays on Magic*. Translated and edited by Robert De Lucca (Cause) and Richard J. Blackwell (*Magic*). Cambridge: Cambridge University Press, 1998.

Agrippa, Henry Cornelius. *Three Books of Occult Philosophy*. Translated by James Freake. Edited by Donald Tyson. St. Paul, MN: Llewellyn Publications, 1995.

Anon. *Certain Sermons or Homilies*. London: [1547] 1562. Edited by Ian Lancashire. Renaissance Electronic Texts, 1.1, University of Toronto, 1994. https://onesearch.library.utoronto.ca/sites/default/files/ret/homilies/elizhom.html.

Anon. *The Second Tome of Homilies*. London, 1623. Edited by Ian Lancashire. Renaissance Electronic Texts 1.1., University of Toronto, 1994. https://onesearch.library.utoronto.ca/sites/default/files/ret/homilies/elizhom.html.

Bargagli, Girolamo. *The Female Pilgrim (La pellegrina)*. Translated by Bruno Ferraro. Ottawa, Canada: Dovehouse Editions, 1988.

Castelvetro, Ludovico. "Commentary on Aristotle's 'Poetics'" (1570). Translated by Andrew Bongiorno. In Lauter, *Theories of Comedy*, 87–97.

Castelvetro, Ludovico. *Castelvetro on the Art of Poetry*. Translated by Andrew Bongiorno. Binghamton, NY: Medieval and Renaissance Texts and Studies, 1984.

Clubb, Louise George. *Pollastra and the Origins of* Twelfth Night: Parthenio, commedia *(1516) with an English Translation*. Farnham, Surrey: Ashgate, 2011.

Contarini, Gasparo. *The Commonwealth and Government of Venice*. Translated by Lewis Lukenor. London, 1599.

da Bibbiena, Bernardo Dovizi. *The Pretenders / I suppositi*. In *Renaissance Comedy: The Italian Masters*. Vol. 2 of 2. Edited by Donald Beecher. Toronto: University of Toronto Press, 2007, pp. 21–100.

della Porta, Giambattista. *Gli duoi fratelli rivali / The Two Rival Brothers*. Edited and translated by Louise George Clubb. Berkeley, CA: University of California Press, 1980.

de Montaigne, Michel. *Essays*. Translated by John Florio. London, [1603] 1613. Early English Books On-line: https://eebo.chadwyck.com.

de Montaigne, Michel. *The Complete Essays*. Translated by Donald M. Frame. Stanford, CA: Stanford University Press, 1958.

Donatus. "A Fragment on Comedy and Tragedy." Translated by George Miltz. In Lauter, *Theories of Comedy*, 27–32.

Donatus. "On Comedy." Translated by S. G Nugent. In Preminger, et al., *Classical and Medieval Literary Criticism*, 305–9.

Donatus. "The Fragment Containing *On Comedy and Tragedy*." In Sidnell, *Plato to Congreve*, 79–83.

Erasmus, Desiderius. *The Praise of Folly*. Translated by Clarence H. Miller. New Haven, CT: Yale University Press, (1979) 2003.

Evanthius. "On Drama." Translated by O. B. Hardison. In Preminger, et al. *Classical and Medieval Literary Criticism*, 301–5.

Ficino, Marsilio. *The Book of Life*. Translated by Charles Boer. Dallas, TX: Spring Publications, 1980.

Ficino, Marsilio. "Book Three: The Book on 'Obtaining Life from the Heavens.'" In Ficino, *Three Books on Life*, 236–393.

Ficino, Marsilio. *Three Books on Life: A Critical Edition and Translation*. Edited and translated by Carol V. Kaske and John R. Clark. Tempe, AZ: Medieval and Renaissance Texts and Studies, [1989] 1998.

Greene, Robert. *Friar Bacon and Friar Bungay*. London, 1594.

Lauter, Paul, ed. *Theories of Comedy*. Garden City, NY: Anchor Books, 1964.

Lavater, Ludwig. *Of Ghosts and Spirits Walking by Night*. Translated by R. H. [Robert Harrison]. Edited by J. Dover Wilson and May Yardley. Oxford: Oxford University Press, 1929.

Maggi (Madius), Vincent. From *On the Ridiculous* (1550). Translated by George Miltz. In Lauter, *Theories of Comedy*, 64–73.

Minturno, Antonio Sebastiano. From *The Art of Poetry* (1563). Translated by Anita Grossvogel, revised by Paul Lauter. In Lauter, *Theories of Comedy*, 74–86.

Munday, Anthony. *A Critical Edition of Anthony Munday's* Fedele and Fortunio. Edited by Richard Hosley. New York: Garland, 1981.

Ovid. *Metamorphoses, Books I–VIII*. Translated by Frank Justus Miller; revised by G. P. Goold. 3rd edn. Cambridge, MA: Harvard University Press, 1977.

Ovid. *Metamorphoses, Books IX–XV*. Translated by Frank Justus Miller; revised by G. P. Goold. 2nd edn. Cambridge, MA: Harvard University Press, 1984.

Pollastra, Giovanni. *Parthenio*. In *Pollastra and the Origins of* Twelfth Night: Parthenio, commedia *(1516) with an English Translation*. Edited by Louise George Clubb. Farnham, Surrey: Ashgate, 2011, pp. 70–227.

Polo, Gil. *A Critical Edition of Yong's Translation of George of Montemayor's* Diana *and Gil Polo's* Enamoured Diana. Edited by Judith M. Kennedy. Oxford: Clarendon Press, 1968.

Preminger, Alex, O. B. Hardison, Jr., and Kevin Kerrane, eds. *Classical and Medieval Literary Criticism: Translations and Interpretations*. New York: Frederick Ungar, 1974.

Proust, Marcel. *Swann's Way*. Translated by Lydia Davis. New York: Penguin Books, 2003.

Robortellus, Franciscus. "On Comedy" (1548). Translated by Marvin T. Herrick. In Marvin T. Herrick, *Comic Theory in the Sixteenth Century*. Urbana, IL: University of Illinois Press, 1964, pp. 227–39.

Roccoboni, Antonio. From *The Comic Art* (1585). Translated by George Miltz. In Lauter, *Theories of Comedy*, 98–107.

Romanska, Magda and Alan Ackerman, eds. *Reader in Comedy: An Anthology in Theory & Criticism*. London: Bloomsbury Methuen Drama, 2017.

Scaliger, Julius Caesar. *Poetices libri septem* [*Poetics*] (1561). Translated by C. J. McDonough. In Sidnell, *Plato to Congreve*, 99–110.

Sidnell, Michael J., ed. *Plato to Congreve/* Vol. 1 of 4, *Sources of Dramatic Theory*. Cambridge: Cambridge University Press, 1991.

Skelton, John. *John Skelton*, Magnyfycence. Edited by Paula Neuss. Manchester: Manchester University Press, 1980.

Spenser, Edmund. *The Works of Edmund Spenser: A Variorum Edition*. General editors Edwin Greenlaw, Charles Grosvenor Osgood, and Frederick Morgan Padelford. 11 vols. Baltimore, MD: Johns Hopkins Press, 1933.

Thomas, William. *The History of Italy*. London, 1549.

Thomas, William. *The History of Italy (1549) by William Thomas*. Edited by George B. Parks. Ithaca, NY: Cornell University Press, 1963.

Trissino, Giovanni Georgio. "From *Poetics*, Division VI (c. 1543–50)." Translated by Anita Grossvogel, revised by Paul Lauter. In Lauter, *Theories of Comedy*, 42–7.

Udall, Nicholas. *Roister Doister*. In *Three Sixteenth-Century Comedies:* Gammer Gurton's Needle, Roister Doister, The Old Wife's Tale. Edited by Charles Walters Whitworth. London: Ernest Benn Limited, 1984, pp. 89–211.

SECONDARY SOURCES

Abrams, M. H. *The Mirror and the Lamp: Romantic Theory and the Critical Tradition*. New York: Norton [1953] 1958.

Adelman, Janet. *Blood Relations: Christian and Jew in* The Merchant of Venice. Chicago, IL: University of Chicago Press, 2008.

Allen, John A. "Dogberry." *Shakespeare Quarterly* 24, no. 1 (Winter 1973): 35–53.

Allen, William. *A Defense and Declaration of the Catholic Church's Doctrine, Touching Purgatory*. Antwerp: by John Latius, 1565.

Alpers, Paul J. *The Poetry of* The Faerie Queene. Columbia, MO: University of Missouri Press, 1982.

Anderson, Judith H. *Words That Matter: Linguistic Perception in Renaissance English*. Stanford, CA: Stanford University Press, 1996.

Andrews, Richard. "Resources in Common: Shakespeare and Faminio Scala." In *Transnational Mobilities in Early Modern Theater*. Edited by Robert Henke and Eric Nicholson. Farnham, Surrey: Ashgate, 2014, pp. 37–52.

Andrews, Richard. *Scripts and Scenarios: The Performance of Comedy in Renaissance Italy*. Cambridge: Cambridge University Press, 1993.

Arendt, Hannah. "Home to Roost." In *Responsibility and Judgment*. New York, Schocken Books, 2003, pp. 227–56.

Arendt, Hannah. *The Human Condition*. 2nd edn. Chicago, IL: University of Chicago Press, [1958] 1998.

Armstrong, Paul B. *How Literature Plays with the Brain: The Neuroscience of Reading and Art*. Baltimore, MD: Johns Hopkins University Press, 2013.

Bachelard, Gaston. *The Poetics of Space*. Translated by Maria Jolas. Boston, MA: Beacon Press, [1964] 1994.

Bahr, Michael Don. "Acting Shakespeare: A Roundtable Discussion with Artists from the Utah Shakespeare Festival's 2016 Production of *Much Ado About Nothing*." *Journal of the Wooden O* 16/17 (2018): 38–55.

Bakhtin, M. M. *The Dialogic Imagination: Four Essays*. Edited by Michael Holquist. Translated by Caryl Emerson and Michael Holquist. Austin, TX: University of Texas Press, 1981.

Bakhtin, M. M. "Epic and the Novel." In Bakhtin, *Dialogic Imagination*, 3–40.

Bakhtin, M. M. *Problems of Dostoevsky's Poetics*. Edited and translated by Caryl Emerson. Minneapolis, MN: University of Minnesota Press, 1984.

Bakhtin, M. M. *Rabelais and His World*. Translated by Helene Iswolsky. Bloomington, IN: Indiana University Press, 1984.

Baldwin, T. W. *Shakspere's Five-Act Structure*. Urbana, IL: University of Illinois Press, 1947.

Barber, C. L. *Shakespeare's Festive Comedy: A Study of Dramatic Form and Its Relation to Social Custom*. Princeton, NJ: Princeton University Press, 1959.

Barkan, Leonard. "Diana and Acteon: The Myth of Synthesis." *English Literary Renaissance* 10, no. 3 (Autumn 1980): 317–59.

Barnaby, Andrew. "The Political Conscious of Shakespeare's *As You Like It*." *Studies in English Literature* 36, no. 2 (Spring 1996): 373–95.

Barton, Anne. "*As You Like It* and *Twelfth Night*: Shakespeare's 'sense of an ending' (1972)." In *Essays Mainly Shakespearean*. Cambridge: Cambridge University Press, 1994, pp. 91–112.

Bassi, Shaul. "Jessica, Sarra, Ruth: Jewish Women in Shakespeare's Venice." In The Merchant of Venice: *The State of Play*. Edited by M. Lindsay Kaplan. London: Bloomsbury, 2020, pp. 173–93.

Bassi, Shaul. *Shakespeare's Italy and Italy's Shakespeare: Place, "Race," Politics*. New York: Palgrave Macmillan, 2016.

Bate, Jonathan. "The Elizabethans in Italy." In *Travel and Drama in Shakespeare's Time*. Edited by Jean-Pierre Marquerlot and Michèle Willems. Cambridge: Cambridge University Press, 1996, pp. 55–75.

Bate, Jonathan. *Shakespeare and Ovid*. Oxford: Clarendon Press, 1994.

Beckwith, Sarah. *Shakespeare and the Grammar of Forgiveness*. Ithaca, NY: Cornell University Press, 2011.

Beckwith, Sarah and James Simpson. "Premodern Shakespeare." *Journal of Medieval and Early Modern Studies* 40, no. 1 (Winter 2010): 1–5.

Bell, Robert H. *Shakespeare's Great Stage of Fools*. New York: Palgrave Macmillan, 2011.

Belsey, Catherine. "Shakespeare's Sad Tale for Winter: *Hamlet* and the Tradition of Fireside Ghost Stories." *Shakespeare Quarterly* 6, no. 1 (Spring 2010): 1–27.

Bennett, Jane. *The Enchantment of Modern Life: Attachments, Crossings, and Ethics*. Princeton, NJ: Princeton University Press, 2001.

Benson, Sean. *Shakespearean Resurrection: The Art of Almost Raising the Dead*. Pittsburgh, PA: Duquesne University Press, 2009.

Bentley, Eric. *The Life of Drama*. New York: Atheneum, 1983.

Berger, Jr., Harry. "Displacing Autophobia in *Faerie Queene* I: Ethics, Gender, and Oppositional Reading in the Spenserian Text." *English Literary Renaissance* 28, no. 2 (Spring 1998): 163–82.

Berger, Jr., Harry. "Marriage and Mercifixion in *The Merchant of Venice*: The Casket Scene Revisited." *Shakespeare Quarterly* 32, no. 2 (Summer 1981): 155–62.

Berger, Jr., Harry. *Second World and Green World: Studies in Renaissance Fiction-Making*. Berkeley, CA: University of California Press, 1988.

Berger, Peter L. *Redeeming Laughter: The Comic Dimension of Human Experience*. Berlin: Walter de Gruyter, 1997.

Bergson, Henri. "Laughter." In Sypher, *Comedy*, 60–190.

Berman, Morris. *The Reenchantment of the World*. Cornell, NY: Cornell University Press, 1981.

Bernard, J. F. "*The Merchant of Venice* and Shakespeare's Sense of Humour(s)." *Renaissance Studies* 28, no. 5 (November 2014): 643–58.

Bernard, J. F. *Shakespearean Melancholy: Philosophy, Form and the Transformation of Comedy*. Edinburgh: Edinburgh University Press, 2018.

Bernet, Rudolf. "Levinas's Critique of Husserl." In *The Cambridge Companion to Levinas*. Edited by Simon Critchley and Robert Bernasconi. Cambridge: Cambridge University Press, 2004.

Berry, Ralph. "*Twelfth Night*: The Experience of the Audience." *Shakespeare Survey* 34 (1981): 111–19.

Bevis, Matthew. *Comedy: A Very Short Introduction*. Oxford: Oxford University Press, 2013.

Billig, Michael. *Laughter and Ridicule: Towards a Social Critique of Humour*. London: Sage Publications, 2005.

Bishop, T. G. *Shakespeare and the Theatre of Wonder*. Cambridge: Cambridge University Press, 1996.

Blits, Jan H. *The Soul of Athens: Shakespeare's* A Midsummer Night's Dream. Lanham, MD: Lexington Books, 2003.

Bloch, Ernst. *A Philosophy of the Future*. Transated by John Cumming. New York: Herder and Herder, 1970.

Bloom, Harold, ed. *Bloom's Shakespeare Through the Ages:* Much Ado About Nothing. New York: Infobase Publishing, 2010.

Bloom, Harold, ed. *William Shakespeare's Comedies: New Edition*. New York: Infobase, 2009.

Bloom, Paul. *How Pleasure Works: The New Science of Why We Like What We Like*. New York: W. W. Norton, 2010.

Bradbrook, Muriel C. *The Growth and Structure of Elizabethan Comedy*. London: Chatto & Windus, 1955.

Bristol, Michael D. *Carnival and Theater: Plebeian Culture and the Structure of Authority in Renaissance England*. New York: Methuen, 1985.

Brokaw, Katherine Steele. *Music and Religious Change in Early Modern English Drama*. Ithaca, NY: Cornell University Press, 2016.

Brooks, Harold F., ed. *A Midsummer Night's Dream*. London: Methuen, 1979.

Brown, J. P. C. "Seeing Double: Dramaturgy and the Experience of *Twelfth Night*." *Shakespeare* 10, no. 3 (April 2014): 293–308.

Bruster, Douglas and Erik Rasmussen, eds. Everyman *and* Mankind. London: Methuen, 2009.

Buber, Martin. *I and Thou*. Translated by Walter Kauffmann. New York: Charles Scribners' Sons, 1970.

Bullough, Geoffrey, ed. *Narrative and Dramatic Sources of Shakespeare*, 8 vols. London: Routledge, 1957.

Calvino, Italo. *Six Memos for the Next Millennium*. Translated by Geoffrey Brock. Cambridge, MA: Harvard University Press, 1988.

Cameron, Euan. *Enchanted Europe: Superstition, Reason, and Religion: 1250–1750*. Oxford: Oxford University Press, 2010.

Canovan, Margaret. "Introduction." In Arendt, *Human Condition*, vii–xx.

Carroll, William C., ed. *Love's Labour's Lost*. Cambridge: Cambridge University Press, 2009.

Carroll, William C. *The Metamorphoses of Shakespearean Comedy*. Princeton, NJ: Princeton University Press, 1985.

Cartmell, Deborah and Peter J. Smith, eds. Much Ado About Nothing: *A Critical Reader*. London: Bloomsbury, 2018.

Cartwright, Kent. "The Return from the Dead in *The Merchant of Venice*." In *Visions of Venice in Shakespeare*. Edited by Laura Tosi and Shaul Bassi. Farnham, Surrey: Ashgate, 2011, pp. 167–83.

Cartwright, Kent. "Secularity Meets Wonder Woman in *All's Well That Ends Well*." In *Sacred and Secular Transactions in the Age of Shakespeare*. Edited by Katherine Steele Brokaw and Jay Zysk. Evanston, IL: Northwestern University Press, 2019, pp. 49–67.

Cartwright, Kent. *Theatre and Humanism: English Drama in the Sixteenth Century*. Cambridge, Cambridge University Press, 1999.

Casey, Edward S. *The Fate of Place: A Philosophical History*. Berkeley, CA: University of California Press, 1998.

Casey, Maud. *The Art of Mystery: The Search for Questions*. Minneapolis, MN: Greywolf Press, 2018.

Cassirer, Ernst. *The Individual and the Cosmos in Renaissance Philosophy*. Translated by Mario Domandi. Mineola, NY: Dover Publications, [1963] 2000.

Cavell, Stanley. *Pursuits of Happiness: The Hollywood Comedy of Remarriage*. Cambridge, MA: Harvard University Press, 1981.

Chaney, Edward. *The Evolution of the Grand Tour: Anglo-Italian Cultural Relations Since the Renaissance*. Rev. edn. Abingdon: Routledge, 2000.

Clubb, Louise George. *Italian Drama in Shakespeare's Time*. New Haven, CT: Yale University Press, 1989.

Cohen, Walter. "*The Merchant of Venice* and the Possibilities of Historical Criticism." *English Literary History* 49, no. 4 (Winter 1982): 765–89.

Coletti, Theresa M. *Mary Magdalene and the Drama of Saints: Theater, Gender, and Religion in Late Medieval England*. Philadelphia, PA: University of Pennsylvania Press, 2011.

Colie, Rosalie L. *Shakespeare's Living Art*. Princeton, NJ: Princeton University Press, 1974.

Cook, Carol. "'The Sign and Semblance of Her Honor': Reading Gender Differences in *Much Ado About Nothing*." PMLA 101, no. 2 (March 1986): 186–202.

Cooper, Helen. *The English Romance in Time: Transforming Motifs from Geoffrey of Monmouth to the Death of Shakespeare*. Oxford: Oxford University Press, 2004.

Cooper, Helen. *Shakespeare and the Medieval World*. London: Bloomsbury, 2010.

Copenhaver, Brian P. "How to Do Magic, and Why: Philosophical Prescriptions." In *The Cambridge Companion to Renaissance Philosophy*. Edited by James Hankins. Cambridge: Cambridge University Press, 2007, pp. 137–69.

Copenhaver, Brian P. "Introduction." In Walker, *Spiritual and Demonic Magic*, viii–xi.

Copenhaver, Brian P. *Magic in Western Culture: From Antiquity to the Enlightenment*. Cambridge: Cambridge University Press, 2015.

Cornford, Frances Macdonald. *The Origins of Attic Comedy*. London: Edward Arnold, 2014.

Couliano, Ioan P. *Eros and Magic in the Renaissance*. Translated by Margaret Cook. Chicago, IL: University of Chicago Press, 1987.

Cox, John D. *Seeming Knowledge: Shakespeare and Skeptical Faith*. Waco, TX: Baylor University Press, 2007.

Craig, Hardin, ed. *The Coventry Corpus Christi Plays*. The English Text Society, London: Kegan Paul, 1902.

Crawford, Jason. *Allegory and Enchantment: An Early Modern Poetics*. Oxford: Oxford University Press, 2017.

Crosby, Alfred W. *The Measure of Reality: Quantification and Western Society, 1250–1600*. Cambridge: Cambridge University Press, 1996.

Cummings, Brian. *The Literary Culture of the Reformation: Grammar and Grace*. Oxford: Oxford University Press, 2002.

Daalder, Joost. "The 'Pre-History of Beatrice and Benedick in *Much Ado About Nothing*." *English Studies* 85, no. 6 (December 2004): 520–27.

D'Amico, Jack. *Shakespeare and Italy: The City and the Stage*. Gainesville, FL: University Press of Florida, 2001.

Danson, Lawrence. *The Harmonies of* The Merchant of Venice. New Haven, CT: Yale University Press, 1978.

Das, Nandini and Nick Davis, "Introduction." In *Enchantment and Dis-enchantment in Shakespeare and Early Modern Drama: Wonder, the Sacred, and the Supernatural*. Edited by Nandini Das and Nick Davis. New York: Routledge, 2017, pp. 1–17.

Daston, Lorraine and Katherine Park. *Wonders and the Order of Nature, 1150–1750*. New York: Zone Books, 1998.

Davis, Philip. *Shakespeare Thinking*. London: Continuum, 2007.

Dawson, Anthony B. and Paul Yachnin. *The Culture of Playgoing in Shakespeare's England: A Collaborative Debate*. Cambridge: Cambridge University Press, 2001.

de Certeau, Michel. *The Practice of Everyday Life*. Translated by Steven Rendall. Berkeley, CA: University of California Press, 1984.

Demastes, William W. *Comedy Matters: From Shakespeare to Stoppard*. New York: Palgrave Macmillan 2008.

de Sousa, Geraldo U. "Shakespearean Comedy and the Question of Race." In Hirschfeld, *Oxford Handbook of Shakespearean Comedy*, 172–89.

Dillon, Janette. "Shakespeare and the Traditions of English Stage Comedy." In Dutton and Howard, *The Comedies*, 4–22.

Dollimore, Jonathan. *Radical Tragedy: Religion, Ideology, Power in the Drama of Shakespeare and his Contemporaries*. 3rd edn. Houndmills, Basingstoke: Palgrave Macmillan, [1984] 2004.

Donno, Elizabeth Story, ed. *Twelfth Night*. Cambridge: Cambridge University Press, 2003.

Drakakis, John. "Historical Difference and Venetian Patriarchy." In *The Merchant of Venice*. Edited by Nigel Wood. Buckingham: Open University Press, 1996, pp. 23–56.

Duffy, Eamon. *The Stripping of the Altars: Traditional Religion in England c. 1400–1580*. New Haven, CT: Yale University Press, 1992,

Dutton, Richard and Jean E. Howard, eds. *The Comedies*. Vol. 3 of 3, *A Companion to Shakespeare*. Oxford: Blackwell, 2003.

Eagleton, Terry. *Humour*. New Haven, CT: Yale University Press, 2019.

Eggert, Katherine. *Disknowledge: Literature, Alchemy, and the End of Humanism in Renaissance England*. Philadelphia, PA: University of Pennsylvania Press, 2015.

Elkins, James and David Morgan, eds. *The Art Seminar*. Vol. 7, *Re-Enchantment*. New York: Routledge, 2009.

Elliott, G. R. "Weirdness in *The Comedy of Errors*." *University of Toronto Quarterly* 9, no. 1 (October 1939): 95–106.

Empson, William. *Some Versions of the Pastoral*. London: Chatto & Windus, 1950.

Erne, Lukas. *Shakespeare as Literary Dramatist*. 2nd edn. Cambridge: Cambridge University Press, [2003] 2013.

Escobedo, Andrew. *Volition's Face: Personification and the Will in Renaissance Literature.* Notre Dame, IN: University of Notre Dame Press, 2017.

Fauconnier, Giles and Mark Turner. *The Way We Think: Conceptual Blending and the Mind's Hidden Complexities.* New York: Basic Books, 2002.

Felheim, Marvin. "Comic Realism in *Much Ado About Nothing.*" In Bloom, *Bloom's Shakespeare Through the Ages:* Much Ado About Nothing, 194–210.

Felski, Rita. *The Limits of Critique.* Chicago, IL: University of Chicago Press, 2015.

Felski, Rita. *The Uses of Literature.* Malden, MA: Blackwell, 2008.

Fernie, Ewan. "Introduction." In Fernie, *Spiritual Shakespeares,* 1–27.

Fernie, Ewan, ed. *Spiritual Shakespeares. Spiritual Shakespeares.* New York: Routledge, 2005.

Ferguson, Margaret W. "*Hamlet:* Letters and Spirits." In Parker and Hartman, *Shakespeare and the Question of Theory,* 291–307.

Findlay, Alison. "The Critical Backstory." In Cartmell and Smith, Much Ado About Nothing: *A Critical Reader,* 21–39.

Fletcher, Angus. *Allegory: The Theory of a Symbolic Mode.* Ithaca, NY: Cornell University Press, 1964.

Floyd-Wilson, Mary. *Occult Knowledge, Science, and Gender on the Shakespearean Stage.* Cambridge: Cambridge University Press, 2013.

Foakes, R. A., ed., *A Midsummer Night's Dream.* Updated edn. Cambridge: Cambridge University Press, (1985) 2003.

Ford, John R. Twelfth Night: *A Guide to the Play.* Westport, CT: Greenwood Press, 2006.

Foucault, Michel. *The Order of Things: An Archeology of the Human Sciences.* London: Routledge, 1989.

Foucault, Michel. "Of Other Spaces: Utopias and Heterotopias." Translated by Jay Miskowiec. In *Architecture/Mouvement/Continuité* 5 (October, 1984): 46–9. http://web.mit.edu/allanmc/www/foucault1.pdf

Frazer, James George. *The Golden Bough: A Study of Magic and Religion.* Abridged edn. London: Palgrave Macmillan, [1890] 1990.

Freedman, Barbara. *Staging the Gaze: Postmodernism, Psychoanalysis and Shakespearean Comedy.* Ithaca, NY: Cornell University Press, 1991.

Freud, Sigmund. *Jokes and Their Relation to the Unconscious.* Translated by James Strachey. London: Routledge & Kegan Paul, 1960.

Freud, Sigmund. "The Theme of the Three Caskets" (1913). Translated by C. J. M. Hubback. In *Character and Culture.* Vol. 9 of 9, *The Collected Papers of Sigmund Freud.* Edited by Philip Rieff. New York: Collier Books, 1963, pp. 67–79.

Friedman, Michael D. *"The World Must Be Peopled": Shakespeare's Comedies of Forgiveness.* Madison, NJ: Fairleigh Dickinson University Press, 2002.

Frye, Northrop. *Anatomy of Criticism: Four Essays.* Princeton, NJ: Princeton University Press, 1957.

Frye, Northrop. "The Argument of Comedy." *English Institute Essays 1948.* Edited by D. A. Robertson. New York: Columbia University Press, 1949, pp. 58–73.

Frye, Northrop. *A Natural Perspective: The Development of Shakespearean Comedy and Romance.* New York: Columbia University Press, 1965.

Gamboa, Brett. *Shakespeare's Double Plays: Dramatic Economy on the Early Modern Stage.* Cambridge: Cambridge University Press, 2018.

Gane, Nicholas. *Max Weber: Rationalization versus Re-enchantment.* Houndmills, Basingstoke: Palgrave, 2002.

Garber, Marjorie. *Shakespeare After All.* New York: Anchor Books, 2005.

Gillies, John. *Shakespeare and the Geography of Difference*. Cambridge: Cambridge University Press, 1994.

Girard, René. "Perilous Balance: A Comic Hypothesis." *Modern Language Notes* 87, no. 7 (December 1972): 811–26.

Girard, René. *A Theater of Envy: William Shakespeare*. Oxford: Oxford University Press, 1991.

Goodland, Katharine. *Female Mourning in Medieval and Renaissance Drama: From* The Raising of Lazarus *to* King Lear. Aldershot: Ashgate, 2005.

Gordon, Bruce. "Malevolent Ghosts and Ministering Angels: Apparitions and Pastoral Care in the Swiss Reformation." In *The Place of the Dead: Death and Remembrance in Late Medieval and Early Modern Europe*. Edited by Bruce Gordon and Peter Marshall. Cambridge: Cambridge University Press, 2000.

Gottlieb, Derek. *Skepticism and Belonging in Shakespeare's Comedies*. New York: Routledge, 2016.

Grady, Hugh. *Shakespeare and Impure Aesthetics*. Cambridge: Cambridge University Press, 2009.

Grady, Hugh. "Shakespeare and Impure Aesthetics: The Case of *A Midsummer Night's' Dream*." *Shakespeare Quarterly* 59, no. 3 (Fall 2008): 274–302.

Graham, Kenneth J. E. and Philip D. Collington, eds. *Shakespeare and Religious Change*. Houndmills, Basingstoke: Palgrave, 2009.

Greenblatt, Stephen. *Hamlet in Purgatory*. Princeton, NJ: Princeton University Press, 2001.

Greenblatt, Stephen. "Invisible Bullets." In Greenblatt, *Shakespearean Negotiations*, 21–65.

Greenblatt, Stephen. "Martial Law in the Land of Cockaigne." In Greenblatt, *Shakespearean Negotiations*, 129–64.

Stephen Greenblatt, et al., eds. *The Norton Shakespeare*. 3rd edn. New York: W. W. Norton, 2015.

Greenblatt, Stephen J. "Resonance and Wonder." In *Learning to Curse: Essays in Early Modern Culture*. New York: Routledge, 1990, pp. 161–83.

Greenblatt, Stephen. *Shakespearean Negotiations: The Circulation of Social Energy in Renaissance England*. Berkeley, CA: University of California Press, 1988.

Greenfield, Thelma N. "*A Midsummer Night's Dream* and *The Praise of Folly*." *Comparative Literature* 20, no. 3 (Summer 1968): 236–44.

Gross, Kenneth. *Shylock Is Shakespeare*. Chicago, IL: University of Chicago Press, 2006.

Guenther, Genevieve. *Magical Imaginations: Instrumental Aesthetics in the English Renaissance*. Toronto: University of Toronto Press, 2012.

Gumbrecht, Hans Ulrich. *Production of Presence: What Meaning Cannot Convey*. Stanford, CA: Stanford University Press, 2003.

Gurewitch, Morton. *Comedy: The Irrational Vision*. Ithaca, NY: Cornell University Press, 1975.

Hackel, Heidi Brayman. *Reading Material in Early Modern England: Print, Gender, and Literacy*. Cambridge: Cambridge University Press, 2005.

Hackett, Helen. "Introduction." In *A Midsummer Night's Dream*. Edited by Stanley Wells. London: Penguin Books, 2005, pp. xxi–lxxxvii.

Hadfield, Andrew. "Shakespeare and Republican Venice." In *Visions of Venice in Shakespeare*. Edited by Laura Tosi and Shaul Bassi. Farnham, Surrey: Ashgate, 2011, pp. 67–82.

Hamilton, A. C. *The Structure of Allegory in* The Faerie Queene. Oxford: Clarendon Press, 1961.

Hankins, John Erskine. *Source and Meaning in Spenser's Allegory: A Study of* The Faerie Queene. Oxford: Clarendon Press, 1971.

Harbage, Alfred. *Annals of English Drama, 970–1700.* Revised by S. Schoenbaum. 3rd edn. revised by Sylvia Stoler Wagonheim. London: Routledge, 1989.

Hardin, Richard F. "*Menaechmi* and the Renaissance of Comedy." *Comparative Drama* 37, nos. 3,4 (2003–04): 255–74.

Hare, Elissa Beatrice. *Enchanted Shows: Vision and Structure in Elizabethan and Shakespearean Comedy about Magic.* New York: Garland, 1988.

Hartman, Geoffrey H. "Shakespeare's Poetical Character in *Twelfth Night.*" In Parker and Hartman, *Shakespeare and the Question of Theory,* 37–53.

Hartwig, Joan. *Shakespeare's Analogical Scene: Parody as Structural Syntax.* Lincoln, NE: University of Nebraska Press, 1983.

Hassel, Jr., R. Chris. *Faith and Folly in Shakespeare's Romantic Comedies.* Athens, GA: University of Georgia Press, 1980.

Heal, Felicity. *The Power of Gifts: Gift Exchange in Early Modern England.* Oxford: Oxford University Press, 2014.

Heller, Agnes. *Immortal Comedy: The Comic Phenomenon in Art, Literature, and Life.* Lanham, MD: Lexington Books, 2005.

Henze, Richard. "Deception in *Much Ado About Nothing.*" *Studies in English Literature* 11, no. 2 (Spring 1971): 187–201.

Herrington, H. W. "Witchcraft and Magic in the Elizabethan Drama." *The Journal of American Folklore.* 32, no. 126 (Oct.–Dec. 1919): 447–85. http://www.jstor.org/stable/535187.

Hibbard, G. R., ed. *Love's Labour's Lost.* Oxford: Clarendon Press, 1990.

Hirschfeld, Heather, ed. *The Oxford Handbook of Shakespearean Comedy.* Oxford: Oxford University Press, 2018.

Hobbs, Jerry R. *Literature and Cognition.* Stanford, CA: Center for Study of Language and Information, Stanford University, 1990.

Hobgood, Allison P. *Passionate Playgoing in Early Modern England.* Cambridge: Cambridge University Press, 2014.

Hokenson, Jan Walsh. *The Idea of Comedy: History, Theory, Critique.* Madison, NJ: Fairleigh Dickinson University Press, 2006.

Holbrook, Peter. "Class X: Shakespeare, Class, and Comedy." In Dutton and Howard, *The Comedies,* 67–89.

Holland, Peter, ed. *A Midsummer Night's Dream.* Oxford: Oxford University Press, 1994.

Hopkins, Lisa. "Comedies of the Green World: *A Midsummer Night's Dream, As You Like It,* and *Twelfth Night.*" In Hirschfeld, *Oxford Handbook of Shakespearean Comedy,* 520–36.

Horkheimer, Max and Theodor W. Adorno. *Dialectic of Enlightenment: Philosophical Fragments.* Edited by G. S. Noerr, translated by E. Jephcott. Stanford, CA: Stanford University Press, 2002.

Hornback, Robert. *The English Clown Tradition from the Middle Ages to Shakespeare.* Cambridge: D. S. Brewer, 2009.

Horvath, Gabriela Dragnea. *Theatre, Magic, and Philosophy: William Shakespeare, John Dee and the Italian Legacy.* New York: Routledge, 2017.

Howard, Jean E. "The Difficulties of Closure: An Approach to the Problematic in Shakespearean Comedy." In *Comedy from Shakespeare to Sheridan: Change and Continuity in the English and European Dramatic Traditions.* Edited by A. R. Braunmuller and J. C. Bulman. Cranbury, NJ: Associated University Presses, 1986, pp. 113–28.

Howard, Jean E. *Shakespeare's Art of Orchestration: Stage Technique and Audience Response*. Urbana, IL: University of Illinois Press, 1984.

Howard, Jean E. *The Stage and Social Struggle in Early Modern England*. New York: Routledge, 1994.

Hughes, Felicity. "Psychological Allegory in *The Faerie Queene*, III.xi–xii." *Review of English Studies* 29 (1978): 129–46.

Humphreys, A. R., ed. *The First Part of Henry IV*. London: Methuen, 1960.

Hunt, Maurice. "Malvolio, Viola, and the Question of Instrumentality: Defining Providence in *Twelfth Night*." *Studies in Philology* 99, no. 3 (Summer 1993): 277–97.

Hunt, Maurice A. *Shakespeare's* As You Like It. New York: Palgrave Macmillan, 2008.

Hunter, G. K., ed. *All's Well That Ends Well*. London: Methuen, 1959.

Hunter, R. G. *Shakespeare and the Comedy of Forgiveness*. New York: Columbia University Press, 1965.

Huston, J. Dennis. *Shakespeare's Comedies of Play*. New York: Columbia University Press, 1981.

Hutson, Lorna. *The Invention of Suspicion: Law and Mimesis in Shakespeare and Renaissance Drama*. Oxford: Oxford University Press, 2007.

Hutton, Ronald. *The Rise and Fall of Merry England: The Ritual Year 1400–1700*. Oxford: Oxford University Press, 1994.

Javitch, Daniel. "The Assimilation of Aristotle's *Poetics* in Sixteenth-Century Italy." In *The Cambridge History of Literary Criticism*. Vol. 3 of 9, *The Renaissance*. Edited by Glyn P. Norton. Cambridge: Cambridge University Press, 1999, pp. 53–65.

Jensen, Ejner. *Shakespeare and the Ends of Comedy*. Bloomington, IN: Indiana University Press, 1991.

Jensen, Phebe. *Religion and Revelry in Shakespeare's Festive World*. Cambridge: Cambridge University Press, 2008.

Johnson, Samuel. *Mr. Johnson's Preface to his Edition of Shakespear's Plays*. London: 1765.

Johnston, Alexandra. "The Emerging Pattern of the Easter Play in England." *Medieval English Theatre* 20 (1998): 3–23.

Kaplan, M. Lindsay. "Jessica's Mother: Medieval Constructions of the Jewish Race and Gender in *The Merchant of Venice*." *Shakespeare Quarterly* 58, no. 1 (Spring 2007): 1–30.

Kastan, David Scott, ed. *King Henry IV, Part 1*. London: Thomson Learning, 2002.

Keilen, Sean. "Shakespeare and Ovid." In *A Handbook to the Reception of Ovid*. Edited by John F. Miller and Carole E. Newlands. London: Wiley-Blackwell, 2014, pp. 232–45.

Kennedy, Judith M., ed. *A Critical Edition of Yong's Translation of George of Montemayor's* Diana *and Gil Polo's* Enamoured Diana. Oxford: Clarendon Press, 1968.

Kermode, Frank. *The Sense of an Ending: Studies in the Theory of Fiction*. Oxford: Oxford University Press, [1967] 2000.

Kermode, Frank. "Voltimand and Cornelius: Doubles in *Hamlet*." In *Forms of Attention: Botticelli and* Hamlet. Chicago, IL: University of Chicago Press, 1985, pp. 33–63.

Kermode, Lloyd Edward. "Experiencing the Space and Place of Early Modern Theater." *Journal of Medieval and Early Modern Studies* 43, no. 1 (Winter 2013): 1–24.

Kiernan, Pauline. *Shakespeare's Theory of Drama*. Cambridge: Cambridge University Press, 1996.

Knoll, Gillian Beth. *Conceiving Desire in Lyly and Shakespeare: Metaphor, Cognition and Eros*. Edinburgh: University of Edinburgh Press, 2020.

Knutson, Roslyn Lander. *The Repertory of Shakespeare's Company, 1594–1613*. Fayetteville, AR: University of Arkansas Press, 1991.

Kreps, Barbara. "Two-Sided Legal Narratives: Slander, Evidence, Proof, and Turnarounds in *Much Ado About Nothing*." In *Taking Exception to the Law: Materializing Injustice in Early Modern English Literature*. Edited by Donald Beecher, Travis Decook, Andrew Wallace, and Grant Williams. Toronto: University of Toronto Press, 2015, pp. 162–78.

Krieger, Elliot. *A Marxist Study of Shakespeare's Comedies*. London: Macmillan, 1979.

Kronegger, Marlies and Anna-Teresa Tymieniecka, eds. *Analecta Husserliana*. Vol. 65, *The Aesthetics of Enchantment in the Fine Arts*. Dordrecht, The Netherlands: Springer Science+Business Media, 2000.

Lakoff, George and Mark Johnson. *Metaphors We Live By*. Chicago, IL: University of Chicago Press, 1980.

Landy, Joshua. *How To Do Things with Fictions*. Oxford: Oxford University Press, 2012.

Landy, Joshua and Michael Saler. *The Re-Enchantment of the World*. Stanford, CA: Stanford University Press, 2009.

Lanham, Richard A. *A Handlist of Rhetorical Terms*. 2nd edn. Berkeley, CA: University of California Press, 1991.

Laroque, François. *Shakespeare's Festive World: Elizabethan Seasonal Entertainment and the Professional Stage*. Translated by Janet Lloyd. Cambridge: Cambridge University Press, 1991.

Laroque, François. "Shakespeare's Imaginary Geography." In *Shakespeare and Renaissance Europe*. Edited by Andrew Hadfield and Paul Hammond. London: Thomson Learning, 2005, pp. 193–219.

Latour, Bruno. *Reassembling the Social: An Introduction to Actor-Network Theory*. Oxford: Oxford University Press, 2005.

Latour, Bruno. *We Have Never Been Modern*. Translated by Catherine Porter Cambridge, MA: Harvard University Press, 1993.

Lawrence, Jason. *"Who the Devil Taught Thee So Much Italian?": Italian Language learning and literary Imitation in Early Modern England*. Manchester: Manchester University Press, 2005.

Lawrence, Sean. *Forgiving the Gift: The Philosophy of Generosity In Shakespeare and Marlowe*. Pittsburgh, PA: Duquesne University Press, 2012.

Lefebvre, Henri. *The Production of Space*. Translated by Donald Nicholson-Smith. Oxford: Basil Blackwell, 1991.

Leggatt, Alexander, ed. *The Cambridge Companion to Shakespearean Comedy*. Cambridge: Cambridge University Press, 2004.

Leggatt, Alexander. *English Stage Comedy: 1490–1990: Five Centuries of a Genre*. London: Routledge, 1998.

Leggatt, Alexander. *Shakespeare's Comedy of Love*. London: Methuen, 1973.

Leinwand, Theodore B. "Negotiation and New Historicism." *PMLA* 105, no. 3 (May 1990): 477–90.

Leinwand, Theodore B. *Theatre, Finance and Society in Early Modern England*. Cambridge: Cambridge University Press, 1999.

Levin, Richard. *The Multiple Plot in English Renaissance Drama*. Chicago, IL: University of Chicago Press, 1973.

Levin, Richard A. *Love and Society in Shakespearean Comedy: A Study of Dramatic Form and Content*. Newark, DE: University of Delaware Press, 1985.

Levinas, Emmanuel. *Totality and Infinity: An Essay on Exteriority*. Translated by Alphonso Lingis. The Hague: Martinus Nijhoff Publishers, 1979.

Levine, Caroline. *Forms: Whole, Rhythm, Hierarchy, Network*. Princeton, NJ: Princeton University Press, 2015.

Levith, Murray J. *Shakespeare's Italian Settings and Plays*. New York: St. Martin's Press, 1989.

Lewis, C. S. *The Discarded Image: An Introduction to Medieval and Renaissance Literature*. Cambridge: Cambridge University Press, 1964.

Lewis, C. S. *Spenser's Images of Life*. Cambridge: Cambridge University Press, 1967.

Lin, Erika T. "Performance Practice and Theatrical Privilege: Rethinking Weimann's Concept of *Locus* and *Platea*." *New Theatre Quarterly* 22, no. 3 (August 2006): 283–98.

Lin, Erika T. *Shakespeare and the Materiality of Performance*. New York: Palgrave Macmillan, 2012.

Lindley, David. *Shakespeare and Music*. London: Bloomsbury 2006.

Lobis, Seth. *The Virtue of Sympathy: Magic, Philosophy, and Literature in Seventeenth-Century England*. New Haven, CT: Yale University Press, 2015.

Locatelli, Angela. "The Fictional World of *Romeo and Juliet*: Cultural Connotations of an Italian Setting." In Marrapodi, et al., *Shakespeare's Italy*, 69–86.

Logan, Thad Jenkins. "*Twelfth Night*: The Limits of Festivity." *Studies in English Literature* 22, no. 2 (1982): 223–38.

Looney, Aaron T. *Vladimir Jankélévitch: The Time for Forgiveness*. New York: Fordham University Press, 2015.

Lopez, Jeremy. *Theatrical Convention and Audience Response*. Cambridge: Cambridge University Press, 2004.

Loriggio, Francesco. "Prefacing Renaissance Comedy: The Double, Laughter, and Comic Structure." In *Comparative Critical Approaches to Renaissance Comedy*. Edited by Donald Beecher and Massimo Ciavolella. Ottawa: Dovehouse Editions, 1986, pp. 99–118.

Lynch, John Patrick. "Introduction." In Berger, *Second World and Green World*, xv–xxiii.

Lyne, Raphael. "Shakespeare, Plautus, and the Discovery of New Comic Space." In *Shakespeare and the Classics*. Edited by Charles Martindale and A. B. Taylor. Cambridge: Cambridge University Press, 2004, pp. 122–38.

Lyne, Raphael. *Shakespeare, Rhetoric and Cognition*. Cambridge: Cambridge University Press, 2011.

Lyons, John D. *Before Imagination: Embodied Thought from Montaigne to Rousseau*. Stanford, CA: Stanford University Press, 2005.

Lyotard, Jean-François. *Heidegger and "the jews."* Translated by Andreas Michael and Mark S. Roberts. Minneapolis, MN: University of Minnesota Press, 1990.

Magnusson, Lynne. *Shakespeare and Social Dialogue: Dramatic Language and Elizabethan Letters*. Cambridge: Cambridge University Press, 2004.

Marciano, Lisa. "The Serious Comedy of *Twelfth Night*: Dark Didacticism in Illyria." *Renascence: Essays on Values in Literature* 56, no. 1 (Fall 2003): 3–19.

Mares, F. H., ed. *Much Ado About Nothing*. Cambridge: Cambridge University Press, 1988.

Margolies, David. *Shakespeare's Irrational Endings: The Problem Plays*. Houndmills, Basingstoke: Palgrave, 2012.

Marrapodi, Michele. "The 'Woman as Wonder' Trope: From *Commedia Grave* to Shakespeare's *Pericles* and the Last Plays." In *Shakespeare and Renaissance Literary Theories: Anglo-Italian Transactions*. Edited by Michele Marrapodi. Farnham, Surrey: Ashgate, 2011, pp. 175–99.

Marrapodi, Michele, A. J. Hoenselaars, Marcello Cappuzzo, and L. Falzon Santucci, eds. *Shakespeare's Italy: Functions of Italian Locations in Renaissance Drama*. Manchester: Manchester University Press, 1993.

Marshall, Cynthia. *The Shattering of the Self: Violence, Subjectivity, and Early Modern Texts*. Baltimore, MD: The Johns Hopkins University Press, 2002.

Martin, Randall. *Shakespeare and Ecology*. Oxford: Oxford University Press, 2015.

Maslen, R. W. *Shakespeare and Comedy*. London: Thomson Learning, 2005.

Matuska, Ágnes. *The Vice-Device: Iago and Lear's Fool as Agents of Representational Crisis*. Szeged, Hungary: Institute of English and American Studies, University of Szeged, 2011.

Mayer, Jean-Christophe. *Shakespeare's Early Readers*. Cambridge: Cambridge University Press, 2018.

Mazzeo, Joseph A. "Universal Analogy and the Culture of the Renaissance." *Journal of the History of Ideas* 12, no. 2 (April 1954): 299–304.

McCoy, Richard C. *Faith in Shakespeare*. Oxford: Oxford University Press, 2013.

McEachern, Claire. *Believing in Shakespeare: Studies in Longing*. Cambridge: Cambridge University Press, 2018.

McGowen, Todd. *Only a Joke Can Save Us: A Theory of Comedy*. Evanston, IL: Northwestern University Press, 2017.

Meeker, Joseph W. *The Comedy of Survival: Studies in Literary Ecology*. New York: Scribner's, 1972.

Mentz, Steve. *At the Bottom of Shakespeare's Ocean*. New York: Continuum, 2009.

Mentz, Steve. "Green Comedy: Shakespeare and Ecology." In Hirschfeld, *Oxford Handbook of Shakespearean Comedy*, 250–62.

Mentz, Steve. "Revising Sources: Novella, Romance, and the Meanings of Fiction in *All's Well That Ends Well*." In Waller, All's Well That Ends Well: *New Critical Essays*, 57–70.

Meredith, George. "An Essay on Comedy." In Sypher, *Comedy*, 3–57.

Moffatt, Laurel. "The Woods as Heterotopia in *A Midsummer Night's Dream*." *Studia Neophilologia* 76, no. 2 (2004): 182–7.

Montrose, Louis Adrian. "'The Place of a Brother' in *As You Like It*: Social Process and Comic Form." *Shakespeare Quarterly* 32, no. 1 (Spring 1981): 28–54.

Morgan, David. "Enchantment, Disenchantment, Re-Enchantment." In *The Art Seminar*. Vol. 7, *Re-Enchantment*. Edited by James Elkins and David Morgan. New York: Routledge, 2009, pp. 3–23.

Morreall, John. *Taking Laughter Seriously*. Albany, NY: State University of New York Press, 1983.

Morse, Ruth, Helen Cooper, and Peter Holland, eds. *Medieval Shakespeare: Pasts and Presents*. Cambridge: Cambridge University Press, 2013.

Moul, Victoria. *Jonson, Horace and the Classical Tradition*. Cambridge: Cambridge University Press, 2010.

Mowat, Barbara. "The Theater and Literary Culture." In *A New History of Early English Drama*. Edited by John D. Cox and David Scott Kastan. New York: Columbia University Press, 1997, pp. 213–30.

Munro, Lucy. "Shakespeare and the Uses of the Past: Critical Approaches and Current Debates." *Shakespeare* 7, no. 1 (April 2011): 102–25.

Myhill, Nova. "Spectatorship in/of *Much Ado About Nothing*." *Studies in English Literature*, 39, no. 2 (Spring 1999): 291–311.

Nelson, T. G. A. *Comedy: An Introduction of Comedy in Literature, Drama, and Culture*. Oxford: Oxford University Press, 1990.

Nevo, Ruth. "Existence in Arden." In *William Shakespeare's* As You Like It. Edited by Harold Bloom. Broomall, PA: Chelsea House Publishing, 2004, pp. 21–37.

Newman, Karen. *Shakespeare's Rhetoric of Comic Character: Dramatic Convention in Classical and Renaissance Comedy*. New York: Methuen, 1985.

Ngai, Sianne. *Theory of the Gimmick: Aesthetic Judgment and Capitalist Form*. Cambridge, MA: The Belknap Press of Harvard University Press, 2020.

Ngai, Sianne. *Ugly Feelings*. Cambridge, MA: Harvard University Press, 2005.

Nikulin, Dmitri. *Comedy, Seriously: A Philosophical Study*. New York: Palgrave Macmillan, 2014.

Olson, Paul A. *Beyond a Common Joy: An Introduction to Shakespearean Comedy*. Lincoln, NE: University of Nebraska Press, 2008.

Orgel, Stephen. *Imagining Shakespeare: A History of Texts and Visions*. Houndmills, Basingstoke: Palgrave, 2003.

Ornstein, Robert. *Shakespeare's Comedies: From Roman Farce to Romance Mystery*. Newark, DE: University of Delaware Press, 1986.

Ortiz, Joseph M. *Shakespeare and the Politics of Music*. Ithaca, NY: Cornell University Press, 2011.

Osborne, Laurie E. "'The marriage of true minds': Amity, Twinning, and Comic Closure in *Twelfth Night*." In Schiffer, Twelfth Night: *Critical Essays*, 99–113.

Ostovich, Helen and Lisa Hopkins, eds. *Magical Transformations on the Early Modern English Stage*. New York: Routledge, 2014.

Palfrey, Simon and Emma Smith. *Shakespeare's Dead*. Oxford: Bodleian Library, 2016.

Palmer, D. J. "'Twelfth Night' and the Myth of Echo and Narcissus." *Shakespeare Survey* 32. Cambridge: Cambridge University Press, 1979: 73–8.

Parker, Patricia and Geoffrey Hartman, eds. *Shakespeare and the Question of Theory*. New York: Methuen, 1985.

Parker, Patricia. *Shakespeare from the Margins: Language, Culture, Context*. Chicago, IL: University of Chicago Press, 1996.

Parks, George B. "The Decline and Fall of the English Renaissance Admiration of Italy." *Huntington Library Quarterly* 31, no. 4 (August 1968): 341–57.

Pellone, E. M. "Shylock's Ghosts." Unpublished essay, 2019.

Pentland, Elizabeth. "Beyond the 'Lyric' in Illyricum: Some Early Modern Backgrounds to *Twelfth Night*." In Schiffer, Twelfth Night: *Critical Essays*, 149–66.

Perry, Curtis and John Watkins, eds. *Shakespeare and the Middle Ages*. Oxford: Oxford University Press, 2009.

Peterson, Douglas L. "Beginnings and Endings: Structure and Mimesis in Shakespeare's Comedies." In *Entering the Maze: Shakespeare's Art of Beginning*. Edited by Robert F. Willson, Jr. New York: Peter Lang, 1995, pp. 37–53.

Peterson, Kaara L. "Shakespearean Revivifications: Early Modern Undead." *Shakespeare Studies* 32. Madison, NJ: Fairleigh Dickinson University Press, 2004: 240–66.

Pfister, Manfred. "Shakespeare and Italy, or, the Law of Diminishing Returns." In Marrapodi, et al., *Shakespeare's Italy*, 295–305.

Plaice, Neville, Stephen Plaice, and Paul Knight. "Translators' Introduction." In Ernst Bloch, *The Principle of Hope*. Vol. 1 of 3. Translated by Neville Plaice, Stephen Plaice, and Paul Knight. Cambridge, MA: MIT Press, 1986.

Platt, Peter G. "'The Meruailouse Site': Shakespeare, Venice, Paradoxical Stages." *Renaissance Quarterly* 54, no. 1 (Spring 2001): 121–54.

Platt, Peter G. *Reason Diminished: Shakespeare and the Marvelous*. Lincoln, NE: University of Nebraska Press, 1997.

Platt, Peter G. *Shakespeare and the Culture of Paradox*. New York: Routledge, 2009.

Pollard, Tanya. "Audience Reception." In *The Oxford Handbook of Shakespeare*. Edited by Arthur Kinney. Oxford: Oxford University Press, 2012, pp. 458–73.

Poole, Kristen. *Supernatural Environments in Shakespeare's England: Spaces of Demonism, Divinity, and Drama*. Cambridge: Cambridge University Press, 2011.

Potter, Lois. Twelfth Night: *Text and Performance*. London: Macmillan, 1985.

Powers, Alan W. "'What he wills'": Early Modern Rings and Vows in *Twelfth Night*." In Schiffer, Twelfth Night: *Critical Essays*, 217–28.

Praz, Mario. "Shakespeare and Italy." In *The Flaming Heart*. New York: Norton, 1958.

Preiss, Richard. *Clowning and Authorship in Early Modern England*. Cambridge: Cambridge University Press, 2014.

Preiss, Richard. "Robert Armin Do the Police in Different Voices." In *From Performance to Print in Shakespeare's England*. Edited by Peter Holland and Stephen Orgel. Houndmills, Basingstoke: Palgrave Macmillan, 2006, pp. 208–27.

Prescott, Paul. "Endings." In *Shakespeare and the Making of Theatre*. Edited by Stuart Hampton-Reeves and Bridget Escolme. Houndmills, Basingstoke: Palgrave, 2012, pp. 50–68.

Presser, Charlotte. "Intertextual Transformations: The *Novella* as mediator between Italian and English Renaissance Drama." In *Shakespeare, Italy, and Intertextuality*. Edited by Michele Marrapodi. Manchester: Manchester University Press, 2004, pp. 107–17.

Radcliff-Umstead, Douglas. *The Birth of Modern Comedy in Renaissance Italy*. Chicago, IL: University of Chicago Press, 1969.

Redmond, Michael J. *Shakespeare, Politics, and Italy: Intertextuality on the Jacobean Stage*. Farnham, Surrey: Ashgate, 2009.

Richards, I. A. *Poetries and Sciences*. Rev. edn. with commentary. London: Routledge & Kegan Paul, [1926; rev. edn. 1935] 1970.

Richardson, Catherine. *Shakespeare and Material Culture*. Oxford: Oxford University Press, 2011.

Ricoeur, Paul. *Interpretation Theory: Discourse and the Surplus of Meaning*. Fort Worth, TX: Texas Christian University, 1976.

Rigolot, François. "The Renaissance Fascination with Error: Mannerism and Early Modern Poetry." *Renaissance Quarterly*. 57, no. 4 (Winter 2004): 1219–34.

Robertson, Kellie. *Nature Speaks: Medieval Literature and Aristotelian Philosophy*. Philadelphia, PA: University of Pennsylvania Press, 2017.

Rodgers, Amy J. *A Monster with a Thousand Hands: The Discursive Spectator in Early Modern England*. Philadelphia, PA: University of Pennsylvania Press, 2018.

Rose, Mark. *Shakespearean Design*. Boston, MA: Belknap Press of Harvard University Press, 1972.

Rosenberg, Tina. "Neo-Nazis in Your Street? Send in the Coup Clutz Clowns." *The New York Times*, September 6, 2017.

Rosenfeld, Gary. "Deconstructing the Christian Merchant: Antonio and *The Merchant of Venice*." *Shofar* 20, no. 2 (Winter 2002): 28–51.

Rovelli, Carlo. *Seven Brief Lessons on Physics*. New York: Riverhead Books, 2016.

Ryan, Kiernan. *Shakespeare*. 3rd edn. Houndmills, Basingstoke: Palgrave, [1989] 2002.

Ryan, Kiernan. *Shakespeare's Comedies*. Houndmills, Basingstoke: Palgrave Macmillan, 2009.

Ryan, Kiernan. "'Where hope is coldest': *All's Well That Ends Well*." In Fernie, *Spiritual Shakespeares*, 28–49.

Saler, Michael. *As If: Modern Enchantment and the Literary Prehistory of Virtual Reality*. Oxford: Oxford University Press, 2011.

Salingar, Leo. *Shakespeare and the Traditions of Comedy*. Cambridge: Cambridge University Press, 1974.

Salkeld, Duncan. "New Directions: Letting Wonder Seem Familiar—Italy and London in *Much Ado About Nothing*." In Cartmell and Smith, *Much Ado About Nothing: A Critical Reader*, 89–109.

Sartre, Jean-Paul. *The Imaginary: A Phenomenological Psychology of the Imagination.* Translated by Jonathan Webber. New York: Routledge, 2004.

Schalkwyk, David. "Music, Food, and Love in the Affective Landscape of *Twelfth Night.*" In Schiffer, Twelfth Night: *New Critical Essays*, 81–98.

Schalkwyk, David. *Speech and Performance in Shakespeare's Sonnets and Plays.* Cambridge: Cambridge University Press, 2002.

Schiffer, James, ed. Twelfth Night: *Critical Essays.* London: Routledge, 2011.

Schleuter, June. *Dramatic Closure: Reading the End.* Madison, NJ: Fairleigh Dickinson University Press, 1995.

Schmitt, Jean-Claude. *Ghosts in the Middle Ages: The Living and the Dead in Medieval Society.* Translated by Teresa Lavender Fagan. Chicago, IL: University of Chicago Press, 1998.

Schutz, Alfred. "On Multiple Realities." In *The Problem of Social Reality: Collected Papers I.* Edited by Maurice Natanson. The Hague: Martinus Nijhoff, 1962, pp. 207–59.

Scragg, Leah. *Discovering Shakespeare's Meaning.* Houndmills, Basingstoke: Macmillan, 1988.

Segal, Charles. "Black and White Magic in Ovid's *Metamorphosis*: Passion, Love, and Art." *Arion: A Journal of Humanities and the Classics*, 3rd series, 9, no. 3 (Winter 2002): 1–34.

Selleck, Nancy. *The Interpersonal Idiom in Shakespeare, Donne, and Early Modern Culture.* Houndmills, Basingstoke: Palgrave, 2008.

Shapiro, Barbara J. *A Culture of Fact: England, 1550–1720.* Ithaca, NY: Cornell University Press, 2000.

Shapiro, James. *Shakespeare and the Jews.* New York: Columbia University Press, [1996] 2016.

Shapiro, James. *A Year in the Life of William Shakespeare: 1599.* New York: HarperCollins, 2005.

Shapiro, Michael. *Gender in Play on the Shakespearean Stage.* Ann Arbor, MI: University of Michigan Press, 1994.

Sharp, Ronald A. "Gift Exchange and the Economics of Spirit in *The Merchant of Venice.*" *Modern Philology* 83, no. 3 (February 1986): 250–65.

Shell, Alison. *Shakespeare and Religion.* London: Bloomsbury, 2010.

Shershow, Scott Cutler. *Laughing Matters: The Paradox of Comedy.* Amherst, MA: University of Massachusetts Press, 1986.

Shuger, Debora Kuller. *Habits of Thought in the English Renaissance: Religion, Politics, and the Dominant Culture.* Berkeley, CA: University of California Press, 1990.

Sievers, E. W. Excerpt from *William Shakespeare* (1866). In Bloom, *Bloom's Shakespeare Through the Ages:* Much Ado About Nothing, 86–8.

Sillars, Stuart John. "'Howsoever, strange and admirable:' *A Midsummer Night's Dream* as *Via Stultitiae.*" *Archiv für das Studium der Neueren Sprachen und Literaturen* 244, no. 1 (2007): 27–39.

Simon, Richard Keller. *The Labyrinth of the Comic: Theory and Practice from Fielding to Freud.* Tallahassee, FL: Florida State University, 1985.

Slights, Camille Wells. *Shakespeare's Comic Commonwealths.* Toronto: University of Toronto Press, 1993.

Smidt, Kristian. *Unconformities in Shakespeare's Early Comedies.* Houndmills, Basingstoke: Macmillan, 1986.

Smidt, Kristian. *Unconformities in Shakespeare's Later Comedies.* New York: Palgrave Macmillan, 1993.

Smith, Bruce R. *Ancient Scripts and Modern Experience on the English Stage, 1500–1700.* Princeton, NJ: Princeton University Press, 1988.

Smith, Emma, ed. *Shakespeare's Comedies.* Oxford: Blackwell, 2004.

Smith, Logan Pearsall. *The Life and Letters of Sir Henry Wotton.* Vol 1 of 2. Oxford: Clarendon Press, 1907.

Snyder, Jon R. *Dissimulation and the Culture of Secrecy in Early Modern Europe.* Berkeley, CA: University of California Press, 2009.

Snyder, Susan. *The Comic Matrix of Shakespeare's Tragedies.* Princeton, NJ: Princeton University Press, 1979.

Sofer, Andrew. *The Stage Life of Props.* Ann Arbor, MI: University Michigan Press, 2003.

Spivack, Bernard. *Shakespeare and the Allegory of Evil.* New York: Columbia University Press, 1958.

Steed, Maggie. "Beatrice." In *Players of Shakespeare.* Vol. 3 of 3. Edited by Russell Jackson and Robert Smallwood. Cambridge: Cambridge University Press, 1993, pp. 42–51.

Stein, Gertrude. "Portraits and Repetition." In *Stein: Writings 1932–1946.* Edited by Catharine R. Stimpson and Harriet Chessman. New York: Library of America, 1998, pp. 287–312.

Stern, Tiffany. *Documents of Performance in Early Modern England.* Cambridge: Cambridge University Press, 2009.

Stern, Tiffany. "Watching as Reading: The Audience and Written Text in Shakespeare's Playhouse." In *How to Do Things with Shakespeare: New Approaches, New Essays.* Edited by Laurie Maguire. Malden, MA: Blackwell, 2008, pp. 136–59.

Stott, Andrew McConnell and Andrew Weitz, eds. *A Cultural History of Comedy.* 6 vols. London: Bloomsbury, 2020.

Storey, Graham. "The Success of *Much Ado About Nothing.*" In *More Talking of Shakespeare.* Edited by John Garrett. New York: Theatre Arts Books, 1959, pp. 128–43.

Strasnicky, Marta. "Shakespeare and the Government of Comedy: *Much Ado About Nothing.*" *Shakespeare Studies* 22. Madison, NJ: Fairleigh Dickinson University Press, 1994: 141–71.

Subbotsky, Eugene. *Magic and the Mind: Mechanisms, Functions, and Development of Magical Thinking and Behavior.* Oxford: Oxford University Press, 2010.

Sullivan, Jr., Garrett A. "'Be this sweet Helen's knell, and now forget her': Forgetting, Memory, and Identity in *All's Well That Ends Well.*" *Shakespeare Quarterly* 50, no. 1 (Spring 1999): 51–73.

Sullivan, Jr., Garrett A. "Shakespeare's Comic Geographies." In Dutton and Howard, *The Comedies,* 182–99.

Sullivan, Patrick J. "The National Theatre's *Merchant of Venice.*" *Educational Theatre Journal* 26, no.1 (March 1974): 31–44.

Sypher, Wylie, ed. *Comedy:* An Essay on Comedy *by George Meredith*; Laughter *by Henri Bergson; Introduction and Appendix, "The Meaning of Comedy," by Wylie Sypher.* Garden City, NY: Doubleday Anchor, 1956.

Sypher, Wylie. "The Meaning of Comedy." In Sypher, *Comedy,* 191–255.

Tartamella, Suzanne. "Jessica's Silence and the Feminine Pyrrhonic in Shakespeare's *The Merchant of Venice.*" *Renaissance Drama* 48, no. 1 (Spring 2020): 83–101.

Thomas, Keith. *Religion and the Decline of Magic: Studies in Popular Beliefs in Sixteenth and Seventeenth Century England.* Harmondsworth: Penguin, [1971] 1973.

Tiffany, Grace. "Names in The Merchant of Venice." In The Merchant of Venice: *New Critical Essays.* Edited by John W. Mahon and Ellen MacLeod Mahon. New York: Routledge, 2002, pp. 353–68.

Tosi, Laura and Shaul Bassi, eds. *Visions of Venice in Shakespeare*. Farnham, Surrey: Ashgate, 2011.

Trilling, Lionel. "Manners, Morals, and The Novel." In *The Liberal Imagination*. New York: Viking Books, 1950, pp. 199–215.

Tsur, Reuven. *Poetic Conventions as Cognitive Fossils*. Oxford: Oxford University Press, 2017.

Turner, Henry S. *Shakespeare's Double Helix*. New York: Continuum, 2007.

Tuve, Rosamund. *Allegorical Imagery: Some Mediaeval Books And Their Posterity*. Princeton, NJ: Princeton University Press, 1966.

Ulrici, Heinrich. Excerpt from *Shakespeare's Dramatic Art* (1839). In Bloom, *Bloom's Shakespeare Through the Ages: Much Ado About Nothing*, 78–9.

van Es, Bart. *Shakespeare's Comedies: A Very Short Introduction*. Oxford: Oxford University Press, 2016.

Verhoeven, Cornelis. *The Philosophy of Wonder*. Translated by Mary Foran. New York: Macmillan, 1972.

Videbaek, Bente A. *The Stage Clown in Shakespeare's Theatre*. Westport, CT: Greenwood Press, 1996.

Wagner, Matthew D. *Shakespeare, Theatre, and Time*. New York: Routledge, 2012.

Walker, D. P. *Spiritual and Demonic Magic: From Ficino to Campanella*. University Park, PA: Pennsylvania State University Press, [1958] 2000.

Wall, Wendy. "Just a Spoonful of Sugar: Syrup and Domesticity in Early Modern England." *Modern Philology* 104, no. 2 (November 2006): 149–72.

Waller, Gary, ed. *All's Well That Ends Well: New Critical Essays*. New York: Routledge, 2007.

Walsham, Alexandra. *Providence in Early Modern England*. Oxford: Oxford University Press, 1999.

Walsham, Alexandra. "The Reformation and 'The Disenchantment of the World' Reassessed." *The Historical Journal* 51, no. 2 (June 2008): 497–528.

Walsham, Alexandra. *The Reformation of the Landscape: Religion, Identity, and Memory in Early Modern Britain and Ireland*. Oxford: Oxford University Press, 2011.

Ward, John O. "Magic and Rhetoric from Antiquity to the Renaissance: Some Ruminations." *Rhetorica* 6, no. 1 (Winter 1988): 57–118.

Warneke, Sara. *Images of the Educational Traveller in Early Modern England*. Leiden: Brill, 1995.

Watson, Robert N. *Back to Nature: The Green and the Real in the Late Renaissance*. Philadelphia, PA: University of Pennsylvania Press, 2008.

Weber, Max. *The Protestant Ethic and the Spirit of Capitalism*. Translated by Talcott Parsons. London: George Allen and Unwin Ltd., 1930.

Weber, Max. "Science as Vocation." In *Max Weber's Complete Writings on Academic and Political Vocations*. Edited by John Dreijmanis. Translated by Gordon C. Wells. New York: Algora Publishing, 2008, pp. 25–52.

Weimann, Robert. *Author's Pen and Actor's Voice: Playing and Writing in Shakespeare's Theatre*. Cambridge: Cambridge University Press, 2000.

Weimann, Robert. *Shakespeare and the Popular Tradition of the Theater: Studies in the Social Dimension of Dramatic Form and Function*. Edited by Robert Schwartz. Baltimore, MD: The Johns Hopkins University Press, 1978.

Weimann, Robert and Douglas Bruster. *Shakespeare and the Power of Performance: Stage and Page in the Elizabethan Theatre*. Cambridge: Cambridge University Press, 2008.

Weinberg, Bernard. *A History of Literary Criticism in the Italian Renaissance*. Vol. 2 of 2. Chicago, IL: University of Chicago Press, 1961.

West, William N. *As If: Essays in* As You Like It. Goletta, CA: Punctum Books, 2016.

Wever, R. *An Enterlude Called Lusty Juventus*. Edited by Helen Scarborough Thomas. New York: Garland, 1982.

Whitney, Charles. *Early Responses to Renaissance Drama*. Cambridge: Cambridge University Press, 2006.

Whitworth, Charles, ed. *Three Sixteenth-Century Comedies:* Gammer Gurton's Needle, Roister Doister, The Old Wives Tale. Tonbridge, Kent: Ernest Benn, 1984.

Wiebracht, Ben. "'The vile conclusion': Crises of Resolution in Shakespeare's Love Plots." *Shakespeare* 12, no. 3 (June 2016): 241–59.

Wilcox, Helen. "Shakespeare's Miracle Play?: Religion in *All's Well That Ends Well*." In Waller, All's Well That Ends Well: *New Critical Essays*, 140–54.

Wiles, David. *Shakespeare's Clown: Actor and Text in the Elizabethan Playhouse*. Cambridge: Cambridge University Press, 1987.

Williams, Deanne. "Shakespearean Medievalism and the Limits of Periodization in *Cymbeline*." *Literature Compass* 8, no. 6 (June 2011): 390–403.

Williams, Gordon. *A Glossary of Shakespeare's Sexual Language*. London: Athlone Press, 1997.

Williams, Kathleen. *Spenser's* Faerie Queene: *The World of Glass*. London: Routledge and Kegan Paul, 1966.

Williams, Raymond. *Marxism and Literature*. Oxford: Oxford University Press, 1977.

Williams, Wes. *Monsters and their Meanings in Early Modern Culture: Mighty Magic*. Oxford: Oxford University Press, 2011.

Williamson, Elizabeth. "Things Newly Performed: The Resurrection Tradition in Shakespeare's Plays." In Graham and Collington, *Shakespeare and Religious Change*, 110–32.

Witmore, Michael. *The Culture of Accidents: Unexpected Knowledges in Early Modern England*. Stanford, CA: Stanford University Press, 2001.

Wittgenstein, Ludwig. *Philosophical Investigations*. Translated by G. E. M. Anscombe. 2nd edn. (Oxford: Basil Blackwell, (1953) 1958.

Wofford, Susanne L. "*The Faerie Queene*, Books I–III." In *The Cambridge Companion to Spenser*. Edited by Andrew Hadfield. Cambridge: Cambridge University Press, 2001.

Wofford, Susanne L. "Veiled Revenants and the Risks of Hospitality: Euripides's *Alcestis*, Bandello, and Shakespeare's *Much Ado About Nothing*." In *Rethinking Shakespeare Source Study: Audiences, Authors, and Digital Technologies*. Edited by Dennis Austin Britton and Melissa Walter. New York: Routledge, 2018, pp. 90–123.

Womack, Peter. "Imagining Communities: Theatres and the English Nation in the Sixteenth Century." In *Culture and History 1350–1600: Essays on English Communities, Identities and Writing*. Edited by David Aers. Detroit, MI: Wayne State University Press, 1992, pp. 91–146.

Woodbridge, Linda. *The Scythe of Saturn: Shakespeare and Magical Thinking*. Urbana, IL: University of Illinois Press, 1994.

Woolfson, Jonathan. *Padua and the Tudors: English Students in Italy, 1485–1503*. Toronto: University of Toronto Press, 1998.

Wrightson, Keith. "'Decline of Neighborliness' Revised." In *Local Identities in Medieval and Early Modern England*. Edited by Norman L. Jones and Daniel Woolf. Houndmills, Basingstoke: Palgrave Macmillan, 2007, pp. 19–49.

Wyatt, Michael. *The Italian Encounter with Tudor England: A Cultural Politics of Translation.* Cambridge: Cambridge University Press, 2005.

Yamada, Akihiro. *Experiencing Drama in the English Renaissance: Readers and Audiences.* New York: Routledge, 2017.

Yates, Frances A. *Giordano Bruno and the Hermetic Tradition.* London: Routledge and Kegan Paul, 1964.

Young, David P. *Something of Great Constancy: The Art of "A Midsummer Night's Dream".* New Haven, CT: Yale University Press, 1966.

Zambelli, Paola. *White Magic, Black Magic in the European Renaissance.* Leiden: Brill, 2007.

Zupančič, Alenka. *The Shortest Shadow: Nietzsche's Philosophy of the Two.* Cambridge, MA: MIT Press, 2003.

Zupančič, Alenka. *The Odd One In: On Comedy.* Cambridge, MA: MIT Press, 2008.

Index

For the benefit of digital users, table entries that span two pages (e.g., 52–53) may, on occasion, appear on only one of those pages.